D0983714

WITHDRAWN

Witch Hunting
in Southwestern Germany
1562–1684

Witch Hunting
in Southwestern Germany
1562-1684

The Social and Intellectual Foundations

❧

H. C. Erik Midelfort

Stanford University Press
Stanford, California
1972

Stanford University Press
Stanford, California
© 1972 by the Board of Trustees of the
Leland Stanford Junior University
Printed in the United States of America
ISBN 0-8047-0805-3
LC 75-183891

*For my parents
and my parents-in-law*

Preface

IN MY wanderings I have incurred many scholarly debts that may never be properly repaid, but that should at least be acknowledged. First, my thanks must go to Timothy Breen, J. H. Hexter, and Hans Hillerbrand for encouraging me to pursue this topic and for helping me to collect my thoughts. In addition, I received invaluable counsel from Howard Lamar and Heiko Oberman. My manuscript received careful and helpful scrutiny from Gene Brucker and Steven Ozment, and while researching and writing it, I have been guided by the genial wisdom of Jaroslav Pelikan.

I received assistance of a more material, but no less crucial, sort from the Deutscher Akademischer Austauschdienst, which made my year in Germany possible. Also, I was able to purchase microfilm through the assistance of Yale University.

My work was eased considerably by the gracious reception given me by the libraries of Karlsruhe, Munich, Stuttgart, Zurich, Tübingen University, and Yale University. Similarly, various state archives displayed a spontaneous readiness to help a novice with difficult manuscript materials: the Generallandesarchiv in Karlsruhe, the Württembergisches Staatsarchiv in Ludwigsburg, the Staatsarchiv in Sigmaringen, and the Hauptstaatsarchiv in Stuttgart. Many of my fondest memories are of the pleasant hours I spent in small-town archives, especially those of Ellwangen, Offenburg, and Rottweil, and I am grateful for the help these archives gave me. Finally, my thanks to the Universitätsarchiv in Tübingen for its unfailing support and assistance.

The pictures in the picture section are reproduced by the kind permission of the custodians of the originals: the Graphische Sammlung of the Zentralbibliothek Zürich, the Hauptstaatsarchiv Stuttgart (HSASt), and the Württembergische Landesbibliothek Stuttgart.

My first encounter with the early modern German script came through the summer institute of the Foundation for Reformation Research in St. Louis, Missouri. Without the help of A. C. Piepkorn's paleography course, my task would have been much harder. Even at their most legible, however, witchcraft records are depressing documents. For helping me retain such composure as remains, therefore, I must thank my wife, Corelyn.

H.C.E.M.

Charlottesville, June 1972

Contents

❧

Eight pages of illustrations follow p. 126

Tables and Figures

❧

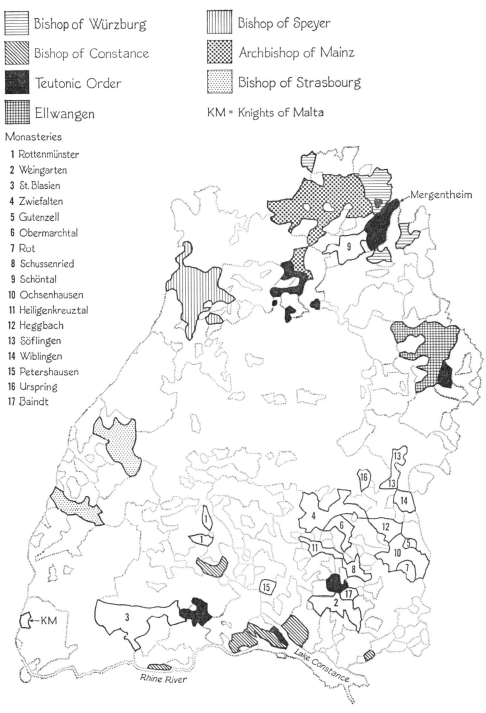

Legend

Bishop of Würzburg		Bishop of Speyer	
Bishop of Constance		Archbishop of Mainz	
Teutonic Order		Bishop of Strasbourg	
Ellwangen			

KM = Knights of Malta

Monasteries
1 Rottenmünster
2 Weingarten
3 St. Blasien
4 Zwiefalten
5 Gutenzell
6 Obermarchtal
7 Rot
8 Schussenried
9 Schöntal
10 Ochsenhausen
11 Heiligenkreuztal
12 Heggbach
13 Söflingen
14 Wiblingen
15 Petershausen
16 Urspring
17 Baindt

Mergentheim

KM

Rhine River

Lake Constance

Southwestern Germany, ca. 1550~1650
Ecclesiastical Lands

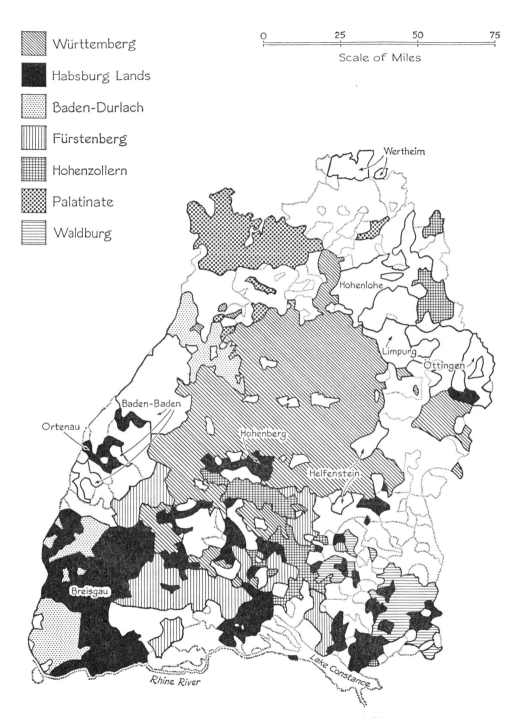

Württemberg

Habsburg Lands

Baden-Durlach

Fürstenberg

Hohenzollern

Palatinate

Waldburg

Scale of Miles

0   25   50   75

Wertheim

Hohenlohe

Limpurg

Öttingen

Baden-Baden

Ortenau

Hohenberg

Helfenstein

Breisgau

Lake Constance

Rhine River

Southwestern Germany, ca. 1550~1650
Larger Secular Lands

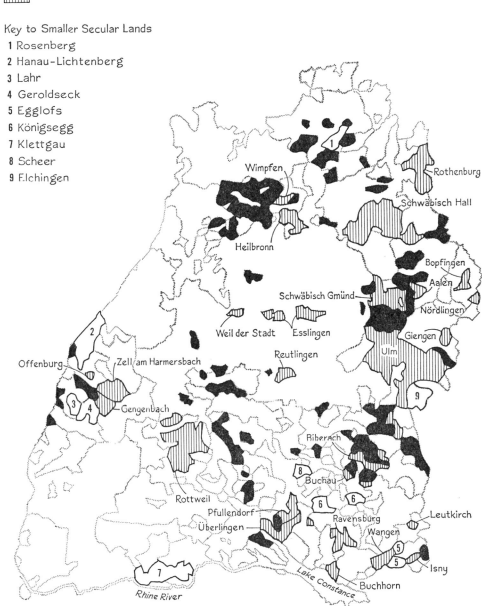

 Imperial Knights

Imperial Cities

Key to Smaller Secular Lands
1 Rosenberg
2 Hanau-Lichtenberg
3 Lahr
4 Geroldseck
5 Egglofs
6 Königsegg
7 Klettgau
8 Scheer
9 Elchingen

Wimpfen

Rothenburg

Schwäbisch Hall

Heilbronn

Bopfingen

Aalen

Schwäbisch Gmünd

Nördlingen

Weil der Stadt   Esslingen

Giengen

Ulm

Reutlingen

Offenburg

Zell am Harmersbach

3 4   Gengenbach

Biberach

8

Buchau

6   6

Rottweil

Pfullendorf   Leutkirch

Ravensburg

Überlingen

Wangen

5

5

Isny

Buchhorn

Lake Constance

7

Rhine River

Southwestern Germany, ca. 1550-1650
Smaller Secular Lands

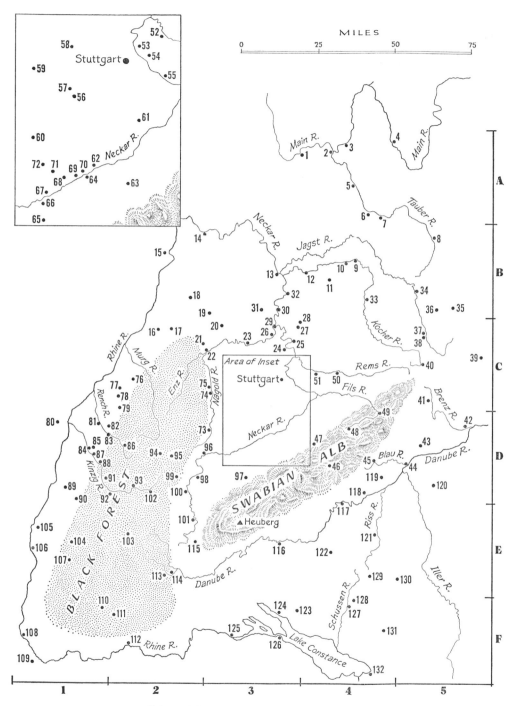

Place Names Mentioned in Text

Key to Map on Facing Page

Place names are listed alphabetically. The number following each place name is the number corresponding to that place on the map or the inset; these numbers are followed by location finders.

Witch Hunting
in Southwestern Germany
1562–1684

Chapter One

Introduction

ANYONE picking up a book on witchcraft is bound to have some questions about the author's attitude toward his subject. Many authors prolong the uncertainty by allowing their prejudices and attitudes to emerge gradually in the course of the text. Such a technique has certain dramatic advantages, but it can also lead to suspicion or confusion concerning the writer's purposes. I shall accordingly state at the outset that I do not "believe" in witchcraft. Thus the reader must not expect to encounter arcane lore or the details of obscene rites in this study; folklore, and even the fate of Kepler's mother, though interesting, are not my concern here.[1] Such a warning would not be necessary if scholars in the field of witchcraft were more adroit in averting the pitfalls of sensationalism or the charms of darkest Africa.

Second, I must report with some disappointment that the evidence I have seen does not support the widespread contention that witches formed organized groups for ritual (or any other) purposes.[2] Despite earnest efforts to uncover such groups, I found that the legal torture practiced by the witch hunters sufficiently explains confessions of ritual activities among witches without concluding that they actually took place. As an inexperienced researcher bent on overturning the solid conclusions of the past, I regret this failure; but its admission may serve to disarm those critics who claim to know the answers without consulting the evidence.

Third, I should point out that our common picture of the witch as an ugly old hag, living alone, and known for her eccentricities is not unlike the sixteenth- or seventeenth-century stereotype. Many scholars delight in upsetting this commonly held view by noting that men, young women, and children, wealthy and poor alike, were all convicted of witchcraft. Though factually correct, this assertion is misleading, for it was only during the largest witch hunts that the stereotype deteriorated dangerously, leaving all social classes and all types of people open to suspicion. By choosing to neglect this distinction, some scholars make their subject seem more mysterious, and themselves more profound, than they are.

Again, it has become fashionable in pursuing local studies of witchcraft to disdain the larger questions raised by more traditional scholars.[3] The implication would seem to be that local history operates on such a radically different plane that it cannot yield important results for general European or intellectual history. But inquiries into the larger issues of witchcraft cannot, in fact, fruitfully proceed in the absence of detailed local studies; and I have taken the further view that local questions, properly asked and exhaustively answered, not only permit but indeed obligate the asker to reflect on the larger issues implied. The mere fact that certain questions first arose in the nineteenth century makes them no less worth answering today, as long as the scholar's categories are not limited by ancient controversies. Accordingly, this study will examine closely the traditionally problematic areas of religion and greed in the light of local, legal, and archival evidence. In particular we shall be very much concerned with regional differences in the style and severity of witch hunting. In these terms, the present study might best be viewed as a form of comparative history.

Another basis for this study is a modest familiarity with social theory and the anthropological study of witchcraft. Anthropologists in particular have long sought to detect patterns in witch hunting, in ways that seem quite applicable to historical research.[4] In my analysis of the largest witch hunts of southwestern Germany, therefore, I shall emphasize those recurring patterns of conduct that point to fundamental social mechanisms at work. A similar concern for the social groups involved in witch hunts calls for close scrutiny of the social class, social status, age, and family patterns, wherever the documents allow. Finally: I shall pay particularly close attention to the dynamics of the large panic trial itself.

My willingness to borrow certain techniques from the anthropologists should not, however, be seen simply as acceptance of a functionalist interpretation of German witchcraft. Many scholars have admonished us not to be too quick to condemn the witchcraft of other (primitive) societies, since it often seems to perform a valuable integrative "function" for them. Thus witchcraft may reinforce ideals of neighborliness and charity while providing sanctions against antisocial behavior; witchcraft accusations seem often to provide legitimate channels for aggression against persons otherwise immune. In this manner, anthropologists have confidently compiled lists of functions that witchcraft may perform.[5] Such functionalism seems especially attractive when applied to historical materials, for it allows historians to interpret their materials without falling prey to petty ethnocentrism. Functionalism seems to foster exactly that inner sympathy with historical societies that historians try to develop in their work. George L. Kittredge argued in this vein in suggesting that witchcraft made real sense in the seventeenth century.[6] More recently, E. William Monter has insisted that Jean Bodin actually won his argument in defense of witchcraft.[7] Both men have shown a laudable willingness to accept early modern thought on its own terms. Among explicit functionalists, Kai Erikson has argued that witchcraft accusations in early New England were a part of that society's attempt to define its moral boundaries and character.[8] The sociologist Guy Swanson has suggested that witchcraft in Europe was a response to ambivalence toward political authority during the Renaissance.[9] And George Rosen, especially, has opposed the assertion that witch trials were attacks of social madness by demonstrating that they often served important social functions.[10]

All of these studies show intelligent application of functionalism to historical study, but they all embody a teleological method and a relativist intent that ultimately yield confusion. But the social sciences have in fact come to examine their functionalist assumptions with increasing precision, and to recognize that functionalism itself very often leads to neglect of the "dysfunctional."[11] The historical application of anthropological theory has also gained in precision and expertise; in a study of witchcraft in Essex, for example, Alan Macfarlane concluded that accusations there, rather than preserving old patterns, actually contributed to social change.[12] He found that in Essex, "witchcraft beliefs and accusations were a neutral weapon, not necessarily only at the command of conservative forces. They might not only be used to 'express moral rules . . . outside the criminal and civil law,' but also to generate the energy for the creation of *new* 'moral laws.' "[13] One need not accept Macfarlane's broad framework to recognize that his is a new and more cautious functionalism, a sympathetic but critical use of anthropology.

A similar caution came to govern my own work. I began my research with the blithe notion that I might discover the functions of witch trials in German society, but after examining the records of the largest witch trials of southwestern Germany I concluded that these major panics served no valid social function, and were indeed dysfunctional. Society was not made stronger and more cohesive by such trials, but weaker and more torn by suspicion and resentment. It may be true that small witchcraft trials, involving one or two suspects, continued to reinforce social boundaries and traditional morals well into the eighteenth century; certainly some small-scale suspicion of witchcraft has prevailed in certain regions down to the twentieth century.[14] On the whole, though, witchcraft cannot be assessed positively.[15]

Recognizing the limits of functionalism brings into question the extent to which all "preindustrial" societies are similar. Many historians have tried to apply the insights of social anthropology to Western materials by arguing that industrialization has been such a powerful force for change that the "world we have lost" was directly comparable to primitive African societies.[16] If so, the reaction of primitive societies to growing industrialization might provide insights into the history of preindustrial Europe. The dangers of such an approach are becoming clear, for sixteenth- and seventeenth-century Europe can scarcely be compared to today's primitive societies. Early modern Europe already exhibited a series of parallel paths to higher social status, a high literacy rate, an extremely diverse but interlinked religious outlook, a typically "Western" family pattern, and a measure of industrial development that preclude all comparisons with today's primitive societies.

Such a cautionary conclusion does not mean that European historians have nothing to learn from anthropology.[17] It does mean, though, that we should stop comparing the details of one society with those of another. If social anthropology is to be useful to historians, it will be on the theoretical level, with respect to the kinds of questions asked, the kinds of problems recognized, and the kinds of methods employed. Thus the present study will not bristle with arcane allusions to the Navajo, Azande, or Cewa. Instead we may hope that the problems delineated here will reflect an appreciation for the "nomothetic," or pattern-seeking, approach. This approach reflects my admiration for the contributions made by social anthropologists.

Models derived from economic determinism or from psychology have also been applied to witchcraft materials, without great success. It is frequently thought, for example, that the confiscation of property afforded the witch hunters an irresistible, gross monetary motive.[18] Corrupt officials no doubt flourished in one or another time or place. But as a general explanation, greed falls short on two counts: in some witch-infested regions confiscation was absolutely forbidden; and where confiscation did occur, the rate was often quite low. Moreover, various other crimes carried the penalty of confiscation. Must we therefore assume that trials for treason or murder were also inspired by greed?

In a similarly imperious way, the defenders of psychological history have on occasion concluded that certain mental aberrations evident in such famous witchcraft manuals as the *Malleus Maleficarum* can explain all subsequent witch hunts. According to these theorists, the celibate inquisitors projected their own feelings of guilt and deprivation onto women, who of course constituted for them an acute temptation. These and similarly far-ranging conclusions reflect more ingenuity and deliberation than solid research, for the German courts of inquisition during the sixteenth and seventeenth centuries were in fact composed of laymen with wives and families. Other scholars have postulated, though without offering evidence, a subtle mother hatred at the root of witchcraft accusations.[19] But despite its subsequent fame, the misogynistic *Malleus Maleficarum* of the fifteenth century was couched in difficult Latin, and was therefore accessible only to scholars. Indeed, one finds only the rarest mention of the *Malleus* in German sermons and trial records of the period, and surprisingly little emphasis on that symptom so dear to its authors, impotence. One may conclude that this sort of generalized psychological approach, based on a few *loci classici*, is inadequate to the study of witchcraft.[20]

Still, social and psychological studies can be more sophisticated, and the best of them have offered complex explanations of witch hunting. Judges, for example, often assumed a semiecclesiastical role in which demands for confession and repentance were no longer strictly judicial, but part of an attempt to save souls. Suspects, moreover, may have suffered from hysteria, epilepsy, hallucinations, and "perturbations of sensory functions," that "for a very large part explain the 'corporal or imaginary visions,' the diabolical persecutions, obsessions, and possessions."[21] But psychopathology provides no golden key to an understanding of witch hunting; though it can help to explain why certain people appeared to be victims or perpetrators of demonic seizures, it cannot make clear why certain periods or regions experienced severe witch hunts. Thus a more sensitive analysis is in order.

It is also clear that greater precision is called for in discussing the dynamics of the witch hunt. In attempting to explain why witch hunts broke out at specific times, scholars have pointed to their temporal conjunction with wars of religion and outbreaks of heresy hunting.[22] There is no doubt some validity in correlating witch hunts with periods of religious conflict and renewal, but the correlation is still incomplete, and the reasons for the beginnings of large-scale witch hunting remain unclear.

The reasons for the decline in massive witch hunts by the middle of the seventeenth century also require attention. It was once fashionable to identify the rise of skepticism in the seventeenth century as a cause of the decline in witchcraft trials. The trials, however, had effectively come to an end before the skeptical opponents of witchcraft had achieved any notable philosophical victories. This fact led other scholars back to the notion that the European world view was changing as the witch trials came to an end, and that the specific arguments against witchcraft advanced in the late seventeenth century were therefore of minor consequence.[23] Still other scholars clearly perceived that "witch trials were done away with everywhere by governments that still believed in sorcerers and witches."[24] Such an insight provides a firm grasp of the complex mechanisms at work in witchcraft trials, and is fully substantiated in the present study. In short, it would seem that witch hunters in many regions stopped hunting and executing witches not because they no longer believed in them, but because they no longer knew how to find them.

If this study has a characteristic emphasis, then, it is the search for the dynamics, the movement in time during individual witch hunts and over the whole period of witch panics. Rather than assume that one witch trial was like another, or that witchcraft can be defined in the same terms for both the sixteenth and seventeenth centuries, I have tried to observe shifts in emphasis, in meaning, and in the functioning of social mechanisms. One cannot assume, as the great scholar Joseph Hansen did, that witchcraft theory ceased to evolve after 1540, and that the trials undertaken after that year were simply automatic responses to set beliefs.[25] Rather, we shall examine in detail the evolution of witchcraft trials and witchcraft theory in a restricted region of Germany.

This brings us to the limitations of space, time, and subject matter that will govern this study. When I first set to work, I envisaged an analysis of all of the witchcraft trials in the entire region called Upper Germany, including Baden, Württemberg, and German-speaking Switzerland. And to have been comprehensive, the study would have had to encompass Alsatian witch trials as well. That I innocently imagined such a task to be feasible can be laid to the common assumption that Swabia had had very few witch trials.[26] When I began poring over the voluminous records of Swabian witch trials, however, I realized how futile and superficial such a general survey of Upper Germany would be. Since a fairly recent dissertation on Swiss witchcraft had roughly summarized the printed literature for that region,[27] I turned my attention to southwestern Germany, for which no rude survey of any sort existed.

The source materials on witchcraft are more extensive than most people would suppose. Sermons, diaries, and local tracts contain useful information, as do the legal records of judicial proceedings and of consultations with learned legal faculties. There is also a large, though often arcane, secondary literature on witchcraft in the German Southwest, which often supplements manuscript materials with information about documents now lost. All of these sources make a thorough survey possible.

But it is indeed striking how few decent surveys of witchcraft exist for Europe, surveys that attempt to list all of the witch trials in a given town or region. With a few notable exceptions,[28] the study of witch hunts has remained impressionistic, and many historians have fallen prey to the most frivolous broadsides and scandalous rumors. Often, reports of thousands of witches executed may be traced to writers who were either delighted or horrified by the spectacle of mass witch trials; in either case, gross exaggeration was inevitable.

Current research on witchcraft must therefore build on a critical appreciation of what *did* happen. Only by patient analysis of all relevant literature can we observe the patterns in a region or period that might help us to an understanding of the witch hunt.

It was with such considerations in mind that I decided to concentrate upon the trials in the German Southwest. To anyone aware of the complexities of German historical geography, however, it is obvious that no modern definition of southwestern Germany really fits the geographical facts of the sixteenth and seventeenth centuries. At that time approximately 350 territories formed a checkered map of lands held by 250 knights and princes, 25 imperial cities, and some 75 ecclesiastical lords.[29] The territories had no special unity, no capital, and no larger organization that could represent them as a whole. Baden and Württemberg at that time occupied only about one-third of the territory that they do today. Under such circumstances, only individual territories had any real unity. Still, for purposes of comparison it was necessary to examine more than just one territory. The only apparent solution was an arbitrary one: I treated the area contained in modern Baden-Württemberg regardless of resulting anachronisms. In this study, then, the term "Baden-Württemberg" will refer to the modern state; for historical purposes, I will call this area the German Southwest. References to Baden or Württemberg will denote the smaller areas these territories occupied prior to the Napoleonic era.

It would take a lifetime to examine all primary sources on witchcraft in the German Southwest, and basic information on witchcraft and witch trials in the area is in fact available from a mass of secondary sources. As I began researching, it became clear that I would have to further limit the scope of my study, and good sense dictated studying only the larger witch trials. More information is available for larger trials, and their dynamics were distinctly different from those of small ones. Specifically, large-scale panics depended on rounds of mass denunciation among those suspected of witchcraft, whereas small trials did not. In fact, long after the large-scale panics had ceased in the German Southwest, we find recurrent cases of witchcraft in which only one or two people were implicated. One may conclude, therefore, that the large trials represented witch hunting at its most virulent, and exhibited an element of sheer panic not manifested in the smaller, intermittent trials.

Thus I decided to examine in detail only the large witch hunts, while keeping the smaller ones in mind for reference and comparison. But it was now necessary to decide arbitrarily what constitutes a "large" witch hunt. After surveying the witchcraft literature on Baden-Württemberg, I decided that any hunt resulting in 20 or more executions in one year could qualify as large. There were 17 or 18 such witch hunts, and I found a measure of reliable information for 14 of them (see Table 5, p. 73). This produced a manageable group with large enough variations in time, region, and severity to yield good comparative material.

To ensure that I was not choosing a falsely weighted sample, I also examined briefly all the trials that had led to the execution of ten or more people in a year (see Table 5). My brief review suggested that I was justified in limiting my attention to the 14 large trials for which information was available. Still, the smaller hunts offered their own lessons, and Macfarlane and Monter have recently studied such hunts with fair success.[30] In two instances, those of Reutlingen and Calw, small scares were so instructive that I included them in the analysis of the large trials in Chapter 6.

With the largest trials delineated, it was easy to establish a formal period to be covered by my research. The first large hunt in the German Southwest occurred in 1562, at Wiesensteig. The last occurred less than 20 miles away in Esslingen, between 1662 and 1665. With the inclusion of Reutlingen and Calw, then, this study covers the period 1562 through 1684.

In sum, what follows is an analysis of witchcraft and witch hunting as they appeared in southwestern Germany. Starting from a short analysis of some basic problems in the interpretation of European witchcraft, we shall proceed to a study of the shifting denominational views regarding witches and of the growth of Catholic orthodoxy. That theoretical vantage point will yield some insight into the patterns in time, space, and confession that characterized all witch hunts in the German Southwest. We shall then be equipped for a narrative analysis of the largest witch hunts and the general crisis of confidence they produced. In the final chapter I shall summarize what is known about the people accused of witchcraft, and I shall try to explain both the popular suspicion directed toward old women at the start of most panics and the breakdown of this stereotype as the panics progressed.

Chapter Two

An Anatomy of Witchcraft

MODERN scholarship has produced a number of competent histories of witchcraft from pre-Christian to post-Christian times.[1] Fortunately this relieves us of the need to present a detailed chronological review of what is generally known. Yet from the viewpoint of the great trials of the sixteenth and seventeenth centuries, certain basic considerations have either been neglected in these narratives or left buried in their footnotes. Before proceeding to the German Southwest, then, we should examine the broad European foundations of witchcraft theory; we should study the basic anatomy before we begin peering through the microscope.

During the sixteenth century, a wide variety of treatises, both scholarly and popular, filled the air with controversy over the nature of witchcraft. Yet amid the seeming chaos of competing views, three basic tenets were recognized as fundamental to virtually all serious witchcraft theory.[2] First, the devil had to have the physical power necessary to work all the evil effects ascribed to him; he could not be a mere tempter. Second, God had to allow the devil the exercise of his powers; i.e., the devil's actions had to agree in some way with the divine plan. And third, the essential pact of the witch with the devil had to be based in some rationale; the pact had to be part of the devil's plan while remaining the responsibility of the witch. Although some regions of Europe, like Essex in England, seem to have adopted a fully diabolical concept of magic and witchcraft only in the seventeenth century, most literate defenders of witchcraft beliefs from the fifteenth century on debated and discussed each of these tenets in trying to awaken their readers to the dangers that threatened.[3] Accordingly, much of the enormous literature on witchcraft found its focus in the controversy surrounding these three issues.

In discussing the power of the devil, all writers of the sixteenth century, both Catholic and Protestant, used the Bible as their basic source.[4] According to the Bible, the devil had deceived and tempted Eve; he had tormented Job and destroyed his crops, cattle, and children; he had carried Christ to the top of the Temple in Jerusalem; and he had possessed with demons those unfortunates whom Christ later healed. Such explicit acts supplied firm evidence that the devil had great physical powers;[5] anyone who might wish to deny the flight of witches, for instance, had to deal with Christ's presence atop the Temple. Real problems arose only when theorists tried to explain exactly by what means the devil moved material things. This was, of course, the fundamental question behind all *maleficium*, or injury by use of evil spirits: How could immaterial, incorporeal substance produce the motion of material, corporeal substance?

Aristotle approached this problem with the concept of the unmoved mover, which he described as causing motion as "the object of desire." Thus an incorporeal being could act not as a physical agent, but only as an object of love.[6] Scholastic thought took over this theory, maintaining that it was the function of all angels to cause local motion; they caused the movements of the heavenly spheres and could move earthly matter as well.[7] The devil and his legion were essentially angels whose fall had only impaired, but not destroyed, their angelic powers. One could argue, therefore, that devils were still able to produce local motion in terrestrial substances. When prompted to construct more adequate mechanical explanations, writers on witchcraft usually shifted to analogy. The authors of the famous *Malleus Maleficarum* explained that "bodily nature is naturally born to be moved locally by the spiritual which is clear from the case of our own bodies, which are moved by our souls. . . . Corporeal matter naturally obeys a good or a bad angel."[8] And if souls could move their bodies, how much easier is such motion for an "entirely immaterial spirit such as a good or bad angel."[9] The renowned French jurist Jean Bodin added to the arguments favoring diabolic powers by reasoning that if the devil could move the soul without the body, it would be still easier for him to move the soul and the body together without disturbing the close union between them.[10] The question of exact mechanism was obviously not considered pertinent. Except for a few Renaissance Aristotelians, even the opponents of the witch trials readily conceded the devil his power to produce local motion.[11]

In addition to powers of local motion, the devil was thought to have previous knowledge of many things. He acquired such prescience, however, only by using his natural talents. By his speed and long experience, for instance, it was clear that the devil could know many things that man could not, and by accurately interpreting scriptural prophesies he would know of things to come. In proposing these ways by which the devil could know the future, sixteenth-century writers were making no original contribution, and very few men of their time seem to have opposed their reasoning.[12]

At the same time, there were certain powers that God had not granted to the devil. No orthodox Christian could ever suggest that the devil had powers of creation *ex nihilo*, or that he could produce an essential change of form. Nor could he work a true miracle, for this would have placed in jeopardy the miracles by which God gave proof of his truth. Therefore, the devil could not raise the dead, part the seas, or work real cures of bodily ailments. Such wondrous things as he seemed to do were accomplished through the use of natural powers that exceeded human comprehension; his acts were not miracles, but marvels.[13]

Just as important as the question of the devil's power was that of divine permission. The devil's power to do certain things posed no real danger unless God permitted him to do them. The primary source in this sort of discussion was usually the Book of Job, whose first chapters showed plainly that Satan had to gain the consent of the Lord before testing and tormenting Job. This argument, too, was generally accepted in its day, and a multitude of writers in the sixteenth century argued against any sort of Manicheism that could relieve God of responsibility for evil by positing an evil principle beyond His control. Both defenders and opponents of witch hunting actually agreed in their opposition to Manicheism, although they often accused each other of falling into this heinous form of heresy.[14]

The problem that arose from God's permission was a moral one: Why had God permitted the devil to work so much evil? Again with fair unanimity, writers of the sixteenth century responded that God used the devil to test the faithful and punish the wicked. The Bible provided many illustrations of both situations, and major differences of opinion arose only in deciding how men should behave in adversity. If one were simply afflicted by the devil with disease and misfortune, then one could do little more than bear the test with the patience of Job.[15] If there were natural remedies to be sought out, however, it was sinful neglect not to use them. "Natural remedies" included both the lawful use of natural medicines and whatever measures could be taken against the perpetrators of evil. Thus murderers should be apprehended and punished, and witches discovered and burned. Bodin followed precisely this argument in asserting that one must pursue witches "with all diligence and complete rigor so that the wrath and vengeance of God may cease."[16] Citing the *Malleus Maleficarum*, Bodin illustrated his case with a German town near Constance whose plague did not subside until the witchcraft in the region had been destroyed. A similar execution seems to have saved the town of Verigny in April of 1579.[17] In these arguments, Bodin (and the witch-hunting school in general) did not exceed the time-worn arguments of the later Middle Ages.[18] The final examples brought forward by Bodin, however, introduced the third crucial assumption in the theory of witchcraft, the pact with the devil.

It was easy enough to prove on biblical grounds that the devil had physical powers, and that God allowed him to use them to test and punish mankind. It was much more difficult to prove man's intentional complicity in such works of evil. To be sure, one could cite the magicians of Pharaoh, the witch of Endor, or Exodus 22:18, which enjoined the faithful: "Thou shalt not suffer a witch to live." None of these passages spoke directly to the point, though, and it was here that the earliest controversies arose and scholastic arguments became most complex. Late medieval theorists had argued, if somewhat inconsistently, that the very production of maleficia required the cooperation of witch and devil.* It was clear that "witches, by the exercise of no natural power, but only by the help of the devil, are able to bring about harmful effects. And the devils themselves can only do this by the use of material objects as their instruments."[19]

But the *Malleus Maleficarum* conceded that "in the time of Job there were no sorcerers and witches, and such abominations were not yet practiced."[20] Evidently, the devil had managed to get along without human assistance in biblical times. To escape these embarrassing

---

* There was rarely any question of witchcraft's being a form of natural magic, for witches were held to be too stupid to have the necessary insight into nature for this sort of magic. See Thorndike, *History*, V: 69.

discrepancies, the sixteenth-century defenders of witch hunting no longer held that the devil *required* the help of witches to produce harmful effects, but simply maintained that it was to his advantage to use it. Only in this way could the devil be sure of the allegiance of his followers, and only by enticing witches into sinful abominations could he confirm them in their guilt and secure them for his kingdom.[21] In addition, men like Bodin held that the devil could actually do more evil with the help of witches than without it. As the body cannot act without the soul, nor the soul alone eat or drink, yet together body and soul can do all these things; so too, the witch and the devil together could do more than either separately.[22] Witch hunters naturally exulted when they discovered palpable evidence of written pacts binding a witch to the devil.[23] Indeed, by the close of the sixteenth century, most commentators found the essence of witchcraft to be this pact, the crucial bond that tied man to the powers of evil.

With the pact, demonic power, and divine permission, all the fatal elements were present, and the theory of witchcraft could stand firmly against attack. One might then deny all manner of incidental details and yet remain stoutly in favor of witch hunting itself. With these three crucial elements in mind, we may review the status of witchcraft theory in Europe. Because scholarship has been particularly confusing in its approach to the medieval origins of witch hunting and to the kinds of opposition that witch hunting provoked in early modern Europe, we shall take up these topics in turn.

Most accounts of European witchcraft assert that early medieval Europe maintained a cautious skepticism, or even disbelief, toward witchcraft.[24] The assertion seems especially plausible in light of the fact that the large witch hunts began only in the later medieval period. Using this fact as a lever, scholars have strained to pry open the mystery of the late Middle Ages. They have sought to explain the seeming growth of credulity and superstition during this era, and to determine what crucial element was added to the theory of witchcraft. By and large, scholars have explained this apparent decline in critical faculties by emphasizing the growth of a scholasticism that sanctioned elaborate demonologies and wild tales of demonic power. Even Saint Thomas has been called before the court of reason to defend himself against the charge of nourishing the "witchcraft delusion."[25] In simplest terms, such scholars have seen the spread of witch hunting as the result of an increasingly widespread belief that demons could appear as men and animals, that witches existed in large numbers, that they could fly, that they attended secret sabbaths, and that they could provoke a wide variety of temporal evils. If such an account is correct, it is clear that the origins of witch hunting were intellectual, and, more specifically, scholastic. And if this is true, it is easy to believe that the witch craze declined when an enlightened Europe regained its healthy skepticism regarding the demonic world.

Our analysis of witchcraft theory can prove useful at this point. If the essential crime of witchcraft resided in a pact with the devil, then the growth of belief in witches' flight and secret sabbaths, or in charms and necromancy, cannot have directly produced those unique elements that made the witch hunt possible. In any event, other scholars have shown that the medieval scholastics did not invent anything new in witchcraft theory, but merely borrowed from their predecessors.[26] But if the scholastics did not invent the superstition of the late Middle Ages, we are thrown into confusion, and we must sharply reexamine the thesis that the earlier Middle Ages were skeptical, and therefore free of superstition about witchcraft.

In fact, the attitude of the early Church was by no means unified or unequivocal. Among its clergy, pagan magic fell under condemnation as a spiritual crime, an atavistic relic of pagan religion. Yet few clerics seem to have denied the physical dangers of harmful magic—a magic to which both Roman and Germanic law attached stiff secular penalties. Theologians like Saint Augustine asserted that spirits could work wonders in the world and take the shape of men and animals.[27] The Church, however, sternly condemned some magical beliefs as clearly superstitious or heretical. The Second Synod of Bracara in 563, for example, castigated the Priscillian belief that the devil could control the weather,[28] and many magical ideas were condemned for their pagan origin or content.

The classic text in this regard has always been a celebrated legal relic of the ninth century, the canon *Episcopi eorumque*. This canon condemned the belief that certain women rode out at night on the backs of animals in the company of the goddess Diana, explaining that they were merely deluded by the devil into thinking that they did such things. Historians have long considered this crucial document convincing proof that the early Church rejected all notion of witchcraft. Unfortunately, they have failed to recognize the canon's constant emphasis on the preservation of God's sovereignty.[29] Such women "wander from the right faith and relapse into pagan errors when they think that there is any divinity or numen except the one God."[30] In other words, the canon *Episcopi* asserted that these women had fallen into serious heresy by attributing divine powers to a mere creature. Such persons were said to lose the faith, "and he who has not the right faith in God is not of God but of him in whom he believes, that is, the devil."[31]

Far from dismissing such simple people as visionaries or lunatics, as so many scholars have supposed, the canon condemned them as infidels: "Whoever therefore believes that anything can be created, or that any creature can be changed to better or worse or be transformed into another species or likeness, except by God himself who made everything and through whom all things were made, is beyond all doubt an infidel [and worse than a pagan]."[32] Nor did the early medieval Church deal lightly with such infidels and heretics. These were no addled dreamers; they were to be uprooted thoroughly from their parishes. Thus bishops were urged to attack vigorously and "eradicate the pernicious art of sorcery and magic invented by the devil, and if they find a man or woman follower of this wickedness, they are to eject them foully disgraced from their parishes."[33]

It is certainly correct to view the canon *Episcopi* as a major statement of ecclesiastical policy toward witches. But far from "flatly contradicting the whole theory of witchcraft" as it would later be established, the canon in fact laid down the guidelines by which the Church judged witchcraft well into the eighteenth century.[34] For the Church, witchcraft was a serious sin regardless of its physical effects; it was in itself a spiritual crime to be treated in the same way as apostasy or heresy. Only those who consider the witches' sabbath or the flight of witches to be the total essence of witchcraft can maintain that there was a radical shift in Church policy between the ninth and fifteenth centuries. Indeed, even Rossell Hope Robbins agrees that "the pact with the Devil was the essence of witchcraft."[35] Evildoing or night flying notwithstanding, "the main crime was knowingly invoking the Devil and opposing the Church; quite secondary was causing disease or death."[36] Such a statement, also Robbins's, renders clearly foolish his perpetuating the fable that the canon *Episcopi* asserted "in effect that belief in witchcraft was superstitious and heretical."[37] The canon had condemned in no uncertain terms any glorification of the devil's powers or worship of the devil. It is important to emphasize this often misunderstood point because it forms a crucial pillar of continental witchcraft belief. Well into the seventeenth century, men would argue, just as the canon had, that witches did not in fact do all they believed they did, but that they were guilty anyway because their will was corrupt. The early medieval Church, in other words, laid down the basic argument that the essence of witchcraft lay in the witch's pact with the devil. Thomas Hobbes and Pierre Bayle even presented secularized versions of this analysis.[38]

Thus we must recognize two distinct views of magic and the devil in the early Middle Ages, neither one of which was "skeptical." On the one hand, secular authorities punished maleficium, or harmful magic, whenever it was discovered; indeed, under Roman law it had been a capital crime. On the other hand, the Church punished witchcraft as a form of apostasy and devil worship with the most severe punishments it could muster in that era; banishment was the explicit threat of the canon *Episcopi*. In sum, two crimes existed side by side, the secular crime of maleficium and the spiritual crime of apostasy.

If it now seems less certain that the early Middle Ages were totally skeptical as regards witchcraft, we have still to explain what happened in the late Middle Ages to provoke widespread witch hunts. We have already suggested that witchcraft beliefs were not simply an awkward agglomeration of peculiar ideas, and that the scholastics did not add or invent any crucial component of witchcraft fantasy. Still, the role of the scholastics cannot be dismissed outright. We need not follow G. L. Burr in his conviction that witches were "postulated into existence by the brain of a monkish logician."[39] But neither can we ignore the fact that although the notion of the witch's pact went back at least as far as the canon *Episcopi*, it was nonetheless open to later elaboration.

The scholastics, in analyzing the pact between man and devil, brought together the secular and religious conceptions of magic and witchcraft, seeking to forge a unity where none had existed. The key to this genuine contribution to witchcraft theory was the view that all magic was demonic. We have seen that the early medieval Church viewed magic as heathen superstition; in the thirteenth century, all magic became heresy. The crucial element for Thomas Aquinas was the *pactum implicitum,* by which all magical practices involved a contract, either tacit or explicit, with the devil.[40] Since no one could seek superhuman effects except by prayer to God without implicitly calling upon the only other superhuman power available, the devil, all magic necessarily involved apostasy from the Christian faith.[41] A modern Jesuit scholar has labeled this step the "moral-theological mistake in the judgment of superstition."[42] It was the crucial link that allowed the Inquisition to shift its attention from outright heretics to magicians and sorcerers, and inquisitors often cited Aquinas between 1323 and 1327 when attacking the invocation of spirits as heresy.[43] Pope John XXII followed the same reasoning in condemning magic as devil worship. His bull of 1326 asserted that magicians "sacrifice to and adore devils; they make or obtain figurines, rings, vials, mirrors, and other objects by which they command demons through their magic art."[44] The confusion of magic and heresy threw open a whole new field of action for the Inquisition, for superstitious magical beliefs and practices were common among both village and city folk. Once heresy was established, execution was the common punishment, since canon law already so provided.[45]

This expanded view of the witch's pact would not have been particularly threatening if the Inquisition had not convinced itself that the forces of evil were legion and well-organized. After successfully stamping out heresy in southern France, the Inquisition of the fourteenth century turned to sorcery and magic, drawing on the theory of the implicit pact with the devil to uncover startlingly large numbers of heretics. At Carcassonne and Toulouse, confessions referred to secret meetings of sorcerers who worshiped the devil in animal form and practiced various kinds of harmful magic. Whether such groups or secret organizations ever existed in any form is exceedingly difficult to determine, but it is certain that the Inquisition at this point was acting on the basis of its long experience with the Albigensian heresy. After more than a century of investigating such group activities, it was only natural that the Inquisition should expect magicians to be similarly organized.[46] In trials occurring around 1335, the Inquisition forced women to confess that they had met for obscene rites and had worshiped the devil, whom they considered the equal of God.[47] Misappropriating the biblical promise that those who sought should also find, the Inquisition indeed sought and found a secret cult of devil worshipers, giving birth in the process to the concept of the witches' sabbath. It took scholars more than a hundred years to catch up with the "facts" unearthed by the Inquisition, and to square them with earlier Church law.[48] The canon *Episcopi* presented certain obvious problems until theologians discovered a loophole suggesting that although riding with Diana was not possible, riding with the devil clearly was.[49] The effect this explanation had on inquisitorial proceedings cannot be overestimated. Now that witchcraft appeared to be an organized cult, one accusation might lead to many. Thus the concept of the witches' sabbath did not change the essential crime of witchcraft, but it made accusations and trials more likely and more perilous.

Even this danger might not have existed if inquisitorial methods had been more reasonable.[50] In fact, the Inquisition conducted trials in secret, used torture frequently, denied counsel or defense to the accused, and demanded the names of accomplices.[51] One might well wonder how the word of a convicted witch, a slave of the father of lies, could be accepted as legal evidence against others suspected of witchcraft. The stock answer was that witchcraft was so horrible a crime that no orthodox, upright Christian could possibly know anything about the crimes committed. Witchcraft, in other words, was a *crimen exceptum*, a crime distinct from all others. Thus Bodin explained that "proof of such evil is so obscure and difficult that not one out of a million witches would be accused or punished if regular legal procedure were followed."[52]

Under such legal circumstances, the idea of the witches' sabbath provided fertile ground for mass trials, and it was the sabbath more than any other trait that distinguished continental witchcraft of the early modern period from sorcery of the earlier Middle Ages. In the European context, in fact, one might well restrict the term "witchcraft" to the group phenomenon, the diabolic cult, as opposed to the individualistic sorcery of all times and places.[53] However, such a distinction should not obscure the fact that the crime involved had not changed. Apostasy and the pact with the devil were still at the heart of witchcraft as they had been in the canon *Episcopi*, even though the circumstances surrounding the charges of witchcraft had changed radically.[54] Proceeding from prosecutions of one or two scattered sorcerers at a time, the Inquisition used the doctrine of *pactum implicitum* to discover large groups. In other words, the late Middle Ages did indeed make two fundamental contributions to the witch hunt, notably the idea that all magic involved a pact with the devil, and the idea that a massive, organized witch cult threatened Christendom.

Traditional scholarship has found that the classical theory of witchcraft was brought to completion in the late fifteenth century by a pope and two Dominican friars. In 1484, Innocent VIII issued a bull against witchcraft called *Summis desiderantes affectibus*. This bull was hardly unique,[55] but it was exceptionally important in the history of witch hunting because it was frequently reprinted. The Pope sorrowfully reported that he had heard of widespread witchcraft in Upper (i.e. southern) Germany, as well as in the rest of Germany. Unmindful of their own salvation and deviating from the Catholic faith, many persons of both sexes were supposedly abusing themselves with evil spirits, causing untold harm to cattle and crops, spreading disease and death among their neighbors, and preventing the sexual act. It was clear that these men and women committed not only the secular crime of maleficium but also a spiritual one if they could "blasphemously renounce that faith which they received by the sacrament of baptism," and "offend the Divine Majesty."[56] And yet despite the papal letters carried by the inquisitors, both clerics and laymen were resisting the proper investigation of these evils. Innocent therefore commanded that this opposition cease and authorized the bishop of Strasbourg to threaten with excommunication, suspension, or interdict all who hindered the inquisitors.

Armed with this authorization, two Dominican inquisitors, Heinrich Institoris and Jacob Sprenger, set to their task with vigor. By 1486, they had executed 48 witches in the diocese of Constance alone.[57] By that date too, they had completed their legal manual on witch hunting, the famous *Malleus Maleficarum*. Although it was in most respects a very derivative work and did not emphasize the witches' sabbath, the *Malleus* did contain detailed information on methods of trying, judging, and sentencing witches. In addition, it emphasized two points that distinguish it from the bulk of earlier witchcraft literature.[58] First, the *Malleus* stated that witchcraft's primary danger lay not in its threat to the Christian faith, but in its physical harm (maleficium) to the faithful.[59] Using one example after another, the

Malleus showed how genuinely destructive witches were and contended that no one could be secure as long as they practiced their heinous arts. In addition to this emphasis on maleficium, the *Malleus* sought to show that the devil was an essential part of all witchcraft, and the entire first book was devoted to just this issue. Thus the *Malleus* completed the task begun by the scholastics by offering a final synthesis of the secular crime of maleficium with the ecclesiastical crime of apostasy.[60]

Second, Institoris and Sprenger found themselves forced by their own logic to insist that secular courts should join the struggle against witches; after all, if the crime they discussed was largely secular in its emphasis on evil magic, they could hardly avoid calling on the secular authorities for help.[61] Also, if the threat was as general as they claimed, the Inquisition by itself could never hope to crush it single-handedly, since many countries and territories forbade the Inquisition to operate within their borders.[62] The appeal to secular jurisdictions was so successful that in the sixteenth century we find the Inquisition involved in witch trials only in Spain and Italy. In France, Germany, and Switzerland, secular courts took over both the task and the methods of the Inquisition, and only in ecclesiastical territories did the Inquisition remain directly responsible for witch hunting. (Indeed, the state proved more efficient in this ecclesiastical role than perhaps it ever was in any other role it has assumed.)

Looking backward from the sixteenth century, it now seems clear that the general development of witchcraft has often been portrayed in a confusing manner. Clearly, all three elements of full-blown witchcraft—divine permission, diabolic power, and especially the pact—existed in the early Middle Ages. The distinctive contribution of the fourteenth century was not so much a fall from healthy skepticism into the sewers of superstition as it was an attempt to combine secular and ecclesiastical thought. The prior example of heresy was clearly decisive in this regard. If this thesis is adequate, it means that the "witchcraft delusion" cannot be simply attributed to scholastic genius. Instead, it grew out of current legal practice, scholastic theory, and the known or suspected practices of heretics themselves. The history of witchcraft thus escapes the narrow confines of *Ideengeschichte* and becomes a problem with crucial legal, intellectual, and social dimensions.

This approach to the history of witchcraft also has important implications for the sixteenth and seventeenth centuries. It is commonly thought that the efforts of Innocent VIII made disbelief in witchcraft a form of heresy. In its most pointed form, this view invokes the notion that, in the early Middle Ages, belief in witchcraft was in itself heretical; seen in that context, the shift of the late Middle Ages is all the more striking. We have tried to cast doubt on this formulation as it applies to the earlier period. How well does it work for the period 1450–1650?

First, it must be noted that Innocent VIII did not lay down any doctrine of witchcraft as required dogma, for though he certainly approved and fostered witch hunting, he made no doctrinal innovations. Similarly, the *Malleus Maleficarum* failed to become generally accepted doctrine, and its influence and authority have been vastly exaggerated by most scholars. In fact, the *Malleus* represented a summation of what was widely known or believed, with an infusion of acidly misogynistic ideas; no court that I am aware of ever tried to enforce belief in its peculiar tenets.

Questions of doctrine raise the general issue of orthodoxy in the sixteenth and seventeenth centuries. To an extent not generally recognized today, men were free to speculate and disagree about witchcraft, at least during the sixteenth century. Neither the law nor the theology of witchcraft was firmly enough established to prevent a wide variety of thought on the subject. Thus a great many thinkers in the sixteenth century were openly skeptical of the more extreme aspects of witchcraft theory. Characteristically, these men have since been regarded as heroes of liberated thought, daring to risk life and property to attack the ecclesiastical orthodoxy. It detracts nothing from their dedication to recognize the plain fact that, in general, the risks these men ran were minimal, since no clear orthodoxy had yet been established.

Lawyers of the sixteenth century worked particularly hard to clarify the confused medieval heritage. Although the medieval Inquisition treated all magic as a capital heresy, secular courts continued for centuries to try and punish only attested cases of harmful magic (maleficium). In sixteenth-century Germany, we can observe a marked ambiguity regarding the distinction between harmful magic and magic that produced no physical harm. A prime example is the criminal code promulgated by Charles V in 1532, the *Constitutio Criminalis*

Carolina, often called simply the *Carolina*. Because this code formed the basic criminal law of the whole Holy Roman Empire, it deserves a brief analysis here. In the crucial article regarding witchcraft (Art. 109), the *Carolina* stated: "Item, when someone harms people or brings them trouble by witchcraft, one should punish them with death, and one should use the punishment of death by fire. When, however, someone uses witchcraft and yet does no one any harm with it, he should be punished otherwise, according to the custom of the case; and the judges should take counsel as is described later regarding legal consultations."[63]

Although it seems clear here that harmless magic was less severe a crime than harmful magic, later jurists could not easily make sense of this attitude. One cannot simply conclude that, as a secular code, the *Carolina* avoided the punishment of spiritual crimes, since blasphemy, perjury, sodomy, and theft of the sacramental host were all capital crimes,[64] whose particular horror lay in their peculiar offense to God. The distinction between harmless and harmful magic seemed illogical to many thinkers, and we will see that many legislators, jurists, and theologians could make sense of this distinction only if diabolical magic were separated from natural magic.* Only then would it make sense to punish natural magic less severely.

Other major sixteenth-century theorists, notably Grillandus, argued that the civil law should not punish beneficial sorcery, such as magic used to cure disease or drive away storms.[65] Such a view did not prevail, however. The electoral Saxon criminal constitutions of 1572 are often taken as the final triumph of the view that harmless magic was as serious a crime as genuine maleficium.[66] These codes drew the rather logical conclusion that "if anyone, forgetting his Christian faith, sets up a pact with the devil or has anything to do with him, regardless of whether he has harmed anyone by magic, he should be condemned to death by fire." Certainly this clause embraced preceding scholastic theory, but it was also clearly a logical interpretation of the *Carolina*. Thus the code went on to say that "if anyone causes harm by magic without such a pact, be he great or small, this sorcerer or sorceress should be executed with the sword."[67] In trying

---

* Much rank nonsense has been written on this point. Men did not become crazed with lust for witch burning in the second half of the sixteenth century; they simply applied logic to the *Carolina*.

to clarify the *Carolina*, the Saxon legislators obviously did not fully accept the theory that all magic involved a pact with the devil. In practice, German courts tended to avoid such technicalities by proving witches guilty of both a pact with the devil and specific damage.

Witchcraft remained controversial in other ways as well, and witchcraft theory in the early modern period simply cannot be viewed as a monolith challenged only by a few heroic and enlightened men. The medieval heritage was diverse and confused enough to ensure continued debate. Thus it should be clear that men could disagree with works like the *Malleus Maleficarum* while in no way regarding themselves as skeptics or opponents of witchcraft theory.

One of the most controversial elements of witchcraft theory was the flight and sabbath of the witches. As we have seen, the canon *Episcopi* denounced belief in both phenomena. The same view was widely held into the seventeenth century, and though spokesmen for this view have been regarded as among the earliest opponents of the witchcraft "delusion," they would in fact be better treated as representatives of an established and respected dogmatic position.[68] It is worth recalling that neither the bull of Innocent VIII nor the final summary of fifteenth-century theory, the *Malleus Maleficarum*, made any detailed mention of the sabbath. Men like Ulric Molitor, who wrote on witchcraft in 1489, have been wrongly labeled as "enlightened" but "too cowardly to draw practical conclusions" from their insights.[69] Indeed, Molitor rejected many aspects of witchcraft as illusory (e.g. transformations into animals, flight, sabbath, copulation with the devil), but he agreed that true witches who had a pact with the devil deserved death. Similarly, he asserted that the devil could not harm men or cause damage of any sort unless he had the prior permission of God. Thus Molitor's views were not the first glimmerings of an enlightened mentality but the echoes of a well-known and respected medieval tradition.[70] In the sixteenth century, we find similar expression of skepticism about the flight and sabbath of witches from Symphorien Champier, Johann Fichard, Andreas Alciatus, Samuel de Cassinis, Franciscus Ponzinibio, and Michel de Montaigne, to mention only a few at random.[71] Yet not one of these men ever denied that true witches should be severely punished.

Other thinkers, like Johann Georg Gödelmann, the Rostock jurist originally from Swabia, tried to reduce the legal abuses of witch hunting and attacked many of the superstitions concerning witchcraft. Gödelmann also denied that witches could raise storms, but he nonetheless conceded that true witches must be severely punished.[72] Indeed the tradition of the canon *Episcopi* remained vital down to the eighteenth century and became the core of what we shall call the Württemberg preaching tradition.

Although most of the controversy regarding witchcraft bore on matters other than opposition to the witch hunt, the sixteenth and seventeenth centuries did produce a great many genuine opponents. Some disputed one of the three basic propositions necessary to any witchcraft theory; these may be called radical opponents, since their criticisms, if effective, would have made witch hunting intellectually indefensible. A second group of writers concentrated their attack not on the theory of witchcraft but on the legal abuses associated with the witch trial. To understand the nature of the debate in southwestern Germany, let us turn briefly to a major proponent of each of these two types of opposition, to the radical Johann Weyer and the pragmatic Friedrich von Spee.

By definition, radical opposition to witch hunting began with the fundamental tenets of witchcraft theory. Without oversimplifying a complex matter, we can distinguish three modes of radical opposition; since witchcraft theory rested on the witch's pact, demonic power, and divine permission, fundamental criticism of witch hunting had to attack at least one of these three concepts. On scriptural grounds, the notion of the pact was probably the weakest.* In addition, it was not theologically clear why the devil had to have human help once he had received the permission of God. For both of these reasons, the notion of the pact with the devil was the object of the first full-scale attack on witch hunting.

Johann Weyer (Wier) was the ducal physician at the court of Jülich-Cleves when he published his famous *De Praestigiis Daemonum* (1563). He there asserted that the devil had far greater powers than were commonly acknowledged.[73] The devil had no need for human aid in plaguing mankind, but delighted in making feeble, foolish old women think they had worked all sorts of magical wonders. Such women did not deserve the stake, but needed Christian instruction.

---

* Isaiah 28:15 was the text most often cited in this regard: "We have made a covenant with death, and with hell are we at agreement."

Far worse in Weyer's eyes were the learned magicians (*magi infames*) who knowingly invoked the devil in their occult arts, but who usually escaped prosecution of any sort. Still, not even these men deserved death. Only the poisoners (*pharmakos* in the Septuagint), those who killed or harmed by natural means, deserved the death so commonly dealt out to others. Further, Weyer attacked the idea of the pact with the devil by bluntly asserting that it did not exist.[74] Though it is often suggested that Weyer was a confused voice crying in the wilderness, and that he was ill treated for his efforts,[75] the most recent thorough account fails to bear out such a view.[76] Not only was Weyer well treated and respected for his work, but he also prompted a whole series of writers to oppose witch hunting and to refresh (if not wholly to expropriate) his arguments. Up to 1630, one can list at least 12 articulate disciples in Germany alone.[77]

Thus Weyer and his school constitute the first mode of radical attack on witch hunting. The other two modes denied either God's permission or the devil's power. In general, these tenets were much more defensible on biblical grounds, but Weyer himself brought into question the permission of God in asserting, in several places, that the devil could never disobey the laws of nature.[78] Since he based much of his argument on biblical exegesis, though, he could not deny that God had often allowed the devil to work wonders. One can find premonitions of a mechanical universe in the sixteenth century,* but only a few rigorous judicial astrologers seem to have drawn this conception to its logical conclusion.[79] Wonders, marvels, and general disorderliness still reigned in the sixteenth century and left much room for demonic action. Only much later, at the end of the seventeenth century, could one find rigorous theories of an orderly nature in which God has forbidden all intrusion by such disorderly, unlawful processes.[80]

Thus the power of the devil was virtually incontestable except for those slight restrictions that we have already noted. Orthodox exegesis of the Book of Job could only result in the conviction that the devil could do almost anything the Lord allowed him to do.[81] In this regard, Weyer actually expanded the power of the devil, for only by inflating the devil's powers could Weyer excuse the women whom

---

* See p. 42 below, and note 55 to that passage, on pp. 238–39.

the devil deceived and deluded.[82] During the seventeenth century, belief in the powers of the devil was often used as a criterion of sound religion, since doubt on this point might reveal skepticism, unwillingness to accept the authority of scripture, or "atheism."[83] Only in the very late seventeenth century could one find fundamental criticism of this point. Working with a completely new metaphysics, the Dutch Cartesian minister Balthasar Bekker argued that spirit and matter cannot influence one another, and since the devil is a spirit, he cannot have physical effects in the world.[84] Another skeptic, Christian Thomasius, refused to go as far as Bekker, but discredited the power of the devil and denied the criminal nature of heresy as well as pacts with the devil.[85] With such men we enter a whole new world of thought; clearly, such fundamental criticism could come only from those who were ready to replace old structures with new. For these reasons, Weyer's attack on the witch's pact provided the most valuable and credible of the radical attacks on the foundations of witchcraft, while by the very excesses of their argument, men like Bekker were to have little real influence.

But even apart from these three modes of radical criticism, it was possible to oppose the practice of witch hunting itself. Jurists produced just such an attack when they protested that trial methods were brutal or unfair and contended that anyone would confess anything in order to escape further torture. Torture had originally been intended as a means of freeing the criminal from the power of the devil so that he could speak the truth.[86] The entire judicial system rested on distrust of circumstantial evidence[87] and on belief in the powers of the devil,[88] and torture and confessions were seen as the only ways of circumventing such dangers. Properly used, torture and confessions might have constituted a workable judicial system. Improperly used, they were the tools of judicial murder.

The dangers of improper trial procedures had long been recognized. The *Carolina* had aimed at preventing many of the worst abuses by regulating the use of torture.[89] Already in 1515, Andreas Alciatus recognized the danger of torturing witches until they named those they had seen at the sabbath.[90] Weyer raised the same point in 1563 when he protested that prisoners were "constantly dragged out to suffer awful torture until they would gladly exchange this most bitter existence for death," and that they quickly confessed "whatever crimes were suggested to them rather than be thrust back into their hideous dungeons amid ever recurring torture."[91] The Rostock jurist Gödelmann agreed in 1584 that improper trial methods accounted for many miscarriages of justice.[92]

Lawyers and those anxious to remain orthodox in their theology thus found a vast body of legal abuses to attack.[93] For example, the renowned Saxon jurist Benedict Carpzov has gone down in history as a merciless witch hunter.[94] But in fact, he worked hard to remove abuses of torture and to eliminate the concept of *crimen exceptum*.[95] The legal or pragmatic mode of attack on witch hunting found its most eloquent expression in the Jesuit Friedrich von Spee. With years of experience as confessor to witches about to be executed, Spee asserted that he had never seen one who really had done the things she confessed. His *Cautio Criminalis* of 1631 is a stinging indictment of German criminal procedures: "a single innocent person, compelled by torture to confess guilt, is forced to denounce others of whom she knows nothing; so it fares with these, and thus there is scarcely an end to accusers and accused, and, as none dares retract, all are marked for death."[96] Spee also charged that the judges were using witch trials and confiscations to enrich themselves. This accusation has more recently been advanced as one of the main reasons for witch hunting in general, and we will examine it carefully later.[97] Spee, moreover, depicted a chain reaction of accusations that had no natural limit; witch trials, he thought, could only be stopped by the interference of a prince. If this were true, it would be a point of great significance. We shall have occasion to examine such social mechanisms later, and to show that, in this matter, Spee was wrong.

Spee's *Cautio Criminalis* exerted a decided practical influence. It may be that the well-known moderating influence of the Swedish army during the Thirty Years War was due partly to his influence on Queen Christina of Sweden.[98] Spee's arguments also persuaded the Elector of Mainz, Johann Philipp von Schönborn, to put an end to witch trials in all electoral lands after 1647.[99] Although Spee published his work anonymously to avoid conflict with his ecclesiastical superiors, even the Roman Inquisition recognized that abuses were common; in 1635 it admitted that "the Inquisition has found scarcely one trial conducted legally."[100] Spee's book appeared in 16 editions (including translations) within 100 years. But since it was not theoretical in purpose, it had very little effect on witchcraft theory; and, unlike Weyer, Spee acquired no widespread following.[101] Only with Christian Thomasius did his work enter the mainstream of witchcraft discussion; but by then, as we have seen, entirely new theoretical concepts were in use.[102] By 1700, when Spee had become well known, witch hunting was once more the sporadic, isolated, and rare event that it had been before 1400. The age of panic was over.

Our close examination of continental witchcraft theory leads naturally to certain broad conclusions. With a tripartite basis of divine permission, diabolic power, and the witches' pact, witchcraft theory in the early modern period was not rigid and monolithic, but flexible and varied. Since a number of diverse interpretations of it could make good theological sense, at least in the sixteenth century, orthodox thinkers could be skeptical of some aspects of witchcraft without feeling drawn into general, or "atheistic," skepticism. In particular, the tradition codified in the canon *Episcopi* provided a constant source of inspiration for men hoping to glorify God and restrict the power of the devil. Such men might still condemn the apostasy inherent in witchcraft while doubting many of the examples of devilish power. Among genuine opponents of witch hunting, a number of approaches were also available. As we have seen, the notion of a pact with the devil was hardest to defend theologically, and it was here that Johann Weyer applied critical pressure. Because Weyer's radical criticism threatened to undermine one of the crucial intellectual foundations of continental witchcraft theory, it irritated witch hunters more than the practical and essentially legalistic criticisms of Friedrich von Spee. However, one need not conclude that Spee's work was without influence. Rather, it is possible that because his criticisms escaped any thorough response, they were better able to influence the attitudes of judges. In recognizing Weyer's work as more radical, one should also recognize that the pragmatic, legal approach was ultimately more effective.

In any event, with this review of the gross anatomy of European witchcraft behind us, we can turn our attention to the situation in southwestern Germany.

Chapter Three

Witchcraft Theories in the German Southwest

As we have seen, medieval witchcraft theory was not a monolithic, uncontested block of superstition, but rather a body of ideas that remained flexible through the sixteenth century and beyond. Nor does it seem that nothing new was added to witchcraft theory during the sixteenth century. Yet the great authority on witchcraft, Joseph Hansen, came to just such a conclusion. He asserted that by 1540 the entire body of law and scholastic theory, as well as a phantasmagoria of occult details, had been so effectively consolidated that it remained essentially unchanged for a century after. Hansen concluded that the outburst of witchcraft trials after 1540 was "nothing but the natural dying out of the medieval spirit, which the Reformation only partially pushed aside and in this matter hardly even touched."[1]

Such an assertion rests on a division of witchcraft theory into a multitude of constituent ideas. After 1540, to be sure, few, if any, really new elements were added to the conglomerate of magic and witchcraft. Subsequent historians have been content to tinker with details of Hansen's analysis, never recognizing that witch trials in no way depended on a particularly full or elaborate doctrine. We have seen that only three relatively simple but crucial ideas were necessary for the witch hunt; in fact, many regions hunted witches successfully without using any complex demonology whatsoever.[2] Hansen's notion that witch trials merely reflected the natural death of the medieval spirit also made intelligent comparisons impossible. Following his analysis, one could only trace the sporadic but relentless growth of modernity and rationalism in Europe. But if one puts aside his framework, a number of interesting questions arise.

The most important single issue for men in sixteenth-century

Europe was religion and the Reformation aroused passions that have continued to hamper witchcraft research down to the present day. Nineteenth-century scholars disputed vigorously the comparative severity of witch hunting in Protestant and Catholic lands. Protestants blamed the witch trials on the methods of the Catholic Inquisition and the theology of Catholic scholasticism, while Catholic scholars indignantly retorted that Lutheran preachers drew more witchcraft theory from Luther and the Bible than from medieval Catholic thinkers.[3] Hansen blamed both sides equally, and by about 1910 the controversy reached a stalemate. Historians have since agreed that both Protestants and Catholics conducted their own witch hunts and have pursued the matter no further.

This stalemate can be broken by examining the evidence anew, beginning at the local or regional level while still keeping broader questions in mind. One possible approach to the problem is to tabulate all data available on witchcraft trials in the German Southwest. For instance, Table 1 shows that there were 480 witch trials in the German Southwest between 1561 and 1670 for which the number of persons executed can be established.[*] Of these trials, 317 occurred in Catholic areas, i.e. in territories or cities whose official governments were Catholic, while Protestant territories accounted for 163 of them.[†] This represents a Catholic-to-Protestant ratio of 1.9 to 1. However, we should not jump to the conclusion that Catholic witch trials were nearly twice as severe as Protestant trials, since at that time Catholics might have greatly outnumbered Protestants.[‡] Indeed, if this were the information available, there could be no escape from the impasse.

Fortunately, we are able to determine roughly how many persons were executed for witchcraft between 1561 and 1670, or at least to

---

[*] For these and all subsequent statistics, consult the Appendix.

[†] In the face of so striking a difference between Catholic and Protestant witch hunting, it may be well to make clear what we mean by a Catholic or Protestant territory. We refer not at all to the religion "of the people," nor even to that of a majority of the people. Even in so well controlled and documented a region as England, the most recent authority (Trimble, *Catholic Laity*) has hesitated to give even a rough estimate of the number of Catholics in the Elizabethan period. In the splintered and shifting German Southwest, the situation is even more obscure. But these demographic uncertainties are not even completely relevant. Trials were conducted by the state and by magistrates at least officially loyal to the state. Theoretical as well as practical reasons, therefore, dictate that the *official* religion of a state designate the faith to which we should impute those witch trials occurring in any particular state.

[‡] Comparative population figures of this sort are nonexistent.

TABLE I

Number of Persons Executed in Witchcraft Trials,
1561–1670, by Religion

Years	Protestant[a]			Catholic[a]		
	Trials	Executions	Executions per trial	Trials	Executions	Executions per trial
1561–70	10	91	9.1	11	10	0.9
1571–80	7	23	3.3	60	350	5.8
1581–90	11	17	1.5	46	313	6.8
1591–1600	21	87	4.1	33	223	6.8
1601–10	25	63	2.5	20	139	7.0
1611–20	25	51	2.0	43	586	13.6
1621–30	20	28	1.4[b]	52	591	11.4
1631–40	19	192	10.1[b]	15	52	3.5
1641–50	4	3	0.8	15	40	2.7
1651–60	4	5	1.3	10	13	1.3
1661–70	17	60	3.5	12	16	1.5
Subtotals	163	620	3.8	317	2,333	7.4
Supplements[c]		82			194	
TOTAL EXECUTED		702			2,527	

[a] Figures include only those trials for which the number of persons executed is known.
[b] The contrast between the 1620's and 1630's is less sharp when we realize that 1620–32 saw 36 Protestant trials and 192 executions, or 5.3 executions per trial.
[c] We can supplement our totals with inexact data from secondary literature:

Protestant trials			*Catholic trials*		
1570–1610 Wertheim	72		1561–1648 Rottweil	76	
1596–1628 Rammersweier	10		1570–1610 Gengenbach	32	
TOTAL	82		1557–1603 Ortenau	15	
			1581–1594 Waldsee	6	
			1601–1676 Stein a. R.	28	
			1615–1629 Weil der Stadt	37	
			TOTAL	194	

establish absolute minimum estimates. In the absence of any systematic bias that would tend to yield more complete information for Catholic than for Protestant trials, we may compare these minimum estimates with some confidence that they represent the situation as it was. Between 1561 and 1670, at least 3,229 persons were executed for witchcraft in the German Southwest. Of these persons, 702 were tried and executed in Protestant regions, while 2,527 were tried and executed in Catholic territory. This represents a Catholic-to-Protestant ratio of 3.6 to 1.

These figures show that regardless of the ratio of Catholic to Protestant populations in the German Southwest, Catholic magistrates conducted only 1.9 times as many witchcraft trials as the Protestants but executed 3.6 times as many people. Thus Catholic magistrates in the German Southwest were nearly twice as zealous (or efficient, or superstitious) as Protestant magistrates, and roughly twice as many people were likely to die in a Catholic trial as in a Protestant one. The reasons for such a striking difference are not obvious and have never been made clear.

One might well be tempted to agree with those Protestant historians of the last century who praised the liberating effects of the Reformation. However, elementary caution suggests that we should examine the matter more closely. Sharp scrutiny of available data reveals that from 1560 to 1600, Protestants and Catholics had roughly equal rates of execution. After 1601, however, the Catholic rate rose while the Protestant rate fell slightly, and Catholics were more than twice as severe as Protestants in the period 1601–70 (see Table 2). Clearly, such a difference could not depend merely on the Catholicism or Protestantism of a certain area, but must depend on the specific kind of Catholicism or Protestantism. To determine how Catholic or Protestant attitudes changed during the sixteenth century, or to explain marked differences in the severity of witch hunting, we must reconsider the controversy over witchcraft in the German Southwest.

As we have seen, witchcraft was a controversial subject in the sixteenth century. The attitude of the Catholic Church was still very much in flux, and only in 1580–81 did it decisively condemn certain popular practices as magic.[4] At the same time, secular thinkers from both the neo-Platonic and Aristotelian schools emphasized the purely

TABLE 2

Comparison of Protestant and Catholic Trials
Before and After 1600

Years	Protestant trials			Catholic trials		
	Trials	Executed	Executed per trial	Trials	Executed	Executed per trial
1561–1600	49	218	4.4	150	896	6.0
1601–70	114	402	3.5	167	1,437	8.6

natural character of magic. Men like Ficino, Pomponazzi, Agrippa, and Paracelsus, for example, insisted that magic need not involve spirits of any sort and could result from a deep and exact knowledge of nature.[5] As noted earlier (p. 23), lawyers also held varying opinions about magic. The German Southwest in particular was a microcosm of the European controversy over witchcraft, and a closer scrutiny of the development of witchcraft doctrines in that region may clarify the emergence of confessional differences at the end of the sixteenth century.

MARTIN PLANTSCH AND THE TRADITION OF EPISCOPI

We have seen (p. 24) that the witch hunting of Sprenger and Institoris formed the basis for the *Malleus Maleficarum*, and that the jurist Molitor attacked several of the inquisitors' conclusions by reviving the tradition of the canon *Episcopi*. Witches could not do all that they confessed to, but they were guilty because of their association with the devil. Thus, already in the fifteenth century, southern Germany felt the pull of two important and divergent points of view. This tension remained characteristic of witchcraft theories in the German Southwest, influencing most discussions at crucial points. In particular, the tradition of the canon *Episcopi* remained so strong there that it produced a theological school of great importance. The first complete statement of this school in the sixteenth century came from Martin Plantsch, a theologian at the University of Tübingen and a disciple of the nominalist Gabriel Biel.

In 1505 a witch was condemned and executed at Tübingen. Such trials were so rare at the time that Plantsch considered his congregation ill-informed on such matters, and he preached against the evils of fear and superstition in 1505. In January 1507 these thoughts appeared in extended form as an *Opusculum de sagis maleficis*.[6] Here Plantsch used a distinctive threefold division of material that would remain the model for sermons throughout the sixteenth century. First, he discussed what witchcraft was and how the devil performed his wonders; second, he considered the question of why God permitted such works; and third, he reviewed the means that men could properly use to guard against witchcraft. More important than Plantsch's tripartite preaching model was his attitude toward witchcraft, an attitude that would reappear in both Catholic and Protestant thought over the next 200 years. As a nominalist, Plantsch believed that God controls and directs everything on earth.[7] Since man suffers only when God wills or allows him to suffer, he contended, one should fear only God: "This is stated against the many who, whenever they suffer or undergo harm, blame or accuse the stars, or demons, or fortune, some [blaming] witches, others [blaming] enchanters."[8] When hardship came, Plantsch urged that men follow Job in recognizing that "the Lord giveth and the Lord taketh away."

In his second section Plantsch analyzed the numerous methods the devil used to harm and deceive mankind, and agreed that witches in league with the devil deserved death. Yet when he dealt with ways of combating witchcraft, he nowhere recommended the direct method of simply executing the witches. Instead, they should repent and seek out the sacramentalia of the Church. If no cure worked, they could only endure the hand of the Lord, secure in the hope of increased reward in heaven.[9] In short, Plantsch laid such stress on the providential meaning of witchcraft that he never dealt with ways of punishing it.

Plantsch also attacked astrologers and believers in fortune. Of course, Christian attacks on such pagan beliefs went back to the classical period, but the Renaissance had seen a resurgence of astrological thought.[10] Ernst Cassirer may even have been correct in asserting that the laws of the *regnum naturae* took on increased emphasis as those of the *regnum gratiae* declined.[11] It is clear in any event that, for many men of the Renaissance, astrology provided the model of natural causation on which men like Kepler later built.[12] Yet such Renaissance thinkers as Pico opposed the determinism that accompanied the revival of astrology, and the Renaissance emphasis on ethical freedom must be viewed in part as a reaction to astrology.[13] Other thinkers followed the ingenious reasoning of Paracelsus, who combined freedom and astrology by asserting that man could influence the stars as well as be influenced by them.[14] In sum, astrology was an emotional and intellectual response to the world that persisted well into the seventeenth century; even Kepler remained fascinated by the possibility that it might explain things that other theories left to predestination.[15]

The opposition to astrology was more often religious than strictly scientific. Luther, for example, rejected the insult to God's providence inherent in Melanchthon's astrological beliefs. But even Luther believed that marvelous and mysterious events might be prefigured in the stars. Specifically, God might use the heavens to communicate with man, as, for example, He had used the Christmas star.[16] As a nominalist bent on maintaining God's sovereign control of the world, Plantsch would have agreed with Luther on this point.

In condemning theories of natural causation as insufficient, Plantsch might also have had the Renaissance revival of atomism in mind. In the later sixteenth century, atomism presented a problem similar to that of astrology, and the scholars who revived the teachings of Democritus, Epicurus, Lucretius, and Hero of Alexandria posed a new threat to the autonomy and freedom of the individual. Because they tended to equate the structure of the world with that of a machine, such theories were denounced by theologians like Calvin.[17] Neo-Stoicism also posed a threat to man's freedom until it could be properly disarmed and combined with Christian doctrine. Stoic doctrines of fate aroused vigorous rebuttal from the major reformers, since the notion of an unchanging fate suggested a rigid determinism like that of astrology or atomism.[18] Only when Stoic doctrines of fate were explained as metaphors was it possible to produce a complete synthesis of Christian ideas and Stoicism.[19]

The revival of various classical systems of thought posed problems for the traditional Christian of the sixteenth century. Common to all such systems was a tacit determinism that might endanger both God's providence and man's salvation. During the religious revival of the sixteenth century, many Christian scholars took steps to secure traditional ideas in the face of this determinism.[20] Indeed, Plantsch's protest was only the first in a series of similar outbursts throughout the sixteenth century. It is significant that this religious movement often drew explicit connections between God's restored providence and the world of witchcraft.

WÜRTTEMBERG AND THE LUTHERANS

The views that Plantsch expressed at Catholic Tübingen became the traditional and accepted ones at Lutheran Tübingen thirty years later. Their first full expression came from Johann Brenz, the reformer of Schwäbisch Hall and later of the Duchy of Württemberg. Like Plantsch, Brenz was a teacher of the Word of God, concerned with moral and spiritual problems. To a degree that many modern scholars fail to recognize, witchcraft theory made sense to men of the sixteenth century; it was not purely a fabric of delusional and irrational elements but part of a consistent world view.[21] Yet Brenz saw even more clearly than Plantsch that ascribing storms, famine, and other misfortune to witchcraft created a moral problem. A careful study of Job in 1526 convinced Brenz that the true source of such catastrophes was God himself.[22] They were God's way of chastising, warning, and testing His people, and must be viewed as specific calls for repentance. One could expect no end to "natural" disasters until people put an end to their godless, wicked way of life; to obscure God's warning on this score was both dangerous and irresponsible.

Brenz's view of hardship was in no way unusual, and in 1535 and 1537 he expressed ideas on witchcraft that were quite commonplace in their time. Commenting on Acts in 1535, Brenz admitted that God "permits Satan through witches and enchanters to work miracles, or to deceive the eyes of spectators by his delusions."[23] In his lectures at Tübingen in 1537 he commented on Exodus 22:18, noting that Roman law also punished those who used magic to harm their neighbors.[24]

A hailstorm in 1539 caused Brenz to adopt a basically new point of view, that of the canon *Episcopi* as reformulated by Plantsch and Molitor.[25] As we have seen, Brenz viewed hail and storms as tests or punishments from God. Yet his congregation had laid the blame on witches. To Brenz, this was a dangerous evasion of the whole point, and basing his argument on Job he insisted that storms came directly from God and that witches could have nothing to do with them.

Still, Brenz had to explain cases of witches who later confessed that they had indeed caused particular storms. Borrowing from Molitor, he constructed an argument that might have pleased the enlightened David Hume; he asserted that the witches confused sequence with causal relationship.[26] According to Brenz, the devil could often tell when God was going to chastise His people with a storm, or he could at least see a storm coming from afar. He could then rush to his faithful, the godless witches, and prompt them to work their magical rituals and mutter their imprecations. When the storm finally came, the simple, deluded witches naturally thought that they had caused it. Using this ingenious theory, Brenz was able to emphasize that storms were awesome warnings from God, and that no witch could take the blame and relieve God's people of their moral duty to examine themselves and repent. At the same time, he could accept both the power of the devil to work evil and the existence of godless witches who had spurned their baptism and given themselves to the devil. Indeed, such apostates deserved death in a way that simple heretics did not.[27] When Brenz turned to Exodus, he knew better than to refer to the damage done by witchcraft. This time he commented: "Thus Satan, knowing of a future hailstorm, excites the witch to try to stir up a storm by her incantations. . . . Witchcraft in itself can do nothing."[28] Brenz's commentaries on 1 Samuel, Psalms, and Galatians made the same point. Divine providence was heavily emphasized, and the basic ideas of the canon *Episcopi* were clearly in full vigor.[29]

Of course, Plantsch and Brenz were not the only thinkers to consider storms and catastrophes as direct warnings from God; such a moralizing tone was widespread from the 1540's on.[30] The trend found its most popular literary expression in the plays of Hans Sachs. As God explained in a *Fastnachtspiel* of 1554:[31]

> Since they all from my goodness flee
> I pull them by the hair to me
> And give them plagues and dire need
> So they are forced to give me heed.

This providential view of nature led a number of men in the German Southwest to follow Brenz in rejecting human agency as a proper explanation of disasters, particularly hailstorms. Around the same time that Brenz shifted from a conventional to a providential view of witchcraft, Johann Spreter, Lutheran pastor of Trossingen in Württemberg, made a similar shift.[32] In an anonymous work on witchcraft from 1540 called *Hexen Büchlein*, Spreter vigorously maintained that witches were in fact responsible for many of the evils of mankind, including hail. Spreter noted at this time that a large number of both learned and ignorant persons held the opposing view that witchcraft was merely a figment of the imagination.[33] Three years later, however, Spreter was much more cautious. In the abridged edition of 1543 he conceded that witches did not really raise storms. He now maintained that the devil alone was responsible, or that the devil could see natural storms coming and inform his witches in advance.

In any event, Spreter now insisted that not even the devil could work harm without the permission of God.[34]

Spreter's shift was indicative of the direction taken by all of Württemberg, and especially by the University of Tübingen, in the second half of the sixteenth century. Brenz's sermon on hail was itself often reprinted, and a chorus of Lutheran ministers and theologians was soon to take up his theories in full. On August 3, 1562, a severe hailstorm devastated wide areas in the vicinity of Stuttgart, Esslingen, Tübingen, and Sindelfingen. A contemporary chronicler compared the destruction of crops by the storm to that caused by a full-scale battle,[35] and a pamphlet from the same year stated that "Württemberg has not been so poor and devastated in the last one hundred years."[36] Irresponsible voices attributed this curse to witchcraft. The Württemberg court preachers Matthaeus Alber and Wilhelm Bidembach, both of Stuttgart, denounced such rumors in a series of sermons. They asserted that God was not dead but alive, and that He sustained the world constantly.[37] God was the source of all good and evil except sin; those who denied God as the origin of evil believed in a weak (*halbmechtigen*) God and were no different from the ancient Marcionites who worshipped two gods.[38] Witchcraft existed, of course, but like Brenz, Alber and Bidembach refused to recognize that magic was physically dangerous. Only God could cause a storm. True, He might allow the devil a hand in stirring up the elements, but witches had nothing to do with it. Again like Brenz, the two preachers asserted that the devil rushed to his deputies, the witches, and prompted them to "work their magic by cooking and shaking their odds and ends together in their 'hail pot.'" When the hail came, as willed by God, "then these poor bedazzled people think that they caused it."[39] Following Brenz closely, Alber and Bidembach went on to say that real witches deserved death, not for the evil they did, but for renouncing God and Christ and intending to harm their neighbors. Still, magistrates must not believe all the denunciations of the vulgar rabble (*Pöbel*). Moreover, many women were so stupid and weak that they would confess anything under torture, and shaving suspects from head to toe in search of the devil's mark was clearly indecent. Accordingly, the two preachers insisted that it was better to let a thousand guilty go free than to convict one innocent.[40] They said that if the tares and the wheat were so difficult to distinguish, it was better to let them grow together until the final threshing day, and they cited a common Roman maxim to the effect that "harsh justice is great injustice."[41] Returning to their central theme, Alber and Bidembach concluded that one might burn witches until neither wood nor fire remained, but hail would continue. Men must first repent of their sins.[42] Only then would God turn from wrath to mercy.[43]

Jacob Heerbrand, the famous theologian at the University of Tübingen in Württemberg, also supported the providential view of witchcraft. In 1570, Heerbrand held a disputation on witchcraft ("De Magia") based on the text in Exodus 7 describing the magicians of Pharaoh. Magicians, he said, obviously had deep knowledge of nature and could often work wonders. Such magic was laudable and might even lead to knowledge of God, as in the case of the Magi who followed a star to Christ.[44] Yet witchcraft went much further and involved a pact with the devil. In Heerbrand's view, witches committed many sins including direct opposition to the explicit Word of God, apostasy from God, and abuse of the Name and Word of God. Yet abuse of the Word could have no physical effects, and all other works of witchcraft were illusory.[45] Using an example with which we are already familiar, Heerbrand asserted that the devil deluded his witches into believing that they actually caused storms; it was in this way that he retained their allegiance.[46]

Like other preachers of his day, Heerbrand moralized over disasters and wondrous signs. A comet in November 1577 prompted him to warn his congregation that God was wrathful and would soon punish His people for their cursing and the faithless lives they led. The comet was a sign that God had already notched His arrow and drawn His deadly bow; indeed, epidemics had already broken out in many places. The remainder of the sermon was a ringing call for repentance.[47]

On June 21, 1579, Heerbrand analyzed the significance of a lightning bolt that had struck the castle in Tübingen two days before, igniting the powder room and blowing out one whole side of the castle. Some might have explained this event by natural causes, but Heerbrand pointed out that God allows nothing to happen at random. Others might have blamed the ministers of God for their immoral lives, but Heerbrand retorted that this was outright slander. The great majority blamed such lightning and storms on witches. "But these

poor simpletons and old women can make storms neither by themselves nor with the cooperation of the devil himself."[48] Once again
Heerbrand described the familiar way in which the devil deluded his
"betrothed associates." Citing Job as an example of how one should
react to misfortune, he noted that Job did not say, "The Lord giveth
and the devil taketh away," but instead perceived clearly the true
Cause of all things. And why had God now chosen to blast the people
of Tübingen? It was clear to Heerbrand that God wished "to awaken
us from the sleep of security."[49] In the rest of his sermon, he emphasized the need for true repentance.

With so many authoritative voices supporting it, it is not surprising
that the branch of witchcraft theory begun by Plantsch and Brenz
continued to flourish in Württemberg. In 1565, Conrad Wolffgang
Platz, the preacher at Biberach, spoke on the sin of charms, magic,
and witchcraft. He repeated the new orthodoxy that witches were
heinous creatures worthy of death, even if they caused no physical
harm. Witches, he said, thought that they could do great harm, "moti-
vated by bitter jealousy and greed." In fact, they were victims of
dementia diabolica, a delusion caused by the devil.[50]

Platz elaborated his theme in traditional fashion 19 years later. At
that time a lightning bolt struck the church steeple at Biberach, causing a fire that did great damage to the roof, bells, clock, and organ,
as well as killing four persons and injuring 30 others. Such a calamity
was surely a message from God; it could not be explained away by
natural causation, the devil, or witchcraft. Rather, Christians should
examine the ultimate cause of such chastisement, "for all natural
causes, called *causae secundae*, as well as the devil and the evil persons
[i.e. witches], are nothing but the tool of God Almighty."[51] Platz
went on to condemn the idea that misfortune comes most often to
the worst sinners, and to denounce the vicious gossip attributing the
lightning to the Lutherans' "new Gospel."[52] The congregation must
recognize that God had chosen such startling means to shake His
people out of their "deep sleep of security," to test and strengthen
their faith, and to teach them repentance.[53]

God could speak in other ways than storms and lightning; He
might use all manner of natural disasters including war, blight,
plague, famine, and flood. Even the high prices brought by the "price
revolution" (and more acutely by bad harvests) were considered

messages from God.[54] In an agricultural community, however, the crucial variable was the weather, and it is natural that God so often chose hail, rain, and frost as His voice. Accordingly, Württemberg's theologians paid close attention to such phenomena. In 1598, Johann Schopff wrote a treatise of 173 pages in which he interpreted a recent spell of bad weather. As the Lutheran abbot of Blaubeuren, he was fully aware of the moral tradition of which he was a part. His first task was to show that storms were not purely natural phenomena. Seizing upon an analogy that would be commonplace a century later, Schopff compared nature to a clock. A clock, he said, seems to move by itself through the natural action of the weights inside it. But Schopff also pointed out that a clock will keep time only if the clock-maker regulates it.[55] So too, hail and lightning were carefully regulated by God, and without His regulation all hail and storms would come at one time.[56]

It was more difficult to dismiss the role of witchcraft in storm raising. Yet Schopff fell back on the tradition of the canon *Episcopi* as developed by the Württemberg theologians and spent 40 pages roundly condemning those who accused witches of causing storms. Just as a king did not share his "supremacy, glory, and majesty," God allowed no others to share in His glory.[57] Those who thoughtlessly accused witches of storm raising were guilty of lese majesty against God Himself, and witches who confessed to causing storms had simply been deceived by the devil. Though Schopff built on the tradition begun by Brenz, he in no way tampered with Brenz's original ideas.[58] In sum, Schopff's work is an excellent example of the strong providential tradition in Württemberg during the early period of orthodoxy.

We should not think that after Heerbrand only preachers in small towns maintained the Württemberg tradition, for witchcraft remained a subject of academic interest at Tübingen as well. In the early morning of September 8, 1601, an earthquake shook the region around Tübingen. Johann Georg Sigwart, a professor of Scripture at Tübingen University, felt that God had used this event to provide him a new text for the fourteenth Sunday after Trinity. In cutting through the vain speculation about the meaning of the earthquake, Sigwart followed the Württemberg preaching tradition to the letter. He denied the superficial explanations of those who spoke of witchcraft, and he proclaimed God as the true cause of the earthquake. "It is therefore un-Christian talk when this almighty work is ascribed to witches and sorcerers. For in this our Lord and God is robbed of His title and name (that He alone is Almighty). . . . And even if God should permit the devil to do such things, it does not in the least follow that witches can do them also."[59] The meaning of the earthquake was clear to Sigwart: God was warning His people to repent of their sins and turn to Him. The only way to avert far worse disasters was to trust God and seek His forgiveness.

Sigwart displayed exactly the same attitude when frost ruined the grape crop in April of 1602. Once again Sigwart condemned those who said that such events occurred by chance or were controlled by the planets. He also conjectured that some would blame this disaster on witches, "as is usual with hail and storms." No such explanation was satisfactory, for God, not the devil, was clearly in control of events. Nor did natural causes provide sufficient explanation for a Christian, since reference to natural causes could not explain why the terrible frost had struck precisely when and where it had. One could only conclude that God was once more calling His people to repent. This same frost prompted a very similar sermon in Esslingen. Lucas Osiander, the preacher there, asserted that people had too quickly forgotten the warning of the earthquake the previous autumn. Now it was crucial that men respond with repentance and not escape blame by making anyone in particular responsible for the frost. All of God's people had to feel the burden of punishment and heed the call for general repentance.[60]

On May 29, 1613, a terrifying hailstorm ruined crops and killed cattle in the fields around Tübingen. Again departing from his prepared text, Sigwart preached on hail precisely as Brenz and many others had for over 70 years. Sigwart cautiously admitted that the devil, when permitted, had great powers and could perhaps even cause storms; had not Saint Paul called him lord of the air? But if the devil was limited, his servants, the witches, were even more limited. How could witches raise fog and water into the air to cause rain when they had to fetch their own water from the brook in a pail? How could they cause thunder and lightning when they had to restart their hearth fires with glowing coals borrowed from neighbors? In a way that was by now stereotyped, Sigwart told how the devil deluded witches into thinking they had caused storms:[61]

For when Satan, that keenly perceptive and swift scientist, notices that according to nature a storm may arise, he suggests to his witches (according to their own confession), and commands them to work their magic, and to cook and stir this or that together in their hail pot, or to dig sand from a stream and to throw it up over themselves. Then at the same time it thunders and hails, not because they caused it but because it was already about to happen without them, either by nature or at God's decree. . . . And although such persons on their own confession are burnt by the magistrates or executed (as is reasonable) some other way, yet this is done not because jurists and theologians think that they really caused hail and storms; but because they did not lack an evil, devilish will, and did renounce God and the Christian faith, and did give themselves to the devil, and were so taken in by him that, following their master, the devil's example, they want nothing more than to bring all kinds of harm and misery to man and beast.

If Sigwart's views on hailstorms and witchcraft were stereotyped, they were not then formulas without meaning or emotional content. Rather, the Württemberg theologians often struggled to phrase their message in the most colloquial style they could. Thus for Sigwart, and probably for his congregation, these words linking providence and witchcraft were still meaningful.

Even in Württemberg, the providential *Episcopi* tradition of Plantsch and Brenz occasionally conflicted with the stern mandates of the *Malleus*. This conflict was particularly sharp in the thought of Christoph Stähelin, doctor of theology and church superintendent at Herrenberg and Dornstetten. On April 18, 1607, a bolt of lightning struck Dornstetten in the Black Forest, causing a fire that reduced 26 households to utter poverty. Stähelin's explanation of this disaster set forth the orthodox view that God alone was its cause. Yet it seemed clear to Stähelin that God might work directly or indirectly, and he spoke at length about the evil men in league with Satan who deliberately set fires, made men and cattle sick, or killed them with salves. Yet Stähelin emphasized again that God was the true origin of man's troubles. This conclusion, he said, was an important refutation of three groups of mistaken men, notably the careless Epicureans who said that misfortune came by random accident; the Papists who blamed all misfortunes on the new teaching of the Gospel; and those who ascribed all signs, wonders, and disasters to the devil and witchcraft.

With regard to witchcraft, Stähelin sought to reassure his congregation by pointing out that witches could do nothing without God's permission. This was slim comfort, however, since he admitted that God did permit witches to do a great deal of harm. At points in his speech Stähelin echoed Brenz, as when he explained that lightning came naturally at the decree of God, but that witches got the causal sequence confused with their own cooking-pot magic.[62] At other times he seemed ready to break with the Württemberg tradition and assert that witches were indeed dangerous enemies of men. In the end, the providential thrust of Stähelin's thought forced him to say that Christians must be wiser than dogs that bite the stone thrown at them instead of the man who throws the stone.[63] He therefore urged his congregation not to avenge themselves on the devil or his human helpers but to see, as Job had, that God is the cause of all things. Repentance was man's only refuge.

The *Episcopi* tradition of Plantsch and Brenz met no theological opposition of any note in Württemberg; in fact it remained dominant and unmodified until the start of the Thirty Years War. Tobias Lotter, minister of the collegiate church in Stuttgart, must have been aware that the sermon on hail that he preached in 1613 was part of that tradition. Expanded into a treatise of 140 pages and reprinted in 1615, the sermon was in every way typical of the Württemberg providential school. Its organization was totally conventional, examining in order the origin, meaning, and practical significance of storms. As usual, the first task was to show that God was the source of storms; they did not occur by random accident, nor were they controlled by the stars or nature.[64] Least of all were witches to blame for such disasters; Lotter explained that the devil simply deluded his witches into thinking that they had caused hail and wind. At times the devil did this by simply foreseeing natural storms in the way that Brenz had suggested. At other times he might form a blue cloud before the eyes of the witches, making them think they were actually high up in the air where they could make the clouds crash together to produce rain and hail.[65] Occasionally God did allow the devil to raise storms, but even then the devil had to use the materials at hand "like a good scientist," for he could not do anything "above or against Nature."[66]

Despite their powerlessness, witches were not to be praised or released. Not only had they renounced God but their will was devilish, and this alone made them worthy of death. Since God was the cause of storms, however, it was foolish to blame the devil and witches for every storm, "as most people do." Repeating Alber and Bidembach's plea for caution, Lotter maintained that many innocent women were arrested through mere rumor or denunciation by another witch. Once arrested, they fell victim to unbearable torture and confessed. "Thus has much innocent blood been shed, which cannot be washed off as easily as Pilate rinsed his hands. Rather, this blood screams daily to God, along with the blood of Abel, for revenge."[67] Borrowing the words of Stähelin, Lotter condemned those who reacted only against the instrument, for they were no better than the dog that bites the stone thrown at it. Lotter furiously asserted that attributing changes in the weather to the devil and witchcraft was a sin against all of the articles of the Lutheran catechism. Men sinned grievously, therefore, when they attributed storms to witches and grumbled that the government should have burned all witches long before. God's people should concern themselves more with the meaning of storms, recognizing why God sends them and repenting of sin. In a curious and informative excursion, Lotter condemned as idolatrous various Roman Catholic practices aimed at warding off storms.[68]

With so much preaching on witchcraft in Württemberg, it is no wonder that the providential interpretation of witchcraft influenced popular works as well. For instance, the Württemberg State Library possesses 72 pages (nine signatures) of an anonymous play called *Hexenspiegel*, which was printed in 1600 in Tübingen. In the late nineteenth century, the play's author was identified as Thomas Birck, a Lutheran writer of didactic dramas and pastor of Untertürkheim in Württemberg from 1585 to 1601.[69] The fragment ends in the middle of act 2, scene 3; this was obviously a very long play, and Birck admitted at the outset that it needed cutting to make it suitable for a two- or three-hour stage production. Birck did not cut the work himself, since he felt that the whole play would provide useful home reading.[70]

It is clear from this fragment that Birck's aim was not dramatic, but didactic. Still, the nineteenth-century scholars Karl Goedecke and Johannes Janssen were clearly wrong to call the play an example of the "crassest witchcraft belief."[71] Instead, the lesson Birck taught was a blend of Weyer's views and the Württemberg providential tradition. Citing Brenz and Heerbrand in column notes, Birck made his position perfectly clear: Witches could not raise storms, fly to the sabbath, or copulate with spirits.[72] These were all delusions of the devil, often made easier during the deep sleep caused by the witches' salve. Thus Birck recognized that some persons really did consider themselves witches, but he demonstrated that these people were essentially harmless. The existing fragment does not make clear what Birck thought the Christian attitude toward such deluded people should be, but in act 2, scene 2, he favored a character who spoke moderately with witches and refused to fear them.[73] Thus we might infer that Birk did not favor capital punishment for witches whose only crime was spiritual. If so, he went one step beyond the tradition that began with Brenz, and he foreshadowed the views of Thumm.

Traces of the Württemberg witchcraft tradition appeared not only in dramatic works but also in the spectacular pamphlet-style "newspapers" that circulated widely in the sixteenth and seventeenth centuries. In one such pamphlet, which described the growth of witch hunting in Württemberg, the author told of a witch who had killed some 400 children, fornicated with priests and demons, and flown often to "Heuchelberg" for the sabbath.* At the end of his sensational story, however, the author denied the reality of the flights, asserting that they were all fantasies induced by the devil. Likewise, witches were deceived by the devil into thinking that their own magic had caused a storm, "which would have come without their actions. . . . For the Lord God is alone the author of thunder and rain."[74] The author made no attempt to reconcile his conflicting accounts of witchcraft, but even more profound thinkers sometimes found this hard to do. In fact, without the strong emphasis of the canon *Episcopi* on the constant providence of God, the arguments of the Württemberg school might easily have lost their cogency.

Theologians outside Württemberg also felt the influence of the traditional Württemberg theory of witchcraft. Like the author of the pamphlet cited above, however, such theologians often failed to integrate fully the various elements of the theory. Typical in this regard was Jacob Graeter, a Lutheran pastor and dean of Schwäbisch Hall, the free imperial city that Brenz had reformed. In two sermons given during the summer of 1589, Graeter tried to clear a path through the

* A play on words. *Heuberg* was the traditional Swabian meeting place for witches; *Heuchelei* is hypocrisy.

jungle of contradictory theories that confused the common people and led them to act "unreasonably."[75] He did not succeed in his attempt to clarify matters, though, for his usual approach was to accept simultaneously both sides of an argument as being true. Thus witches did indeed work much harm to neighbors, crops, and cattle.[76] On the other hand, the devil usually acted deceptively, and most of his works were "Beschiss, Betrug, und Blendwerck" by which he repeatedly "duped, deceived, and dazzled" mankind.[77]

Graeter showed the influence of the Württemberg providential tradition when he set out to explain why God permitted witchcraft. God, he said, chose this way to punish our disbelief and superstition, undermine our security, and keep us in fear. Man's only proper response was prayer and repentance. Graeter insisted that magistrates must punish witchcraft, but he also admitted that this was no real solution. After all, if witchcraft was a punishment for sin, the only way to improve matters was to stop sinning.[78] At several points Graeter followed Heerbrand's example by introducing confessional polemics, and by denouncing Roman Catholicism as superstitious and naturally inclined to foster witchcraft.[79]

The same tradition influenced a Lutheran preacher who has often been depicted as one of the most bloodthirsty of all witch hunters.[80] Around 1600, David Meder was general inspector of churches and schools in the county of Hohenlohe and preacher in the residential town of Öhringen. Meder noticed that the people of Hohenlohe were confused and divided on the subject of witchcraft, and that judges apparently had misgivings about taking part in witch trials.[81] He therefore delivered eight sermons intended to clarify the subject of witchcraft.

In his first sermon, Meder drew widely from Scripture, history and, the consensus of all learned faculties to prove that witches existed; interestingly enough, he used the canon *Episcopi* to help make this point (see pp. 15–16).[82] Among the sins and vices of witchcraft Meder included poisoning, murder, theft, and storm raising, which shows that he thought witchcraft was not just a spiritual crime. Still, Meder's argument was weak on one crucial point. He asserted that witches could cause bad weather "because they understand how to bewitch storms with the help of the devil, or rather how to misuse the weather that God sends according to the course of nature, and thereby produce damage.[83] Clearly, Meder was confused by the precise example of storm raising used so often by the Württemberg school. He insisted that witches really caused much damage and flew through the air, stole milk, and harmed their neighbors with powders and salves. Yet he recognized that all of these misfortunes were ultimately willed by God to test and chasten His people.[84] When he tried to deal with storms again, Meder once more echoed traditional Württemberg views:[85]

The fact of the matter is that the devil, being highly experienced with nature, sees when God wants to cause a storm naturally, and knows how to use it to harm both men and the fruits of the field. He travels at once to his witches and tells them to take their witch cauldrons or pots, together with the requisite materials, and cook up a storm. And they actually do hope for the kind of storm that ruins the grain in certain fields while sparing other fields. When the storm comes, they think nothing less than that they caused it.

Meder had too little of Brenz's moral sensitivity to maintain the same point of view consistently. He borrowed the above example practically verbatim from the Württemberg school, but since he failed to grasp the moral reasoning behind it he contradicted it elsewhere.[86]

The thought of the Württemberg school apparently convinced Meder that the devil's snares and delusions made finding true witches much more difficult than most people thought. Thus magistrates should not rely on mere village rumors or other circumstantial evidence.[87] Above all, Meder insisted that evidence gained through torture or denunciation should be discarded. Torture, he said, was often used so mercilessly that innocent people were compelled to confess, and they were not allowed to recant afterward.[88] Meder also reproved the courts for admitting denunciations of one witch by another, "as if the devil cannot lie, and as if witches do not gladly besmirch other, innocent people."[89] The only solid kinds of proof were testimony from two or three God-fearing, impartial witnesses, or a truly voluntary, unforced confession.[90] In sum, Meder was clearly influenced by the Württemberg providential view of witchcraft. His legal arguments were in fact very similar to those advanced by Friedrich von Spee almost a generation later.

Considering the strength of the spiritualizing tendency among thinkers on witchcraft in the German Southwest, it is not surprising that in 1590 Daniel Schrötlin, a hospital preacher in Stuttgart, dealt mildly with a 13-year-old girl who thought that she had caused storms. By telling her that she was only imagining things and placing her in a good home, Schrötlin showed the brighter side of the Württemberg tradition.[91] Yet it must be stressed that the spiritualizing view of witchcraft was open to radically different interpretations. On the one hand, it might convince men that witches were in no way dangerous, and that if their only crime was a spiritual one, death was too extreme a punishment. Such was the view of Johann Weyer (see pp. 25–26) and later of the Württemberg theologian Theodor Thumm. As we have seen, the *Carolina* spoke only of harmful and harmless magic, while theologians in Württemberg made a similar distinction between magic of the demonic and nondemonic sorts. After examining the controversy over witchcraft, Thumm declared that in his opinion there were three kinds of witches. First, there were those who labored under melancholy fantasies and were totally deceived by the devil; these were the same harmless women whom Weyer had defended. A second group did have an actual pact with the devil but caused no harm. The third group had an express pact with the devil, worshiped the devil, and with his help sought to harm their neighbors.

Thumm felt that magistrates should take care to distinguish between these three categories. The first group of mentally ill persons was not to be punished at all. The second group needed warnings, the Word of God, and instruction, though the most stubborn cases might be banished. On no account should people of this sort be executed, for the New Testament said that no one should die for defection from the faith, and Roman law agreed that "thoughts should not be punished" (*cogitationis non esse poenam*). Thumm supported this point of view by quoting from contemporary jurists, and by citing a letter from Brenz to Heerbrand (though it seems likely that Brenz really meant that only people with diseased imaginations should not be executed).[92] Thumm finally admitted that truly harmful witches deserved death, but even then not because of their pact with the devil. Though these views of Thumm's were a logical extension of the Württemberg preaching tradition, they also represented a clear departure from it. Thumm added a new note to the controversy surrounding witchcraft, and his ideas show one direction that the spiritualizing, providential tradition could take.

On the other hand, the spiritualizing view of witchcraft also implied that without involving charges of specific harm done, an accusation of witchcraft could readily implicate a large group of people. As a purely spiritual crime, witchcraft was independent of the normal rules of law; there was no damage to be proved, no "kind of deed" (*speciem facti*) to be investigated, and no writ of habeas corpus possible. It might well have been spiritualizing logic of this sort that led so many jurists to deny any legal distinction between harmful and harmless witchcraft, or to assert, as the Württemberg Landesordnung of 1567 and the Saxon Constitutions of 1572 both did, that the real distinction to be made was between diabolic and natural magic. As taught by followers of Brenz, however, the spiritualizing and moralizing view of witchcraft was more likely to have had a moderating influence. Telling men to examine themselves rather than their neighbors seems to have had good results; though the Duchy of Württemberg had its share of witchcraft trials and executions, there were relatively few large panics.

Certainly Württemberg preachers and theologians were partly responsible for Württemberg's relatively moderate record, but they also gained invaluable support from the legal faculty at the University of Tübingen before 1630. For instance, the laws of Württemberg already recognized in 1567 that the fundamental crime of witchcraft lay in the pact with the devil, for unlike the *Carolina*, the Landesordnung of that year did not distinguish between harmful and harmless magic, but rather between devilish and nondevilish magic. Thus in 1567 Württemberg adopted a law embodying the same new and important distinctions that the Saxon Constitutions were to make five years later. Surely the theologians of Württemberg were pleased to see their thought so swiftly reflected in statute.[93]

During the sixteenth century, Tübingen jurists did not discuss witchcraft often or in great detail. Still, their occasional opinions show definite restraint in regard to procedures used against witches. During his Tübingen years (1535–52), Johann Sichard stressed in his lectures that confessions were to be used very cautiously to avoid abuses.[94] Much later, in 1598, the legal faculty demanded the release of a woman who despite repeated torture would not confess that she was a witch.[95] In a hitherto unevaluated opinion for Karl II of Baden-Durlach (1553–77), the Tübingen faculty carefully considered the

problem of denunciation by other witches. The faculty decided that
denunciations were not convincing enough proof of guilt to justify
torture, since witches were unreliable witnesses and could not be
trusted.[96] Thus the moderate views of Tübingen's theologians and
jurists touched and influenced other parts of the German Southwest.

The writings of the famous Tübingen jurist Johann Harpprecht
show a steady progression from an unformed, conventional point of
view to a providential view in harmony with Brenz, and finally, in
the 1620's, to full agreement with Thumm. In his commentary on
Roman law in 1599 Harpprecht had not yet placed the pact with the
devil at the heart of the crime of witchcraft. By 1615, however, he
showed clear sympathy for Weyer, though he also asserted that even
if witches could not fly or do any of the harm ascribed to them, they
still deserved death. The witches' pact with the devil was a "crime
against the king of kings" (*scelus in Majestatem Regis Regum*),
which was of course much worse than ordinary lese majesty. But in
1630 Harpprecht came once more to the subject; this time he could
do no better than simply accept Thumm, stressing the unusual conclusion that the mere pact with the devil was not in itself worthy of
death.[97]

The equally important Tübingen jurist Heinrich Bocer underwent
a somewhat similar progression. In a work published in 1599, he was
content to speak of witchcraft in terms reminiscent of the *Carolina*,
while making no mention at all of the pact with the devil. In lectures
given in 1604, however, Bocer demonstrated the influence of Weyer
and the Württemberg providential tradition, for in denying that
witches could raise storms, he specifically mentioned a sermon that
he had once heard in Tübingen.[98] In full agreement with the spiritualizing and providential school, he asserted that it made no difference
whether witches really did all that they confessed; the essential point
was that their will was corrupt. Bocer's colleague Christoph Besold
held a similar point of view, but he dealt even more severely with
witches. The pact with the devil was alone such a terrible crime, said
Besold, that no actual physical harm need be proved to justify death
by fire. Turning the providential tradition against itself, Besold asserted that treating witchcraft mildly would surely bring the punishment of God in the form of war, famine, or plague. These two jurists
(and many others after them at Tübingen) showed clearly the dan-

gerous extremes to which the Württemberg providential tradition could be carried.[99] By 1630, the orthodox views originated by Brenz were no longer unanimously accepted. Thumm and Besold had interpreted the providential tradition in such diametrically opposite ways that nothing new appeared in Lutheran thought on the subject in the seventeenth-century German Southwest. Among jurists and theologians alike, the debate hovered between the two classic extremes.

Conrad Dieterich, the prolific preacher at Ulm during the Thirty Years War, more than once sharply condemned the lax attitude that had grown up around the subject of witchcraft. He said: "I despair when I hear that we would sooner run out of wood than witches if ever we began a purge in both town and country." Showing none of Thumm's moral discrimination, Dieterich demanded death for fortune-tellers and those who ruined the weather. Yet in an allegorical sense, Dieterich discovered witchcraft in the heart of every mortal, and he felt that God's punishment was fully justified. Dieterich's example shows that Lutheran preachers outside Württemberg had a very traditional, hard-line view of witchcraft. Like Spreter, Graeter, and Meder, this preacher from the imperial city of Ulm failed to grasp the fundamental impulse that had produced the Württemberg providential tradition.[100]

Johann Jacob Faber also adopted a hard line when a witch panic broke out in the imperial city of Esslingen, where he was a minister. In a lengthy tirade he tried to set an example of "righteous zeal" by attacking witchcraft.[101] Though Faber asserted that witches actually did harm to men and cattle, the primary crimes in his view were the pact with the devil and fornication with demons. Citing Brenz's formula regarding storm raising, Faber conceded that much of the devil's work was pure deception.[102] Still, the pact of men with the devil was no delusion and deserved the sternest treatment; Faber therefore attacked Thumm's view as totally misguided.[103] On the other hand, Faber sounded a note of legal caution in regard to the "almost inhuman" practice of torture, admitting that even the innocent might be forced by torture to confess.[104] Though torture might be necessary in cases of witchcraft to ferret out the associates of witches, Faber insisted that great caution was called for in its use.

Many jurists also held such a traditional view of witchcraft. G. L. Lindenspur drew the same harsh conclusions as his master, Besold, while Tübingen's greatest jurist of the seventeenth century, Wolfgang Adam Lauterbach, argued that witches deserved death whether they harmed others or not, or whether their pact with the devil was explicit or merely tacit. Such a stern view of witchcraft survived into the eighteenth century among lawyers at Tübingen.[105]

Yet the moderating tradition of Brenz and Thumm received legal support from the Tübingen jurist Erich Mauritius. Citing Weyer, Thumm, and Harpprecht, Mauritius made it clear that the mere pact was not to be punished as severely as genuinely harmful witchcraft.[106] Similarly, the ferocious and argumentative Tobias Wagner, a minister at Esslingen, gloried in his conversion of a man who in 1642 had signed a desperate pact in his own blood with the devil. Instead of hauling the unfortunate and depressed (*schwermütig*) man to court, Wagner exhorted and prayed with him for four weeks. When the man repented of his sin and turned to Christ, he was set free by the town consistory. Wagner concluded that the man was spared "because he had fallen much more on account of sad attacks of depression than from the egoistic thirst for sensual pleasure."[107] Wagner said that a few weeks after this man's conversion, another one came to him with a pact written in blood binding him to the devil. Once again it would seem that the powers of the Gospel brought the sinner to his senses.[108] Yet Wagner could take a very stubborn and stern attitude in condemning witches for the great harm they did, and for the enormity of their demonic pact. In the foreword to Faber's *Specimen zeli justi*, Wagner even asserted that witches were so thoroughly sunk in sin that repentance was impossible. Must we therefore conclude that his earlier converts were backsliders?[109] It seems clear that Wagner, like so many others of his age and ours, was unwilling to assert a doctrine and follow out its implications with relentless logic.

Two of Wagner's colleagues at the University of Tübingen held to a more consistent theory by repeating the ideas of the Württemberg storm-and-disaster tradition in the style set by Thumm. Johann Adam Osiander, whose voluminous and chaotic works are both a tribute and a disgrace to Lutheran orthodoxy, wrote a commentary on the Pentateuch in which he analyzed Exodus 22:18 at length. His conclusion condemned the notion that anyone should be executed for the pact with the devil; such persons need correction and healing, not the sword.[110] Eleven years later, Osiander expanded his chance reflections on witchcraft into a *Tractatus Theologicus de Magia*. This work presented 140 separate theses, and marked an extreme of erudition and confusion.[111]

Despite his apparent and serious faults, however, Osiander's position was fairly clear on the fundamental question under discussion here. He recognized three basic points of view concerning the crime and punishment of witchcraft. Both Catholics and Calvinists went to one extreme in demanding execution for the apostasy and blasphemy involved in witchcraft, regardless of whether any maleficium was involved. Others took a far too lenient point of view, following Weyer in considering all witchcraft a hoax or delusion. But a third group found the proper mean between these two extremes: "*Our* theologians walk a middle path and make distinctions among witches" (*Media via incedunt* nostri *Theologi et distinguunt inter sagas*).[112] Osiander proceeded to introduce as the characteristic *Lutheran* position the tripartite distinction used by Thumm. Osiander asserted that the purely spiritual crime of apostasy or heresy could not be punished with death, and that the severest treatment permissible was banishment from the Christian world.[113] In short, Osiander's thought represents the witchcraft theories of Plantsch and Brenz taken to their furthest extremes.

Georg Heinrich Häberlin, another colleague of Wagner's, was professor of theology at Tübingen and superintendent of divinity students. In 1683, he was summoned to join a ducal commission investigating witchcraft at Calw. In a sermon at Calw, Häberlin emphasized the devil's role as deceiver. In addition, the devil was personally so strong that he had no need for the help of puny human beings. So it was that the devil often deluded witches into thinking that they had caused great harm: "Often a witch sets up her hail pot and cooks and stirs away in it, until she imagines that she has personally caused a storm that [actually] comes at the will of God and through natural causes."[114] Häberlin therefore appealed to the townspeople of Calw to inspect and reform themselves, rather than to blame others for their misfortune. In both words and sentiment, Häberlin stood firmly in the tradition begun by Brenz. His thought shows clearly that viewing witchcraft as an essentially spiritual crime, as Württemberg theologians so often did, had a moderating influence on witchcraft theory. Other theologians elsewhere, and jurists even in Württemberg, might turn the theory to other ends, but when interpreted in a world of thought permeated by the idea of providence, witchcraft seemed less dangerous. By analyzing all life and history in terms of God's will, thinkers who followed Brenz were able to deflect much of the terror associated with witchcraft into the pious channels of repentance.[115] In this way, Lutheran theologians and preachers in Württemberg evolved an independent and important theory of witchcraft. So far as can be determined, the Duchy of Württemberg was the only major territory in the German Southwest to be so thoroughly dominated by a theological orthodoxy in this regard.

A NOTE ON THE CALVINIST POSITION

For the sixteenth century, at least, the development of Calvinist witchcraft theory in the German Southwest was roughly parallel to that of Lutheran theory. After gaining footholds in several imperial cities, the Reform tradition won a major victory in the Palatinate. From their stronghold at Heidelberg, Calvinist professors were free to sort out their ideas on witchcraft.

Perhaps the most illustrious member of the Heidelberg faculty to take a position was Thomas Erastus, whose *Disputatio de Lamiis seu Strigibus* (1572) violently attacked the work of Weyer. In addition to interpreting Exodus 22:18 in such a way as to condemn modern witches, Erastus went on to assert that these faithless men and women renounced God and worshiped the devil, murdered and seduced their neighbors, fornicated with demons, and professed monstrous and illicit acts.[116] However, Erastus was willing to concede that witches did not actually work magical wonders, and that those who killed did so by means of poison. Even so, he insisted that these persons were not madmen, and that they deserved death for attempting to use the help of the devil to harm others.[117]

The essential crime for Erastus was the pact with the devil, and on this point he argued in the same terms as Weyer and Brenz. Like Brenz, Erastus considered the diabolical pact to be possible, making the crime of witchcraft possible as well. Without being overly schematic it is possible to see once again in Erastus a dangerous misinterpretation of Brenz's thought. Both Brenz and Erastus reduced witchcraft to a spiritual crime. Erastus, however, lacked the emphasis on providence that had prevented Brenz from urging an all-out purge of witchcraft, and so he adopted a rigorous and credulous theory of witchcraft. He was not the only one at Heidelberg to do so, for both the theologian Hieronymus Zanchi and the entire legal faculty agreed that witchcraft was a hideous crime.[118]

However, Heidelberg also had proponents of the opposite view. Not only did Franz Balduin pause in his commentaries on Justianian's Institutes to warn of the dangers of witch trials,[119] but the mathematician Hermann Witekind was among the first to defend Johann Weyer. Witekind's work of 1585 was hardly as daring or as original as Weyer's, but under the pseudonym "Augustin Lercheimer" he repeated many of Weyer's arguments and emphasized the need for new attitudes toward the silly, deranged women who often confessed to witchcraft. As a Calvinist, Witekind's emphasis on the providence of God came naturally, and he asserted with great moral fervor that God plagues mankind to test the faithful and punish sin.[120]

In the matter of storms, Witekind held that the Bible showed God to be in constant control of the weather. He then explained that the devil could often see a storm coming and then spur a witch to "cause" it. Witekind urged that men should rather practice the patience of Job than the impatience of the witch hunt, and he saw a specifically Stoic element in patient acceptance. Citing Seneca, Witekind asserted that men have a tendency to ascribe their misfortunes to human causes "on whom we can avenge our misfortune and harm, for God, the true cause, is seated too high for us to reach or understand."[121] The providential tradition thus found one eloquent spokesman at Heidelberg who thought in precisely the opposite way from his colleague Erastus. Indeed, Witekind surpassed even Brenz by urging that no one should be executed for merely spiritual crimes. If the courts really burned all those who turned from Christ, he said, there would not be wood enough in all the world to complete the task.[122] Witekind was a forerunner of the attitude that Thumm and Osiander in the next century were to make a part of Lutheran thought in the German Southwest.

In the Palatinate, the views of Balduin and Witekind became dominant. Friedrich III, Elector between 1559 and 1576, put an absolute ban on witch hunting, and we hear of no serious panics after his reign.[123] For that matter, very little is known about subsequent Calvinist witchcraft theory in the German Southwest. The Reformed tradition of the seventeenth century is, if possible, even darker than the Catholic tradition.

CATHOLICS IN THE GERMAN SOUTHWEST

It is likely that at least half of the German Southwest remained staunchly Catholic during the Reformation. It would be fascinating to compare the Catholic areas to the areas dominated by the Württemberg providential tradition to determine if the areas with unusually severe witch panics had equally severe schools of thought on witchcraft. Unfortunately, many questions of this type cannot be satisfactorily answered until we know more in general about Catholic thought in the German Southwest. One reason for our surprising lack of information about the Catholics is actually obvious. Of all the universities in southwestern Germany, only Freiburg provided a focus for Catholic intellectual life. Heidelberg, Strasbourg, Tübingen, and Basel all became Protestant. In addition, the University of Freiburg in the later sixteenth century was hardly distinguished by brilliant or even prolific thinkers in theology or law. These faculties were apparently not much interested in publishing.[124] Therefore we must listen carefully to the few Catholic voices we do find.

We have already analyzed the work of the nominalist Martin Plantsch, who laid the foundations for the providential school in Swabia. The next Catholic of the Southwest to discuss witchcraft was probably Johann Zink. This Aristotelian philosopher and physician on the faculty of Freiburg held a spiritualizing view of witchcraft in many ways surprisingly similar to that of Plantsch or Brenz. In a tract of the 1540's on the power of the devil, Zink readily conceded that the devil used witches to perform "not little miracles" (*non parva miracula*).[125] Speaking more cautiously, he asserted a bit later that witches actually used three means in working their wonders (*miranda*): the help of devils, the operation of nature, and the deception of simple human fraud.[126] From this point, Zink moved more firmly to a thoroughly spiritualized attitude. When confronted with the objection that actually the devil was responsible for any harm done and that witches should therefore be treated mildly, Zink rejoined that "the witches have at least persuaded themselves that they do these [evils], and even if they cannot really work such [evils] they do at least thirst perpetually with a burning soul for the ruin of men."[127]

If one pardoned such malevolent creatures, "all corners would soon be full of witches." The simple fact that they had dealings with the devil ("quod cum daemonibus rem habent") was enough to send them to the stake.[128] Zink agreed, therefore, in all essentials with Brenz, even to the ultimate reduction of the crime of witchcraft to malevolence.[129]

A contemporary of Zink's at Freiburg advocated a viewpoint closer to that of the *Malleus*. Georg Pictorius, a classicist in the arts faculty with interests ranging from folk medicine to mythology, became active as a physician after 1540.[130] In a work on demons and witchcraft he drew largely on classical authors to prove that the devil did work true miracles and could actually subvert nature.[131] Whether he meant that demonic miracles were fully as miraculous as those of Christ or the saints remains unclear, for the worthy Pictorius was totally innocent of theology. In discussing ways of driving off demons, he listed fire, sword, and threats, as well as prayers and science.[132] After a long list of the various sorts of ritual magic, Pictorius turned briefly to witchcraft itself and concluded that Scripture very properly condemned witches to death. Not only did witches betray Christ and turn to obscene service of the devil, but they also caused disease and death among their neighbors.[133] Perhaps because of his interest in medicine, Pictorius displayed far more erudition and curiosity than moral sense regarding the problems of sexual congress with spirits. His final sentence summarized a view that agreed fully with the *Malleus Maleficarum*: "If the witches are not burned, the number of these furies swells up in such an immense sea that no one could live safe from their spells and charms."[134]

Pictorius may have been extreme in his uncritical acceptance of traditional materials. At any rate we do not find such a total lack of moral concern in other Catholic writers of the Southwest. Indeed, most Catholics, like their Lutheran counterparts, saw the hand of God in extraordinary events. Nor was it peculiarly Lutheran to deny human agency in "natural" catastrophes. In a catechism published in Freiburg, the Roman Catholic Bartholomeas Wagner felt compelled to deny, like Heerbrand, the responsibility of the clergy for hailstorms. Wagner insisted that the peasants must give up their dreadful cursing and swearing before blaming such storms on their priests' absence from the parish or for their not properly blessing the weather.[135]

Similarly, the famous Catholic preacher Jacob Feucht sounded a ringing appeal for repentance when God chastised mankind with a long chain of misfortunes, high prices, storms, floods, strange diseases, wars, and earthquakes.[136]

Hence Catholics of the sixteenth century shared with Lutherans their emphasis on the importance of providence. The general idea of providence, however, was not always applied consistently to the theory of witchcraft. Reinhard Lutz, a preacher of Sélestat who originally came from Rottweil, demonstrated this ambiguity in a tract on four witches burned in Sélestat in 1570. For Lutz it was clear that God was the author of all good and of all punishments. Yet God often used good and evil angels in achieving His ends. The devils in turn often used human agents. Even if it was true that witches actually did no real harm, they richly deserved execution, since they "seek with their devils only the harm and corruption of other creatures and also think that they themselves cause those things which the devil does by the decree of God."[137] In this analysis, Lutz repeated the views of Brenz and Zink precisely. But a few sentences later he spoke angrily of the "damned witches" who gave themselves to the devil, "with whom they exercise their carnal lusts and harm and corrupt cattle, men, etc."[138] Lutz clearly agreed with the providential view in principle, but continued to regard witches as physically dangerous.

We know of only one other Catholic of the German Southwest who discussed witchcraft during the sixteenth century. Jodocus Lorichius, one of the more distinguished theologians of Freiburg in the later sixteenth century, wrote a small volume on superstition.[139] This work is valuable chiefly as a picture of the grotesque mass of superstitions among the common people and even among the learned. For Lorichius, magic and witchcraft were primarily forms of blasphemy. He displayed none of Pictorius's curiosity about the ritual and sexual aspects of magic but concentrated on condemning all magic as demonic. He asserted that blessings and holy signs have only a limited power against the devil.[140] Man must not rely on them as a defense against witchcraft; the proper defense required fear of God and a pious life. When disease and trouble came, men should first examine themselves for sin and then search for natural causes. Even if the disease were unnatural, no form of magic was to be used against it. Lorichius claimed that Job knew very well that all his troubles came from the devil; yet it was really God who gave, and God who took away. In such circumstances, Lorichius urged his readers to accept Job as a model. Once again we find Job at the center of a spiritualized view of witchcraft.[141] As with Plantsch, Brenz and his tradition, and Zink, Job served for Lorichius as a towering archetype of the providential view. In his view of witches, however, Lorichius was every bit as stern as Brenz or Zink. Death and confiscation were the only proper punishments for so heinous a blasphemy.[142]

Although the intellectual world of the Catholic Southwest is not well known for the sixteenth century, we know even less about the seventeenth.[143] In 1604 Friedrich Martini, doctor of laws and professor of canon law in Freiburg, published an interpretation of two crucial clauses of the *Carolina*: Articles 109 and 218.[144] The first of these clauses demands our immediate attention, for in these comments, Martini spelled out his attitude regarding the crime of witchcraft.* Martini wrote specifically to refute a view of witchcraft that he found distressingly common among his Lutheran opponents. "It is disputed whether witches are to be killed simply because they give themselves to the devil, attend nocturnal sabbaths, and fornicate with the devil, even though they do not kill any person with poison and do not harm crops and cattle."[145] Martini found that Johann Fichard, Johann Gödelmann, Laurentius Kirchovius, "et alii nonnulli" actually denied that the pact with the devil was sufficient cause for execution. These men, whom he labeled the patrons or defenders of the witches, followed Weyer in rejecting capital punishment for purely spiritual crimes, and in discarding the pacts as "mere fantasies of deluded minds."[146] Martini refuted their "vain rhetorical tricks" in a detailed analysis that depended heavily on Martin Delrio and Albert Hunger, a professor at Ingolstadt. The key to his theory lay in his distinction between "magus" and "maleficus." Both types of magician contracted at least a tacit pact with the devil, but the maleficus was far more terrible than a simple magus. A magus worked for his own pleasures and sought to harm no one, whereas a maleficus worked to harm all things. The magus thought that he actually forced demons to do his work, whereas the maleficus reverenced the devil as lord and master. Again, the magus learned his arts only from books, but "the maleficus is seduced by the devil himself" (*maleficus ab ipso daemone seduci-*

---

* For Martini's treatment of *Carolina* 218, see below, pp. 165–66.

tur). And finally, the "magus did not expressly renounce God and all His saints," while the maleficus did so regularly.

Turning to the *Carolina*, Art. 109, Martini found an example of the precise distinction he had just made. The patrons of the witches were sadly mistaken, he said, when they read the law as if it distinguished between harmful and harmless magic. The true distinction was between *magia simplex* and *maleficium*. In this way Martini bent the words of the *Carolina* to divide "Zauberey" into fully demonic and nondemonic forms. In such an interpretation, the essential crime was spiritual, i.e. the pact with the devil. It was just this distinction that had brought about the reform of so many German witchcraft laws from the mid-sixteenth century on. It was the sort of spiritualizing analysis, equating sin and crime, that the great Saxon jurist Carpzov followed in the seventeenth century (see above, pp. 23–24). Martini did not stop there, however; he emphatically denied that witchcraft was only a spiritual crime. Flight to the sabbath and coitus with demons were definitely possible. Blasphemy and idolatry, moreover, were public crimes and not merely mental crimes.[147]

In this manner Martini reinforced the strain of thought running from the *Malleus Maleficarum* through Binsfeld and Delrio. In the German Southwest he belonged to the Catholic tradition of Pictorius and Lutz, as opposed to the more "providential" and moralizing view of Plantsch, Zink, and Lorichius.

After Martini, formal Catholic witchcraft theory seems to have virtually dried up, aside from an unenlightening Freiburg disputation in 1631.[148] One could argue that this was a sign of maturity, i.e. that Catholics were now putting their minds to better use. Another construction, however, seems more likely. We observed that among Catholics the tension between the traditions of *Episcopi* and the *Malleus Maleficarum* remained strong during the sixteenth century. In this the Catholics resembled their Protestant brethren. Indeed one could argue that the forces of tension, the existence of real issues, were partly responsible for the Catholic literature that survives on the subject. The cessation of Catholic literature on witchcraft in the German Southwest may well be an indication that the vital tension was gone, that discussion was no longer fruitful. Certainly the aridity of the 1631 Freiburg disputation would support the conclusion that Catholics could no longer debate real issues.

There are other indications of what was happening. During the sixteenth century it is roughly correct to say that there were no serious differences between Catholics and Protestants over witchcraft. Both confessions had representatives from the two schools of witchcraft theory, the providential *Episcopi* tradition and the persecuting *Malleus* tradition. During the sixteenth century these views were so chaotically jumbled together that scholars have understandably concluded that Catholics and Protestants did not have serious differences on this subject. However, by the end of the sixteenth century we find evidence that a specifically Catholic view had crystallized, although the symptoms of this process are diffuse.

In large measure the process may have been a reaction to Protestant pressure. During the late sixteenth century, as confessional differences became clear, each denomination worked at developing a position that excluded all the errors and hints of error of their opponents. In the effort to provide an unambiguous image, each denomination or confession came to reject practices and doctrines that had formerly been part of the common domain and had seemed unimportant.[149] Protestants like Jacob Heerbrand of Tübingen now condemned Catholic rites, blessings, and paraphernalia as "mera vere Diabolica, impia, et blasphema magica."[150] In other cases Catholic scholars were singled out and attacked as magicians.[151] Another Lutheran scholar suggested that "the miserable papacy" naturally had more witchcraft and more trials than the Protestant areas.[152] A preacher characterized Catholicism as superstitious and therefore naturally inclined to witchcraft. In contrast, he pompously maintained that "no truly Protestant woman could become a witch."[153]

One Catholic response was that the real source of witchcraft was the Reformation itself, a position held by the learned Martin Delrio.[154] Other Catholic preachers blamed storms and disasters not on witchcraft but on the new heresy of Luther.[155] In times so filled with charge and countercharge, the Catholic party may easily have been led to attack specific doctrines of witchcraft as if they were part of the Protestant threat. This would seem to explain why Cornelius Loos, a Catholic priest, suffered savage repression in 1592 and was forced to recant the ideas he had learned from Weyer. The condemnation of Loos specifically attacked his assertions as heresy.[156] Before this judgment there had been no real Catholic orthodoxy on witchcraft.

In response to Weyer, and indeed to the whole Brenzian school, Catholics retaliated by rejecting the *Episcopi* tradition or by explaining it away. After 1600 we do not hear of German Catholics proclaiming the theory that witches could really do no harm, a theory that numerous Protestants continued to hold.[157] Characteristically, Catholic controversy now shifted away from the theory of witchcraft and into the realm of legal procedure. The work of Friedrich von Spee, thoroughly procedural in essence, thus emerges as about the only kind of protest open to a Catholic in the seventeenth century.

In another context we have noted Martini's condemnation of Weyer and his Lutheran colleagues as patrons of the witches. For Martini it was now a specifically *Protestant* theory that witches were not to be executed for merely spiritual crimes.[158] A few years later, in Schwäbisch Gmünd, Weyer's ideas were specifically linked to the "illusions of non-Catholic writers" (see below, p. 120).[159] Some Protestants even came to agree with the Catholic analysis. In 1687 a Lutheran scholar found this Catholic notion acceptable and described a specifically *Lutheran* theory of witchcraft, one that he thought achieved a firm middle ground between the lenient views of the Weyer school and the strict school of both Catholics and Calvinists.[160]

In this way the strong providential tradition nourished by Brenz and his followers in Southwestern Germany seems to have provoked the Catholic front to solidify its ranks against it. Such a hypothesis might explain the growing severity of Catholic witch hunting in the seventeenth century. One could argue that so long as both Catholics and Lutherans retained an ambiguous attitude toward witchcraft, so long as both fronts nourished the traditions of both the *Episcopi* and the *Malleus*, both parties might conduct trials of roughly equal severity. When the Catholics lost this flexibility and rejected the *Episcopi* tradition, however, one could anticipate a rise in the severity of witch hunts conducted in Catholic regions and could then account for the markedly more severe witch trials conducted by Catholics after 1590 or 1600.

SUMMARY

In summarizing the witchcraft theories prevalent in the German Southwest, we cannot fail to notice that during the sixteenth century all three major confessional groups were split between a strongly providential point of view (the *Episcopi* tradition) and a strongly fearful point of view (the *Malleus* tradition). Scholars have wrongly sought to portray witchcraft theory as monolithic, when in fact diversity or at least polarity was the rule. Other scholars have incorrectly attempted to show that, from the beginning, the Reformation fostered a new attitude toward witchcraft. It now seems more plausible to recognize that at least until 1590 or 1600, Lutherans, Calvinists, and Catholics alike shared a common basis in the two major traditions handed down from the Middle Ages. Among sixteenth-century Lutherans, the polarity was perhaps least clear because of the overwhelming domination of the *Episcopi* tradition of Plantsch and Brenz in Württemberg. Other Lutherans, like Graeter, Spreter, or Meder, relied at times specifically on the *Malleus Maleficarum*, and yet they all showed a characteristic confusion or hesitation on the subject of storms and other harmful witchcraft. Among the Calvinists at Heidelberg, too, the conflict of opinion became exceptionally clear in the dispute between Erastus and Witekind. Yet there also one notes the willingness of Erastus to concede that witches may really do no harm. Among Catholics the same split appeared between Zink and Lorichius on one side, and Pictorius and Martini on the other. The fundamental question was whether witchcraft was physically harmful or not. In all three confessions it was *not* a simple matter of how thoroughly Lutheran, Calvinist, or Catholic one was.* It was also not an issue between enlightened rationalists and fanatic obscurantists. The basic argument was really between two groups of pious men. One group laid so much emphasis on God's control of human events that Job was the only proper model and repentance the only proper response. Hunting witches was not necessarily illicit for them, but morally distracting.† The other group felt far less strongly the will of God in everyday life. For them, witchcraft was a hideous blasphemy and a real threat to all living things. The only response possible for them was to follow Exodus in searching out and uprooting the hidden enemies of life.

---

* This is a fair assessment despite the fulminations of Johann Adam Osiander against what he conceived to be the monolithic Calvinist and Catholic attitude toward witchcraft (*De Magia*, pp. 287–92). One could perhaps sustain the argument that Catholic writing tended to be more theoretical, especially after Delrio.

† For Witekind the execution of confessed witches *was* an injustice, because for him the women were plainly mad or feebleminded. He did not deny that a true pact with the devil was worthy of death.

Although these two traditions coexisted in each confession during the sixteenth century, it seems likely that the Catholics lost their diversity by about 1600. Reacting against the Protestants, they effectively eliminated the *Episcopi* or providential tradition from their ranks. With the strength of Brenz's school in Württemberg, and with the agreement between Erastus and Witekind that witches might really do no harm, it is understandable that Catholics might draw the conclusion that both Lutherans and Calvinists were soft on witches. From a Catholic point of view, the Protestants were now "patrons of the witches."

Although the Catholics stiffened their front in this way, evidence shows that the Lutherans in the German Southwest did not. The seventeenth century continued to be a period of vigorous controversy for Lutheran theologians and lawyers alike. The difference between Lutheran and Catholic theories in the seventeenth century, therefore, was that the Lutherans retained a strong tradition of doubt regarding the power of the devil, whereas Catholics successfully eliminated it. This shift partly explains the severe Catholic record in the seventeenth century in contrast to that in the sixteenth century, when Catholic and Protestant witch hunts were about equal in severity.

Still, the Lutheran regions of the German Southwest also had their witch hunts in the seventeenth century. The providential tradition did not after all put a total ban on witch trials. If nurtured, that tradition could issue in the thought of men like Weyer or Thumm, who found mere spiritual crimes to be unworthy of capital punishment. To be fully effective, however, the seeds of the *Episcopi* tradition needed proper soil in which to grow. Unfortunately, in most regions of the German Southwest the soil seems to have been too hard until it was harrowed by actual witch panic.

Chapter Four

Patterns of Witch Hunting in the German Southwest

❧

AFTER surveying the intellectual basis of witchcraft in the German Southwest, we are in a better position to examine the actual witch hunting there. The patterns arising from such an examination will rise to haunt us time and again.

Generally speaking, witchcraft trials came late to Germany. Mass witch hunts seem to have appeared first in southern France and Switzerland in the fourteenth and fifteenth centuries. We know of only a handful for Germany in the fifteenth century and the first half of the sixteenth century.[1] In fact, between 1520 and 1576 concern about witches declined to such an extent that the *Malleus Maleficarum* was not once reprinted.[2] Trials during the early Reformation period were very rare in Germany, although they were common in northern Italy.

TEMPORAL PATTERNS OF WITCH HUNTING

Protestant scholars used to attribute this decline in witch hunting to the healthy attitude of the reformers toward Roman Catholic superstition.[3] Catholic scholars from the sixteenth century on, however, have stressed the Reformation as an actual cause of witch trials.[4] Luther, it was said, was so obsessed with the devil that he mentioned the devil more often than Jesus Christ in his Small Catechism.[5] Other scholars have suggested that witch hunting was a reaction to despair and hard times and that this sort of social crisis appeared first in the later sixteenth century.* Up to now, regrettably, the pattern of trials

---

* There can be little question that the second half of the sixteenth century saw times of plague and famine, but not for the first time. The treatment of the Jews at the time of the Black Death in the fourteenth century is instructive.

has remained a mystery. Why the period of the Peasants' War or large portions of the Thirty Years War were free from persecution of both witches and Jews is unclear. However, we cannot treat the witchcraft trials of the late sixteenth and seventeenth centuries as a natural and automatic chain reaction resulting from the "medieval witchcraft delusion" as its sole cause. Certainly the German witch hunts depended on medieval theories to a large extent. But the story is more complex. Something must have happened in the later sixteenth century to make Germany suddenly more enthusiastic about witch hunting.

Recent studies have tried to link a resurgence of witch hunting to the spirit of the Counter-Reformation, dogmatic, contentious, aggressive.[6] After all, witch hunting was characteristic of the "Age of the Counter-Reformation." This is a familiar and attractive theory, but one that has been peculiarly hard to verify. Only when its proponents examine some particular event do they begin to speak in terms that can be proved or disproved. W. G. Soldan, in the last century, and R. H. Robbins, more recently, have tried to make the Jesuits responsible for the introduction of witch hunting into Germany.[7] It is clear that the Jesuits, like almost everyone else, supported witch trials. But they were not the first to do so, nor were they unanimous in their purpose.[8] The common accusation that Jesuits used witch trials to eliminate Protestant enemies has proved especially hard to substantiate. Even the great scholar George Lincoln Burr had to confess that he saw no evidence to support this conclusion.[9]

Turning from general allegations regarding the Counter-Reformation, we find that other scholars have examined changes in the law. Legal historians have pointed out that witch trials were dependent on new kinds of trial procedures connected with the reception of Roman law and the inquisitorial process. Early German law had been a private legal system in which all actions required a private plaintiff. This type of system had serious disadvantages, since no single person might know enough about a crime or might dare to accuse another. A further stumbling block was the severe treatment of accusers, and especially of false accusers. In a private-accusatorial trial, if a case was not proved, the plaintiff had to pay the penalty.[10] During the sixteenth century an alternative system, the inquisitorial trial, found increased application. The state or court took over the functions of accuser. Such were the origins of the public prosecutor in Germany. But in the sixteenth and seventeenth centuries, the judge, defense, prosecutor, and torturer were all incorporated in one man or one panel of men. The legal consequences of this intermediate stage in legal development were dangerous.[11] A legal historian can therefore argue that decisive changes in law and procedure opened the way for mass witch trials.[12] Witchcraft appeared in the compilations of Württemberg law for the first time in the Landesordnung of 1552.[13] The influential Electoral Saxon Constitutions of 1572 far surpassed in clarity and rigor the more confusing *Carolina* of 1532. Following the Saxon model, the Elector Palatine and the Margrave of Baden-Baden published codes in 1582 and 1588 that punished the heretical aspects of witchcraft as severely as maleficium.[14] These laws testify to the growing spiritual emphasis evident in many sectors of German life after 1550. In addition, the careful regard of the *Carolina* for sufficient evidence (*Indizien*) before applying torture was forgotten.[15]

If the second half of the sixteenth century was a period of new aggressiveness in religion and new carelessness in law, it was also a period of new fascination with and fear of the devil. These are qualities that are naturally hard to measure. It is difficult if not impossible to compare periods in the attempt to discover which was the more fearful, but an index of popular literature dealing with the devil can be constructed. The second half of the sixteenth century saw the rise and climax of a new genre of literature, the devil-book.[16] In its most typical form it concentrated on a human vice or weakness like swearing, drinking, or dancing, and showed how devilish it was.[17] Other works of this genre gave popular analyses of the power of the devil and his servants, the witches and magicians. The general effect of these pieces was to suggest that the devil was everywhere.

The first work of this sort appeared in 1552, a "Sauffteufel" (Devil of Drunks), which was reprinted 17 times.[18] The 1550's saw seven first editions of such devil-books and 17 reprints. The real explosion, however, came in the 1560's. The public appetite for this sort of book was insatiable. Between 1560 and 1569, 14 first editions of the devil-books appeared on the German market. At the same time 70 reprints appeared. In 1569 the shrewd publisher Sigmund Feyrabend took advantage of popular interest in the devil by printing a fat folio volume containing 20 of the best or most sensational devil-books.[19] By con-

TABLE 3

Devil Literature in Germany, 1550–1600

Years	First editions	Reprints	Independent copies
1550–59	7	17	21,000
1560–69	14	70	78,000[a]
1570–79	6	5	8,600[b]
1580–89	9	9	14,400[c]
1590–99	1	4	4,600

[a] Plus 1,000 copies of 1569 *Theatrum Diabolorum* of 20 devil-books, or 20,000 additional copies.
[b] Plus 1,500 copies of 1575 *Theatrum* of 24 devil-books, or 36,000 additional copies.
[c] Plus 1,500 copies of 1587–88 *Theatrum* of 33 devil-books, or 49,000 additional copies.

servative estimate, the 1560's saw nearly 100,000 individual copies of devil-books on the German market.* By sixteenth-century standards this was an enormous figure. The hunger for devil-literature slackened a little in the 1570's but revived in the 1580's. It finally withered away in the 1590's, although we hear echoes of this genre until the end of the seventeenth century (see Table 3). Faust literature also took firm root in this soil and saw 24 editions in the last 12 years of the sixteenth century.[20]

A further indication of popular fascination with the subject of the devil and witchcraft was the publication of another large folio volume in 1586 containing exclusively works pertaining to witchcraft. Both this *Theatrum de Veneficis* and the *Theatrum Diabolorum* must have fostered excitement by their technique of presenting authors with radically opposing views.[21]

It may be justifiable to conclude that this bulk of popular literature both reflected and fostered a new fear of and interest in the devil. Conditions in southwestern Germany, where plague was once again beginning to claim its toll and where legal and religious tensions reached new heights, resulted in mass witchcraft trials in the 1560's.[22] No

---

* Grimm uses the conservative estimates of ca. 600 copies for a first edition and 1,000 copies for subsequent reprints. He estimates also that there were probably 1,000 copies of the first edition of the *Theatrum Diabolorum* and 1,500 copies of it each time it was reprinted and enlarged (1575, 1587–88); Grimm, "Teufelsbücher," p. 532. Bavaria and the Catholic electors were quick to recognize the dangers of this sort of literature and forbade their possession and sale in their territories. Bavaria was the first to use censorship, in 1565; Grimm, p. 540.

longer would witch trials end with one or two executed; indeed, the year 1562 witnessed 63 witches burned at Wiesensteig.

In spite of the sudden explosion of large witch hunts, however, small trials continued even during the later period to far outnumber the large panics. In the peak years of 1561–1670, trials resulting in the execution of one or two persons accounted for some 60 per cent of all witchcraft trials.[23] This fact makes it hard to maintain that the witch hunting of the early modern period was radically and qualitatively different from earlier medieval "sorcery" trials. In the Southwest, however, it is true that the period before 1562 was marked by virtually no large witch hunts.* Similarly, after the great trials at Esslingen and Reutlingen between 1662 and 1666, we hear of no mass executions of witches in the Southwest, despite a continuance of individual, local, small witchcraft trials well into the second half of the eighteenth century.

The century between 1562 and 1666 was different. In addition to a much higher number of small trials involving one or two suspects, we now find mass trials—genuine panics.†

Another index of witch trial frequency in the German Southwest is the number of individual courts or jurisdictions to conduct such trials. From 1400 to 1500 we know of 14 towns in the Southwest that conducted trials for witchcraft. But during the 1560's alone, at least 21 conducted witch trials. In the 1570's this figure jumped to 50. During the 1580's 48 towns had trials. The first three decades of the seventeenth century were as bad or worse. In the year 1616 alone, 20 towns were busy with witchcraft trials. In 1629, 31 separate regions were seized by the panic, but from then on the number dropped sharply to between one and six per annum. After 1650 there were even a few years when no trials have been recorded at all.

When we turn to the number executed, it becomes even more evident that the years 1562 to 1666 represent a special period in the history of witchcraft in the Southwest. Between 1400 and 1560 we know of over 88 executions. Yet we have no record of more than three execu-

---

* However, Sprenger and Institoris claimed to have executed 48 witches in the diocese of Constance between 1482 and 1486; *Malleus Maleficarum*, II, Q. 1; cf. Müller, "Heinrich Institoris," p. 397, n. 2.

† For sources of the following information, see the Appendix, which lists all known witch trials in the German Southwest.

TABLE 4

Frequency of Small Witchcraft Trials Where Outcome Is Known,
1561–1670: Number of Suspects Executed

Years	0 executed		1 or 2 executed		Total trials where outcome is known	
	Prot.	Cath.	Prot.	Cath.	Prot.	Cath.
1561–70	1	2	5	7	10	11
1571–80	0	3	3	11	7	60
1581–90	2	3	5	12	11	46
1591–1600	3	3	10	12	21	33
1601–10	4	1	10	5	25	20
1611–20	6	6	15	10	25	43
1621–30	7	6	8	19	20	52
1631–40	4	1	7	5	19	15
1641–50	1	3	3	8	4	15
1651–60	2	0	2	10	4	10
1661–70	6	2	6	10	17	12
TOTAL	36	30	74	109	163	317

SOURCE: Data are taken from the Appendix.

CONCLUSIONS: In this period, 51.9 per cent of all trials where the outcome is known (480) were small (249), i.e. with at most two suspects executed; 67.5 per cent of all such Protestant trials (163) were small (110); 48.8 percent of all such Catholic trials (317) were small (139); and 34 per cent of the total of such trials (480) were Protestant (163) and 66 per cent Catholic (317).

tions in any one town during a given year. Similarly, after 1671 no court executed more than four persons in any one year. Between 1561 and 1670, however, we know of well over 3,200 executions in the Southwest. Of these, only 236 persons were executed in small isolated trials involving only one or two witches. Even trials resulting in up to ten executions in a single year accounted for only 31 per cent of the total number executed. On the other hand, the large panic trial executing 20 or more persons in a single year now accounted for 40 per cent of all executions. The large trial became the decisive new style of witch hunting after 1562. (See Tables 4 and 5 and Appendix.)

Since the large witchcraft panic trial was precisely the new and different component in witch hunting at its worst, the next chapter examines in detail some of the largest. But first we must consider the general picture presented by these trials.

It is clear that the period 1562–1666 forms a genuine unit in the history of witch hunting in the German Southwest. Within this period,

TABLE 5

Frequency of Small Witchcraft Trials Where Outcome Is Not
Known, 1561–1670: Number of Suspects Involved in Trials

Years	1 suspect		2–5 suspects		6+ suspects		Number of suspects unknown	
	Prot.	Cath.	Prot.	Cath.	Prot.	Cath.	Prot.	Cath.
1561–70	2	1	0	1	0	0	1	3
1571–80	0	4	0	0	0	1	0	6
1581–90	3	1	2	5	0	0	0	8
1591–1600	11	3	0	2	0	2	1	3
1601–10	24	1	1	7	0	2	2	3
1611–20	38	1	10	5	1	4	0	2
1621–30	34	5	7	2	1	0	2	2
1631–40	13	0	3	2	0	0	0	0
1641–50	8	2	3	1	0	2	1	0
1651–60	30	8	5	4	1	1	3	1
1661–70	41	1	8	3	1	0	5	2
TOTAL	204	27	39	32	4	12	15	30

SOURCE: Data are taken from the Appendix.
CONCLUSIONS: Where outcomes (i.e. executions, acquittals, or other dispositions) are not known, there were more Protestant trials than Catholic, but the Protestant trials were more often small. There were 247 Protestant trials where only the number of suspects was known, 82.6 per cent of which had only one suspect; there were 71 Catholic trials where only the number of suspects was known, 38 per cent of which had only one suspect. (The disproportionation in totals of Catholic (101) and Protestant (262) trials is due to oversampling of the Protestant regions.)

moreover, certain other patterns may be discerned. For example, misfortune of one sort or another provided the occasion for most witch hunting. Storms, plague, famine, and the like drove simple men to search for the causes. As we have seen in the sermon literature, preachers were well aware of this fact. In a synod of 1594 in Württemberg, preachers even complained specifically that "if men or animals get sick, the people at once blame evil women, whereby the innocent fall under suspicion of witchcraft."[24] During a plague and grain famine in Geneva in the years 1542–45, some 40 persons were found guilty of witchcraft and executed.[25] Such cases could be multiplied ad infinitum. They all reflect what some scholars call scapegoating. Of course, in a literal sense there are significant differences between this sort of social mechanism and that involving the ancient Jewish scapegoat, which was sent off into the wilderness bearing the *sins* of the entire community. No one had held the goat physically responsible for previous misfortune. Even if the term is a misnomer, however, the phenomenon of discovering human agency and human conspiracy to account for troubles has been well known throughout Western history.[26]

Not all loose accusations of witchcraft produced trials, of course, and not all trials ended in execution. In fact, in some places where we have detailed evidence there is good reason to suppose that over half the persons accused of witchcraft were acquitted. In Switzerland especially, the rate of acquittal seems to have been very high.[27] By their very nature, however, acquittals attracted little attention. Both contemporary publicists and later historians have been overwhelmingly interested in witchcraft executions. Consequently the secondary literature on witch hunting in the German Southwest has very little to say regarding acquittals for witchcraft. Even so, we know of 66 trials during the peak period 1561–1670 in which no one was executed. Thus 14 per cent of all the trials whose outcome is known produced no executions at all (see Table 4). This figure does not begin to include many trials in which ten or 20 accusations might result in one or two executions and 18 or 19 acquittals. At present our general data are far too fragmentary to allow a more specific statement than this. Only in isolated cases do we have complete enough records to determine how many persons were ultimately accused in a panic, and how many of them regained freedom.

The term acquittal really meant little more than cessation of proceedings. At any moment the accused, even though once acquitted, might be brought in for further investigation. The concept of double jeopardy did not generally exist. An investigation continued until sufficient evidence accumulated to produce conviction. If a sufficient amount of evidence did not at once emerge, the suspect might be released pending further inquiry. He was certainly not considered "proved innocent." The case was simply "not proved." When further facts came to light, or when other denunciations of the suspect were registered, the trial might be resumed.

In addition, even if a suspect was proved innocent of witchcraft in one instance, that was no reason why he could not be guilty of witchcraft in other cases. A person could become a witch at any time in life. It is not surprising, therefore, that suspects "acquitted" of the crime of witchcraft often found themselves accused again one, five, or ten years later. Many of the acquitted learned that they could not resume a normal life, and so they moved to a different region in the hope of escaping their past. Under these varied circumstances our generalizations about the numbers of the acquitted are even less reliable. Their true proportion among the accused of the German Southwest will probably never be known.

Looking further at the temporal pattern of witch trials in southwestern Germany, it is clear that after 1632 witch hunting went into a steep decline, only to revive in a last burst of energy in the 1660's. In some parts of Germany this early pause in witch hunting is perhaps the result of invasions and occupations by foreign troops. The Swedish troops in some parts may have been especially effective in suppressing "this social war among the natives."[28] In 1647 Johann Seifert, the German translator of Spee's *Cautio Criminalis* and field preacher among the Swedish troops, even dedicated his translation to Queen Christina of Sweden and to her army officers, in recognition of the salutary influence the Swedes had had in Germany.[29] Yet as we shall see, a Swedish solution will not work for the German Southwest.

The chronology here is most instructive, since the years 1634 through 1640 were for southwestern Germany the most terrible and devastating of the whole Thirty Years War. In this period, plague and famine swept the countryside repeatedly. In five years Württemberg lost three-quarters of her population.[30] In the midst of such massive social dislocation, witch hunting declined. One could perhaps speculate that the terror of these years was so intense that people simply had no time or need to hunt witches. Such a theory would be an evasion of the question. Three hundred years earlier the sudden devastation of the Black Death had indeed resulted in swift, wholesale persecutions—of Jews. Catastrophe could and often did result in witch hunts too, as we have already noted. It will not do to assert that in some way the misery of the Thirty Years War was unique.

One of the crucial elements that seem to have suppressed witch hunting after 1634 was firm military control. When military control broke down, witch hunting might resume. To explain the decline of witch hunting after 1634, we should also note that by the late 1630's, men did not have to speculate on the *internal* causes of plague and famine. With roving bands of soldiers everywhere, the process of scapegoating could find a much more obvious target for its hostility than witches. For a few years, we might say, the soldier took up the burden of guilt so long carried by witches. The obvious difference between the two situations was that the soldier could defend himself or escape much more easily than the local hag.[31] It is clear, therefore, that although the natives must have known whom to blame for many of their ills, they could do very little about it. The scapegoating mechanism was allowed to proceed only part of the way.

A further note on the military complications of witch hunting may give a more concrete picture of the shifts in scapegoating during the Thirty Years War. At their winter camp at Durlach in Baden in 1643, the Bavarian army suffered a destructive plague among the horses. The local army leaders at once suspected that witches were responsible, especially those who had been banished from their home towns and had married soldiers, thereby obtaining a perfect opportunity of "working their evil."[32] By this stage of the war, women and other hangers-on often outnumbered the regular soldiers in camp by a ratio of four or even five to one.[33] They constituted a special problem for any army and must have been resented by its leaders. In communications with the government in Munich, the army leaders urged that witch trials be permitted at once. A few years earlier, two Bavarian army officers had apparently used witch hunts to great effect. The cautious officials in Munich, however, reminded its army that proper procedures were at all times to be employed, and that a mere *Schultheiss* or village mayor did not have sufficient authority to conduct witchcraft trials. By close government control in this case, it would seem that the army was denied a chance to uproot the internal causes of its troubles.[34] In line with our earlier speculation, it may be noted that at least among army men the proper scapegoat remained witches.

A few months later a different band of troops did get the witch hunt they wanted. In December 1643 Bavarian troops under Von Sporck occupied the free imperial city of Schwäbisch Hall, some forty miles northeast of Stuttgart. Apparently the same rumors and suspicions ran through this group of troops as we saw among those at Durlach. Soldiers' wives were suspected strongly of witchcraft. The colonel decided apparently on his own to conduct a trial by use of the old test of immersion in water. Being of a scientific nature, however, Von Sporck decided to prove the validity of this test by showing that an innocent person would float.* Offering a reward of 12 thalers

* This is in direct contrast with the English test in which the innocent were supposed to sink.

to any unsuspected citizen of Schwäbisch Hall who would undergo the test, the colonel found only one volunteer, a Jew named Löb. After floating three times, he collected his reward. The colonel now felt justified in subjecting soldiers' and officers' wives to the same test. Many were found guilty and executed.[35]

It is fascinating to note that a Jew during this time of stress felt confident enough to undergo such a test. In this region at least, it would seem that witches had so seized the popular imagination that Jews, far from being a constant potential scapegoat, could be used to *prove* the validity of the "Haller Hexenbad." Such examples illustrate well the peculiar way in which the objects of displaced aggression shifted during wartime conditions. It is of course impossible to know how many women, made desperate by the suspicions of their neighbors, fled to a nearby army where they might find protection for a price. Without strict controls forbidding witch trials like those among the Swedish armies, it becomes easy to see how the Bavarian army could fall into the position of witch hunting.

The notion of a shift in scapegoat is an attractive speculation, but one that cannot yet be documented. Succeeding chapters show that other changes during the Thirty Years War made witch hunting more difficult.

The last large flare-up of witch hunting came in the 1660's. For most of southwestern Germany the worst period had been 1627–32, but for Württemberg the peak came only between 1661 and 1670, when at least 77 persons were tried for witchcraft. This fact is especially hard to explain, since by that time the people were once again recovering from the horrors of war. This decade was not generally a notoriously repressive one in the rest of the German Southwest, although witch panics did take place in both Reutlingen and Esslingen between 1662 and 1666. Both of these free imperial cities were completely surrounded by Württemberg. Therefore, it looks as if a generally moderate region of the Southwest, a duchy and two adjacent imperial cities, at last fell victim to the fear of the devil. Unaccountably, all three were Lutheran.

REGIONAL PATTERNS OF WITCH HUNTING

Turning from temporal patterns of witch hunting in southwest Germany, we note that regional diversity affected the zeal shown in witch hunting. Recent sociological studies have shown how important a knowledge of regional variations is for understanding social movements.[36] Not only political units but geographic regions—valleys, forests, regions with the same type of soil or with similar patterns of land tenure or family life—influence the way people interact and the ideas they develop about themselves. However, I could discover no geographic basis for witch hunting in the German Southwest.[37] Panic was not more severe in mountainous areas, as some have asserted.[38] Nor were witch hunts more common or severe in towns with stagnant populations, as others have suggested.[39] Differences in conditions of land or tenure seem not to have had any effect. The crucial question may well be whether family structure and the status of women varied enough to change the pattern of witch hunting. However, this is a field of inquiry that is only beginning; we will have no firm results until the research in this exciting type of historical and comparative anthropology reaches greater maturity.[40]

Generally during the sixteenth century we can observe a movement of witch hunting from the more cultured northwest and southwest (the Rhine basin) toward the center and east. It would seem that witch hunting in part at least spilled over from France and Switzerland into Germany. Thus the fifteenth century saw trials at Heidelberg, Constance, Ettenheim, Ravensburg, Breisach, Waldshut, Triersberg, Eisingen, and Stein (i.e. in the west and south). In the sixteenth century the infection spread generally northeastward, affecting many of the smaller territories before 1560. Among the Catholic towns and territories hit by witch hunting were Bretten, Tübingen, Ringingen, Blaubeuren, Saulgau, Pforzheim, Waldsee, Stuttgart, Rottenburg, Bottwar, Oberndorf, Hechingen, Schiltach, Gundelfingen, Weissenhorn, Freiburg, Constance, the Ortenau, Horb, and Zell am Harmersbach. It is noteworthy that of all these towns only Zell a. H. was an imperial city. When we turn to the Protestant areas afflicted with witch hunting before 1560, we find Ulm, Schwäbisch Hall, Esslingen, Constance, Heilbronn, Dornstetten, Crailsheim, and Niedernhall. Of these eight towns, the first five were free imperial cities.* It is obvious that imperial cities were the earliest major contributor to Protes-

---

* Constance must appear as an imperial city in the Protestant list. The town lost its imperial privileges during the Interim (1548–50) and fell to the status of a Habsburg territorial town.

tant witch trials, in sharp contrast to the Catholic picture. It is of course necessary to remember that the imperial cities were among the earliest converts to the Reformation, and that it is only logical they might also provide several of the earliest examples of Protestant witch trials.

When we review the large amount of secondary literature on witch hunting in the German Southwest, it becomes evident that some of the largest territories had very few witchcraft trials. The Calvinist Palatinate seemed relatively free of panics. So too were Lutheran Württemberg and Lutheran Baden-Durlach. Similarly, the large city territory of Ulm experienced very few witchcraft trials. From the secondary literature, one is tempted to conclude that large territories were in fact less prone to panic than smaller, weaker ones. (This was a commonplace in nineteenth-century historiography.) In part, this conclusion is no doubt justified, but an examination of primary sources still surviving for Württemberg suggests a somewhat different picture.

We have two large series of overlapping sources by which to study witchcraft in seventeenth-century Württemberg: the consultations of the Tübingen legal faculty and the records of the Württemberg Oberrat, a supervisory council that sat in Stuttgart.[41] The great majority of witchcraft cases in these two sources falls in the seventeenth century. Despite scanty documentation for the sixteenth century, these records suffice to demonstrate that even a large territory like Württemberg could have a high number of witchcraft trials. In the seventeenth century, the Tübingen legal faculty was part of the regular legal machinery of Württemberg and had to be consulted under certain circumstances. In theory it should have been consulted in every witchcraft trial.[42] If it was consulted by local courts in every case of witchcraft, a high number of records of these transactions has been lost. It seems more likely that local courts often simply avoided consulting the Tübingen jurists. Even so, the huge series of consultations housed in the Tübingen University Archive contains records relating to 217 persons accused of witchcraft in the seventeenth century. The records of the Württemberg Oberrat, housed in the State Archive at Ludwigsburg, contain the reports of 245 separate witchcraft cases in the seventeenth century. Curiously enough, the overlap between these two series is very slight. In no more than 47 instances do we find the same case discussed in the records of both Tübingen and Ludwigs-burg. It is clear that neither series of records alone can give a true picture of Württemberg witch hunting, nor is there any assurance that the simple combination of both series gives a complete account. We can say, however, that during the seventeenth century, at least 415 persons were accused of witchcraft in Altwürttemberg. This is about four times as many as one could derive from all the secondary litera-ture on witch trials in Württemberg. Unfortunately we cannot even estimate how many of these 415 were ultimately executed.

A study of the geographic distribution of witchcraft trials in Würt-temberg has further surprises. Trials were most common in the Stutt-gart-Cannstatt area. Next came the region Brackenheim-Besigheim-Bietigheim to the north of Stuttgart and the region Böblingen-Sindel-fingen to the southwest of Stuttgart. Together these three regions ac-counted for at least 88 witchcraft cases in the seventeenth century. In contrast, the southeast around Blaubeuren and Münsingen and the northwest around Maulbronn were remarkably free of witch trials in the seventeenth century. (Consult the map of place names in the front of the book.)

What remains then of the observation that the large territories seemed less prone to witch hunting than their smaller neighbors? It is obviously inaccurate if we take it to mean that a large territory like Württemberg had very few witch trials. Yet it retains some value when we notice that none of the 415 cases of Württemberg witchcraft in the seventeenth century was a large-scale panic trial. All of them were of the small individual type so common before 1560.* It seems possible that both the Palatinate and Baden-Durlach had similar ex-periences. By avoiding the large witchcraft trial in which many were executed at once, these large territories gained a reputation for un-usual moderation.

If the largest territories often escaped large-scale panic trials, the same can generally be said for the very smallest territories of the Ger-man Southwest. We know of no cases in which imperial knights or the petty nobility tyrannized their people and wrought wanton de-struction. In this regard, the common generalization relating small territories and severe witch hunts is inaccurate for the German South-

---

* Later we examine a few apparent exceptions to even this modified generalization —Oberkirch (1631) and Calw (1683-84).

west. In fact, from secondary sources we might conclude that as a group the lower nobility were the most exemplary magistrates of all. Yet their situation has been so neglected and their records so scattered that a true picture cannot emerge at this time. Often they were so insignificant that their courts could not even rule in capital crimes like witchcraft.

Where, then, did the large trials occur? They took place in the middle-sized territories, in the imperial cities, and in the church lands. The trials that executed ten or more in one year occurred in middle-sized territories like the Ortenau, Hohenberg, and Breisgau, all three under Habsburg rule; in Baden-Baden, Fürstenberg, Helfenstein, Waldburg, Wallerstein, and Hohenzollern. They occurred in imperial cities like Constance, Offenburg, Gengenbach, Reutlingen, Nördlingen, Esslingen, Schwäbisch Gmünd, Rottweil, and Schwäbisch Hall. And finally they occurred in Oberkirch, jointly under the bishop of Strasbourg and the duke of Württemberg; in Freudenberg under the bishop of Würzburg; in the monastery of Obermarchtal; in the *Fürstpropstei* Ellwangen; and in Mergentheim under the control of the Teutonic Order. In succeeding chapters we examine these three groups more closely.

PATTERNS OF DECLINE

After surveying the patterns of witch hunting in the German Southwest at its peak, it remains for us to observe the ways in which witch trials gradually disappeared.

By the end of the Thirty Years War, witch hunting was beginning to encounter official government opposition in southwestern Germany. We later examine the crisis of confidence that brought many magistrates to doubt their own procedures in witchcraft trials. By the year 1621 a man had to pay dearly for denouncing five men and a woman in the town of Horb as witches. Instead of proceeding by torture until all six confessed, the court ruled that the denunciations were malicious slander and ordered the accuser to pay costs, and sent him off to war.[43] In 1640 a man from Wolfach complained that his wife had been accused of witchcraft; and another man was fined ten gulden in a similar case.[44] In 1654 in Marbach, a district town of Württemberg, simple accusations of witchcraft were again punished.[45] In a similar situation in 1665 in Sindelfingen, a person was convicted of slander in a mysterious poisoning, and forced to pay two gulden as a fine.[46] Two years earlier the executioner of Ettenheim had complained of lack of business and, in particular, of a dearth of witches.[47] Finally, in 1672 the council of Altdorf in the *Landvogtei* Schwaben (a Habsburg land) flatly prohibited all accusations of witchcraft and threatened a severe penalty for infractions of this new rule.[48] In the same year a witchcraft trial in Kappel on the Rhine produced the usual accusations and confessions, but with the extraordinary result that all were let go. The local pastor was admonished to instruct the children involved in the trial and to give them better doctrine.[49] By 1674 this sort of treatment was becoming usual. In that year a woman from Derendingen near Tübingen was warned and punished for calling her in-laws witches, and a year later a woman was simply warned and denied communion for referring to the devil as her lord.[50] Only a decade earlier she might have been in serious trouble. Although regular witch trials continued to take place, caution was becoming more usual. The punishment for idle accusations grew in severity—as, for example, in 1682 when the court at Ettenheim forced a woman to retract her denunciation of another woman and fined her one hundred gulden.[51] Similar actions continued during the eighteenth century, with the state and legal apparatus now being used to defend persons accused of witchcraft.* This is essentially the position in which courts find themselves today, when superstition erupts in denunciations or rumors of witchcraft.

The way in which witch trials came to an end is a fascinating, largely unexplored topic. The transition was not simply from punishing witchcraft to punishing accusations of witchcraft. Instead, after a crisis during the Thirty Years War, a new complex of crimes gradually entered the picture. Rather than witches being accused of a pact with the devil or carnal intercourse with spirits, it became increasingly common for persons to be found guilty of casting charms (*Segensprechen*), fortune telling (*Wahrsagen*), and magical treasure hunting (*Schatzgräberei*). In an earlier period these crimes would have implied a pact with the devil and would have led to demands for information about the sabbath, intercourse with spirits, the persons

---

* E.g., in Sindelfingen in 1738, a woman was fined for evil language in denouncing others as witches (Weisert, *Geschichte der Stadt Sindelfingen*, p. 130); and in Owen in 1761, a woman complained of being accused of witchcraft (Rooschüz, *Owen*, p. 74).

harmed by such magic, and finally accomplices. In this way simple superstitions could be made to imply the whole cult of witchcraft. In the late seventeenth century and increasingly in the eighteenth, such superstitions were punished merely as superstitions, or in certain cases as fraud. Thus the number of cases involving *veneficium* or *maleficium* dropped off sharply, whereas trials for *Segensprechen*, *Wahrsagen*, *Schatzgräberei*, and the *Passau Art* (by which a man was supposedly rendered safe from bullets) rose dramatically.

Some people actually did practice these kinds of magic, as we know from the survival of many of their books.[52] Adepts and novices alike tried to force demons to reveal the location of hidden treasure. Other forms of casting spells undoubtedly also persisted, quite unaffected by theological movements and shifts in the view of the devil. In 1751 it was still necessary to warn the gravedigger of Derendingen not to hand over to anyone the personal effects, hair, or fingernails of unbaptized children, for they might be used in superstitious magic.[53] In a case of treasure hunting in 1705, one man from Schorndorf so thoroughly believed in the possibility of wealth beyond his fondest dreams that he was defrauded of a small fortune (912 gulden). Certainly here and elsewhere in the eighteenth century the law was as much interested in the crime of fraud as in the punishment of superstition.[54]

In addition, courts now began to view poisoning as simply a different kind of murder. Instead of being linked to the action of spirits and at least a tacit pact with the devil, poison was now recognized more and more as simply a physical agent.[55] The central government of Württemberg in the eighteenth century dealt repeatedly with cases of simple poisoning. Similarly, infanticide, a crime far more common in the seventeenth century than one might have supposed, came to be detached from its association with witchcraft. When in 1738 a person from Urach was accused of killing a 13-week-old child, the indictment stated that the method used was "mouse poison." We find no hint of witchcraft; the crime had become simple murder.[56] Another murder case from 1740 stated that the murderer used *Mauspulver*.

Gradually the courts developed a psychological perspective that enabled them to understand cases of witchcraft in a more sophisticated way and to handle them more as we do today. For example, in 1730 a woman of Eberhard, near Nagold in the Black Forest, was accused of apostasy and harmful magic (*Abfall von Gott* and *malefi-cium*). Despite the fact that an overzealous pastor considered her thoroughly guilty, the court ruled that she was melancholy and feebleminded, and let her go unharmed.[57] Such an attitude, coupled with a clear discrimination of the very real crimes often at the root of an accusation of witchcraft, spelled the end of witchcraft as a crime in the German Southwest. If the crimes of magic and witchcraft could be adequately explained by such categories as fraud, theft, murder, poisoning, and mental illness, the utility of the concept of witchcraft vanished. When a child was thought to be bewitched in 1742, the officials of Nagold found it sufficient simply to forbid the parents to consult persons unskilled "in arte medica."[58] Hysterical fear of witchcraft in this region was dead.

Although this perspective shows the external shape of legal changes in the seventeenth and eighteenth centuries, scholars have not detected a major reason for the cessation of witch hunting. However, we will now see that this change emerged from zealous attempts to enforce the law.

Chapter Five

The Large Witchcraft Trials Begin, 1562-1618

THE LARGEST witch hunts in the German Southwest may have escaped attention altogether. Several localities are said to have experienced "large" witch hunts, but today most or all of the documents relating to them are lost. We can, therefore, report nothing more than the bare fact that a certain number of persons were said to have been executed in a certain year. Rather than attempt to build a narrative around such a frail skeleton I have simply presented the bare details in Table 6.

Even though our interest may be primarily in systematic analysis, we must start with a certain amount of basic information in narrative form. To understand the dynamic shape of a witch hunt, moreover, a narrative account is essential. What follows, therefore, is a series of descriptions of the witch hunts I have examined in detail. Rather than presenting full descriptions including all of the folklore, terror, and "local color" for each of the hunts, I have tried to present the dynamic features: how a panic began, rose, and fell, in the sharpest detail, while at the same time providing enough supporting information to give the reader some feeling for the documents, some general sense of what went on.

Perhaps the most common model for understanding the witch hunt has been the chain reaction. Many scholars have assumed that accusation of one person led (by torture) to denunciations of many more, and so on until an entire community was suspect. The popular literature is full of stories of villages in which virtually the whole population was exterminated in witch hunts. This domino theory of witch hunting is indeed roughly accurate for the initial phase of a panic, but it gives us no way of understanding how a witch hunt ever ended

TABLE 6

The Largest Witch Hunts in the German Southwest

Panics examined in detail (over 20 persons executed in one year)			Panics not examined in detail (over 10 persons executed in one year)		
Place	Year	Executed	Place	Year	Executed
Wiesensteig	1562	63	Wurzach[a]	1575–76	33
	1583	25	Breisgau[a]	1576	55
Rottenburg	1578	7			
	1580	9[b]			
	1582	8	Reute i.Br.[a]	1582	38
	1583	12			
	1585	9	Waldsee	1586	16
	1590	3	Nördlingen[c]	1590–94	35
	1595	6	Ingelfingen	1592	14
	1596	36	Freiburg i.Br.	1589	18
	1598	1		1603	13
	1599	10			
	1600	17	Hirrlingen	1599	10+
	1601	15	Hohenzollern	1598	18
	1602	1			
	1603	6			
	1605	6			
	1609	4			
Rottweil	1580	30?			
Obermarchtal	1586	22			
	1587	25			
	1588	6			
Ellwangen[d]	1611	100	Dornhan	1608–9	16
	1612	160			
	1613	50			
	1614	27			
	1615	33	Haslach	1615	10
	1616	13			
	1617	0	Sindelfingen	1615–16	12
	1618	10			
Schwäbisch Gmünd[e]	1613	11			
	1614	27			
	1615	?			
	1616	?			
	1617	?			
Offenburg	1627	7			
	1627–28	5			
	1628	17			
	1629	32			

TABLE 6 (*continued*)

Panics examined in detail (over 20 persons executed in one year)			Panics not examined in detail (over 10 persons executed in one year)		
Place	Year	Executed	Place	Year	Executed
Ortenau	1627	4			
	1628	39			
	1629	22			
	1630	14			
Gengenbach	1627–31	70?	Hüfingen	1631	10
Baden:					
Steinbach	1628	33			
Bühl	1628–29	70			
Baden	1627–31	90			
Wertheim	1616–17	50?			
	1629	10			
	1630–32	2			
	1633	11			
	1634	16			
	1641	2			
	1642	4			
	1644	3(+?)			
Mergentheim	1628	17			
	1629	94			
	1630	13			
	1631	1			
Oberkirch:					
Cappel	1631	20			
Ulm	1631	9			
Renchen	1632	12			
Sasbach	1631?	63			
Oppenau	1631–32	50			
Esslingen	1662	28[f]	Saulgau	1650–80	"Many"[a]
	1663–64	1			
	1665	8[f]			
Reutlingen	1665–66	14[g]			
Calw	1683–84	2[g]			

[a] Although trials in which more than 20 persons were apparently executed in one year were conducted in these places, no substantial material was located concerning them.

[b] This number is for Rottenburg and Horb.

[c] Nördlingen is not technically in the German Southwest, and its archive will not be usable for several years.

[d] All figures for Ellwangen except for the year 1617 are estimates. There were burnings on 17 separate days in 1611, on 17 days in 1612, 6 in 1613, 10 in 1614, 14 in 1615, 7 in 1616, and 5 in 1618.

[e] In Schwäbisch Gmünd for 1613–17, 59 persons were executed and 8 died in prison.

[f] Estimates.

[g] These trials do not strictly fulfill the criterion of 20 persons or more executed in one year, but for other reasons they are of interest.

without total depopulation. For this reason we shall examine the ways in which witch trials ended, with a view to refining the crude and inadequate idea of chain reaction.

The first large witch hunt in the German Southwest occurred in Wiesensteig on the Fils River in the small county of Helfenstein. During the early sixteenth century Wiesensteig remained resolutely Catholic, perhaps as a result of the influence of the reputable collegiate chapter there and the good administration of the bishops of Augsburg.[1] Nonetheless, popular pressures for reform led in 1555 to an invitation to Jacob Andreae, the famous Tübingen theologian, to lecture there. Andreae's lectures were quickly followed by those of other reformers, among them Leonhard Culmann, Mailänder, Hallberger, and Metz. From the start they split into factions, arguing among themselves the merits of Luther, Osiander, and Zwingli. However, the success of the Reformation in Wiesensteig depended more on the counts of Helfenstein than on popular demand or dogmatic unity. The zeal of the two brothers, Sebastian and Ulrich von Helfenstein, for reform proved to be of short duration. Sebastian died in his prime in 1564, and Ulrich fell prey to disease and to the urgings of his devoutly Catholic wife. Moreover, the Bishop of Augsburg, Otto Truchsess von Waldburg, began legal proceedings in the Reichskammergericht against Helfenstein to recover certain church funds that the brothers had used to pay the reformers. For all of these reasons, Ulrich was persuaded to receive a visit from Peter Canisius, and finally to return to Catholicism in 1567. The attempts of Duke Christoph of Württemberg and Margrave Karl von Baden to reconvert Ulrich to the Reformation were fruitless.

It was in this situation of religious turmoil, fear of war, epidemics, and severe hailstorms that Ulrich lashed out against witches. In 1562 he had several women arrested after a terrific storm on August 3. Damage from hail was so extensive that Duke Christoph wrote on the wall of his Stuttgart castle, "Balingen [where very few grapes were cultivated] produced more wine this fall than Stuttgart [with many vineyards]."[2] Ulrich's prompt action in Wiesensteig apparently found wide approval in some circles. In Esslingen, for example, Pastor Thomas Naogeorgus took up the hue and cry against witches with such vigor that the Esslingen city council warned him on August 18 not to stir up the people so irresponsibly.[3] Nevertheless, the officials of Esslingen felt so unsure of themselves that they wrote to Wiesensteig for advice and information. In reply we learn that Ulrich had already executed six of the suspected women as witches, and that a number of Wiesensteig witches claimed to have seen citizens of Esslingen at the witches' dance. Here we see the perfect illustration of why the concept of a witches' sabbath was of such grave structural importance. With information of this sort, a witch panic might spread from an original location to disturb all of the surrounding countryside.*

Despite the panic at Esslingen, all three of the persons arrested there were ultimately let go. It may well be that the sermons preached by Alber and Bidembach in nearby Stuttgart influenced the Esslingen council to moderate its procedures. In any event we know that Ulrich von Helfenstein was distressed at such lenience.[4] Within a short time he had executed 41 of the godless women of Wiesensteig.[5] On December 2, 1562, he approved the execution of 20 more.[6] In some such way we reach the total reported in a sensational pamphlet of 1563, which described "the true and terrible acts and deeds of the sixty-three witches and sorceresses who were burned at Wiesensteig."[7]

It is unfortunate that we can know no more about this first massive witch hunt in the German Southwest. The trial documents themselves were either lost long ago or destroyed, perhaps in the great fire of 1648, when two-thirds of the city went up in flames.[8] The early seventeenth-century chronicler Oswald Gabelkofer touched the subject without illuminating it.[9]

That a Protestant town near the reforming influence of the University of Tübingen came to have the first large witch hunt in the whole region indicated that Wiesensteig in 1562 was not controlled by men of the Tübingen persuasion. The superintendent of Wiesensteig was the unorthodox Lutheran Leonhard Culmann, a follower of Andreas Osiander.[10] It would make sense, in the absence of other proof, that Culmann could not have been steeped in the witchcraft doctrines of Brenz, Alber, Bidembach, and Platz, and that he might well have taken a hard line against witches as the cause of great harm. At least in the similar situation of Naogeorgus in Esslingen, this was the case. Naogeorgus in his sermons so stirred up the populace that he pro-

* Esslingen was over 30 miles from Wiesensteig.

voked rebuke from the Esslingen city council. Surely the printing of Alber and Bidembach's sermons on witchcraft was aimed at counteracting the influence of Naogeorgus.[11] When the three suspects at Esslingen were released, Naogeorgus was every bit as angry as Ulrich von Helfenstein had been.[12] When we inquire into Naogeorgus' background, we find that he too was unorthodox, and certainly not in the Brenzian tradition. Martin Crusius, the great chronicler, noted that after this witch panic in Esslingen, Naogeorgus was dismissed for his theological irregularity and died a year later, in December of 1563, in Weissenlohe in the Palatinate.[13] It seems curiously significant that the social disruption of witch hunting first reached epidemic status under the influence of Protestant preachers not trained in the spiritualizing Tübingen tradition.

The polemicists of the nineteenth century argued whether Wiesensteig was Protestant or Catholic at the time of this witch hunt in 1562. It seems obvious that the town and territory must be chalked up to the Protestant side. If this was a Catholic victory, however, scholars should have seen that it was only partial, for 21 years later, when Wiesensteig had clearly returned to the Catholic faith, witches were once again burned. At least 25 were executed there in 1583.[14] Again shortly before 1605 the Count of Helfenstein seems to have brought 14 more witches to justice.[15] Aside from these violent outbursts, it was quiet in the upper valley of the Fils, at least until 1611, when four women from Württemberg and one man were burned at Wiesensteig.[16] We have no record of any other witch trials at Wiesensteig, but since such judicial records are lost or scattered, we cannot argue from silence that there were no more trials. However, there were no more large witchcraft panics, or we would hear of them from other sources.

ROTTENBURG

Rottenburg and Horb, a few miles up the Neckar from Tübingen, were the two chief centers of the northern part of the county Hohenberg. In 1581 they had about 2,750 and 1,660 inhabitants respectively.[17] Hohenberg was itself part of the Habsburg lands in southwestern Germany which together were called "Vorderösterreich." Although the Reformation made early progress in Hohenberg, by the mid-sixteenth century the Habsburgs had succeeded in leading their territory back to Catholicism.[18] By the years 1528–30 Rottenburg knew the problem of witchcraft and even seems to have found a special potion that led stubborn suspects to confess when the most extreme tortures failed. Unfortunately there is no record of what this drink might have contained, but we do know that something like it was used in other trials.[19] At any rate, it must have been used with some discretion, for it was not until 1559 that Horb burned any witches, whereas Rottenburg did not purge itself of witches until 1578. In that year Horb executed nine women and Rottenburg seven.[20] Despite the damage done by a violent storm that set fires in Horb and ruined some crops that year, an exceptionally fine harvest was brought in at the end of the summer. By then, of course, the witches responsible for this obviously insignificant destruction were dead.[21] In the next 11 years both Rottenburg and Horb lived in fear of the witches. In the summer of 1580 perhaps nine witches were executed at Horb and Rottenburg.[22] Two summers later, in 1582, eight or more were executed in Rottenburg.[23] In 1583 at least 12 were executed in Rottenburg and 13 in Horb.[24] Unfortunately this diligence was not successful in eradicating all the witches. After burning nine more women at Rottenburg in 1585, however, the magistrates did order a pause, saying that if they continued to burn witches at this rate there would soon be no women left in Rottenburg.[25]

Such a sentiment did not long persist. In 1589 Horb convicted and burned five women "who had made a pact with Satan and were rumored to have brought harm to the people."[26] During the next year, Rottenburg found three more witches and committed them to the sword and fire.[27] That same year saw a most curious example of the way witchcraft and the Counter-Reformation occasionally worked together. The accusation has been made that Catholics used the witch hunt to get rid of their Protestant subjects, although there is no indisputable instance of this. By 1590 the trials in Rottenburg had been undermining social confidence for some 12 years. As was usual in such situations, the social status of those accused tended to rise as time passed. So it was that Agatha von Sontheim zu Nellingsheim, a member of the lower nobility, was suspected of witchcraft in 1590. Denunciations from confessed witches had now reached out credibly even to the nobility. In desperation her relatives, the Herren zu Ehingen, tried to save her by having the trial stopped. Unfortunately for them, the Habsburg Archduke Ferdinand took the position that the law was no respecter of persons or wealth. Even so, a commission was set up in Augsburg to study the case. Together they worked out a compromise in 1594. The lords of Ehingen could save Agatha by paying the sum of 10,000 gulden and by restoring their recently reformed lands to the Catholic faith. We do not know which of these two demands they found easier to meet, but here, at least, the law did "respect" persons—or more accurately money and religion.[28]

Rottenburg now had a breathing spell of nearly five years. But in 1595 at least six witches were executed, and here we have extracts from the original documents to work with.[29] In June of that year these women were interrogated and tortured until they confessed. The motifs in the confessions were seduction by a man dressed in green or black, greed for money (which the devil gave readily enough, but which always turned out to be dung or broken pottery), and acute depression or unhappiness with marriage. Invariably the women also admitted causing grave damage to crops and livestock.[30]

The worst year of all at Rottenburg was 1596. In all, 35 witches were executed and one person died in prison. We have information concerning 19 of them. The confessions have constant reference to depression, sadness, trouble, or distress before the women were enticed into witchcraft. The devil was said to be at first a great consolation to them. Perhaps in their emotional distress they projected their desires onto the figure of the devil. Regardless of how answers were extorted from them, it is significant that one of the women explained her actions by asserting that "not everything they say about God is true."[31] Combined with their depression seemed to be a dissatisfaction with conventional religion. It would overstrain the evidence to see this remark as symptomatic of covert Protestantism, but the remark does support the contention that the most suspect women were independent in both habits and thoughts. The commonest method the devil used to console the women was with money. Often the witches confessed that times had been so severe that they did not know how to feed themselves or their children.

The trials and executions in Rottenburg were so sensational that professors at Tübingen found their students deserting the classroom. Martin Crusius noted in his diary on May 7, 1596, "Today ten witches were burned at Rottenburg, four tied to each stake.* In lecturing on Thucydides I had few listeners since they had gone up [to Rottenburg] to watch." On June 1, 13 more were executed, and on July 21 again 12, tied to four stakes. In addition, one person died in prison, presumably from severe torture.[32]

As was common when trials became so frequent, even members of the *Ehrbarkeit* (the non-noble governing elite) fell under suspicion. In 1596, for example, the wife of the *Schultheiss* of Schwaldorf was denounced, questioned, condemned, and executed. Political motives might have colored this charge, but under more stable conditions, denunciations like this were thrown out. Witch hunting so thoroughly shook up normal bonds of social trust that the most respected members of the community were no longer immune to attack.[33]

This pattern repeats itself in many of the trials. We know of none in Rottenburg in 1597, but in 1598 one woman was executed. By 1599 there was a rapid rise to ten or more executions.[34] In 1600 some 17 were executed, including the wife of the *Schultheiss* of Hirrlingen. Again the social status of the accused went up during the panic.[35] The next year saw no letup as 15 witches were burned in Rottenburg.[36] In 1602 even the old city *Schultheiss*, Hans Georg Hallmayer, came to be suspected of witchcraft. Crusius noted that this man, who was first mentioned as *Schultheiss* in 1570, "burned 180 witches while he was *Schultheiss*."[37] Even if this is an exaggeration, certainly his reputation as a severe governor was well established. The essence of his crime in 1602 was having sexual relations with Satan "in the assumed form of a hospital maid here." By 1602 any crime could be viewed as witchcraft. Hallmayer was thrown in prison, confessed his pact with the devil, and died in his cell.[38] One can well imagine the fear, distrust, and dismay that spread when it became apparent that the most zealous witch hunters were themselves tainted with witchcraft. Lower officials too were not trustworthy. In 1605 Christoph Wendler, the lieutenant of the *Vogt* (bailiff) of Rottenburg, was arrested and sent to Innsbruck, where he was condemned for extortion. As punishment, the government of Vorderösterreich confiscated one-third of his property. Crusius noted that Wendler too was suspected of witchcraft.[39]

---

* How this works out arithmetically is not clarified. Crusius, *Diarium*, I: 89, 103.

The attack on high local officials seems often to have shaken communities out of their descent into utter panic: the very machinery of witch hunting became so suspect that townsmen grew wary of it. In Rottenburg in any event, we know of no executions in 1602. In the next decade the hunt proceeded by fits and starts. In 1603 six persons were executed and six more in 1605.[40] Four more met the sword and fire in 1609.[41] But four years later, when women were accused of witchcraft in Rottenburg and in the outlying villages of Hirschau, Wurmlingen, Wendelsheim, and Hailfingen, all of the suspects were released when the magistrates received legal counsel from Jacob Halbritter of the University of Tübingen that the evidence did not suffice to permit formal charges against them.[42] This new note of caution characterized Rottenburg's later confrontations with witchcraft.[43] It had taken 30 years and at least 150 lives to attain this degree of sophistication.

A NOTE ON ROTTWEIL

Moving up the Neckar River, we briefly note Rottweil. In the sixteenth century, Rottweil was one of the oldest, proudest, and largest imperial cities in the German Southwest, with a large subject territory of 28 villages and a city population of 5,100.[44] As the seat of the imperial *Hofrat* (a high court for settling interterritorial disputes) and with formal ties to Switzerland, Rottweil managed to assert her independence of neighboring Württemberg and Breisgau. Economically, it was a center of cloth and hardware production (especially sickles).

From the records remaining in this venerable city, we can reconstruct the outlines of about 60 witchcraft executions in the sixteenth century (1566–99), and another 71 in the seventeenth century (1600–1648).[45] Rottweil never came even close to executing 20 persons in one year,* according to all the records except for an anonymous pamphlet of 1580. This *Newe Zeittung* of 1580 reported the witch hunting of Swabia and noted that "in Rotweil [sic] they burned a good part of the witches, thirty in all, who had miserably killed many small children."[46] Now 30 in one year would be a severe witch hunt indeed. However, since the Rottweil documents are in fairly decent order,

---

* For the years 1580–84 we know of 22 executed, and in the period 1589–91 we know of 14 executed. These were the peaks.

TABLE 7

Rottweil Witchcraft Trials

Year	Executed	Year	Executed	Year	Executed
1566	1	1581	9	1590	8
1572	2	1583	6	1591	2
1574	2	1584	4	1593	1
1575	1	1585	2	1596	1
1577	2	1586	1	1598	7
1579	1	1588	1	1599	2
1580	3[a]	1589	4	1600–1648	71

SOURCES: Ruckgaber, "Hexenprozesse," pp. 174–96; Rottweil Stadtarchiv, Criminalakten: II/I/V/9/# 14–26; *Zwo Newe Zeittung*, sig. A1v.

NOTE: For the years 1584 and 1589–99 I have improved the data given by Ruckgaber on the basis of the Criminalakten in the Rottweil Stadtarchiv.

[a] There were 30 reported in *Newe Zeittung*.

we must remain skeptical of this larger, totally unsubstantiated number.

Table 7 summarizes what we know of the Rottweil witch hunt with a list of executions so far as we can reconstruct them.

In the confessions of the Rottweil witches we find all of the elements we have found before: seduction by the devil masquerading as a man in red, black, or green clothing, the offer of help by the devil to assist the witch in particularly troublesome matters (money, food), a thorough denial of God and Christianity, the sabbath with dancing and feasting, and harmful magic.[47] At Rottweil, as in other places, the men charged with witchcraft were very often guilty of a purely secular crime like theft or murder, and had magic or demonolatry added to the charge. They would therefore have suffered death even if witchcraft had not been part of their crime.

An extraordinary number of those executed in Rottweil came from outside the town. Of 42 executed between 1561 and 1600 whose origin is known, 37 came from outside Rottweil, many from villages under the jurisdiction of the city, but some came from as far away as Geislingen (near Ulm) and Hof (north of Bayreuth). After 1600 the same rough relation persisted, with 55 out of 71 executed having origins outside Rottweil.[48] In the case of nearby villages, these facts suggest that for some obscure reason the suspicions and accusations of the countryside failed to infect the city. But we might also surmise that at least in the case of real strangers, their execution reflected a xenophobia and hatred of the unusual and of the rootless and occasionally criminal vagabonds who roamed the land. The officials of Rottweil did indeed fear that a band of arsonists was at work in the Neckar valley.[49]

Even if Rottweil had no truly "severe" panic as the *Newe Zeittung* reported, the witch trials there do fit the pattern that reveals itself throughout the German Southwest.

OBERMARCHTAL

In 1580 the Premonstratensian monastery of Obermarchtal was an imperial abbey whose territory of 64 square miles included ten villages and a population of about 700 on the southeastern edge of the Swabian Alb.[50] This region of Swabia was a checkerboard of imperial abbeys and small secular territories. Proper background studies and supplementary archival materials are lacking to explain the reasons for the beginning of witch hunting in Obermarchtal in the 1580's. Records show that it suffered one extremely severe witch hunt and others well into the eighteenth century.

Between 1571 and 1591 the abbot of Obermarchtal was Konrad Frei, an efficient administrator who zealously pulled the abbey into financial solvency, especially by the collection of debts outstanding.[51] One might suspect that here, as elsewhere, witch hunting was a lucrative business, but according to all documents that survive, the witches of Obermarchtal were poor peasants. It could hardly be otherwise since there were no towns, mines, or other sources of wealth nearby. In this situation of sparse sources, it is indeed unusual to have an exhaustive study of the trials at Obermarchtal.[52] But its author, Robert Dengler, was also unable to discover why the 1580's brought so sharp a fear of witchcraft, although he confidently asserts that a long pause in witch trials between 1596 and 1627 was due to the political situation of concern over the succession to Jülich-Cleves.[53]

Whatever the immediate cause, Melchior Hurm of Rottenburg was arrested, condemned, and executed on May 18, 1581, for a combination of witchcraft and murder. It was highly unusual that a man should be the first in a series of witchcraft trials, and we may be justified in emphasizing his crime as an actual murder the details of which were perhaps so shocking that devilish inspiration was ascribed to him.[54] It was not until five years later that 15 women and seven men were executed in at least seven separate burnings, from June through September 1586. Then there seems to have been a hiatus of several months, until June 1587 saw at least 13 more executions (12 women and one man). During the rest of the year 11 more women and one man were burned. Finally in 1588, the unusually severe panic subsided, with only six executions (four women and two men).[55] In all the subsequent history of Obermarchtal we know of only 30 more executions. In a population of around 700, three years had claimed the lives of nearly 7 per cent of the inhabitants.

The reason for such severe trials in a small, secluded territory like this is apparent from the procedural details. The documents of confession and examination show the emphasis placed on finding accomplices. From 1586 and 1587 some 24 lists of denunciations survive, lists in which confessed witches named their *Gespillenen*. Waldburga Kepplerin, for example, gave the names of 11 persons she had seen at the dance.[56] On the other hand, there is no emphasis on the devil's mark as a form of *indicium* leading to torture.[57] Generally these denunciations alone were sufficient to warrant torture. When Ursula Bayer denounced eight persons, we know that four of them were executed with her on June 16, 1586. Two others were later executed (one in 1593), and only two escaped trial and torture.[58] In Obermarchtal, torture led invariably to denunciations, which in turn led to further trials. It is easy to understand how these panic trials began and expanded; the wonder is that they came to an end at all. Part of the reason may have to do with the personality of the judge, Bernhard Bitterlin, a harsh man. But since he continued as *Vogt* well into the seventeenth century, we can find no reason for the wave of trials between 1586 and 1589. We know that Bitterlin did not change his mind concerning witchcraft, for in 1627–28 he condemned at least seven persons to death for witchcraft.[59]

Aside from these details, the Obermarchtal materials are simply too weak to provide further structural information. We cannot be as sure as Dengler is that most of the persons executed for witchcraft were women of loose morals simply because they confessed to sexual crimes, or that they were guilty of infanticide because they admitted to it.[60] The problem is much more complex, because torture and a predesigned list of questions might bring anyone to confess those crimes. Only in the few instances where women actually turned themselves in can we suspect that Dengler is right in calling these women neurotic, eccentric, and visionary.[61]

The trials at Obermarchtal represent, unfortunately, a lurid flash in the Swabian landscape that raises many more questions than it solves.

ELLWANGEN

At the beginning of the seventeenth century, the *Fürstpropstei* (princely prebend) of Ellwangen was a Catholic territory of approximately 155 square miles, dominated by the city of Ellwangen with its collegiate church and the castle overlooking the town. Until 1460 Ellwangen had been the seat of an important imperial Benedictine monastery; but in that year, because of poor administration and lack of proper discipline, Pope Pius II transformed the monastery into an exempt, secular collegiate chapter headed by a Fürstpropst (prince-provost), with 12 canons of knightly birth and ten choir-vicars.[62] This "secularization" meant that canons were no longer monks obedient to the rule of Benedict but were members of the secular clergy. As an "exempt" institution, the Fürstpropstei was not subject to the normal episcopal discipline of Augsburg but was subject to the pope directly. In Ellwangen a spiritual council (*geistlicher Rat*) performed the duties of local ecclesiastical supervision.[63] In secular affairs, the Fürstpropstei was also almost totally independent of external supervision and control. Although Württemberg retained a duty to protect Ellwangen (*Schirmherrschaft*), after the mid-sixteenth century this duty became virtually meaningless. It is fair to say that by 1600 the Fürstpropstei enjoyed an independence from both ecclesiastical and secular influence that many larger territories might well have envied. At any rate, there was generally a lively competition for the election to Fürstpropst from the sixteenth century on.[64]

We are well informed about the judicial machinery of the Fürstpropstei, which reflects much of the independence from external controls that was common in Ellwangen. By 1466 a criminal code was promulgated especially for Ellwangen.[65] During the sixteenth century, however, judicial procedures changed as more and more emphasis came to be placed on the inquisitorial form of action (see p. 68) and on intervention by the princely court-council (*Hofrat*) in all phases of criminal procedure.[66] Fortunately, an *Instruction* of Fürst-propst Johann Christoph von Westerstetten, written some time between 1605 and 1613, survives to inform us of those rules and criminal procedures prevailing at the exact time of the massive witch hunts.

In an apparent attempt to reduce abuses of torture, the Fürstpropst declared that any defendant was to be brought to a confession, either willingly or by torture, only in the presence of the *Stadtvogt* (city bailiff), the *Stadtschultheiss* (city supervisor), the secular councilors, two or three members of the court, and the city clerk.[67] It should be noted that so large a company of supervisors seldom if ever met as directed. Later, on the same day that this usually tortured confession had been exacted, the prisoner was to be *besiebnet*. This involved a solemn confirmation of the confession before seven men and was regarded as important proof that the accused was now telling the truth voluntarily. According to the *Instruction*, the court was to convene, still on the same day, and make a final judgment. The court then informed the *Stadtvogt* and the secular councilors of the sentence, so that preparations could be made for the punishment (usually execution). The court also presented the sentence to the Fürstpropst, since he retained the right of mitigating all sentences.[68] In witchcraft cases, for example, the prince almost invariably changed sentence of death by burning to death by the sword, with the corpse then given over to the flames.

On the second day, according to this *Instruction*, the convict was to be told of the sentence passed on him in his absence, and was given the opportunity to confess and take communion. On the third day, if all went as prescribed, the sentence was to be executed.[69] Actually trial procedures took longer than this ideal pattern, and we may presume that the Fürstpropst hoped mainly to render litigation more efficient, even if this three-day model was usually out of reach. By the eighteenth century, however, an elaborate set of formalities had again become standard, as a report from 1738 makes clear.[70] As a symbol of its legal independence, Ellwangen never permitted appeals to higher courts in criminal cases.[71]

When it came to witchcraft cases, these general procedures did not seem to provide definite enough guidance. In addition to records kept of previous witchcraft cases in 1528 and 1588–89 in which some 12 or 13 persons were executed, the authorities at Ellwangen collected a set of descriptions of witchcraft procedures from electoral Mainz (i.e. from the residence of the electors at Aschaffenburg) and from the Habsburg territories of Bregenz and Hoheneck.[72] In the specific sets of questions formulated for the interrogation of witches by a councilor of Ellwangen in 1611, the order and wording of questions seem to have been directly borrowed from the *Directorium* from Bregenz.[73] Somewhat later, the authorities in Ellwangen seem to have been perplexed about what rules should apply for the confiscation of witches' property. On this occasion they requested and received a copy of the latest version of an electoral Mainz mandate covering the problem of "how to deal with the punishment of witches by confiscation."[74] Here again, it seems, outside models helped to formulate the policies of Ellwangen, but only to the extent that Ellwangen officials found the advice reasonable.

The magistrates of Ellwangen might seek out yet another form of outside help, namely, the consultation of legal faculties concerning specific points of law. When necessary, they consulted the faculties of both Freiburg i. Br. and Ingolstadt.[75]

All in all, Ellwangen presented a fairly common picture of the medium-sized territory in southwestern Germany. There are no striking structural characteristics that would lead one to expect the kind of ferocious witch hunt that exploded between 1611 and 1618. Only its isolation and independence from outside control rendered Ellwangen perhaps more susceptible to a runaway panic than other territories its size.

The quiet years before 1611 may well have been a time of frustration and despair. We know from later testimony that storms were frequent and crop damage often severe in the years after 1605. We also know that an extraordinary number of cattle and horses sickened and died in ways that seemed mysterious if not nefarious to the people of Ellwangen. Perhaps the last straw in this kind of environmental burden was the plague that broke out in the region in 1607 and worked with deadly effect among the undernourished population.[76] During the witch trials we hear mention of epidemics and "contagion," which continued to spread through Ellwangen, Schwäbisch Gmünd, and the surrounding area.[77] In 1618 one writer described these epidemics as supernatural in origin, since they were unfamiliar even to experienced doctors.[78]

The year 1611 also brought the first Jesuits to Ellwangen. Unfortunately the ocean of documents does not tell us how or why the Ellwangen witch hunt began. There are perhaps 100 separate folders of material relevant to these trials, but they contain judicial documents almost exclusively — records of examinations, confessions, and sentences, with confiscation data but no descriptive materials, no diaries, and few letters.[79] This being the case, any account is bound to be some form of speculative reconstruction.

On April 7, 1611, Barbara Rüfin, the 70-year-old wife of Caspar Rüf from the village of Rindelbach, was arrested and brought into Ellwangen on suspicion of witchcraft. At that time she was suspected primarily of desecrating the host, which she received during the Eucharist; indeed, she readily admitted that she occasionally had to adjust the host to prevent it from falling out of her mouth. In addition, she had a reputation for witchcraft. Over the years even her husband had come to consider her a witch, "and often remarked that women here were burned, and that she should turn herself in to be examined."[80] In the next few days, however, the details of denunciation and accusation began to accumulate as various relatives and neighbors were asked to tell all they knew about Rüfin. By April 12 she was suspected of killing cattle by means of salves and of attempting to kill her own son by putting quicksilver in his soup. After that incident, her son was heard publicly condemning her *mer als 100 mal*, as a witch.[81] In the extensive documents relating to this case, a garish light is thrown on a number of folk beliefs as well as social situations conducive to witchcraft accusations.

Rumor and reputation played an understandably large role. An example is the tale told by Veit Miller, aged 39, on April 9. He explained that

his father, now dead, used to tell often how years ago more than 30 head of cattle of all sorts, mostly horses, got sick. They had gone then to a witch at Lustnau named Biren Ketterin, who is now dead, to ask advice on where this misfortune might come from. The witch came into their house and said that such misfortune originated with evil persons. But she would cause the witch responsible to reveal herself. As soon as she left their house, she said, a person would come asking for three things. If they gave her these things, their situation with the cattle would get worse than before. Then the above-named Barbara Rieffin, hardly after the witch left them, came into their house and asked for a shawl, a butter box, and a cradle. But she was refused. In addition to these three she asked for a pan to bake in. But all were refused. And after all of these things were refused in this way, his parents had peaceful success with their cattle.*

In a flood of testimony like this, the cloud of suspicion and isolation surrounding the old lady became darker and darker. Her own family relationships seemed to contribute to her isolation. She had trouble with her husband, although he claimed under interrogation on April 9 that he actually called her a witch only when he was angry. More serious was her relationship with her daughter-in-law, Agatha. Agatha testified on April 11 that she had married Barbara Rüfin's son Basti (Sebastian) against his mother's will. She could never seem to satisfy her mother-in-law. From the start she had been *ein arme dirn*, not good enough for Basti. Apparently in reaction to this loss of her son's primary affection, Barbara had tried to poison him about nine years earlier.[82] This explicit in-law tension found no socially approved expression and must have built up until Basti simply exploded by calling his mother *ein allte Unhold* (an old witch).[83]

By April 12 enough accusations had accumulated that the investigators (Dr. Carl Kibler, one of the Council; the *Schultheiss*; and the city clerk) felt it necessary to ask Barbara Rüfin for her side of the story. Again, as before, she denied all guilt, claiming that she knew nothing (*kein dingle!*) of what made certain cattle sicken and die. She swore on pain of death she had eaten all of the soup that Basti claimed was poisoned. But under pressure she broke down in sobs.

It should be clear that up to now no torture had been used, only the patient collection of evidence and the attempt to make divergent stories square with one another. By April 20 enough evidence was present that the examiners decided on torture. That day they stretched her twice for periods of 15 minutes each time, and still the old lady held on. She insisted on her innocence and trusted that God would manifest some sign confirming it.[84]

Hard, stubborn, courageous as she might be, torture finally broke her. On April 22 she was tortured seven separate times, and by the end of the day she had confessed to all charges brought against her.

---

* The spelling of Rüfin's name varies throughout these documents. The storyteller apparently tried to cover the fact that Rüfin seems to have asked for four items.

She admitted desecrating the host, copulating with the devil, attempting to poison her son, having a pact with the devil, and ruining crops; and she identified a number of her accomplices. Remarkably enough, when she was questioned the next day without torture, she denied all that she had earlier confessed. Under torture, however, the confession slowly, painfully, reemerged. By April 25 the old lady was totally confused. She asserted that she trusted in God, but that the devil forbade her to go to church. She attended a witches' dance, she said, but asserted that if she were a witch, she would confess it. She showed her examiners a devil's mark on her foot the size of a kreuzer (a common coin), which the torturer, Meister Wolff, examined. After admitting a long string of crimes, she ended her testimony for that day with a *revocatio omnium*. Even the examiners recognized that the 70-year-old woman had become *ganz wankelmuetig* (completely confused).[85]

This state of mind reappeared on May 6, when the examiners confronted her ruthlessly with a list of 18 counterarguments drawn from her own words. In this list we obtain an incredible view of the witch-hunting mind at work, rigorous, methodical, logical. For example, if she were innocent, how could she have *known* that a demon had taken her place beside her husband while she was out at the nocturnal sabbath? Or again, if she claimed to be guiltless, how could she explain *knowing* that an associate's lover-devil was named Little Feather (*fedterlein*)?[86] It did not occur to her examiners that she might not have "known" these facts but simply have invented them. Surely part of the *révolution mentale* separating that age from this was a growth in the sense of the impossible. But just as important a part was a redefinition of the term *knowledge*.* Torture, as we saw earlier, rested on the hope of uncovering facts that an innocent person simply could not know. We see here what that could mean in practice.

The extraordinarily instructive case of Barbara Rüfin (with some 200 pages of legal documents) came to an end on May 6 and May 9, when she finally without torture confessed to the charges brought against her. On May 16, 1611, she was executed with the sword, her body burned, and all her belongings confiscated by the Fürstpropstei of Ellwangen. Her trial was remarkable for her stamina and courage,

---

* Febvre, "Sorcellerie." See also the account of the witch trials at Wertheim in Chapter 6, pp. 138–43.

as well as for the pragmatic, methodical way in which her examiners had questioned everyone concerned, and had gone to some lengths to determine whether alleged damage done in past years really had occurred (e.g. had a certain cow died mysteriously? Had a certain storm ruined certain crops?). Perhaps it is fortunate that after this first burning in Ellwangen not everyone had to undergo so thorough and thoughtful a trial.

As time passed, the examiners became increasingly skilled in forcing people to confess. They seem to have decided that legally only three denunciations were needed to show probable guilt. If in addition the devil's mark could be found (any spot on the body that was insensitive to probing with a needle or that failed to bleed when probed), the examiners could move without delay to torture. For most of the witches executed after Rüfin, these two criteria were prominent. This increase in efficiency meant that for many witches it took two weeks or less to move from arrest to execution.

Certainly officials in Ellwangen saw a need for this new efficiency in the ever-mounting number of persons denounced by persons crazed by torture. By the end of the year 1611, at least 17 execution days had been held in which surely well over 100 persons died. The year 1612 saw another 17 burnings, with probably at least 140 executed. The annual letter of the Society of Jesus mentioned a total of 167 executed for that year.[87] For 1613 we have records of some six execution days. On September 13, after four of the burnings for that year, Father Johann Finck, S.J., wrote from Ellwangen, "Up to now [starting in 1611] 303 have been burned, mostly from Ellwangen. In addition three more have been caught, and even from the better families, two girls and a boy who was my pupil earlier in Dillingen. I do not see where this case will lead and what end it will have, for this evil has so taken over, and like the plague has infected so many, that if the magistrates continue to exercise their office, in a few years the city will be in miserable ruins."[88]

Others explained that the severity of Ellwangen's panic arose from the fact that three priests and an organist were found guilty of witchcraft and executed in June 1615, after suffering a painful degradation from holy orders.* They had confessed to performing black magic

---

* The priests each had a hole cut in their right hands, in their tonsures, and in their foreheads, and then had salt and vinegar rubbed in these spots to expunge all traces

during mass. One even admitted that for four years he had baptized all children in the devil's name. This obviously explained why so many witches were found in Ellwangen. From a psychological point of view, it seems certain that if even priests might be witches, the normal communal sense of the impossible had suffered a critical blow. The normal mechanisms of shutting off a witch panic no longer existed when the very foundations of society were felt to be shifting in this way.* At the same time, accusations and convictions of highly placed and undoubtedly honorable men must have shaken some people into the recognition that something had gone wrong.

Part of the new official rigor with regard to witchcraft was designed to speed the process leading to torture. With Barbara Rüfin, the court was baffled and delayed by extensive testimony from neighbors and friends; the members only slowly made up their minds about the essential parts of the crime of witchcraft, carefully collating material and developing questions for her next interrogation. By midsummer of 1611, much of this labor was dispensed with, for lists of general questions came into general use. The princely advisor, Dr. Carl Kibler, for example, drew up a list of 30 questions that began by asking if the accused could say the Lord's Prayer, the Ave Maria, the Creed, and the Ten Commandments, but then moved on directly to the question of who seduced her into witchcraft. How did this seduction occur? Why did she give in? Where? When? What was the devil like? What did he promise? What was it like to have sexual relations with him? Why did she not break off the relationship when she realized that he was a devil? And so on and on.[89]

As a result of questionnaires (*Fragstücke*) like this, we have no problem understanding the remarkable uniformity that soon characterized almost all of the witches' confessions. We do not need to theorize that the witches must have had some cult in order to explain their agreement on the most minute details.[90] The questions asked supply us with a sufficient answer. By constant use of these formulas it was even possible to set the pattern or sequence of events in a witch's confession.

---

of sacramental chrism. Finally, their fingernails were ripped out, and they were given secular clothing. *Zwo Hexenzeitung* (Nuremberg, 1615), fol. 2r-v. For two of these priests, cf. Ellwangen Kapitelrezesse, WSAL B387, Bü. 799, fol. 264r-v.

  * See other accounts of trials in Chapters 6 and 7.

Typically the witches of Ellwangen confessed first to some form of sexual seduction, perhaps at the instigation of another person already a witch.[91] Only later did these persons discover that their seducer was the devil. In fact the whole German Southwest was remarkably poor in that vivid imagery that pictured the devil as a goat or a cat or a monster. Among the trials that I have examined, the devil was always extremely manlike, even if hooves or "a hard and cold nature" could betray his true identity. The subsequent discovery that their lover was the devil, however, never deterred the witches from next renouncing God, His servants and saints, as well as their own baptism, or from undergoing a new, devilish baptism. Next they confessed desecrating the holy sacrament (usually by stamping on the host, mixing it with dung, or employing it in magical potions) and digging up the bodies of dead babies for use in the witches' salve. Following this first section of spiritual crimes (which could rarely be proved by any means beyond denunciation and confession), the typical confession turned to the actual harm done (maleficia). First to be mentioned were storms; then came sickness and death for cattle and people. Finally, in a third section, witches described the sabbaths[92] they attended and were obviously under great pressure to name as many other witches they had seen at the sabbath as possible. We may note that these sabbaths were often the only time or place that one witch was thought to have contact with others, and they therefore provided the crucial link from one accusation to the next.

The Ellwangen officials were occasionally extremely successful in eliciting long lists of persons seen at the sabbath. Weier Anna, for example, denounced 24 different persons, and the *Schweizerin* 17.[93] A woman called simply Cleva denounced a string of 29 persons, but then revoked several of them.[94] The effect of such lists may well be imagined. In some cases they were used fully 23 years after they were written down: some of the denunciations from 1588 played a role in 1611.[95] In addition, witches very commonly denounced persons in other towns and in completely different jurisdictions. In this way the germ of witch hunting could pass from town to town very much like an epidemic. To assist their neighboring regions, the officials at Ellwangen even assembled a book of persons denounced from regions outside the Fürstpropstei, alphabetically by town.[96]

With all of these genuinely legal procedures in use against the witches, it is perhaps not surprising that witch panics broke out. But in addition, official corruption had its own part in the trials at Ellwangen. On August 4, 1611, for example, the *Hofrat* heard the case of two men who complained, apparently with reason, that the *Schultheiss* of Rötlin was spreading the rumor that they were witches, like their wives, who had already been executed.[97]

In other cases, it seems that guilt was presumed before confession or sentence made it legal. In some cases, for example, a suspect's property would be inventoried even before he confessed. This procedure was clearly a preparation for confiscation, but it introduced dangerous elements into purely legal matters. In yet another case in 1616, Johann Grezing, an administrator for the Fürstpropstei, fell under suspicion of witchcraft. The Fürstpropst Johann Christoph von Freiberg proceeded to appoint a new man to his position before Grezing had confessed. Taking Grezing's side, the Ellwangen chapter argued that this was both unfair and tactless, since if Grezing should emerge innocent, he could be restored to his rightful position only with great difficulty. They argued that this was especially so in cases of witchcraft, which was "by its very nature difficult to prove."[98]

In general, however, this kind of high-level corruption or mismanagement was not so widespread, or at least so evident, as that of the torturers and guards. We know of two guards, Ulrich Felger and Melcher Hauber, for example, who divulged trial details and other secret information both to other suspects and to the public at large. In addition, both admitted raping a number of female suspects in prison. For his crimes Hauber was sworn to absolute secrecy, with death as the threatened punishment for perjury.[99] These breaches of secrecy were a serious matter, since in theory the entire judicial process rested on the *independent* agreement of many people on the same details—details they could know only if they were guilty. If these details, e.g. the names of persons already denounced for witchcraft, became known to others suspected of witchcraft, then the denunciations under torture would soon pile up against these other persons until they too were drawn into the whirlpool. In the case of Felger, we find not only this kind of crime but also extortion and blackmail. Georg Weixler, the chapter scribe, had a wife, Magdalena, who was accused of witchcraft. Felger carefully told her everything she should say to escape frightful torture, all in return for Magdalena's ring, necklace, and other possessions. After taking advantage of her sexually, Felger also tried to extort money from both Georg Weixler and Magdalena's father in Kempten. When these attempts failed, he tried to escape but was caught. Under interrogation he revealed that Magdalena's name had been sold to a desperate suspect, *die Gurtenschneiderin*, for a silver cup. After another escape he was extradited from Limpurg in August 1614, and executed on November 6.[100]

The glimpse that Felger's case yields us of the terror and wretched corruption at the base of the witch-hunting ladder makes one marvel that the examiners were so ignorant of the way in which some suspects obtained the names of those they denounced.

Still one more obvious reason exists for the massive proportions of the witch hunt at Ellwangen. A few of the confessions were obtained completely voluntarily. We may well recall that it was just such a case that convinced a skeptical Jean Bodin that witchcraft was a reality.[101] In Ellwangen, apparently a few of the witches were totally convinced of their own guilt and turned themselves in for examination. One such was Maria Ostertag, a girl of 16 who had herself imprisoned on July 11, 1613, and confessed without any prompting or torture that she had been seduced into witchcraft by her aunt (who had already been executed) in the hope of easing her hunger. Now she could not bear the torments of the devil any longer and wished to pay for her sins. She even voluntarily displayed her devil's mark, on the right shoulder, and denounced at least 34 others as witches. In describing her crimes, she emphasized the horror of her sexual seduction and of her subsequent sacrilege, but did not stress genuine maleficia. It may be suggested that she saw herself as so thoroughly guilty that mere temporal harm shrank in her sight before the more terrible affront to God. In condemning this repentant girl to death by the sword, the court accorded her the unique privilege of a decent burial in the churchyard, instead of reducing her to ashes. On August 21, 1613, this sentence was executed.[102] Her example was so touching that Father Johann Finck was moved to write: "God has comforted us especially through a girl of 16, who last month was executed with six others. She could no longer endure the persecutions of the devil and placed herself voluntarily in custody. With tears she explained that she would rather bear death and the stake than put up with the tyranny of the devil any longer. Standing, she received the death blow."[103]

An even younger girl provided another instance of this sort. In 1611, Margaretha, the seven-year-old daughter of Jacob Gebelin from the village of Sinzenberg, aroused general fear and suspicion when she boasted of riding away at night to witches' dances. On August 26 of that year she was thrown in jail, where she confessed voluminously to all manner of dealings with the devil. Yet the magistrates considered her age and the fact that she had been baptized by a Lutheran preacher and decided to turn her over to the Jesuits for proper training in the "Christian Catholic" faith. The Jesuits tried exorcism, holy oil, and other Catholic ceremonies generally omitted by the "Lutherans and other heretics," but all to no avail. Four years later, in 1615, little Margaretha still claimed to work witchcraft, did not repent her association with the devil, and refused to obey her father and other authorities.[104] At this stage the magistrates decided to consult men more learned in the law than they. The jurists of the University of Freiburg i. Br. responded that 11 years of age was too young to be tried for crime, but that if she did not improve in the custody of an honorable woman, she could be executed at age 14. The jurists at Ingolstadt, however, noted that she had already had ample time to repent and should be executed at once. We do not know what policy the magistrates decided on, but we do find that they examined her again one year later (May 16, 1616) and found that she was as much a witch as ever. Apparently the milder advice of Freiburg had prevailed.[105]

It would be inaccurate to imply that the techniques described here provoked no protest. We already have noted that Georg Weixler denounced the guard Ulrich Felger and maintained that his wife was innocent. He even transcribed a moving letter of hers to him: "I know that my innocence will come to light, even if I do not live to see it. I would not be concerned that I must die, if it were not for my poor children; but if it must be so, may God give me the grace that I may endure it with patience."[106] Weixler no doubt wrote his account of the matter to clear himself of charges of complicity with Felger in attempts to free his wife, but it is just as clear that Weixler saw his wife's execution as a gross miscarriage of justice.

In a rather different case, Michael Dier (or Dirren), one of the judges of the court of Ellwangen, endured the agony of seeing his wife convicted and executed for witchcraft. Convinced of her innocence, he seems to have announced his opposition to this sentence publicly. Perhaps partly as a result of this intransigent attitude, he soon found himself accused of witchcraft, and was arrested on October 21, 1611. Under pressure (and almost certainly torture), he confessed. Yet as late as November 8 he maintained that his wife had been done an injustice and that he was as innocent "as Christ on the cross."[107] These protests were of no avail, and he joined a group of other convicts in the fifteenth burning, on November 19, 1611.

It seems clear that these kinds of inarticulate protest were easily controlled by Ellwangen officials. It was more serious when a neighboring territory, Öttingen, accused them of malfeasance in 1618. In an angry mood the Ellwangen magistracy replied in a *Grundtlicher Gegenbericht* that charged Öttingen with malicious calumny.[108] Judging from this *Gegenbericht*, it seems that Öttingen had attacked Ellwangen's reasons for conducting witch trials as well as the procedures employed. In addition, Öttingen suspected that Ellwangen had added indecently to its treasury by confiscating property from those persons executed. In a heated defense, Ellwangen retorted that these charges were wrong on all counts. First, it was obvious that 1611 had been a year of great witchcraft. "It is undoubted that a work of witchcraft was made manifest to several persons by the fatal decree and admonition of God." The large number of supernatural storms and mysterious diseases was ample proof. If officials had not acted quickly, they would have sinned against the innocent, whom they were obliged to protect. In addition, the magistrates were justified in seeking out witches in order to convert them to God and save their eternal souls. For this reason, they could assert they had been models of "getrewer Christlicher eyffer, discretion, und angelegene Sorgfaltigkeit." As to the procedures used, they insisted that more than 100 of the executed had actually confessed their crimes without torture or any compulsion. (This is surely too high an estimate, but it made a good argument.) The witches rejoiced at a chance to enter God's grace again and to end their miserable lives as Christians. Another proof of the justice of the Ellwangen proceedings lay in the fact that a "rather sizable number" were denounced as witches but were found innocent.* In addition, when Ellwangen witches denounced persons outside the Fürstpropstei as witches, the magistrates of these territories and imperial cities caught and punished them. Moreover, impartial, noble observers

---

* We should like to know how large this *zimlicher anzahl* was, but records of these cases were not carefully kept.

in Ellwangen at the time of the witch trials supposedly found nothing out of order, even though Ellwangen's speedy justice had seemed risky to them. And finally, if Öttingen meant to imply that witchcraft was a purely spiritual crime (and therefore deserving only spiritual punishment), the Ellwangen officials could assure themselves and their opponents that all of the witches had confessed murder and other serious secular crimes. Thus they could assert that not one case of presumable innocence had been unjustly condemned. It was therefore to be wondered at that Öttingen chose to afflict the already wretched territory. Ellwangen could remind itself that "attacking the good deeds of the honorable is the empty pleasure of the evil persons" (*probris bonos notare sunt solatia vana pessimorum*).

In turning to the charge of outrageous profit from confiscations, the Ellwangen officials were briefer and more to the point. First, they claimed that not one heller had gone into their pockets, but that all money confiscated had really gone for food and lodging for the witches, with the excess for pious causes (*usus pios*). This procedure was justified not only by tradition but also by the consideration that these witches caused so much individual harm that no private satisfaction was possible.[109] So the money was spent on pious causes that helped both the community and the souls of the witches.

It is not clear exactly what had brought Öttingen into this case, but it seems certain that that Protestant territory could exercise no real influence on Ellwangen. In its independence from effective outside controls, witch hunting had to proceed more or less until the judges tired of it.[110] By 1618 apparently they had reached this stage. In that last year of the great panic we know of perhaps six burning days, with possibly ten executed. In a way this was a last spasm of the hunt, for 1617 had recorded not one witchcraft case.[111] After 1618, Ellwangen had a respite from this sort of panic until it was caught up in the general wave of witch hunting in 1629.* Even then it was far more cautious than between 1611 and 1618.[112] By 1618 perhaps Ellwangen was regretting some of the effects of its actions. In that year officials expressed the fear that people were avoiding Ellwangen because of its reputation for witchcraft. Pupils, especially, were sent elsewhere rather than risk an education at so infamous a town.[113] Certainly the

---

* In 1619 a man held on suspicion of witchcraft died in prison after an eight-year confinement; WSAL B389, Bü. 230f.

opinions of neighbors like Öttingen, even if they had no legal force, must have made officials reconsider what they had done. Their defense, written in 1618, could well be the kind of passionate self-defense that springs from glimmers of self-doubt. At any rate, by then the worst was over.

SCHWÄBISCH GMÜND

In 1600 Schwäbisch Gmünd was an imperial free city of some 6,000 inhabitants, 30 miles east of Stuttgart and only 16 miles southwest of Ellwangen.[114] During the Reformation the city had been able to maintain an uneasy Catholicism that it gradually made more severe and exclusive during the last decades of the sixteenth century. Even so, the city showed reluctance in 1588 and 1597 to allow the Jesuits a free hand in the town. It seems unlikely that by 1600 there were more than a very few Protestant families left in the city.[115]

As in Ellwangen, the "quiet" decade before the Thirty Years War brought storms and cattle disease to Gmünd. In terms of human population, however, these epidemics do not seem to have been so devastating as the one in 1575 in which 2,000 reportedly died.[116] Nonetheless, agrarian conditions no doubt brought Gmünd to a state of tension that required only a push from outside to bring on a real panic. In 1613 this sort of external influence appeared when officials at Ellwangen reported to Gmünd that certain inhabitants of Gmünd had been denounced as witches.[117] Throughout the following year, Gmünd maintained close formal relations with Ellwangen, since the imperial city did not employ an executioner of its own and borrowed this dishonorable official from Ellwangen as often as it needed one.

Once Schwäbisch Gmünd began conducting trials of its own, the city developed its own procedures. In content, however, the confessions were very similar to those of Ellwangen. On June 13, 1614, for example, Anna and Catherina Jelerin were executed after tortured confessions were extracted from them. According to their confessions (they are virtually identical), they took up dealings with the devil 24 years earlier, renounced God and His saints, spurned their baptism, copulated with the devil (but without pleasure), and caused much harm by means of storms and potions.[118] In these confessions, as in those of Ellwangen, a balance was carefully maintained between spiritual and secular crimes. Witches in this region were clearly thought guilty of both types of crime. It makes little sense on the basis of such documents to try to determine which crime, the apostasy or the maleficium, was "crucial." Obviously, the act of apostasy came first in time. But it is just as obvious that magistrates became aware of and genuinely afraid of witchcraft only when harm was done.

The concept of witchcraft in the region of Ellwangen–Schwäbisch Gmünd placed extremely heavy emphasis on the sexual seduction of witches by the devil. This detail was almost never omitted from the confession of a female witch. Yet despite this morbid sexual interest, the witches were not made responsible for impotence and infertility as they so often were in the *Malleus Maleficarum*. This seems to be true throughout the German Southwest and makes up a bit of the negative evidence showing that a century after its composition the *Malleus* was relatively uninfluential on the local level. Certainly its Latin and scholastic language tended to make it accessible only to scholars and not to many lawyers or even to the average judge.

The townspeople of Gmünd needed no such theoretical treatise to bring their witches to justice. The denunciations of convicted witches proved sufficient. In one case, a desperate woman denounced over 200 different persons. Starting in the autumn of 1613, the trials brought ten women and one man to execution by the end of that year (one man and one woman died in prison); during 1614 at least 27 more persons were executed.[119] By 1617 the chronicler Dominikus Debler counted 78 persons who had been formally tried for witchcraft. Of that number, no fewer than eight died in prison and only 11 in all were set free. In addition, an unusually high number (16) endured death by fire without the mitigation of strangulation or decapitation.[120] Confiscation of property normally accompanied conviction for witchcraft in Gmünd.

Again as in Ellwangen the panic reached out to touch persons high on the local social scale. By 1617, trials had claimed the lives of the wife of a *Bürgermeister*, the wife of a *Schultheiss*, and a priest who was said to have baptized in the name of the devil.[121]

With the Gmünd documents in fragmentary condition and seriously disordered, further speculation is avoided regarding specific numbers of persons denounced, accused, or executed. Although 1617 is said to represent the worst year of all, we have no documentary proof that such was the case.[122] We do know that opposition emerged

to the Gmünd witch hunts. For example, Jacob Kemblin was so outraged that the court should execute his wife Catharina for witchcraft
that he took the case to the *Reichskammergericht* in Speyer and spent
"all my goods and possessions" in judicial formalities there. He failed
to cultivate a temperate tongue, however, and was heard wishing
that "hail and thunder" would smash in the city hall. This sort of
insult and affront to city authority was not taken lightly, and Kemblin
was hauled before the magistrates of Gmünd; there he was forced
to retract his defamatory and calumnious remarks and to promise
never to repeat them.[123]

Much more weighty was the influence of Dr. Leonhard Kager, a
lawyer and counselor for the city of Gmünd. Born in 1538 in Füssen,
south of Augsburg, he had lived in Gmünd from at least 1584. Certainly Kager was one of the most respected men in the community,
and at his death in 1616 perhaps one of the wealthiest.*

In October 1613 during the first trials for witchcraft, Kager was
called on to advise the court on several peculiarly difficult matters.
On October 9 he read an "Information" to the city Council. On the
next day he composed an appendix to this Information. Together and
with full references, these documents form a "Consilium in Causa
Maleficarum, Lamiarum, et Veneficarum" which he turned over to
the Council on December 16. But this was not the end. In early January
1614, he appended a "Responsum Juris in eadem causa."[124] Together
these form a 62-page consultation whose prime intent was to urge
caution and great discretion in the treatment of the crime of witchcraft. It is a stroke of great luck that this remarkable document survives.

Kager argued, for example, that the only law that certainly applied
in this case was imperial law, namely, the *Carolina*. The penalties
for not abiding by that code had been severe in recent years.[125] Gmünd
must, therefore, exercise great caution in matters of torture and imprisonment. Kager did not of course deny such a crime as witchcraft.
In fact he appealed to theologians for proof that witchcraft was the
most horrible crime of all. But even granting this, he insisted on
drawing distinctions. The flight of witches to their sabbath, for ex-

---

* He owned a three-story house with nine rooms and a large silver collection; Weser,
"Alte Gmünder, XIV." Kager and his wife set up a trust for needy students that was
still functioning in 1911.

ample, was for Kager an illusion caused by the devil. Storm-raising too was a delusion.[126] In addition, he insisted on sharply separating harmful magic (*maleficium*) from the mere pact with the devil. He maintained that only in this way did the *Carolina*, Article 109, make sense. If only the pact could be proved, then the defendant must be given some arbitrary punishment less than death. Kager in these ways represented the older, *Carolina* school of thought, and had resisted the common emphasis on the spiritual crime of witchcraft, an emphasis that had made maleficium theoretically irrelevant and had penetrated most German legal codes in the second half of the sixteenth century.*

Kager's greatest effort, however, went not into the theory of witchcraft but into the procedures by which these evildoers could be discovered and punished. He held that far too often the wrong kinds of evidence were used. Reputation (*fama*), for example, was valid only when it was supported by men of good character. If instead accusations and arrests were based on "mere talk" or on the "evil claptrap of the common rabble," then it is not truly *fama* but *vana vox populi*. Similarly, Kager conceded that a true devil's mark, like the one found on Barbara Secklerin's back, was a serious indication of guilt. Together with her evil reputation it might justify torture, "but only if the degree and mode of torture permitted by the laws and by the *Carolina* are properly observed and not exceeded."[127] On this basis, Anna Bullinger, who had withstood torture four times, should be let go.[128]

Again, Kager noted that confessions were a notoriously weak form of proof. Many women claimed that they confessed only to avoid torture. In such cases Kager urged that since grave doubt existed about the truth of the confession, the accused should be set free. "For it is better and holier that many criminals be dismissed than that one innocent be condemned." Just as confessions and reputation did not provide firm ground, neither did loose accusations of witchcraft. As we saw in Ellwangen, the habit of calling persons one disliked witches was widespread. Kager went so far as to say that this evil habit had so spread among the "common rabble" that for the slightest offense men and women, young and old, called one another witches. It was

---

* See earlier discussions, on pp. 23–24, 52–53, 69.

worse in Gmünd, he said, than anywhere else he had ever seen.[129] For this reason, Kager said that he had often urged the Council to take action, but now he had even drafted an Edict for their approval, by which such loose talk would be severely punished. We know that the Council at least took this advice of Kager, and published the Edict.[130]

After this criticism of the legal value of reputation, rumor, and confession, it is no surprise that Kager also found the denunciation of witches by other witches a worthless procedure. He noted that the reason many women were so steadfast that they died confirming their lists of denunciations was "the simple product of agony and fear of further torture" (*auss lautter Martter unnd forcht nach weitterer tortur beschehen*). Indeed, many held to their stories merely to escape being returned to prison.[131] In a "Fernere Information" of May 4, 1615, Kager repeated his denunciation of the Gmünd prison, which he called evil and filthy. According to Kager, prisons should be used only for retention, and not as a *species torturae* or a perpetual confinement.[132] In addition, the word of a witch was not worth much in the first place, for Kager asserted that witches often tried to implicate the innocent. Women, moreover, could be deceived by illusions of the devil. The devil could even assume the form of innocent persons so that witches might think they had seen them at the sabbath.[133] For all of these reasons, therefore, Kager held that the testimony of witches was too weak and fluctuating to build a foundation for the accusation of someone else. And certainly persons accused by witches who later withdrew their accusations were not to be tortured until better evidence accumulated.[134]

Kager had argued a consistently moderate case, with great emphasis on procedure. Coming as it did at the beginning of the Gmünd witch trials, it might seem curious that his distinguished voice was so little heeded. Fortunately we can reconstruct the major reasons why the Council chose to reject Kager's ideas, for a "counter-consilium" exists, written apparently by one of the Gmünd prosecutors, who attacked Kager point by point.[135]

Fundamentally, Kager's opponent disagreed on the proper definition of witchcraft. Kager, he said, divided witchcraft into crimes of "simple theft, homicide, adultery, and human lese majesty." Although this seemed to follow the *Carolina*, he said that Kager chose this type of definition to exclude heresy and the "crime of divine lese majesty" from consideration. In other words, Kager was concerned with the old distinction: harmless vs. harmful witchcraft. Instead of this old-fashioned literal distinction, the counter-consultant presented the dichotomy of *maleficium* vs. *magia.*[136] Relying on Friedrich Martini, the jurist of Freiburg whom we discussed earlier, this writer drew out the common and necessary conclusions from assuming that the *Carolina* was actually distinguishing in Article 109 between demonic and nondemonic magic. He asserted it was against all reason that the slightest physical harm should merit a fiery death but that the most severe spiritual crimes should escape more lightly. In this way Kager's opponent spiritualized the crime of witchcraft, as most other late-sixteenth-century witchcraft theorists had also felt forced to do. The crime of apostasy, with or without real harm done, now merited the full punishment of the law.

In addition, Kager's opponent asserted that the *Carolina* was not the only guide for action and that regional customs might in many cases prevail.* More important, discretion might direct that laws could even be broken to secure the conviction of notorious criminals. Citing an opinion of the Ingolstadt legal faculty to the Duke of Bavaria in 1590, he concluded that "on account of the enormity of the crime, it is permissible to go beyond the laws." Now if this was the case, it was clear that a local court did not need to consult higher legal authorities for every case of witchcraft.†

When Kager had gone on to state that it was better and holier to release many guilty than to convict one innocent, our counter-consultant turned himself into verbal pretzels trying to show that this made no sense:

It is evil to let a guilty man go free. But if one must choose between two evils, letting the guilty go free or condemning the innocent, it is safer to do the former. Thus Bossius, *in tit. de delicto* n. 23, says that we sin more justly in pardoning than in condemning. But whoever sins is neither holy nor good; for sin is not good, to say nothing of better, nor is it holy, to say nothing of holier. Therefore, the previously cited rule is badly stated— "better and holier"—*on the contrary, it is a sin.*

---

* This was legally true, but many imperial cities relied heavily on the *Carolina* as proof of their imperial status and as defense against the expansionist claims of larger territories.

† The *Carolina*, Art. 109, had said, rather ambiguously, that consultation *was* necessary in cases of witchcraft.

In addition to this remarkable logic, he argued that witchcraft was a *crimen exceptum*, freed from the normal legal restrictions and precautions. In fact, God punished men for weak toleration of such crimes. Witches therefore must never be let go.* In cases of doubt, defendants may be put to the judgment of God.† The real crime, he insisted, was lenience; judges were responsible for the commonwealth, and not merely for individuals. It might be best for individuals (*respectu nominati*) to apply Kager's rule, but it would certainly not be best for the state (*respectu reipublicae et boni publici*). Obviously the issues of individual and society were as alive then as now.

Turning next to the flight of witches and to their marvelous deeds, including storm-raising, the counter-consultant employed two rather modern tactics to get the better of Kager. First, he asserted that we know from experience that witches really fly, for we have heard their confessions. Against these hard facts the windy arguments of mere reason cannot prevail; for "experience is the efficacious teacher of things"!‡ Nor could the canon *Episcopi* be used to disprove the flight of witches, since modern authorities agreed, he said, that this document did not refer "to our witches" (*ad lamias nostras*).[137] Second, when we confront a doubtful case, the commonest opinion is most likely to be true, for "the greater truth may be presumed to reside with the greater number." And although a few scholars had cast doubt on various aspects of witchcraft, there could be no doubt which opinions were held by the majority. In this way Kager's opponent maneuvered himself to the side of both democracy and empirical knowledge!

In a vexed tone he complained that he could not see what Kager really wanted. If, for example, confessions of witches were not to be accepted as valid proof of guilt, "not one of a thousand confessed and convicted witches would have been burned." He also insisted that not all witches were demented or delirious. This of course was the agony of those who defended the witches, like Johann Weyer. They

---

* He seems to have lost track of the main point, that we do not know *who* the witches are. Kager would never have argued that known witches be released.

† This bears a distinct parallel to the notorious idea of the crusaders against the Albigensians, that God would know His own, thereby excusing the accidental slaughter of innocents.

‡ This appeal to empirical knowledge of witchcraft became increasingly pronounced during the seventeenth century. Joseph Glanvill in England enshrined it; see his *Sadducismus Triumphatus*.

could not prove that *all* the women executed for witchcraft had been mentally ill. They could not disprove *every* case of flight. Consequently, men like Kager's opponent could slip past the closest reasoning by granting that *sometimes* flight and storm-raising and the pact with the devil were illusory, but that sometimes they actually did occur.

The counter-consultant also tried to prove that denunciation of others by confessed witches provided an adequate degree of suspicion so that two denunciations of the same person could lead to torture. Nor did all denunciations have to agree in every detail for this to be true. He cited an opinion of the Freiburg legal faculty: "In exceptional crimes, agreement as to time and place are not required." When Kager asserted that witches were clearly such dishonorable persons that their word was worthless, he was forgetting that no matter how malicious and infamous a person may be, "yet he purges himself and supplements any judicial lack through torture."

Kager had tried to circumvent many of these criticisms by demonstrating that many aspects of witchcraft were simply incredible and impossible. His opponent retorted that this was not for a mere layman to judge, but for philosophers and theologians. "Our Weyerian adversaries" claim that witches merely imagine all of their actions, but here again we find mere physicians and lawyers meddling with church matters.

In dealing with specific procedures to be used with recalcitrant suspects, Kager's opponent carefully described the kinds of torture to be used and admitted that restraints had to be exercised. No one, for example, was to be left hanging in strappado for more than an hour at a time (most authorities thought 15 minutes sufficient). Torture could also be repeated, "but not too often." If after two sessions the accused had not conceded any new and suspicious information, he was to be let go, "but this is not useful in practice"! Repeatedly he defended the use of confessions and evidence gained by torture in these trials against the humane restrictions of Kager. In trying to explain why Kager had gone so far in the wrong direction, the counter-consultant could only think that Kager had studied in the wrong camp. We have already seen Kager condemned as a Weyerian. One of Kager's major sources, the Lutheran Johann Georg Gödelmann of Rostock, was even condemned as the "patron of the witches" (*patro-*

cinium lamiarum).[138] But beyond these false prophets, Kager had also drawn heavily on the "illusions of non-Catholic writers." In the fierce atmosphere of Counter-Reformation Gmünd, this blow was vital. It is noteworthy that Kager's opponent agreed with Martini in ascribing the pernicious ideas of leniency toward witches to Protestants (see p. 64).

Basically all of these arguments against Kager may be reduced to a few crucial ones. (1) Witchcraft is primarily a spiritual crime and need not involve harm to require the death penalty. (2) Witchcraft is a special crime; therefore the ordinary rules of law do not apply. (3) Judges must be concerned with the safety of society and should therefore be ready to sacrifice individual rights. (4) Torture and confession have a quasi-religious function in bringing a suspect back into the realm of normal humanity; therefore denunciations of others as witches may be believed and acted on legally.

Against these conclusions, Kager must have seemed dangerously lenient, old-fashioned, unconcerned for society as a whole, and suspiciously Protestant. At any rate, the mounting toll of accusations tells us clearly who won the argument in 1614. Kager's wife and maid even gained a reputation for witchcraft.[139]

Chapter Six

The General Crisis of Confidence, 1627-1684

THE LARGEST witch hunts in the German Southwest have so far represented a scattered and amorphous type of panic. Although the 1580's
and 1590's did see unusually vigorous action along the Neckar valley
in Rottenburg, Horb, Oberndorf, Sulz, Rottweil, and Hechingen, and
although the witch hunts in Ellwangen and Schwäbisch Gmünd were
clearly related, still until the late 1620's one finds little evidence of an
entire region going into convulsive frenzies of social purgation.[1] Yet
in the five years between 1627 and 1632 that is exactly what happened.
We find massive witch hunts during those years in Mergentheim
(seat of the Teutonic Order), the Margravate of Baden-Baden, the
imperial free cities of Offenburg and Gengenbach, the Habsburg Ortenau, the county of Löwenstein-Wertheim, and the district of Oberkirch (formally a part of the bishopric of Strasbourg, but administered
by Württemberg).[2]

With regard to region, all of these territories were in the north and
west, with an almost total blanketing of the area now known as central Baden. Essentially only the Palatinate and Baden-Durlach in that
region avoided witch panic during those years. Because these trials as
a group so clearly militate against any merely "accidental" view of
why certain places had severe witch trials at certain times, it is well
to consider first the area and the period as a unit. As Trevor-Roper
said in a different context, "a wholesale coincidence of special causes
is never plausible as the explanation of a general rule."[3] Therefore we
must search for general causes of the witch panics in these seven distinct and independent territories of the German Southwest.

Examination of previous trials has shown that communal misfortune very often triggered suspicions of witchcraft. It would also

seem likely that fears of witchcraft would increase during times of increased stress, such as the threat of war. Indeed, the first witch hunts of major size in southwestern Germany in the 1560's exemplify just this conjunction of misfortune and fear of war. We now examine the period 1627–32 for stress of this sort.

In the matter of misfortune it is clear that plague was once more on the rise. Epidemics of various sorts had come in waves ever since the 1520's, but during the seventeenth century their severity increased, and they reached out to touch large areas instead of isolated villages. The year 1611 had seen plague in 46 towns of the German Southwest, and had surely been part of the trigger in the Ellwangen trials. Now again in the mid-1620's a new wave of disease and death began to roll across the Southwest. With troops and hangers-on roaming about Germany, plague was far more easily spread than under normal peacetime conditions. Peasants from the countryside tended to overcrowd towns and produce fertile ground for epidemics. In addition, the war brought famine to large sections of Germany, reducing the powers of resistance of the populace. Plague and other epidemics claimed many more lives during the Thirty Years War than all the bloody deeds of gun and sword.[4]

Fully 200 of the 299 towns of the German Southwest possess records of some sort of epidemic between 1500 and 1680. These 200 towns had their own indigenous diseases and chronic epidemics, but when considered as a whole, certain patterns become clear. (See Fig. 1.)

The build-up of epidemics in the 1620's probably caused many persons to suspect witchcraft. In 1626 at least 31 southwestern German towns suffered plague. However, outbursts of plague did not always trigger witch hunts. Between 1633 and 1636, the German Southwest experienced its worst and most widespread plague. Parts of Württemberg, for example, lost 80 to 90 per cent of their population (e.g. Maulbronn and Königsbronn).[5] Yet this period of the middle 1630's was also one of rapid and general *decline* in witch hunting. One would have to conclude either that plague had nothing to do with witch hunting or that a new social process was at work during the second wave of plague, inhibiting the witch hunt.

During the Thirty Years War it would seem unnecessary to demonstrate that there was a fear of war. The problem is more complex, however, for we seek to understand why certain regions were perhaps

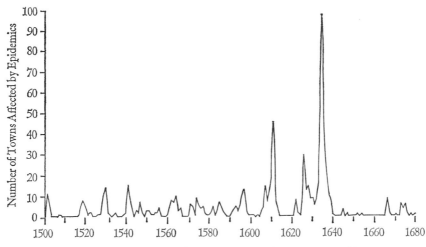

Fig. 1. Epidemics in the German Southwest, 1500–1680.
SOURCE: Keyser, *Deutsches Städtebuch*, IV, 2, 1: *Badisches Städtebuch*. IV, 2,
2: *Württembergisches Städtebuch*.

under greater strain than others. The German Southwest was generally spared the devastation of major military operations until 1632 or even 1634. The chronicler of Salem Abbey near Lake Constance, for example, noted that 1630 (the year of Gustavus Adolphus's landing in Germany) had been most notable for a snowfall in May and for the extraordinarily abundant wine harvest that fall.[6] Such a picture of tranquillity did not often obtain farther north. By 1622 the Margrave of Baden, Georg Friedrich, had encountered the imperialist forces at Wimpfen and had been defeated. In the ensuing months the imperialists reduced the Palatinate and Heidelberg to submission, restored Wilhelm, the son of Eduard Fortunat, to his lands in Baden-Baden,[7] and forced the new Margrave of Baden-Durlach, Friedrich V, to abandon his territory.[8] The war bruised the German Southwest, therefore, in the northern and western sectors, precisely those regions subsequently afflicted with witch panics of major proportions. Yet when war came to Swabia ten years later, it failed to trigger witch hunts of any size at all.

The years 1622–23 saw the total disruption of coinage. Money became so depreciated that prices soared out of sight. Food prices, moreover, did not need monetary policy to rise. The year 1625 had had a cold spring and bad harvests from Würzburg across Württemberg to the whole Rhine valley.[9] The next year found famine along the Rhine as a result of wet cold weather and wretched harvests.[10] These conditions of themselves drove prices beyond what many laborers could afford.

Again as with the plague and war, these additional hardships of inflation and famine were not peculiar to the 1620's. In fact, as with epidemics, conditions in the German Southwest grew generally far worse in the 1630's. At Speyer, for example, rye prices increased only 9.2 per cent between the periods 1610–19 and 1624–29. But between 1630 and 1639 they more than tripled what they had been in 1624–29.[11] We confront a situation, therefore, of increased hardship during 1625–30, but hardship that was incomparably less severe than that of the succeeding decade. The reason witch hunting developed to such extreme dimensions during this period has always been unclear. The witch hunt cannot have been a simple product of superstition and hardship, for later hardships failed to provoke the response they did in the late 1620's. At least one element is missing if we consider merely the superstitious witchcraft beliefs of a region and the catalytic disasters that may have triggered panic. That element is mood—the mood of villagers, townspeople, lawyers, governors, and judges. Mood is not easily measurable; yet it clearly depends on more than superstition (or enlightenment) and hardship (or physical well-being). Mood is affected by national or even international surges of feeling, by experience, by local history.

The national mood in Germany between 1625 and 1629 was certainly one of despair among Protestants and jubilant rejuvenation among Catholics. These were the years of Wallenstein's triumphs, the failure of King Christian IV of Denmark, the deaths of Christian von Braunschweig and of Ernst von Mansfeld. And in 1629 Emperor Ferdinand II proclaimed his Edict of Restitution by which Germany was to return to the ecclesiastical situation of 1552; all church lands secularized since that date were to be returned to Catholicism. Ever since 1627 this Edict had been a growing plan in the mind of Ferdinand.[12] One region most seriously affected by the Edict was the duchy of Württemberg, which lost 14 large monasteries—the very foundation of the remarkable system of higher education in Württemberg.[13] These were years when it seemed that Protestantism would not survive. It was this conjunction that caused Trevor-Roper to point out that "the witch trials multiplied with the Catholic reconquest.... The ideological struggle of the Reformation and Counter-Reformation ... had revived the dying witch craze."[14] Certainly it is suggestive that of the seven towns or territories that experienced severe witch hunts between 1627 and 1632, six of them were Catholic.[15]

National mood affords one clue to the terror of the late 1620's, and local experience with witch hunting provides another. General misfortune failed to trigger witch hunts in the middle 1630's, although it seems clearly implicated in the witch panic of 1627–32, because by 1632 the magistrates were learning—learning by that most painful teacher, experience—that the judicial process did not always serve justice. Local history, the memory of recent events, therefore, may provide a more flexible and dynamic factor than overly mechanistic explanations in terms of superstition and misfortune. We now consider the scene of the particular trials.

ORTENAU

The Landvogtei Ortenau was one of the most northerly of all Habsburg lands on the right bank of the Rhine. It lay along the Kinzig River and the flat lands of the Rhine plain. At its center was the imperial free city of Offenburg, a town whose geographic location led to constant struggles between the Vogt of Ortenau and the city over jurisdiction, taxes, and religious affairs. This was especially the case because political boundaries did not agree with ecclesiastical ones.[16] This overlap became especially crucial during the Reformation, since the feudal lord of the Ortenau, Wilhelm von Fürstenberg, was an avid proponent of Reform. After the Schmalkaldic Wars, King Ferdinand was able to push the Fürstenbergs out of the Ortenau and establish closer control over the region. Even after the return of the province to Catholicism, however, friction persisted between the Ortenau and Offenburg.[17]

Despite constant threats to Offenburg's sovereignty, however, the two could agree apparently that witchcraft was a crime so horrid that joint efforts at its eradication were necessary. We have abundant records that Offenburg and the Ortenau repeatedly compared notes and even drew up detailed lists of persons denounced in the neighbor's territory. This was no doubt the commonest way that witch trials spread from place to place. No "Witch Finder General" was necessary as in England, since denunciations usually implicated people from a wide region.[18] We will note later that the witch hunts in Offenburg seem to have been imported in this way from the Ortenau.

Because we possess a detailed and excellent study of the trials in the Ortenau, at this point we simply summarize the gross outlines.[19] In 1627 four women were accused of witchcraft and tortured. All four of them confessed and provided their examiners with long lists of accomplices. During 1628 these lists bore fruit in at least 39 executions on nine separate days. The next year saw hardly any relaxation as at least 22 persons met death at the stake. And finally, in 1630 at least 14 persons were executed, seven in each of two burnings. All told, 79 persons had been condemned in only three and a half years.[20] A contemporary noted that a total of 86 witches had been executed.[21]

Psychologically the Ortenau trials are of some interest. The commonest pattern of confession was to recount one's seduction by the devil and denial of God, followed by copulation with the devil, attendance of a sabbath, and magic that harmed men, animals, and crops.[22] What led women to these deeds? It seems that the most reasonable answer to men in the seventeenth century was that the devil offered sympathy and comfort to women in distress. Since such answers were usually forced from the suspects, we can tell nothing from them about the real psychology of the witches, but it is noteworthy that the judges found this emphasis on a need for comfort credible.[23]

During these murderous trials, very few of the accused escaped death. We have records of only one such, a certain Agnes Schneider, whose endurance survived even the terrible chair, a special iron apparatus heated from below. The trials ended, however, just as abruptly as they began. After 1630 a long period of peace ensued, as if the Ortenau had purged itself, or, rather, had undergone an experience from which it emerged the wiser. The records at our disposal are not conducive to proving such a thesis decisively, but we find it more reliably in the hunts to which we now turn our attention.

OFFENBURG

Offenburg was one of three imperial cities in the Kinzig valley, that ancient Roman route from the Rhine to the headwaters of the Danube. With Zell and Gengenbach, the three formed an enclave between

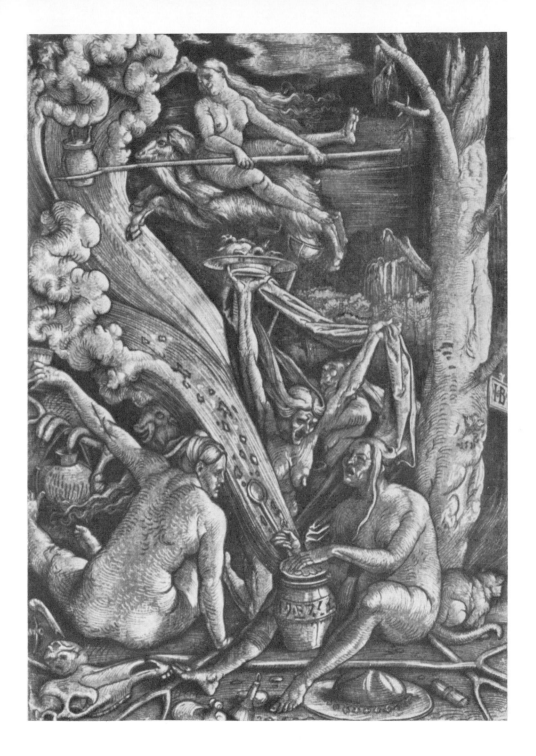

Witches' sabbath, a 1510 woodcut by Hans Baldung, in Philipp Reclam, *Hans Baldung Grien: Hexenbilder* (Stuttgart, 1961), no. 6.

Sixteenth-century punishments, a woodcut from Tengler, *Laienspiegel* (Mainz, 1508),
reprinted in *Der Kelheimer Hexenhammer* (Munich, 1966), p. 69.

Above: Witches carrying a huge cat, from *Newezeitung und ware geschicht dieses 76. Jars* (Hans Cudium von Hof, 1576). Original in Zentralbibliothek Zürich.
Below: A Theatre of Witches, title page from *Theatrum de Veneficis* (Frankfurt a. M., 1586). Original in Landesbibliothek Stuttgart.

Above: "A terrible story of the devil and a witch at Schiltach near Rottweil during Passion Week of 1533," broadside from 1533. Original in Zentralbibliothek Zürich.
Below: "A terrible story of three female witches and two men," at Derneburg in the Harz during the month of October 1555, with a report that witnesses saw the devil carry off a woman being executed for witchcraft. Original in Zentralbibliothek Zürich.

Hexenspiegel.

Ein vberauß schöne vnd

wolgegründte Tragedi / darinnen augenscheinlich zusehen / was von Vnholden vnd Zaube-
rern zuhalten seie. Ob sie können wittern: Jm Lufft fahren: Nächtliche Zusam-
menkunfft / Gastungen vnd Täntz halten: Mit dem Teuffel der Bulschafft pflegen / vnd Kinder zeu-
gen: Jhren Leib groß vnd klein machen / oder in vnuernünfftige Creaturen verendern: Den leuten
die verschloßne Wahr / bey nacht stelen: Menschen vnd Vieh beschädigen / vnd wider heilen: Zukünff-
tige ding wissen / vnd wahrsagen: Vnd durch was mittel ein Christ sich vor jnen hüten / oder wann er
schaden empfangen / wie er sich verhalten: Vnd welcher massen die Obrigkeit sie angreiffen / bewahren /
verrechten / befragen vnd straffen: Vnd wie auch die Pfarrer vnd Seelsorger /
nach dem Gesatz vnd Euangelio / mit jhnen
handlen sollen.

Auß Keyser vnd Königen / Chur vnd Fürsten / Gra-
uen / Freyherrn / vnd andern Adenlichen Personen Erfahrungen
vnd Bedencken: Beuorab auß ettlichen Concilien / vnd vilen guten Büchern
der fürnembsten reinen Lehrern der H. Schrifft / der Rechten vnd Artzney / der Philosophen vnd Ge-
schichtschreibern / trewlich zusamen getragen / vnd mehr dann mit zweyhundert denckwürdigen Historien / den Satz vnd Gegensatz besagende / zu erörterung der warheit / reichlich erklärt: vnd allerhand
Sachen / wie auch der fürnembsten Länder / Herrschafften / Bißthumb / Klöster / Stiffi /
Stät / vnd Personen Namen / in Alphabetische Register /
richtig gebracht.

Exod. 22.

Die Zauberin soltu nicht leben lassen.

Auß des Durchleuchtigen hochgebornen Fürsten vnd Herrn /
Herrn Friderichen / Hertzogen zu Württenberg vnd Teck / Graue
zu Mümpelgart / Herrn zu Heidenheim / Rittern beider Königlichen
Orden in Franckreich vnd Engelland / gnädiger
Bewilligung gedruckt.

Zu Tübingen /

Getruckt bey Georgen Gruppenbach /
ANNO M. DC.

"Mirror of witches: an exceedingly beautiful and well-founded tragedy," by
Thomas Birck. Title page of *Hexenspiegel* (Tübingen, 1600). Original in
Landesbibliothek Stuttgart.

Left: Ellwangen: sample of a confiscation list showing payments on behalf of various persons executed, 1613–1615. Original in WSAL B412, Bü. 77.
Right: Schwäbisch Gmünd: first page of a list of persons executed for witchcraft, 1613–1614. Original in HSASt B177, Bü. 122.

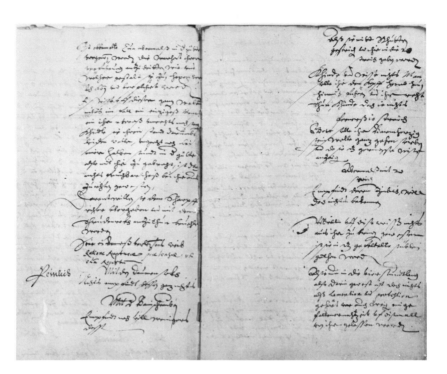

Above: Two pages from the interrogation of Eva, wife of Endres Benther in Mergentheim, 1629. This document shows the shift from questioning without torture to questioning with torture (*peinlich*), and the corresponding shift in the kind of confession elicited. Original in WSAL B262, Bü. 90.

Below: "The true and terrible deeds of the 63 witches burned at Wiesensteig" (1563). A major source for the first large witch hunt in the German Southwest. Original in Landesbibliothek Stuttgart.

Mergentheim in the seventeenth century; drawing by Matthaeus Merian in
Topographia Franconiae, 1656 (Kassel, 1962, p. 60).

the larger territories of the Ortenau, Fürstenberg, and Württemberg. Surrounded by neighbors more powerful than they, these towns had to watch jealously over their rights to avoid slow assimilation or outright subjugation.[24] Between Offenburg and the Habsburg Ortenau, as we have noted, there was constant tension as the Landvogt of the Ortenau tried repeatedly during the sixteenth and seventeenth centuries to increase his influence in Offenburg.[25]

During the Reformation Offenburg held itself formally Catholic, although the magistrates did have to deal with Protestant sympathies among the citizenry.[26] They encountered more trouble among the surrounding villages within Offenburg's district, but even there they lost only six parishes of episcopal Strasbourg territory to the Protestants. To guard against infection of the populace with noxious notions, however, the town felt constrained to close its gates on Sundays and festival days to prevent citizens from walking the short way to Weingarten, where services were Protestant.[27] In many other ways the town fathers acted paternalistically and repeatedly stepped in to protect morals and proper decorum. The Kirchenordnung of 1560, for example, expressly prohibits all persons from appearing in the streets and fields during Sunday services. Later ordinances, like that of 1596, conferred citizenship only on persons willing to swear allegiance to the "true Catholic Church."[28] All the evidence points to the fact that Offenburg's magistrates took their duties seriously and tried to create a tight moral company, a miniature Kingdom of God.[29]

After a few isolated witch trials in the sixteenth and early seventeenth centuries, Offenburg had a quiet spell of some 20 years. Authorities in the Ortenau even accused Offenburg of being lax in its prosecution of witches in 1608.[30] Local pressure for witch hunting in these years seems to have come almost entirely from the guilds, against the moderating, cautious attitude of the Council.[31] In 1627 trials began again, this time with great vigor, and strongly influenced by denunciations made by witches in the Ortenau and in Gengenbach.[32]

On October 31, 1627, the so-called Quiet Council of Offenburg heard a report from the Ortenau officials that the witches executed in Ortenberg (the district center of Ortenau) two days earlier had denounced Symon Haller and Catherin, wife of David Holdermann. When Haller heard this, he threatened to shoot the officials of the Ortenau, who hauled him in for questioning nonetheless. The Council in Offenburg inquired carefully into what he had confessed and whom he had denounced as accomplices, and made plans to read the reply only to men whose wives were not implicated.[33] Six days later, after hearing from the Ortenau, the magistrates of Offenburg decided to arrest and torture the woman Catherin Holdermann (also called Brenn Catherin). Under torture, however, she proved obstinate. On November 9 the Council ordered that the priest talk to her. It was natural of the Council to look out for her spiritual welfare, but unfortunately the priest was in close liaison with the magistrates. Confession in this case took on legal overtones. On November 12 the Council noted that "Brenn Catherin was admonished to confess by the priest, but she still insists on her innocence." It is not quite accurate to say that the clergy played no part in the trial of the Offenburg witches.[34]

In view of Catherin's refusal to confess, her investigation was suspended until Symon Haller could be brought to trial. On November 9 he was delivered to Offenburg by the officials of Ortenau. He was soon tortured, but as a poor man his prison cell must have been torture enough. We learn that he had no heat and no blanket against the November cold. Again and again he protested his innocence. At this impasse the Council must have decided that their methods were antiquated, for they ordered a workman to fashion a "chair like the one at Ortenberg for the witches." These chairs, often spiked and capable of being heated, were usually very effective. A few days later, Catherin Holdermann confessed herself a witch, and Symon Haller's confession soon followed. They denounced others, and by the end of the year seven persons had been executed.[35] During 1628, 21 more were executed in five burnings and one suspect died of wounds received in torture. In 1629, the worst year of all, 32 persons were executed.[36] Since Franz Volk's excellent study of the trials is easily accessible, we forgo further treatment of them here.

Political elements seem to have been at work in the Offenburg panic. We have already remarked that members of the Council whose wives were implicated in witchcraft would not be requested to attend meetings of the Council. Clearly they would not be forced to rule in matters affecting them so closely; yet this kind of exclusion was also a clever way of eliminating political opponents. The wife of Stettmeister Megerer (a member of the Council) was executed in January 1628. This man had long been active in the affairs of Offenburg and had been in charge of the torture of women suspected of witchcraft. When confronted with the arrest of his wife, Megerer's only explanation was that the judges hated him and his wife.[37] Such charges were not taken kindly, and Megerer was forced to give up his offices and to pay a fine of 100 *pfund*. When this former official applied for a permit to leave Offenburg, he was refused. This only led to further accusations from Megerer that the court was unjust. In February of 1630 the poor man died, crushed by an accusation from the witches of the Ortenau that he too was guilty of witchcraft.[38]

Megerer was not the only councilor to have personal experience of the witch panic. On December 1, 1628, Stettmeister Philipp Baur lost both wife and daughter to the craze.[39] Angered by the proceedings, Baur resigned his post and denounced the court, saying that his daughter had been executed only to disgrace him. The Council no doubt feared that these charges from public officials would jeopardize its authority; Baur was, therefore, refused permission to resign. In soothing terms the Council told him "not to take the situation so hard."[40]

Political trials did not end there. Stettmeister Weselin lost his wife to the trials, and shortly thereafter Stettmeister Kaspar Hag found his son-in-law, Jacob Linder, accused of witchcraft. The young man resisted torture at first, but then learned that his wife had ordered a mass sung for him.[41] This information broke his resistance, and he was executed in February 1629. Later in that same year the wife of Stettmeister Philipp Beck was executed. When the court tried to collect the trial costs from him, he angrily responded that this was nothing more than an attack on his property.[42] The trials in 1629 also claimed the life of Stortzen Ness, the wife of the town's artillery officer and daughter-in-law of a councilor. Most important, perhaps, was the execution on November 23, 1629, of Ratsherr Hans Georg Bauer, a man of considerable importance in Offenburg.[43] At last the trials had claimed a member of the Council itself. One does not need an especially vivid imagination to visualize the frantic situation in Offenburg as councilors, who normally got along well enough, turned into bitter enemies. Accusation and insinuation must have hung like a cloud over the town. The cold language of the reports from the Council masks the most vicious of factional battles.[44]

The escalation of trials into the ranks of the town's councilor-judges themselves seems to have had effects similar to those in other trials. In December 1629, hardly two weeks after the Council executed one of its own members, proceedings began against a woman, Gotter Ness. When she proved stubborn, she was placed on the never-failing chair. But still she refused to confess her guilt. This was the first person in Offenburg to withstand this grade of torture, and the Council was apparently thoroughly nonplussed. On December 3 they ordered her sent home.[45] At last they seem to have recognized that some of the suspects might be innocent. Giving themselves time to reconsider recent events, they ordered that "witch-hunting should end until after Christmas."[46] When the holidays were over, the councilors tried once more to make their judicial machinery function. They arrested the daughter of Gotter Ness, Maria, who had been denounced on five separate occasions. In addition, they summoned Hans Georg Holdermann's wife, Magdalena, and Jacob Burck's wife, Ursula. When confronted with the chair, all three confessed. On Wednesday, January 23, 1630, they were all condemned to death by the sword, with their corpses to be burned afterward. All was ready for a Friday execution, but on Thursday the town scribe reported that "the three criminals pretend their innocence, and swear in the face of God that they are not witches." For a confident Council this would have been no more than a nuisance. Torture could once again bring them back to their confessions. But this time, plagued by doubts, the Council ordered the women to be examined by the regimental mayor[47] and by the scribe. In addition, the priest was asked "if in the meantime he had absolved them of anything." The priest would no doubt again have broken his sacramental oath of secrecy if he had had anything to report, but on Friday, January 29, he and the scribe could only repeat that all three "have revoked their confessions and insist, on the peril of damnation, that they are not witches, and would answer in the presence of God for their statements." After further consultations and inquiry, the Council concluded on February 8, 1630, that the women should be let go and on no account suffer for their earlier confessions.[48] The Council, which had so resolutely hunted for three years, collapsed in the face of its own doubts. This collapse ended the bloody trials in Offenburg, although a few small echoes resounded in 1631, 1639, 1641, and 1642.[49] Indeed, by 1631 the Council was even using the war as an excuse for discontinuing the trials. When a citizen accused the wife of Michel Dietrich, she was, to be sure, brought in for torture, but the newly sophisticated Council was skeptical and recommended that "the priest conduct a sacred mass in which her case shall be entrusted to God Almighty." With the determination that the woman was mad, the Council sent her home for observation.[50] Thus the suggestion of Franz Volk that it was the Swedish occupation that brought these trials to an end seems to have rested on pure conjecture.[51] The Swedes did not occupy Offenburg until September 11, 1632; they did not even land in Germany until the summer of 1630. Surely it stretches the evidence to conclude that the Swedish acted the role of pacifier here as they did elsewhere. After all, the Swedes were forced to leave Offenburg in 1634, after the Battle of Nördlingen, and yet no large panic of witch hunting followed. It seems more likely that witch trials came to an end in a way completely dependent on developments within Offenburg. As we have seen, the Council showed signs of indecision and doubt at the end of 1629, and concluded by dismissing four women in a row. As Volk remarked, "We can explain the devastating impression made by the behavior of Gotter Ness only by recognizing the presence of this kind of skepticism."[52] No single great man, no Weyer, Montaigne, Scot, or Spee, was responsible for the end of the witch hunt in Offenburg. It was instead a shift in public opinion and especially in the opinions of the faction-ridden Council that brought a new, practical *cautio criminalis*.[53] The Council seems to have made up its own mind that witchcraft trials were a doubtful expedient at best. The magistrates worked through their own crisis of judicial procedure, learned their lesson, and brought witch trials to a halt.

A NOTE ON GENGENBACH

Less than ten miles up the Kinzig River from Offenburg lay the imperial city of Gengenbach, a town of perhaps 1,100 inhabitants in 1600.[54] Like Offenburg it showed an early interest in the Reformation, but fell back to Catholicism during the Counter-Reformation conducted by Cornelius Eselsberger in 1547.

We have already heard in Offenburg of the investigations into witchcraft at Gengenbach during 1627. From serious scholars we learn only of minor witch hunts there in 1573, 1590, 1599, 1604, 1617, 1659, 1661, 1662, and 1682.[55] Yet all of these trials, involving perhaps

20 persons in all, do not prepare us for the report of a popular historian that between 1627 and 1631 some 70 or more witches were executed at Gengenbach.[56] This was clearly the worst period of all for many locations around Gengenbach, but with the curious silence of more sober scholars on this point and with no documentary evidence to support this claim, we must for the moment remain in the dark about a panic that may well have been even more terrible than that of Offenburg.[57]

BADEN-BADEN

We have had occasion to note the Catholic victory at Wimpfen in 1622 and its immediate result in Baden-Baden. Although that territory had been formally Protestant for 28 years, it now was pushed rapidly back to Catholicism. The Jesuits arrived in large numbers; Protestant pastors were banished; subjects were persuaded or actually forced to attend Catholic services; wealthy recusants were given stiff fines; others were imprisoned or banished. By 1640 the land looked to one observer as if it had never been Protestant.[58] This turmoil and rapid religious change provide a crucial background for the Baden witch hunt panic. Wild claims have even circulated that the Jesuits fostered a witch hunt against crypto-Protestants, and Catholics have struck back with extraordinary vigor against such claims.

However, two facts seem to be beyond dispute. First, no one has found evidence of any large witch hunts in Baden-Durlach, that part of Baden that remained Protestant throughout.[59] Second, within the lands of Baden-Baden, witch hunting was severe only in the districts (*Ämter*) of Baden, Bühl, and Steinbach. If this is the case, it is not enough to assert simply that the return of Catholicism brought witch hunting in its wake. In some places it did, and in others it did not.

Part of the reason for this spotty record of witch panic in Baden-Baden seems to be the personal influence of Dr. Matern Eschbach, one of the most important councilors at the court of Margrave Wilhelm of Baden-Baden. He was a zealous witch eradicator. When the wave of witchcraft trials began to sweep this region of Germany in 1627, he busied himself for over a year in the town of Baden, ferreting out witches (September 16, 1627, to October 3, 1628). Having built a reputation at this work, he was called repeatedly, from October 3, 1628, through April 10, 1631, to the towns of Bühl and Steinbach as well as Baden, where he conducted examinations, advised on the amount of torture to apply, and heard ratifications of confessions (*Besiebnungen*). During this time, Eschbach and his colleagues established a fierce reputation as unrelenting torturers and left a trail of some 200 reports by which we can at least gauge their activity.[60]

In 1628, for example, Eschbach found 33 witches in Steinbach, nine of whom were men. One was even the Margrave's appointed supervisor (*Stabhalter*), Hans Heinz, in Steinbach, a man who became suspect after his mother and sisters were executed as witches.[61] One can only speculate whether political or religious motives also played a part in the elimination of this government official. In addition, hundreds of denunciations were registered, the inevitable result of asking suspects under torture to name all persons they had seen at the witches' dance.

In Bühl, a short distance from Steinbach, Eschbach was even more successful. There during 1628 and 1629 he found at least 70 persons guilty of witchcraft, including the wife of a member of the Bühl district court. Twenty-three of the total executed, or one-third, were men. Denunciations during these trials implicated the local supervisor, the scribe's wife, the *Spitalmeister* in Baden (director of the city hospital, which usually served as a geriatric nursing home as well), the church superintendent of Baden, and other honored persons. The trials were noteworthy for bringing denunciations of children by their own parents, and of parents by their children,[62] thus heralding the last phase of massive witch hunts in which children were common participants.*

For the town of Baden itself, where Eschbach started, our secondary sources become unaccountably vague. By computation, however, it would seem that Baden tried 97 persons between 1627 and 1630 and executed some 90 of them.[63] Baden was the only town of the three to conduct torture in such a way that at least six could withstand the repeated pain. Even so, an overall average of 3 per cent acquitted must be a near record for efficiency or brutality.

In general these trials produced an average of 15 denunciations per suspect. One woman denounced 150 persons. One can imagine, therefore, how quickly an entire town might come to suspect itself of

* See below, pp. 139–41.

witchcraft. Nor could one hope to avoid the panic by escape and then safely return when things had cooled off. The *Spitalmeister* of Baden fell under suspicion of witchcraft, fled, and later returned. It then appeared that the strongest *indicium* against him was his flight to escape investigation. Under torture he confessed, confirmed his confession, and was condemned to die. Then he suddenly recanted his confession and stood firm under another session of torture, thereby escaping execution.[64]

An estimate of the number of Protestants executed as witches in Baden seems to be about five. Out of 200 this number is virtually insignificant, but still inconclusive, since most older persons in Baden-Baden had been raised as Lutherans. It has been easy to argue without evidence that there were many other crypto-Protestants persecuted as witches.[65] Although this aspect of religion in the Baden witch trials is likely to remain a mystery, it is clear that the clergy did break their sacramental oath of secrecy by informing the magistrates what the suspects said to them in the confessional. In this fact surely the anti-Catholics should find sufficient evidence of nefarious behavior that they could in the future refrain from totally unproved assertions.[66]

By 1631 the territory of Baden-Baden had executed nearly 200 persons in three and one-half years. On April 10, 1631, the trial records come to an end. Once again the faithful Swedes have been called in as an external force to explain the sudden decline in witch hunts. This time at least there were Swedish troops in Germany, but unfortunately none so far south. Again it seems more likely to posit an internal cause—a recognition on the part of the judges that if every denunciation were followed up, the entire population would be burned. In the absence of proper documentation, this must remain speculation, but speculation in any event not contradicted by anything we know from other accounts.

OBERKIRCH

During much of the seventeenth century the territory of Oberkirch, although formally one of the bishop of Strasbourg's domains, was administered by Württemberg.[67] During these years, therefore, a fundamentally Catholic land was governed by Protestants, the reverse of the situation in Baden-Baden after 1622, except that by the rules of their contract, the dukes of Württemberg were prevented from promoting any change of religion. In addition to this vague structural similarity, Oberkirch itself lay adjacent to the Ortenau and to Baden-Baden, as well as only a few miles from Offenburg and Gengenbach. Although officials from Württemberg had succeeded in suppressing popular desires for witch hunts in 1612 and 1615, the power of all the surrounding examples of witch panic finally infected Oberkirch too in 1629.[68] The chief supervisor (*Oberamtmann*) in that year wrote to the ducal government in Stuttgart suggesting "that we pursue justice and should uproot such noxious weeds in this territory as in fact our neighbors have done for some time in Offenburg, Ortenberg, Bühl, Baden, and Steinbach."[69] Not only the model but also the first denunciations came from neighboring magistrates in Baden-Baden and the Ortenau. Trials began late in 1629. From our records it is clear that courts were set up in each of the six townships of Oberkirch.* In each case trials were under the joint direction of the *Schultheiss* and the ducal commissar, sent from the central court (*Hofgericht*) in Tübingen. In addition, seven respected men of the community assembled to hear the ratification of confessions in a process called *Besiebnung*; and another 12 town leaders acted as judges (*Richter*) in these cases.

Documents apparently do not survive in large enough numbers to give an account of how many persons were executed in 1629 or 1630. In 1631, however, our documents become surprisingly full. In Cappel, for example, an investigation at the beginning of January 1631 examined the *Schultheiss*, Georg Koger, and 33 others, asking them to name all the persons they suspected of witchcraft. In this way a large list of denunciations accumulated. After a pause during the spring, the court at Cappel began to arrest those suspects most often denounced in the preceding investigation. Between July 8 and July 11, ten persons were forced to confess witchcraft, including the now familiar charges of sexual seduction by a man who turned out to be the devil, denial of God and all His saints, accounts of harm done to neighbors and cattle, and the usual lists of further denunciations. On July 15 all ten ratified their confessions, and two days later they were condemned to death by sword and fire.[70] On July 21 the cycle began again and reached completion on the 30th, with ten more persons

---

* Oberkirch, Oppenau, Sasbach, Renchen, Cappel, Ulm (not to be confused with Ulm on the Danube).

condemned to death. In their confessions the usual psychological details were also volunteered: the women always said that they had given themselves to the man dressed in green in return for money. When the money turned out to be mere broken pottery, however, they still felt compelled to carry through with their part of the bargain. This type of story could well reflect an ambivalence toward sexual matters either by the women or by their questioners—an ambivalence that could at first conceive of no reason but money for such carnal deeds, but that could later understand the charms of such a seduction even when payment had proved fraudulent.

The impression of such ambivalence is reinforced by a second kind of anecdote. All of the women involved at Cappel admitted that they found the devil unnaturally hard and cold and that when they realized this was no man, they had cried out "God preserve me." This cry had caused the devil's instant disappearance. And yet, when the devil turned up again a week or two later to tempt these women, they did not flee again to the protection of God. These contradictory details surely reflect the mixed feelings of that age (like many others) toward sexual pleasures.

Meanwhile, elsewhere in Oberkirch, witch trials proceeded logically and relentlessly. From incomplete records dealing with the tiny district of Ulm, we gather that nine persons were executed in September 1631. On September 8 the legal faculty of Strasbourg had advised Ulm authorities that all nine deserved death even though only five of them actually confessed doing harm to men or cattle. In an elaborate analysis of Article 109 of the *Carolina*, the jurists showed that witches who had done no harm had to be punished in some other way than execution by fire. But many other forms of execution were still available. And since executions "provoke disgust at their confessed denial of God and bond with Satan, and also since scant penitence, conversion, and improvement" could be expected of them, all nine persons richly deserved execution. This is a good example of the rigorous "spiritualizing" attitude that we analyzed earlier. Abhorrence of crimes of the spirit did not entail legal blindness, however. In the same consilium the Strasbourg jurists insisted that with torture great caution was necessary "so that people are not brought by intolerable pain of torture to admit things that truthfully they should not confess." It would be wrong to describe the Strasbourg faculty as confused; they simply asserted that witchcraft was a horrible crime but that great care was required in dealing with witchcraft trials.[71]

Again with fragmentary records we learn that the township of Renchen continued to have witch trials during March 1632. On March 24, 12 persons were condemned to death, including the wife of the *Schultheiss*, Heinrich Heuser, and the wife of one of the judges, Adam Schitten.

The worst trial seems to have come in the township of Sasbach. In an undated list of persons denounced for witchcraft there, 150 names are given, of whom we know from later notations that at least 47 were executed. We may be reasonably certain, however, that some 16 or 17 more were executed, despite the lack of specific statements to that effect.[72] Among the 63 executed we find a large number of highly honored and respected people, including the *Stabhalter*, his wife and daughter, and a member of the court. At least two other court members were denounced, one by seven persons. Others close to the court were also implicated. Such accusations and convictions must have done much to undermine the normal faith in magistrates; in fact, this type of episode could be called the crucial crisis of confidence in witch hunting. As people came to trust their magistrates less and less, the magistrates came to distrust the judicial process.

Perhaps the best-documented example comes from Oppenau, a small town upstream from Oberkirch. Oppenau had a well-publicized series of trials from June 21, 1631, through March 5, 1632, when the records end abruptly in midparagraph. By then 50 persons had been executed in eight separate burnings.[73] By March 1632 some 170 other persons had been denounced for witchcraft.[74] In a town of only 650 inhabitants one can easily imagine what suspicion on this scale would mean to social bonds of trust. By January the court had begun to have doubts concerning its own procedures. Five persons had been formally charged with witchcraft and were about to be tortured. In a protest to the examiners on January 19, they pleaded their total innocence and insisted that whatever they said under torture would be lies. They further asserted that only envy, hatred, and hostility (*Neid, Haass, und Feindtschafft*) accounted for their arrest in the first place. The court, like that of Offenburg in similar circumstances, was by now so perplexed that it decided to consult persons learned in the law. On January 24, 1632, the legal faculty of Strasbourg advised that torture cease at once, that mere denunciations and unproved assertions had no value at all, and that seeing other persons at the witches' dance did not constitute valid evidence against them.[75] With the Oppenau court already so thoroughly in doubt, this consilium must have been the final blow to whatever witch-hunting zeal remained among the magistrates. At least we have no trouble understanding why the March 5 record of deliberations broke off in mid-paragraph. The crisis of confidence in their own rectitude had once again brought judges to a halt. With so many persons implicated in other ways, one can well imagine that the public at large had also lost confidence in their magistrates. Once again there is no need to call forth the Swedes as explanation for the end to panic.[76]

WERTHEIM

The county of Löwenstein-Wertheim in the most northerly part of modern Baden-Württemberg lay for the most part along the Main River. During the sixteenth century the noble house of Löwenstein-Wertheim split in the way so common in Germany and produced a Catholic and a Protestant line. During the Thirty Years War this split meant that control of the whole county shifted back and forth between the two lines according to the fortunes of war.

According to one scholar these confessional tensions had already led to witch hunting by 1616–17, when Bishop Julius Echter von Mespelbrunn of Würzburg attempted to restore the town of Freudenberg to Catholicism.[77] The town did "belong" ultimately to the bishops of Würzburg but was held in fief by the counts of Löwenstein-Wertheim. Legally, therefore, the right to govern church affairs was moot at best.[78] Apparently Bishop Julius did not wait for secular courts to decide matters. When the male line of the counts of Wertheim ended in the sixteenth century, even the secular control of the town became controversial, and in 1612 Bishop Julius took it over, declaring the feudal relationship void. Using as reason the plague of 1611, which had killed over 500 persons in Freudenberg, or about half the population, the bishop announced that the judgment of God was clear: the town must return to Catholicism. The property of those who remained Protestant was confiscated and, according to Vierordt, witchcraft accusations were leveled at other Protestants. Thus in this one instance the witch hunt may have served the Counter-Reformation.

More than 50 witches were executed.[79] Since the documents proving
these assertions were not recently accessible, we may conjecture that
Vierordt tended to regard witchcraft accusations as an attack on
Protestants simply because they coincided with a return to Catholicism. It is curious that subsequent histories of Wertheim, Julius Echter
von Mespelbrunn, and witch hunting have neglected Vierordt's conjecture altogether.[80] The case demands more study.

After Freudenberg was restored to Catholicism, Wertheim was
ruled by two Protestants, both of whom were deeply involved in
alchemy, magic, and dream interpretation.[81] These diversions might
have been harmless enough if the townspeople of Wertheim had felt
secure. But on Christmas Eve of 1628, 13 citizens presented the counts
with a petition, approved by the three ministers of Wertheim, urging
an attack on witchcraft, "since many places [especially Bamberg and
Würzburg] are beginning to uproot this weed."[82] Worse than normal
witchcraft, the most recent crisis involved "our dear children [who]
even without this poison prefer evil over good." They implored the
counts, "with earnest zeal to investigate the people suspected of witchcraft because of their reputation and common slander, and to have the
guilty ones given exemplary punishment. In this way not only do you
obey the command of God the highest Judge, but you further the
honor of God, and free and purge this filthy and desecrated land from
the wrath and punishment of God."[83] If the magistrates took a firm
stand, God could be expected to set limits for the devil, and protect
the youth from such wretched seduction.

Taking their advice, the counts ordered an investigation, which led
to the arrest of two boys, aged ten and five, the sons of Barthol Klein,
a chimney sweep. The children claimed to be witches and reluctantly
supplied the names of other witches whom they had seen at the
dances. By mid-February 15 accomplices were known. Examination
of the boys' grandmother led to a quick confession and 33 new denunciations.[84] A second questioning produced 22 more suspects. In this
way the total rose quickly, until by the end of February at least 86
persons had been denounced. In March the panic was intensified by
more children who claimed, like the Klein boys, to have attended
witches' dances. Nine children from the village of Bettingen alone
underwent examination. With so many suspects, it is surprising that
only nine women and one man were executed during 1629. This is

all the more remarkable since the cautious council of Wertheim took advice from Würzburg in procedural matters.[85] The suspicions awakened in that year, however, poisoned Wertheim for 15 years; trials of persons first named in 1629 continued until 1644.

Wertheim was not the only place to experience "infected" youth. Such trials in fact became increasingly the major pattern in later seventeenth-century witch hunting. Indeed, only a few miles down the Main River, at the residence of the Archbishop of Mainz, a "New Treatise on the Seduced Child-Witches" thundered against the rapid increase in childhood witchcraft. The author asserted that the first reason for such conditions was the sins of the parents, for whom witch-children were a fitting punishment. But more important, such witchcraft was due to the sins of the children themselves. One should not think that they were innocent merely because they were young. Their cursing, coveting, and immoral words and games were proof enough that these children had fallen into mortal sin. The only reason children in general were presumed innocent was their imperfect reason. When they came to full reason "and know the difference in value between gold and an apple," then they might be treated as adults. In addition, hardened malice could "supply their years" and bring them into real mortal sin.[86] In this way the writer found it not surprising that children should fall into criminal witchcraft. And when one added the curses that parents often bestowed on their offspring, the actual seduction of children by their own parents into witchcraft, the improper use or total neglect of baptism, the parents who actually dedicated their babes to the service of Satan, and the evil company kept by children—then it was even likely that children would fall into witchcraft often.[87]

Such at any rate was the contemporary explanation of the sudden emergence of children in large numbers in witchcraft trials. Actually there were two forms of involvement possible. The child could seem bewitched and undergo examination to determine the source of the charm; this was what happened, for example, at Salem, Massachusetts. Or the child might actually be a witch, or at least accompany witches to their dances. In that case, as at Wertheim, the magistrates were eager to learn from the children whom they had seen at the dance. In both forms one encounters childhood witchcraft throughout the rest of the seventeenth century. It is worth remarking that Sweden's great hunt at Mora was of this type and involved more than 300 children.[88]

Most important perhaps, the emphasis on children involved a dangerous shift in stereotype. As long as witches were thought to be women—and even when men came to be caught up as witches—it was unlikely that suspects would volunteer such demonic information about themselves. If they did, they were usually executed. But children occupied a curious middle ground. We have seen one treatise argue that children really could be full-fledged witches. An equally strong tradition held that they might indeed go along to the witches' dance, put that they were not themselves guilty of witchcraft. In this intermediate position, they could make denunciations and recount the dramatic dances they had witnessed with impunity. For many of them it must have been an ideal or at least unique way of getting adult attention.

After 1629 witch hunting subsided for a few years. Once again incautious scholars have attributed this decline to the ubiquitous Swedes, who at this time had not yet landed on the Baltic coast.[89] We know of only two witchcraft cases between 1629 and 1633, one of which involved a suspect who leaped from the city wall to her death when guards came to move her from the tower to a different cell.[90]

In 1633, however, panic broke out again. Over 60 persons were accused of witchcraft, and 11 executed. Once again Wertheim demonstrated a surprising ability to discriminate between mere suspicion of guilt and true guilt. Records do not survive to show why so few of the accused were executed. However, the close interest of the counts of Wertheim in all of these trials may have played a moderating role. The counts occasionally rebuked their councilors for irregular judicial procedure, and they always insisted on having the last word in witchcraft cases.[91]

During 1634 some 16 women were seriously suspected of witchcraft and executed in trials that once again involved schoolboys. Four of the boys were so severely "infected" (*inficirt*) that they were put under lock and key in the hospital and watched day and night by the schoolmaster, who tried to deny the boys' claims that they flew off to dances at night. Examination of these boys led to a number of further denunciations, including ten more children. At a different time the son of the rector of the Latin school was denounced. This boy's father was so upset that he implored the magistrates "to rather do justice to the boy so that his soul may be healed, and so that I can be more certain of his eternal salvation."[92]

From the mid-1630's on, witch hunting went into decline, and after 1648 no more cases are known in Wertheim. However, the trials between 1642 and 1644 are worth mentioning, when Wertheim was under Catholic control.[93] In 1642 an 11-year-old girl accused Anna, the widow of Hans Senkeisen, of witchcraft. When examined, Anna Senkeisen in turn denounced eight more women as witches. Three of these were arrested at once and interrogated. The inevitable result was ten more denunciations.

This batch of denunciations had now reached out to the tavern keeper (*Kellerwirth*), Johann Hotz, aged 71, and his 57-year-old wife Anna. As highly respected citizens, these denunciations raised far more interest and speculation than previous trials and began to call the whole trial procedure into question. We have noted a number of instances already in which, as time passed, the status of those denounced rose. The Council deliberated over the Hotzes for two years, and were so undecided that they consulted the legal faculties of both Ingolstadt (Catholic) and Marburg (Lutheran). Under the threat of torture, Hotz and his wife agreed to confess anything the court required. After doing so, they still maintained that they had simply lied to escape torture. This was a concept foreign to the judicial mind, as this passage in the trial record indicates.[94]

Q. Why in that case did she confess that she was a witch?
A. She confessed out of fear of torture.
Q. How could that be, since she confessed everything so circumstantially, and repeated it again, in such a way that everything was consistent throughout. From that fact it must follow irrefutably that she was a witch.

The examiners simply could not imagine the *creation* of a coherent story that agreed so well with what they already knew. If this poor woman could tell the story, it must be true![95]

Not everyone in town agreed, however. At a wedding in February 1634, Nicolaus Schürer became inebriated and insisted in loud tones that his sister, Anna Hotz, was not a witch but that she and her husband had been forced to confess, and that if Anna died she would be a martyr. Schürer also insinuated that vulgar greed was one of the motives for the trial.[96] Although the court seemed unsure of what to do with Hotz and his wife, that did not mean it was ready to accept public criticism from the brother of the accused. As in Ellwangen or Offenburg, magistrates were always sensitive to such contempt of court, and so they swiftly arrested Schürer, examined him, and fined him for spreading slanderous rumors about the court.[97]

Although the court acted promptly to suppress public criticism of witch trials, and although it eventually condemned Herr and Frau Hotz to death in 1644, the growing doubt about the system seems to have affected it too. Not only had the magistrates been unusually careful throughout the lengthy trial of the Hotzes; we know of no further executions in Wertheim.[98] Once again a kind of crisis of confidence in the old system seems to have precipitated a change to newer procedures, if not a change in basic ideas.

MERGENTHEIM

When the lands of the Teutonic Order were secularized in Prussia during the Reformation, its members did not simply disappear. In fact, the Teutonic Order lived on even after all of its lands had been incorporated in other states. From 1525 to the Napoleonic era, however, the seat of the Order was Mergentheim, a city of about 2,000 inhabitants in 1500. The Reformation made no inroads in Mergentheim, it seems—until the Swedes arrived in December 1631. As late as 1823 only 6 per cent of the population was Protestant.[99] The Order obviously maintained a firm ecclesiastical grip on its territory of approximately 77 square miles.[100] In Catholic territories like Mergentheim, we see once again that curious blend of church and state that we first met in Ellwangen. In matters of jurisdiction, these quasi-spiritual territories employed secular officials to conduct trials and especially to pronounce sentence. In this way the Church remained undefiled by the blood of criminals. It is also possible that the leadership thereby cut itself off from the life of its subjects and could not easily control irresponsible officials. It is suggestive anyway that the largest witch hunts in all of southwestern Germany occurred in Ellwangen and Mergentheim, a coincidence that certainly reflected the similar preoccupation of other Catholic ecclesiastical territories with witch hunting throughout Germany.[101]

As in Ellwangen, too, the trial records are virtually complete, especially for the two main towns of Mergentheim and Markelsheim.[102]

The trials in Mergentheim originated in connection with the trials at Würzburg. Bernhard Reichardt, a magistrate and wealthy man of Markelsheim, had tried to give his young son, Johan Bernhard, a decent education by sending him to school at Neuen Münster in Würzburg. In December of 1627, however, the father became convinced that his son had been seduced into witchcraft there, and transferred Johan Bernhard to the Jesuit school at Dettelbach. By mid-March 1628 the authorities in Würzburg were aware that this nine-year-old boy had been involved in witchcraft and wrote politcly to the Teutonic Order in Mergentheim to ask for assistance in extraditing the child to Würzburg for questioning. Johann Caspar, Administrator of the Teutonic Order, responded at once that the boy was to be delivered up formally to the authorities at the border.[103] By the end of March he was under the jurisdiction of the Würzburg authorities. Far from merely questioning him, the Würzburg court got Johan Bernhard to sign a confession on April 8 that he had been seduced into witchcraft by a classmate. Among other horrors, he had denied God, Mary, and all the saints and angels. With his own blood he had written "Ich, Johannes Bernhardus Reichard, hab mich dem Teüfel vergeben."[104] He had flown to numerous dances and, although only nine years old, had had intercourse with the devil on numerous occasions. Like adults, Johan Bernhard always found the devil "hard as horn" and "of a cold nature." Implicating his *complices*, the boy noted that he had seen three other persons known to him at the dances.

One month later, on May 9, 1628, the authorities at Würzburg burned Johan Bernhard Reichardt and four others. Johann Caspar in Mergentheim heard of the execution only after it had occurred, but agreed fully that it had been justified.[105]

The discovery in Mergentheim that children might be guilty of witchcraft was to have serious consequences. About a month after the execution of young Johan Bernhard, we find the complaint of Velltin Beckh, citizen and tailor in Mergentheim, that his sons had been suspended from school "for no good reason." Beckh requested that Johann Caspar look into the matter. On July 6 and 7, 1628, Johann Caspar set up an *Inquisitio* into the scandal of the three sons of Velltin Beckh. A commission listened to testimony from eight children ranging in age from eight to 14, and from the three sons, aged 12 through 15.[106] This evidence indicated that the two older sons pretended at least to have had dealings with the devil, to have gone to marvelous witches' dances, and also that the oldest claimed to have learned "whole handfuls" from the devil. All three admitted that they were called *Schlotthetzen* (lit. "chimney drivers" or witches). It is also reasonably certain that the eldest son, Georg, had publicly sung indecent songs about the Holy Ghost and had seduced a maid. When questioned concerning these charges, the boys admitted their reputation but claimed that they were joking when they spoke of learning from the devil and of flying to sabbaths. Georg was especially adamant that he had spoken "nicht im ernst sonder Narrenthey." He admitted his dealings with the maid but insisted that "God knows I am free from witchcraft." His younger brother, Gottfried, was not so firm. Under questioning, the boy denied that his mother flew to dances, but soon confessed that he himself had flown by use of a black salve smeared on his pitchfork. Under pressure he even denounced two women and one man, a tailor.

Investigations like this one could only tantalize officials. By mid-July they were convinced that witches had got out of hand in Mergentheim and were provoking God's rage. Something had to be done about the slanderers of God. Unsure how to proceed next, they wrote to the bishops of Bamberg and Würzburg for information and advice. Officials in Würzburg replied on July 20, 1628, that, aside from the case of Johan Bernhard Reichardt, they had not heard of any further witchcraft among subjects of the Teutonic Order. Bamberg was more helpful. On the 29th of July the bishop offered the services of Dr. Ernst Vasoldt as advisor. Johann Caspar eagerly seized the opportunity to gain the aid of a man so experienced in witch trials. Vasoldt was a wealthy man and an important councilor to the bishop of Bamberg. His manner of living testified to his importance. In traveling from Würzburg to Mergentheim, about 22 miles, he consumed food and lodging costing 46 fl. 16 kr.* Since he stayed in Mergentheim from September through December 1628, his food bill there was also high: 91 fl. 47 kr. When his fees and expenses had all been paid, his visit to Mergentheim had cost 570 fl. 49 kr., a tidy sum when compared with the 12 fl. his servant received for the same period.[107]

Vasoldt's presence must have had a reassuring effect in Mergent-

---

* The abbreviation fl. means florin (or gulden); kr. means kreuzer; there were 60 kreuzer in one gulden.

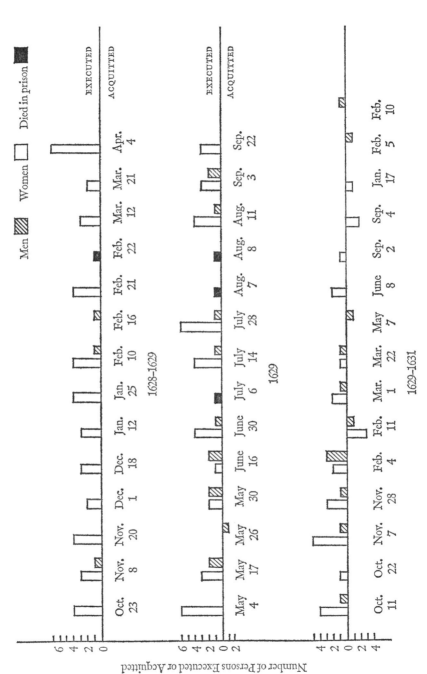

Fig. 2. Executions and acquittals in Mergentheim, 1628–1631.

heim. Here at last was someone who knew what he was doing. Now Mergentheim would not have to repeat the frustrating and inconclusive examinations of the preceding year, when a number of women had been found suspect but no action taken against them.[108] In September 1628, five arrests were made of women long suspected of witchcraft. The process speeded up in October, when at least nine persons were arrested. On October 23 the first batch of four witches, confessed and condemned, reached the stake.[109] By the end of the year, 17 had been executed in five burnings. More important, by December 5, 1628, Vasoldt had helped and approved the efforts of local officials to draw up lists of persons denounced as witches. In Mergentheim the list extended to 140 names, to which 27 more were soon added.[110] For the neighboring township of Markelsheim, Vasoldt and others approved a list of 134 suspected persons. With such handy lists, Vasoldt could safely return to Bamberg. Using these and many similar lists, the Mergentheim officials executed 91 persons during 1629 in 23 separate burnings. Four more persons died in prison, presumably of wounds suffered in torture. Finally, in 1630, the fires declined, consuming only 14 persons in six sessions. On February 10, 1631, the last witch was burned.

The extraordinarily rich documentation for these Mergentheim trials is analyzed in Figure 2. Of the 136 persons formally tried for witchcraft, four died in prison, and ten were acquitted. The overall acquittal rate was therefore 7.35 per cent. Almost 93 per cent were either executed or tortured to death.[111] Yet these simple numbers hide many of the problems involved in determining acquittal rates. A more sophisticated technique is required. On December 5, 1628, the court approved several lists of persons denounced as witches by the persons already examined. To what extent did the court follow up these denunciations, and to what extent did it wait for further evidence? The answers to this kind of question reveal some of the difficulties involved in talking loosely of persons acquitted, and of acquittal rates.

Of the 167 persons named in Mergentheim, the court later tried only 30, or 17.9 per cent.[112] The court seemed actually to be discriminating carefully among the denounced rather than relentlessly following down every last denunciation. Adding the list of 134 names from Markelsheim, we have a total of 301 names of persons denounced by December 1628.[113] Of this number, 224 were never formally tried

(74.3 per cent), whereas 77 (25.7 per cent) were tried and convicted. Even if we asserted that only one-quarter of all persons denounced were finally tried, we would still be on shaky ground, for it seems clear that at least 29 of these additional 134 persons were already *dead* at the time of denunciation. Correcting for this error and assuming a similar error in the 167 names from Mergentheim, we have 236 names of living persons suspected, and 77, or a ratio of 77/236 (32.6 per cent), who reached trial.* It may be true, therefore, that roughly a third of all living persons who were ever denounced as witches were ultimately tried. But this does not mean that denunciations were relatively weak pieces of evidence; quite the contrary.

The judges, in deciding whom they should arrest and examine, paid close attention not only to the fact of denunciation but also to the *number* of times a person was denounced. It usually took three denunciations to start judicial action in Mergentheim, and there are masses of such lists, with each suspect's name lined up with the three or more persons who denounced him.

A contemporary but undated document purports to list "all of those persons of Mergentheim and Markelsheim who have been denounced as witches." Eighty-two persons were named, meaning that this is either an early list, since it is much shorter than the 236 names we have compiled, or that it was selective.† The latter seems to be the case, since of 75 names that we can be sure of, 38 persons were executed. Thus, of this group of denunciations, 51 per cent were ultimately tried and executed.

Still another undated list gives the 17 persons *most often* denounced as witches.[114] These were obviously the persons in whom the judges had the most interest. At least thirteen of these (or 77 per cent) were executed. Since of those persons who were definitely tried, 122 out of 136 (or 90 per cent) were executed, we can appreciate how closely this last group of "most often denounced" approximates the group ultimately tried.

---

* I.e., if we assume that 21.6 per cent of the 167 persons were already dead, only about 131 living persons are left. Subtracting 29 from 134 leaves 105 denunciations from Markelsheim, or 236 altogether. The correction for dead suspects is drawn from WSAL B262, Bü. 83, pt. 2.

† WSAL B262, Bü. 85. Seven of the names are so vague that we cannot be sure whether they represent persons executed or never tried. We are left with a working group of 75.

The point of all this analysis is to cast doubt on those efforts to find rates of acquittal easily by comparing the number executed to the number let go.[115] It is impossible to determine realistically how many were "let go"; in a sense almost everyone who survived a witch panic was "acquitted." The crucial difference between judicial procedures then and now is that during panics, the suspect was *presumed guilty* once he had been arrested. This fact alone justified torture, since all men agreed that innocent persons should not be tortured. Therefore it is not surprising that a high percentage of those arrested and tortured for witchcraft (75 to 90 per cent) were ultimately condemned and executed. If there really are places that show a higher rate of acquittal than this, we might look to the kinds of persons arrested in the first place. If the judges of Mergentheim had arrested all suspects, even those presumed innocent, their acquittal rate would be high, perhaps seven to ten times higher than it was. In other words, this is an area where great caution is necessary before conclusions are drawn.[116]

From a more general point of view it now seems obvious that to sustain a massive witch hunt, a very low rate of "torture-failure" was necessary. Sustaining the psychology of panic required a constant reinforcement of the mechanism in which all persons presumed guilty were found guilty. During panics, I would suggest that the "true" acquittal rate (persons presumed guilty but found innocent compared with the total presumed guilty) was always low, perhaps as low as 5 to 10 per cent.[117] Any rise in this "true" or rock-bottom rate of acquittal usually signaled a crisis of confidence in the system. Used mercilessly, torture could extract any confessions desired from almost anyone. When suspects proved stubborn, they were often simply tortured to death. At the height of Mergentheim's panic, we found four deaths in prison, the only such deaths reported during 1628–31. These deaths would confirm our view of the ruthlessness of torture at the height of panic. Suspects who died in prison did not discredit the judicial system at all. Their bodies were usually burned as if they had already been proved guilty. A rise in the number of suspects who somehow withstood repeated torture, or the adoption of more humane methods of torture (especially with regard to the repetition of torture) would necessarily demonstrate that innocent persons might indeed be suspected of witchcraft, might even be "seen" at a witches' dance, and might have to undergo torture.[118] The shock that accompanied this discovery was not usually so eloquently expressed as by Friedrich von Spee, but it must have been common at the conclusion of every witch panic of major proportions.

Fortunately for this whole model, Mergentheim does reveal a rising rate of acquittal during 1630–31. Although overall only 7.35 per cent of those presumed guilty were acquitted, of the last 18 tried in 1630–31, nine were acquitted and released, or one-half.[119] This rapidly rising rate of acquittal signaled an end to witch panic at Mergentheim. Every person let go was living proof against the judicial system of denunciation and torture, proof that innocent persons might be suspected and tortured.

This analysis answers one question, but raises another. What caused the crisis of confidence among either judges or the populace, the crisis that permitted more humane methods of torture and more acquittals? I would suggest that it could arise in a number of ways. At Ellwangen certainly the suspicion that officials were corrupt must have fostered a lack of credibility between the judiciary and the populace. In Rottenburg and Ellwangen, officials sensed that if they continued trying and burning witches, no women would be left in the town. Even more devastating was the execution of magistrates or their wives as witches, as in Rottenburg, Offenburg, Baden-Baden, Ellwangen, Oberkirch, and Wertheim. If magistrates and honorable men were witches, whom coudl one trust? Finally one should not underestimate the power of human protest. In a number of cases (in Schwäbisch Gmünd, Ellwangen, Offenburg, Wertheim) individuals spoke out against the trials in progress. In each case, the protest was ignored or actively silenced; but perhaps such doubt affected the judges. To protect their reputation for unswerving justice, they had to strike down impertinent objections, which they saw as contempt of court. But later, when they had time to reflect, such protests may have played a part in influencing their opinions.

Such considerations must have been of small consolation to Thomas Schreiber, wealthy innkeeper in Mergentheim, whose criticism of the trials there brought him to the attention of the magistrates.[120] His case is so extraordinarily evocative of the mood of a town during a witch hunt that it deserves to be better known.

At age 30, Thomas Schreiber had a wife, Anna, and four small children. His inn, the "Hirsch," prospered. His relatives in Heidenheim, Württemberg, included a *Bürgermeister*, a town clerk, a beer brewer, and an innkeeper, all solid, even wealthy, citizens. Thomas Schreiber had a strong sense of justice. When the trials in Mergentheim had run only two months, he had already lost faith in the judicial procedure. On December 1, 1628, when Martha, wife of Bürgermeister Hans Georg Braun, was executed, Schreiber was heard by many persons exclaiming that she had been done a gross injustice.* Schreiber even let slip that "King Nero" had also conducted such bloodbaths. Six weeks later Schreiber was again appalled when the extremely wealthy widow of Lorenz Gurren was convicted of witchcraft, and executed on January 12, 1629. When attending the execution of the lady, he had the temerity to express amazement over her confession. The *Amtmann* Max Waltzen turned to him and said pointedly, "Ha, ha, those who know the devil should not be so amazed." That kind of talk perturbed Schreiber, and when magistrates began avoiding him, he prepared to flee. During this time he repeatedly denounced the court for its unjust trials and declared that "if anything happens to me, let every pious Christian fear for himself." He also prayed that "God might preserve everyone from Neuenhaus [the jail and torture chamber], for even the most pious if put in there would be found to be a witch." The trials, he insisted, were bloodbaths, and the magistrates were out to "wash their hands in my blood."

Other records show some of the reasons for the behavior of the magistrates toward Schreiber. On December 12, 1628, Martha Dökherin claimed to have seen Schreiber at a witches' dance. On January 29, 1629, a second woman denounced him. Schreiber's terror grew as he sensed that things were closing in on him. He arranged to have money sent out of town to a place where he could later pick it up. On February 1, 1629, he left town, and fled to Ansbach, and later to Hohenlohe. He left in such a hurry that he later had to write his wife to send him his cloak, shoes, black hat, and a pair of green trousers. He wrote also to his friend, the Latin teacher Georg Allemahn, asking him to examine the case secretly to see whether it was safe to return. In a letter to Bürgermeister Paul Nachtraben, Schreiber again ex-

---

* Someone tried to conceal the implication of the appearance of Hans Georg Braun's wife in these trials by slicing her name and sometimes all of the "B's" (in alphabetical lists) out of the documents. These efforts were not thorough enough to ensure success.

plained why he had left and protested his innocence. He noted that he feared trial because torture led people to confess lies. In yet another letter to his wife he comforted her with the thought, "Oh what pains these unjust judges will have to suffer in hell!" Finally in a tiny note no larger than three inches by four, he told his wife to meet him at Ebersheim in Hohenlohe.

Unfortunately this note and perhaps the other letters were intercepted by the magistrates in Mergentheim. On February 9, 1629, they wrote to Hohenlohe that Schreiber was staying in Ebersheim, and to kindly detain him until extradition papers could be prepared. By February 10, Schreiber was back in Mergentheim answering questions. He admitted at once that the trials seemed like bloodbaths to him but he could not be sure that anyone had been done an injustice. When asked if he had not defended the witches "and held that witchcraft was mere fantasy," Schreiber replied that "he had always said [that witch trials were legitimate] only if no one is done an injustice." At this point the authorities in Mergentheim were apparently confused. There were only two denunciations of Schreiber as a witch, not enough for torture, and Schreiber was too important a man to be dealt with lightly. The first deficiency was remedied on February 13, when Catharina, Georg Reissen's wife, denounced Schreiber. We may suspect that Schreiber's name had been suggested to her, as indeed it may have been to the preceding two women.*

Schreiber's friends were another matter. On April 10, the authorities in Mergentheim received a supplication from friends and relatives in Heidenheim, Langenau, Ellwangen, Dinkelsbühl, and Aalen. They protested the lengthy incarceration of Schreiber without specific charges, admitted that he might have sinned against the magistracy set up by God, but pleaded that his youth and his four little children be mitigating factors.

Instead of considering Schreiber's children, the court wrote to Würzburg for advice. On May 6, 1629, the authorities at Würzburg replied that (1) because three persons had denounced him, (2) because he had fled, (3) because he had attacked the judicial system, Thomas Schreiber might be tortured. The court in Mergentheim proceeded to this step on May 19. Once again Schreiber called the ever

---

* This suspicion gains force from the fact that the first denunciation of Schreiber came shortly after the execution of Martha Braun, whose trial he had protested.

mounting trials a bloodbath,* but claimed to be glad that God was letting him suffer. Dr. Baumann interrupted to insist "as surely as God is in heaven, this is justice." Schreiber countered by swearing "as truly as Christ died on the cross, and God created me, I am innocent." He also asked, "Cannot the learned make mistakes in this matter too?" That was the last straw; he was given over to torture. After hanging for the length of a *Pater noster*, he admitted that he had committed adultery three years ago with a woman who turned out to be the devil. In addition he had denied God and said that "men die like cattle." The rest of his confession proceeded readily as he admitted attending witches' dances and named those whom he had seen there. He claimed that he had never harmed anyone by magic, since his only reason for giving himself to the devil was *Pullschafft* (sexual intercourse). He confessed that he had stolen the host from the Eucharist, and proved to be incapable of repeating his rosary. For a man with so many relatives in Protestant Heidenheim, this incapacity must have seemed particularly significant. He confirmed this confession on May 22, naming seven *complices*, and ratified these confessions and denunciations again on May 25, 26, and 28. Clearly the authorities wanted to establish beyond all doubt the voluntary nature of his confession.

In letters to his wife during this time, Schreiber continued to protest his innocence, and with great emotion took leave of his family. Fortunately, he could look forward to meeting them again in heaven, but even this did not create resignation. He urged his wife to marry again and noted that she had always repeated an axiom that now had especially bitter relevance: "Whoever is chosen for eternal life must undergo thistles, thorns, and strife." In the only note we have from Anna Schreiber, written in a very crude hand, she begs pardon for ever giving him the idea that she thought him guilty of witchcraft, and wishes she were dead. The letters are certainly as touching and revealing as the famous one of Mayor Junius in Bamberg, or that of Weixler in Ellwangen.

The case of Thomas Schreiber is better documented than most, but it reveals the shock and fear that pervaded a town in the grip of panic. Friendships broke down as men lost confidence in one another; families were rent with grief and self-accusation. This case reveals most

---

* Thirty-three persons had been executed since he had been captured.

clearly the danger of attacking the judicial system in the midst of spasms of witch hunting. Doubts, if any, were for the judges, not the populace. Theoretical statements, especially in Latin, were also tolerable. But specific attacks on men and policies were contempt of court and brought swift retribution. On May 30, 1629, Thomas Schreiber was beheaded and burned. Yet how can one measure his contribution to the crisis of confidence in Mergentheim?

The fires continued to burn after the protest of this innkeeper "zum Hirsch." But the growing awareness that he had been right after all brought witch hunting to a close in Mergentheim before the Swedes arrived to enforce such a policy. The panic had lasted two and a half years, had cost 126 lives, and had disrupted the lives of hundreds more. If this was social catharsis, it nearly killed the patient.

ESSLINGEN AND REUTLINGEN

After the horrors of the Thirty Years War were past, and before the renewed destruction of the wars with France, the German Southwest enjoyed a period of reconstruction. Towns were rebuilt and repopulated, often by immigrants from Austria or Switzerland. Generally it was a time of peaceful growth. Several localities even came to punish accusations for witchcraft. It is curious that during the healthy decade of the 1660's, Württemberg experienced widespread witchcraft trials and that the imperial cities of Reutlingen and Esslingen both had the worst scares of their history. All of these areas were Lutheran.

Part of the reason for this late Protestant upsurge of witch hunting may perhaps be ascribed to the breakdown of the Brenzian orthodoxy, described in detail earlier. Although Johann Adam Osiander and Georg Heinrich Häberlin maintained a consistent Brenzian formulation, men like Tobias Wagner and Johann Jacob Faber in Esslingen became disturbed at the real threat of witchcraft during the 1660's. They were by no means isolated. Faber's *Specimen Zeli justi* was prefaced by the poems of no fewer than 14 theologians, pastors, friends, and relatives, who all complimented Faber for his rigid stance.[121] We cannot be sure that similar ecclesiastical shifts were also at work in Reutlingen, but with Württemberg no longer unanimous, it seems at least possible that Reutlingen's pastors demonstrated the same kind of "righteous zeal" as Faber and his colleagues 18 miles away in Esslingen.

The two imperial cities also reveal other similarities in their style of witch hunting; it will repay us to compare them. In both cases the witch panic began with children, in the pattern now familiar from Mergentheim and Wertheim 25 years earlier. As Faber noted, in agreement with the treatise from Aschaffenburg, mentioned above, children had of late lost all sense of obedience and were therefore easily seduced into witchcraft.[122]

In Esslingen a boy of ten from Vaihingen voluntarily confessed to witchcraft in 1662, setting off a wave of similar confessions.[123] The children were taken into custody and examined closely over a long period; they had every chance to condemn others as witches, and yet were too young to be punished severely. One of those denounced was a youth of 16, who in turn denounced 17 more from Vaihingen and Württemberg. He was executed, as were all of the persons he denounced whose fate we know.[124] The panic was under way. It spread rapidly in 1662, until at least 56 persons were suspected of witchcraft. Many persons seem to have been executed at first, but the Council soon developed misgivings. In August and September of 1662 the magistrates consulted the legal faculties of Tübingen, Strasbourg, and Altdorf.[125] Perhaps the rebuke from Tübingen for too extravagant use of torture sobered the Council.[126] At any rate, the years 1663 and 1664 saw numerous arrests and examinations, but only one execution. Even Strasbourg, whose reputation for punishing witches was severer than Tübingen's, now cautioned that not all diseases were caused by witchcraft.[127] In its doubt, the Esslingen Council decided to go easier on the children, sending four home, instructing two to be more careful in future, and retaining two girls as maids to help with prisoners.

In 1665 the witch trials again began to bear unwholesome fruit in Esslingen as at least eight persons were executed. In a number of cases, however, Esslingen overruled the advice of Strasbourg and followed the milder suggestions of Tübingen. The Council released a man with only a fine and four weeks imprisonment who Strasbourg said deserved death. During 1666 the panic subsided completely. The last 11 persons tried were let go with minor punishment or none at all.[128] Such acquittals at the end of witch hunts were symptomatic of the often observed crisis of confidence.

One prominent element has not yet appeared in this account: politics. Scholars have remarked that these witch hunts lasted only while

Daniel Hauff was chief justice, a man whose knowledge of the witch-craft literature was extensive, but who used his special reading of Job and Corinthians to refute men like Weyer, Fichard, Alciatus, and Thumm.[129] Hauff ran the trials rigorously until his death, when they abruptly ceased. As one scholar put it, "Does that seem like an accident?"[130] Others have suspected personal and perhaps political motives in the trials at Esslingen. We have seen, in Offenburg, how viciously accusations could be used against public officials. When Sara, the wife of Councilor Johann Schauer, was repeatedly denounced for witchcraft, her husband required assurance that the trial was not politically inspired. On advice from Tübingen he secured the release of his wife.[131]

All told, at least 214 persons had come under suspicion of witchcraft, at least 79 had been arrested, and at least 37 were executed in Esslingen during the years 1662–66.[132] Surprisingly few of these people came from Esslingen itself, with by far the greater proportion living in two small villages subject to Esslingen.[133]

A similar pattern obtained in Reutlingen at the same time. As in Esslingen and many other imperial cities, the period after the Thirty Years War was one of ever more serious competition with Württemberg for economic power. Many such cities stagnated, even as the city oligarchies tightened their grip.[134] In Reutlingen, oligarchy degenerated into outright tyranny when Johann Philipp Laubenberger was promoted from city judge to Bürgermeister in 1665. He held tenaciously to this post until his death in 1683.[135] During his tenure Reutlingen experienced the only real witchcraft panic of its history.[136] In this way his reign is comparable with that of Judge Hauff in Esslingen. Another similarity is in the influence of children. In 1665 a 12-year-old boy, thought to be possessed by the devil, denounced a number of persons as witches and was believed. The boy was soon joined in the tower by two more children who both had their own ideas of who was responsible for recent witchcraft. Later they were joined by a fourth child. A day of general prayer was set aside for the four, but to no avail. In a consultation from Strasbourg the court learned that for their sexual relations with the devil the children deserved death but that their age argued against execution. If they reached their majority without visible improvement, they were to die. In the meantime their denunciations had other effects. Within a year and a half, 22 persons had been formally accused of witchcraft, and 14 had been executed.[137]

In Esslingen there were rumors of political accusation. In Reutlingen such rumors took on real shape when Magdalena Efferenn, wife of one of the town councilors, was accused of witchcraft in 1665. She fled at once to her parents in Tübingen. Her husband, Heinrich, was the one serious opponent of Laubenberger's plans for controlling the city. Despite continued pressure on him, Heinrich Efferenn remained in Reutlingen. Finally he too stepped down from the Council and fled Reutlingen after being fined 20 gulden for unauthorized dealing in poison.[138] As an apothecary, his position was easily attacked; the mysteries of drugs and poison had always been closely related to witchcraft.[139]

Authorities in Württemberg, however, recognized these trials as political suppression and granted the Efferenns asylum anywhere in Württemberg. The repeated attempts of Reutlingen to extradite Magdalena from Württemberg proved fruitless. From a position of safety in Württemberg, Efferenn now began a vigorous attack on the false denunciations made by the three small children in the Reutlingen tower, and on the ruthless administration of Laubenberger.[140] In 1667, however, witch trials appeared in Cannstatt, where the Efferenns were living. Worried that Magdalena's reputation might bring them to ruin, and thinking that the situation in Reutlingen was calm enough, they returned to Reutlingen. In 1668 the Efferenns were arrested there and put on trial. But doubt had by then become pervasive; Efferenn won his legal battle, yet the fight over a three-year period had cost him all his wealth.[141]

The scholarly accounts at our disposal do not suggest more than 14 executions in Reutlingen betwen 1665 and 1666. Yet because the trials there bear such extraordinary resemblance to those of Esslingen, we have sketched an account. Obviously contemporaries considered the Reutlingen trials of major size and importance. A song published in 1666 in Augsburg told of 40 sons and daughters who supposedly died in the witch hunt there, and exhorted readers to learn from the terrors of Reutlingen to mend their ways and turn to Christ, "who wants to save us from the devil and all evil."[142]

Although the style and lesson of this song were at least one hundred years old, the great age of witch hunts in the German Southwest drew to a close with its refrain. It was not so much that formal theology had changed. Nor could one prove that the Enlightenment or a rise of formal skepticism had come this early to the German Southwest. The examples here have indicated, however, what had happened to make panic-stricken witch hunting a thing of the past by 1670. One community after another had learned by painful experience that judicial procedures were not perfect, that even judges might be witches, and that if allowed to proceed by its own massive mechanism, the witch trial procedure could implicate and eradicate every person in town. Place after place must have suffered that crisis of confidence, which can be seen in so many of the better-documented witchcraft panics; a crisis that shook local society to its roots and destroyed the trust in the tradition of magistrates and institutions that had permitted the hunts in the first place. More important, the magistrates themselves lost faith in their judicial apparatus. An example from Württemberg will make this point clearer.

CALW

The district city of Calw on the edge of the Black Forest in the Nagold valley enjoyed a position as Württemberg's most important industrial city. In the seventeenth century Calw and surroundings supported over 400 master weavers, over 1,000 clothmakers, and several thousand spinners.[143] Although the town did not experience any technically "large" witch hunts in this period of economic growth, it did suffer a panic that is worth considering as a conclusion to our series of large witch hunts.[144] For Calw came perilously near to a bloody series of witch trials that could have claimed more than 50 lives. The crucial question is, therefore, how did Calw avert disaster?

Trouble began as early as 1673, when a woman was suspected of poisoning several of her neighbors. On the advice of the legal faculty of the University of Tübingen, however, she was released. Much of the evidence against her came from children who were not trustworthy. The rest, the faculty said, was the result of hearsay and jealousy.[145] Four years later, a similar charge was leveled against Bartholomaeus Sieben, the illegitimate ten-year-old son of Agnes Hafnerin, a widow. Once again, however, sufficient evidence was lacking to prove that the boy had killed the schoolmaster's son, Johann Crispen, with a poisoned cookie. On questioning, Bartholomaeus explained that his aged step-grandmother, Anna Hafnerin, with whom he and his mother and two unmarried aunts lived, had given him poisoned powders and had encouraged him to harm his classmates. Because he was too young to be tortured, and his step-grandmother too weak, the court decided, with advice from Tübingen, to let him off with a public beating.[146] The beating and warning seem to have done no good; the whole family remained suspect. They were a poor family—so poor that Bartholomaeus slept in the same bed with his mother and grandmother through his sixteenth year.

In 1683 their neighbors openly suspected them of heresy. That year an 11-year-old neighbor boy, later described as having "a melancholy complexion," began to speak strangely of witches and dances. On close questioning he asserted that Anna Hafnerin, now 80 years old, had seduced him into witchcraft, that he had renounced God in words written with his own blood, and had traveled to many witches' dances, where he met many of his classmates.[147] This boy confessed that he had flown off to dances even when observers testified that he had spent the night in bed. Instead of concluding from such statements that he was dreaming, parents became worried that the devil was carrying off only the souls and not the bodies of their children. To prevent such occurrances, they began forcing their children to stay awake and interrogated them thoroughly after they had slept about what had happened and what they had seen.[148] In such a charged situation it was natural that the children of Calw began to tell the wildest stories, often with promptings and suggestions from their parents. On September 7, 1683, 19 of these children were examined by the spiritual and secular magistrates. One was only six years old. In general their statements focused on Anna Hafnerin and on her stepdaughter's son, Bartholomaeus.[149]

The magistrates also examined the two prime suspects, who finally confessed that they were witches. Bartholomaeus admitted now that he had indeed poisoned the schoolmaster's son six years earlier, and that he had been devoted to the devil ever since. The old lady admitted that the devil had seduced her long ago with the promise of money, which she never received, and that she had perverted a number of children into witchcraft. Both suspects pleaded mitigating factors, however, such as extreme age or youth, ignorance and lack of an express pact with the devil.

TABLE 8

*Age Distribution of Children Claiming Involvement
in Witchcraft, Calw, 1683–1684*

Children	Age 3–9	Age 10–12	Age 13–17	Age unknown	Total number
December 1683:					
Number of boys	8	7	2		17
Number of girls	3	10	1		14
Spring 1684:					
Number of boys	5	6	1	2	14
Number of girls	9	9	3	3	24

SOURCE: For 1683, UATüb 84, Vol. 22, pp. 933–34; for 1684, WSAL A209, Bü. 691, 51, pt. 2.

Such pleas did not help them when the Tübingen legal faculty considered their case. The professors agreed that the problem of evidence was great and that accusations from persons under 20 did not carry much weight, but finally decided that by their acts, even if not explicitly, Bartholomaeus Sieben and Anna Hafnerin had pacts with the devil. And the pact alone, according to Johann Brenz and his tradition, was sufficient crime to merit death. In December the two were executed.[150]

The witchcraft trials might have ended there if the town had not been so thoroughly aroused. Accusations and rumors continued to spread. The excited children began to tell of other adults whom they saw at the sabbaths. In a temperate consultation the Tübingen legal faculty on December 20, 1683, considered the 31 children now involved, ranging in age from three to 17, and argued that most of them were either dreaming or simpleminded (see Table 8). Those who confessed real crimes like blasphemy were to receive canings before their classmates. A day of lectures was to be set aside for the clergy and magistrates to tell the schoolchildren how horrible the devil's service was. Referring to the stupendous witch panic in Sweden, the faculty urged strict prohibition of rumor and the reporting of all infractions.[151] Despite this good advice, the faculty had to admit that several adults had serious *indicia* against them, and that they could be examined under torture.

This advice assured the continuance of unrest and tension in Calw. By spring, 1684, the town was so filled with hatred and suspicion that

Friedrich Karl, Administrator of Württemberg, appointed a commission of four jurists and a theologian, Georg Heinrich Häberlin, to examine the situation in Calw and report at once to the Oberrat in Stuttgart. Moving quickly, the commission assembled in Calw one week after receiving its instructions and interviewed all of the children and adult suspects.[152] By that time there were 38 infected children. (See Table 8. Some names from December 1683 had been dropped and others had been added; now the girls outnumbered the boys.) At the same time these children had implicated a total of 77 adults.* In one instance, 21 children all agreed that Anna, Wendel Kohler's wife, was a witch. The commission took a very dim view of the loose rumors that flew about and the patently irresponsible way that parents had suggested stories to their children and had kept them in an excited state by preventing them from sleeping. They concluded that the panic had its origins in the melancholy of Veit Jacob Zahn (now 12 years old), whose spleen also seemed to show signs of affecting his judgment.[153] From this youth most of the other children had received their ideas. Mild torture had even been used against the children to produce wild and dramatic denunciations. Their dreams and illusions were to be disregarded. When the children claimed to be off on flights, they had often in fact been seen in their beds, and the commissioners insisted that the devil could not separate body and soul. The children, therefore, could not have flown anywhere. In addition, these types of spectral evidence were simply too risky and full of deception to provide any firm evidence. The children's stories varied so much that they were worthless. In summary, the commission laid so much emphasis on the deceptive powers of the devil that they could not condemn anyone for witchcraft. Nevertheless, on their recommendation three women were banished: Agnes Hafnerin (the mother of Bartholomaeus), her unmarried sister Anna Hafnerin, and the much suspected wife of Wendel Kohler. They were banished not so much because they were guilty as because they would be in grave danger of life and limb if they remained in Calw. "For the tranquilization of

---

* The persons accused had between one and 21 denunciations against them (WSAL A209, Bü. 691, 51, pt. 1):

	1	2–4	5–10	11–20	21	Total
Men	10	3	1	0	0	14
Women	39	14	6	3	1	63

deranged Calw," it was best that they go away. Anna Kohler and her husband were warned that they must leave, since "they would not be able to earn a living or even subsist among the embittered people of Calw."[154] Other suspects were warned to lead quiet lives for at least a year and were not even to leave their houses. Even leaving Calw was not a sure escape from popular wrath and rumor. One of the Hafnerin sisters was killed by a mob in Weil der Stadt.[155]

The situation remained so uncertain in Calw that the commission prohibited all talk of witchcraft, all rumors, and all vengeful acts against suspected neighbors. One-quarter of the local militia was called forth, from sections of Calw most distant from the trouble spots. When even that measure proved insufficient, the central government in Stuttgart finally sent in an "understanding captain and a platoon of 40 soldiers" to keep order. The commission rebuked the rabble especially for trying to take the law into their own hands.[156] There was of course a long tradition by which neighbors could legally control one another, but this situation had gone much too far.[157]

To calm this sort of frenzy, the commission instituted special days of prayer and repentance. Specific prayers were changed to emphasize the devil as deceiver, and catechetical instruction was reformed. Häberlin preached sermons explaining how deceptive the devil was and how little men really had to fear from witchcraft.[158] In fact, one of the devil's worst tricks was to get a town so excited that it uprooted the wheat with the tares. Witches too were often deceived into imagining that they had done many evil deeds. Häberlin emphasized not suspicion of neighbor but sobriety, chastity, and watchfulness as the best weapons against magic.[159] Here at a crucial juncture, therefore, we find a staunch proponent of the Johann Brenz school effectively attacking the panic that almost got out of hand. The commissioners agreed that "if one tried to burn all the witches in Calw and anyone touched by such a vice, even here [in the Black Forest!] one would sooner run out of wood than such people."[160]

This is a perfect example of what had happened to the desire to hunt witches. Although the urge remained strong among the superstitious populace, the magistrates had learned that one could not accurately tell who the witches were. None of the commissioners disbelieved in the devil or in witchcraft. In fact, they rather emphasized the power of the devil—to deceive. The crisis of confidence in mass denunciations brought mass witch hunting to an end in Calw with only the two executions in December 1683. The commissioners did agree that those two had been true witches. But mass denunciations especially by children could produce nothing but hatred and tension, tension so great that innocent persons were warned to leave town and troops had been necessary.

The commission recognized, in a way symbolic for all the German Southwest, that witch hunts could destroy a community, that they might themselves be a form of devilish delusion. In this way all over the German Southwest, the crisis of confidence brought an end to massive witch hunting while permitting the small trial to persist undisturbed. It was only a partial victory to be sure; but one no less important for that.

Chapter Seven

The Social Foundations

❧

IN THE PREVIOUS chapter we examined the individual processes at work in each of the largest witch hunts of the German Southwest. We now turn to some of the recurrent or basic social realities that affected the course of witch panic. In general, two types of factors have been most popular and plausible in the secondary literature, namely, the material interests of the witch hunters and the social position of the witch. We shall examine these two factors in turn.

CONFISCATIONS

Fortunate is the hunter of straw men in the field of witchcraft. Nothing would be easier than to line up a number of nimble-penned authors and knock them down with footnotes blending dust with acid. To understand the real problem of confiscation in legal procedure is more difficult. Certainly the case is more complex than Robbins suggests when he asserts that "without the bait of quick profits, few secular courts would have followed so facilely the lead of the clerics" into witch trials.[1] Indeed, the very legality of confiscations was controversial in the sixteenth and seventeenth centuries.

The law of confiscations in Germany was complex, partly because the German emperors continued the fiction that the Holy Roman Empire of the German Nation was in fact a legitimate descendant of the ancient Roman Empire. This meant that a two-thousand-year-old tradition in law had to be considered and reconciled before any final judgment could be made. The study of Roman law was not antiquarian but highly practical.[2] In addition to this confusing attitude in early modern Germany, the specific law of confiscations as stated in the *Carolina* of 1532 was a classic of incoherence.

In Article 218 of the *Carolina* a number of common abuses are listed, with an order that they be eradicated everywhere. Among these abuses one reads: "Item, at certain places when a criminal is punished with death, except in cases of lese majesty or in other cases where the criminal has not forfeited life and property, the wife and children are reduced to beggars and the property is confiscated by the lord."[3] At first sight the abuse here mentioned is any kind of confiscation. Second, it seems that the crime of lese majesty was here set parallel to other crimes in which life *and* property were not forfeited, i.e., crimes where confiscation did not follow execution. Yet, third, it is clear that lese majesty somehow formed an exception to the rule that such abuses were to be abolished. Read in this manner this clause made no sense at all. At first it seemed to assert that lese majesty was a crime not requiring confiscation, but then it appeared as an exception to the law forbidding confiscation. No wonder that at this point legal minds were perplexed and at cross purposes.

One of the first scholars to note the difficulty in the wording of the clause was Friedrich Martini, whom we last saw arguing that witches deserved death for their spiritual crime alone, regardless of actual harm done. From his position at Freiburg he also contended that confiscation in cases of witchcraft was perfectly legal, and that previous scholars like Peter Binsfeld, Andreas Fachinaeus, Jacob Menochius, and Julius Clarus had all stumbled either from ignorance of German conditions or from use of a corrupt text.[4] Martini chose a radical solution to the text of Article 218 and argued that an extra word had crept into the printed text of the law. One word might in some cases make very little difference, but in this instance, the word was "not." Martini felt that the only way to make sense of the confused clause was to read the abuse as: "Item, at certain places when a criminal is punished with death (except in cases of lese majesty or in other cases where the criminal has ☆ forfeited life and property), the wife and children are reduced to beggars and the property is confiscated by the lord."[5]

Read in this way, the clause at least made sense. It said that except when a criminal was sentenced to lose both life and property, the lord should not confiscate his property after execution. Such a reading also agreed better with the Roman legal tradition from which Martini drew with ease. Moreover, this interpretation agreed perfectly with German customs.[6] For all of these reasons, Martini was certain that the law of Charles V had not overturned the traditional law but had merely corrected abuses. The *Carolina* certainly permitted confiscation in a few stated cases, but forbade the unrestrained use of this punishment.

Martini had had to tamper forcibly with his text, however, to produce so clear a conclusion. Such tampering was bound to offend some lawyers who felt that no mere interpreter could change the text under discussion. Such a one was Dr. Leonhard Kager of Schwäbisch Gmünd, whose efforts to moderate the judicial procedure there we have already discussed. After noting that some jurists absolutely forbade all confiscation, he showed that others, including Fachinaeus and Binsfeld, allowed confiscation only when no relatives of the third degree in ascending or descending lines were still alive. But a third position, that of Friedrich Martini, would allow confiscation under any conditions, "regardless of near blood relatives."[7] Conceding that Martini had made a strong case for believing that the *Carolina* had been badly printed, and that in this way a superfluous "not" had crept in, Kager insisted that the law had nevertheless been in effect for over 80 years without challenge and had been considered correct by "many Reichstags and Deputationtags." At the same time these bodies had often modified the *Polizeiordnung* by which many minor offenses were regulated.[8] Ultimately Kager simply argued that it was out of place for legal counselors to try to change the law; the law must stand until the legislators reformed it. From his own point of view, Kager asserted that any law of confiscation should be flexible enough to take account of surviving relatives or children. Whereas the magistrates should always reimburse themselves for all expenses from the property of convicts, yet no de jure right to confiscation could exist when relatives survived. In closing, Kager pointed out that even Martini had warned of the indiscriminate use of confiscation and the dangers of disregarding "parents, children, and wives on the pretext of custom."[9]

As we remarked in the preceding chapter, Kager's thoughts did not go unanswered. The counter-consultant, whose arguments so generally prevailed in Gmünd, also answered Kager's objections to confiscation. Relying heavily on Martini, this man urged that the *Carolina* did not need reform in the ordinary sense, because the mistake was simply "an obvious, palpable error in typograhy [sic]" and not a legislative error. Seizing the high legal ground of equity, he urged "that what is wrong and counter to manifest laws cannot be law."[10] With extreme erudition and express gratitude to Martini, the counter-consultant cited numerous precedents that dealt with improperly copied laws and documents. Now that the law was understood, courts could confiscate the property of witches with good conscience.[11] That is just what Gmünd did.

This local controversy in one town reflects the uncertainty that persisted in the wake of the poor wording of Article 218. Martini's contribution was recognized in glowing terms by the major writers on confiscation after him, but most remained unsatisfied by his abrupt amputation of a whole word that had appeared even in written drafts of the *Carolina* in 1530 and 1531. Perhaps the most subtle change suggested for this clause came in 1629 from Melchior Goldast, who favored simply reading "mit" for "nit" (*nicht*). This had the same effect as Martini's deletion of the word altogether.[12] More recent scholars have even managed to retain the "nit" completely, but agree that the clause needs reconstruction to avoid misunderstanding. Clearly the *Carolina* intended to allow confiscation in some cases, while forbidding its indiscriminate use.[13]

We can well understand, however, why many territories felt compelled to establish their own rules in so nebulous and ill-defined a subject. On April 13, 1612, for example, the Elector Archbishop of Mainz decreed that when witches without surviving children were executed, one-half of their property was to be confiscated; when children did survive, the fisc received "one child's portion," i.e., the state was treated as an additional child.[14] This, he said, was an improvement over the traditional practice, where witches without children lost all their property to the state.[15] In addition, the decree guarded against abuses by the *Schultheiss* by withholding information concerning the property of a defendant until after final sentence was passed. After regulating those problems arising from wills and marriage pacts (which usually established each partner's share in various kinds of property), the decree concluded by ordering all debts to be promptly paid in money, grain, wine, or land.

Other areas too were concerned with confiscation. A survey of the 15 jurisdictions whose large witch hunts we described in detail gives some idea of the diversity of practice that resulted. For three of these (Wiesensteig, Obermarchtal, and Reutlingen) we have no information either way to make us conclude that property was or was not confiscated. Of the other 12, three jurisdictions, Rottweil, Offenburg, and Württemberg, absolutely forbade confiscations.[16] We can say of the remaining nine that a policy of confiscation in some form was in force, at least part of the time. For Rottenburg, for example, we know that in 1650, 50 years after the worst hunts, a policy of taking one-third of a witch's property was applied.[17]

In the Ortenau we can be sure that confiscation was regularly practiced. Officials there even tried to take over the lands of persons executed in Offenburg. A contemporary commentator noted that such a scramble for the lands of witches was an abuse only too common.[18] In a case in the Ortenau, the surviving family was so outraged at an attempt to take advantage of their misfortune that they took their case to the Reichskammergericht in Speyer. Instead of inconclusively deliberating for decades in the manner popularly ascribed to it, the court decisively ruled that the attempt of Ortenau officials to take property of Offenburg citizens was illegal. On October 30, 1628, in the name of Emperor Ferdinand II, the court declared,[19]

Since both in the common written civil and criminal [Roman] laws as well as in the well-constituted order and legislation of the Holy Empire it has been salutarily provided that confiscations and seizure of properties have been introduced not by general right (*de jure communi*) but by special custom or statute (*speciali Consuetudinis vel statuti*) and should not be permitted for any except those who passed sentence or judgment, the other properties of the condemned person lying in other lordships or territories should be inherited by the normal heirs. Since the *Schultheiss*, *Meister*, and Council have been most graciously and gently privileged and enfranchised by various of our predecessors in the Empire, Roman emperors and kings, the citizens of Offenburg may and should legally be deprived of their property neither in civil nor in criminal cases by anyone other than the court judgment of the city of Offenburg.

This seemed clear enough. Except in cases where confiscation was already customary, it was not to be used without special permission.

In Baden, confiscation was apparently customary and unchallenged. Both church and state received their "fair share."[20] One finds a different kind of complaint, however: that the corruption of some officials led to payoffs by which the rich escaped execution through bribery. One suspect protested to the judges, "I know how it works; one burns the poor and takes money from the rich."[21] Such so-called *Taschen-richter* were by no means new in the seventeenth century. Reutlingen provided another example.[22] In the Bishop of Strasbourg's nearby town of Ettenheim, similar opportunities for corruption were clear, since inventories of a suspect's wealth were recorded before the person even confessed. Numerous scholars have voiced the understandable suspicion that greed did play a common role, and that wealthy persons were even preferred as suspects in witchcraft cases.[23] It may be that the rich were on occasion found suspect in witch trials in numbers exceeding their proportion of the region's population. But it stretches the available evidence to suggest that greed and corruption prompted every witch hunt or that they even dominated those trials where we have proof of corruption.

Unfortunately no full-scale statistical studies have been conducted to determine the ratio of persons of great wealth involved in witch trials compared to their fraction of the population. Yet it is beyond question that most of the people executed were poor.[24] A witch at Wiesensteig in 1562 even protested, "Why don't rich women get arrested too?"[25]

In search of appropriate materials for statistical study, we conclude our survey of the largest witch hunts. In Oberkirch we know again that confiscation occurred. Some of the records relating to these measures survive, but not enough for rigorous analysis.[26] Similarly with Wertheim and Esslingen, we can say only that confiscation probably took place.[27] The documents of Schwäbisch Gmünd, too, are so fragmentary and in such confused order that no systematic conclusions can be drawn. Out of the 15 witch hunts of major proportions, 13 of them prove unsatisfactory for any detailed analysis of confiscation policy.

Fortunately, the two remaining witch hunts, at Ellwangen and Mergentheim, provide enough documents to begin a more rigorous type of social analysis. It is mere luck that these two places were also the seats of the two worst witch hunts in the entire German Southwest.

Officials in many territories felt confused at the conflicting interpretations of confiscation law and attempted to establish regulations for regions under their own jurisdiction. Ellwangen was particularly interested in learning how to cope with a panic situation in 1611 and 1612. In Chapter 6 we observed the various legal models and answers to specific lists of questions that Ellwangen officials solicited from other territories. In the matter of confiscation, the Ellwangen magistrates were obviously interested in the practice of Electoral Mainz, since they wrote in 1612 asking specifically about the Mainz Decree of April 1612, and received a detailed answer as well as a copy of the Decree.[28] Indeed the information may have helped to moderate Ellwangen's policy of confiscations, since Ellwangen officials dealt favorably with a steady flow of petitions for mitigation of confiscation.[29] At least 40 such petitions survive from 1612 alone. We know therefore that Martini's stern rule of total confiscation did not apply at Ellwangen.[30]

A disorganized sheaf of papers contains a fair amount of information regarding the actual confiscations in Ellwangen.[31] We can establish, for example, that heirs often made their payments to the state in installments. In addition, often several heirs owed sums of money on account of one ancestor or relative who had been executed. Depending on how much the various heirs had inherited, the sums owed by the heirs varied. Commonly certain persons might owe three times what others did, all to the account of the same person. These complicating facts often make it difficult to determine the total sum charged to the estate of persons convicted of witchcraft. By neglecting dubious cases and by combining the many cases of overlap and payments made in installments, one arrives at a few relatively firm figures. From the beginnings of confiscation in 1611 through January 1613 we have firm records of 94 families who had to pay confiscations. Table 9 analyzes their payments.

Nearly 60 per cent of all persons from whom property was confiscated in these years paid 50 gulden or less; and nearly a quarter had to pay more than 100 gulden. To establish some comparative value for these figures, we note that Ellwangen paid its guards at a rate of nearly 100 gulden per annum. A small householder was usually assessed at between 100 and 500 gulden.[32] It is generally true, therefore, that most confiscations entailed amounts easily payable by most families. Those persons whose confiscation ran up to 200, 500, or even 1,000 gulden were among the extremely wealthy of Ellwangen. They were paying usually between one-tenth and one-half of the estate.

In the years after 1612, although the numbers of families affected by confiscation increased, the amounts taken actually decreased (see Table 9). Several lists that we have assembled indicate that between

TABLE 9

Ellwangen Witchcraft Confiscations, 1611–1615

Gulden confiscated	Persons involved, Feb. 1611 to Jan. 1613		Per cent of total	Persons involved, Feb. 1613 to Sept. 1615		Per cent of total
	Number	Per cent		Number	Per cent	
0–4	6	6.4%		12	7.8%	
5–10	17	18.1		30	19.6	
11–15	8	8.5		13	8.5	
16–20	7	7.5		14	9.1	
21–30	5	5.3		17	11.1	
31–40	7	7.5		13	8.5	
41–50	6	6.4		13	8.5	
0–50			59.7%			73.1%
51–60	4	4.3		5	3.3	
61–70	2	2.1		3	2.0	
71–80	1	1.1		7	4.6	
81–90	1	1.1		2	1.3	
91–100	7	7.5		4	2.6	
51–100			16.1			13.8
101–120	2	2.1		1	0.7	
121–140	4	4.3		3	2.0	
141–160	1	1.1		5	3.3	
161–180	1	1.1		1	0.7	
181–200	2	2.1		1	0.7	
201–250	1	1.1		3	2.0	
251–300	5	5.3		5	3.3	
301–350	1	1.1		0	0	
351–400	1	1.1		0	0	
401–500	3	3.2		0	0	
501–600	0	0		0	0	
601–700	0	0		0	0	
701–800	0	0		0	0	
801–900	0	0		1	0.7	
901–1,000	1	1.1				
1,001–1,100	1	1.1				
101–1,100			24.7			13.4
TOTAL	94	100.5%[a]		153	100.3%[a]	
Median amount confiscated	31–40 gulden per family			21–30 gulden per family		
Mean amount confiscated	98 gulden per family			55 gulden per family		
Total amount confiscated	9,220 gulden, 22 kreuzers			8,374 gulden		

SOURCE: Compiled from Supplicationes in WSAL B412, Bü. 54, nos. 3, 4, 5; Confiscationes, 1611, in B412, Bü. 63; and Kapitel-Rezesse, B387, Bü. 798.

[a] Error due to rounding off.

February 1613 and September 1615 at least 153 families were affected, an increase of 59, but only 8,374 gulden were collected compared to 9,220 gulden in the earlier period.[33] The amount taken per family dropped from 98 to 55 gulden, and the median amount dropped correspondingly. These figures are suggestive but do not prove any one explanation conclusively. It could be argued on their basis that the witch hunters singled out the wealthier persons first and thus experienced diminishing returns in their gruesome business. A more likely explanation involves two other factors. First, it is generally true that witch accusations were only acted on when a certain number had been gathered against the same person. One would expect persons under torture to agree most easily on the notorious, the eccentric, or the wealthy, since they were the best known persons in town. This would explain the extraordinary number of innkeepers and midwives who were arrested for witchcraft. In cases where political motives can be discounted, this would also help explain the large number of councilors and their wives, as well as other public officials, who came under suspicion of witchcraft, apparently only because they were better known. Second, one could argue that as people learned what was going on in the panic, some no doubt felt that denunciations had been leveled in their own direction, as in the case of Thomas Schreiber in Mergentheim. When it came to flight, the wealthy had an advantage, a factor that could help account for the decline in wealthy persons convicted of witchcraft in Ellwangen.

Mergentheim presents even more complete records of confiscations. Again it is clear, as everywhere else in southwestern Germany, that total confiscation was not commonly applied. Here too we find records of successful petitions asking for reductions in fines and confiscations.[34] Johann Caspar, administrator of the Teutonic Order in Mergentheim, even declared that although by law he could legally confiscate all the property of a witch, yet "out of lordly leniency and many other reasons" the amount taken was almost always reduced.[35] On January 9, 1629, he explained that "not only the poor and those of little property but also the rich, of large property, will not have reason to complain" about the extent of confiscations in Mergentheim.[36] A cursory glance through the records, however, might lead the unwary to conclude that words did not reflect reality. In a number of cases we find lists of *völlige Confiscationen* (complete confiscations);

analysis of these lists and comparison of them to other records of inventories taken down after execution reveal that *völlige* here merely refers to the full sum required, as opposed to the smaller installments in which it might be paid.[37] It did not mean that a person's whole estate was forfeit.

Like Electoral Mainz, Ellwangen, and many other places in the German Southwest,[38] Mergentheim officials paid close attention to the numbers and ages of surviving dependents in determining how much should be confiscated. Often we can follow with arithmetical precision the process by which such sums were set. When Brigitta, wife of Theobald Obenhaubt, was executed, for example, her property was assessed at 1,000 gulden, which now had to be divided among her husband, seven children, and the state. Her husband received the major share, two-thirds; the remaining 333 gulden were divided in eighths—giving Mergentheim only 40 gulden, or one child's portion.[39] When there were no dependent children, the state did better, collecting 200 gulden from the 600 gulden estate of Paul Braunwart's wife.[40] When men were executed, the state still used restraint. Peter Weit (executed on November 8, 1628) left an estate of 1,158 gulden, of which the state took only 250 gulden. Many persons below a poverty line of about 100 gulden escaped without paying any confiscation at all. Of 87 persons for whom figures are fairly sure, we know that 21 paid no confiscation.[41] The state seemed to exercise its option to seize all the property of a suspect only in cases of flight to avoid prosecution. In this way Hans Arnold, a young man with no dependents, lost his whole estate of 200 gulden.[42] Jacob Frey, the *Obernwirt*, fled after his wife was arrested (she was executed May 17, 1629), leaving an estate of 2,033 gulden, with debts of 1,667 gulden. The state took the remaining 366 gulden.[43]

By combining overlapping lists and eliminating repetitions for Mergentheim, we establish a group of 84 persons for whom we know exact figures on the amount confiscated and total property either from tax assessments or inventories. The data in Table 10 reveal that, on the average, a person lost 14 per cent of his property when he was executed for witchcraft. Over half lost 8.8 per cent or less. All told, 13 per cent of all property owned by witches was confiscated. Below 100 gulden, one seems almost never to have lost anything to the state; the one exception we know of was Waldburga, wife of Jost Böhme,

TABLE 10

Mergentheim Confiscations as Percentages of Assessed Valuation
(Gulden)

Assessed property valuation	Confiscated		Assessed property valuation	Confiscated	
	Amount	Per cent		Amount	Per cent
0	0	0%	619	25	4%
18	0	0	621	200	32
33	0	0	650	20	3
35	0	0	663	50	8
44	0	0	682	70	10
64	0	0	699	70	10
65	0	0	718	100	14
76	0	0	720	40	6
80	80	100	725	233	32
88	0	9	734	200	27
89	0	0	780	50	6
97	0	0	796	130	16
107	5	5	800	30	4
136	0	0	800	25	3
142	20	14	800	100	13
169	10	6	843	400	47
175	20	11	853	53	6
200	200	100	888	111	13
204	25	12	903	25	3
209	40	19	1,000	40	4
211	32	15	1,039	100	10
224	10	5	1,084	300	28
243	20	8	1,158	250	22
248	40	16	1,284	103	8
267	40	15	1,343	400	30
268	25	9	1,528	200	13
302	0	0	1,550	200	13
302	29	10	1,698	80	5
307	20	7	1,745	100	6
320	170	54	1,837	400	21
323	50	16	2,584	1,000	39
329	15	5	2,857	250	9
340	46	14	3,000	715	24
352	200	57	3,400	500	15
363	25	7	4,678	500	11
450	56	12	5,515	500	9
492	50	10	5,520	688	12
509	60	12	5,686	400	7
583	50	9	6,874	240	4

SOURCE: WSAL B262, Bü. 79, no. 1; B262, Bü. 89, no. 24.

NOTE: Each entry represents one person executed for witchcraft in the years 1628–31, except for the first entry of 0 gulden, where eight of those executed were reported as having nothing at all. The total number of persons was 84; total value of assessed property was 78,074 gulden; total amount confiscated was 10,272 gulden, or 13 per cent, with an average of 14 per cent confiscated and a median of 8.6 per cent confiscated.

TABLE II

Mergentheim Confiscations by Economic Class

Assessed wealth (*gulden*)	Per cent confiscated	Assessed wealth (*gulden*)	Per cent confiscated
0	0.0%	701–800	16.9%
1–100	10.0	801–900	14.2
101–200	21.9	901–1,000	3.4
201–300	12.4	1,001–2,000	15.4
301–400	18.6	2,001–3,000	23.9
401–500	11.1	3,001–4,000	14.7
501–600	10.3	4,001–7,000	8.5
601–700	11.1		

whose heirs were apparently forced to give up all of her property.[44] Above 100 gulden the rate of confiscation fluctuated widely, depending on the number of dependents surviving. But in any general category of wealth, whether rich or poor, no systematic exploitation was at work, as Table 11 indicates.

In addition, one can say that neither the poor (below 100 gulden) nor the rich (over 1,000 gulden) predominated. It would be worth knowing, however, how this distribution of witches' wealth compared to the wealth distribution from tax assessments of the city population in general. Even without this information one can conclude that in Mergentheim a strikingly large number of wealthy persons were convicted of witchcraft. Nineteen persons of the 84 had more than 1,000 gulden (or 22.6 per cent). On the basis of crude parallels, this would seem to be much more than among the population at large.[45] Proportionately there were more wealthy convicted of witchcraft than among the citizenry of Mergentheim. Yet before we rush to the conclusion that the wealthy were, after all, singled out and attacked for witchcraft in a maneuver to confiscate their wealth, it is worth noting that the six wealthiest persons on whom we have exact records paid an average of only 9.5 per cent of their estate in confiscations. If there really had been a program to penalize the rich, these wealthiest should at least have suffered the *average* amount, or 14 per cent. In addition, as in Ellwangen, the wealthy were better known, and perhaps on that account more vulnerable to denunciation.

As in Ellwangen, this seemed to imply not only that the wealthiest were more often accused but also that they were among the first to

TABLE 12

Three Periods of Mergentheim Confiscations

Category	Property confiscated	Assessed property	Per cent confiscated
First period: October 28, 1628, through March 12, 1629			
Total	8,523 gulden	45,219 gulden	
Average per person	258 gulden	1,560 gulden	17.5%
Number of persons[a]	33	29	28
Second period: March 21, 1629, through August 11, 1629			
Total	5,629 gulden	35,313 gulden	
Average per person	131 gulden	802 gulden	15.5%
Number of persons[a]	43	44	41
Third period: September 3, 1628, through June 8, 1630			
Total	2,659 gulden	17,228 gulden	
Average per person	92 gulden	783 gulden	9.2%
Number of persons[a]	29	22	21

[a] The number of persons varies in each group in a given period, because often one may know a man's assessed property without knowing what he had to pay in confiscation. To compute the percentage confiscated, it is legitimate to use only those data that are complete for both assessment and amount confiscated. Thus the number of persons considered in the "Per cent confiscated" column is always smaller than in either of the two other groups.

be executed. When we pull our data into temporal sequence, after roughly the ninth execution a general decline is evident in the amount of property confiscated. Dividing into thirds the 31 executions for which we have useful data, we note that the first third accounted for over half of all the property confiscated during the whole panic. The average confiscated was, similarly, twice as high in the first period as in the second, and 2.8 times as high as in the third period. Diminishing returns were a basic fact by 1630. These analyses are presented in Table 12.

Despite rich documentation, we do not know exactly how much the Teutonic Order managed to collect. One document from January 3, 1631, states that a total of 11,187 gulden 20 kreuzers 1½ pfennigs had been received. A later addition corrected this to 12,425 gulden 23 kreuzers.[46] Totaling each of the individual sums that were delivered to the Order gives 16,898 gulden, a figure that accounts for 110 of the 122 persons executed at Mergentheim. The total collected must have come near 20,000 gulden. The money was slow coming in; by the end of 1629, 2,621 gulden in debts were still outstanding. By the end of 1630, operations had become a bit more efficient, with 1,791½ gulden outstanding. Yet six months later, only 123 gulden of this sum had been collected. The reason for this slowness was not only inefficiency but reluctance and resistance among some of the debtors.[47] The normal solutions to such objections to confiscations were either to lower the amount owed or to spread payments out over a longer period.

As for the uses to which these confiscated funds were put, costs of trials, though high, by no means consumed even one-third of the sums collected. A good example of the kind and magnitude of costs is found in a record of January 3, 1631 (see Table 13).

Before one assumes that somehow the court managed to quaff the heroic amount of wine listed, it must be recognized that this list simply records what the middleman did with these funds and foodstuffs. He gave all the grain, oats, and wine to the *Rentmeister* of Mergentheim. The profit was used for matters not related to witch trials but for *pios usus* like schools and hospitals.

To conclude our reflections on confiscations in the German Southwest, it should be obvious, first, that no unified theory or legal inter-

TABLE 13

Court Costs in Mergentheim, 1631

Explanation	Court costs
Cost to build prison and pay workers	716 fl. 8½ kr.
Dr. Vasoldt (legal counsel)	573 fl. 13 kr.
Dinners (formal, expensive affairs) for examiners	1,084 fl. 58 kr.
Dinners for servants	125 fl. 30 kr.
Dinners for executioner and his servant	133 fl. 12 kr.
Food for the witches	1,429 fl. 23 kr.
Court costs [for consultations?]	36 fl. 58 kr.
Payment to examiners of their due wage	242 fl.
Payment to the court clerk	215 fl. 20 kr.
Payment to the guards	968 fl. 34 kr.
Costs for the execution (wood, chains, straw, etc.)	1,615 fl. 29½ kr.
Payment in wine	2,277 fl. 26½ kr. 1½ pf.
Payment in grain	72 fl. 22½ kr.
Payment in oats	69 fl. 3½ kr.
TOTAL	9,559 fl. 47½ kr. 1½ pf.

SOURCE: WSAL B262, Bü. 78, no. 10.
  fl. = gulden   kr. = kreuzer   pf. = pfennig

pretation prevailed. Some territories flatly prohibited confiscation in cases of witchcraft, whereas others regulated it severely. Second, even where confiscation did apply, it is difficult to conclude that the lure of great wealth provoked magistrates into trials that they would otherwise not have allowed. When we confront the contemporary charges of corruption and graft, we must be careful not to overgeneralize. When Friedrich von Spee emphasized the greed of jurists for the profits of witch trials,[48] and when in 1592 Cornelius Loos denounced the "new alchemy by which gold and silver were coined out of human blood," they obviously had serious abuses in mind.[49] It will not do, however, to accept their furious condemnations as a true picture of witch trials everywhere. In Ellwangen and Mergentheim, for which documentation is full, we have no evidence that judges gained exceptional wealth from the witches. Similarly, when Johann Jacob Faber protested favoritism toward the wealthy and cited the popular maxim, "Die Armen in die Aschen, die Reichen in die Taschen" (burn the poor, soak the rich), he may well have had an instance of such corruption in mind.[50] But our evidence certainly demonstrates that the wealthy and powerful often fell victim to the witch hunts.

Third, we can in fact conclude that a fairly even distribution of wealth emerges among those executed for witchcraft, with even some disproportion toward the wealthier. Since the wealthy were not badly treated in the proportion of property confiscated, it seems more appropriate to explain this disproportionate number of wealthy by the fact that they were the best known persons in town, and surely in part the most cordially disliked. For example, a good number of these wealthy persons were substantial creditors; one man had lent over 5,400 gulden to some 80 persons.[51] Some of the old hatred of the Jewish moneylenders may have been transferred to men like him. Certainly it is obvious that at places like Ellwangen and Mergentheim, wealth did not exempt one from suspicion or permit an easy escape through bribery; nor did poverty veil one in such obscurity as to avoid suspicion.

THE WITCH

Turning from confiscations to the other social aspects of witch hunting, we obtain a different vantage point from which to evaluate this complex mechanism. If it was true that suspects were poorer (or less commonly wealthy) in the later phases of a witch panic, it was also true that the proportion of men usually rose in the later phases.[52]

The assembled information regarding the ratio of men to women in our 15 separate hunts is summarized in Table 14. In two early hunts (Wiesensteig and Rottenburg), we find overwhelming proportions of women (98–100 per cent). These trials were also in two regions that proved most persistent in witch hunting. Wiesensteig repeated the spasm of 1562–63 a mere 20 years later, whereas Rottenburg continued to execute people at a high rate over a 30-year period. It is as if the stereotyped identification of witches and old women suffered so little shock that the crisis of credibility or confidence that we found elsewhere could not operate in these places.* One could speculate that those hunts that produced high proportions of men among the executed (20–40 per cent) would tend to have trials that ended abruptly, and would tend to resist backsliding into panic again. More work must be done to test the hypothesis that severe shock to stereotypes of witchcraft tended to inhibit future panic. It would be a good chance to test and develop dissonance theory from a novel point of view.[53] Certainly it is significant that the proportion of women dropped from 87 per cent in the first six large hunts to 76 per cent during and after the crisis of confidence of 1627–31. In summary, it is fair to say that, as a hunt developed, the number of men suspected usually rose, and that from the 1620's on men were generally more prevalent. One stereotype had broken down, a stereotype by which society had been able to hunt its hidden enemies without inviting social chaos.

In an earlier chapter we have already noticed another stereotype that disintegrated: that of age. If witches were predominantly old before 1600, more and more trials after 1600 came to feature children as central actors.[54] Children were not only bewitched like those at Salem, Massachusetts; they were witches themselves. The iron Bishop of Würzburg, Philipp Adolf von Ehrenberg, even executed his own young nephew.[55] From 1627 on, every large witch hunt began with children.

This suggestion concerning sex and age in the dynamic of witch hunting agrees well with what we know regarding the persons executed in the Würzburg trials. In a well-known list from 1629, 160 persons were named, in 29 burnings.[56] When we group these execution days, the patterns of sex and age become clear (see Table 15).

Clearly the proportion of females dropped rapidly, from 85 per cent to a low of 21 per cent before recovering slightly in the last group of

* See Chapter 6 for a description of the crisis of confidence.

TABLE 14

Males and Females Executed in Large Witch Hunts
of the German Southwest

	Sex of persons executed		
Place and year	Female	Male	Per cent women
Wiesensteig:			
1562–63	63[a]		100%
1583	25[a]		100
Rottenburg, 1578–1609[b]	147	3	98
Rottweil, 1561–1600	36	6	86
Obermarchtal, 1586–96:			
1586	15	8	65
1587	24	1	96
1588	4	2	67
1589	1	0	100
1590	1	0	100
1592	1	0	100
1593	3	1	75
1596	1	0	100
TOTAL	50	12	81
Ellwangen, 1611–18:			
1611	91	7	93
1612	73	23	76
1613	10	4	71
1614	16	11	59
1615	20	13	61
1616	8	5	62
1618	2	0	100
TOTAL	220	63	78
Schwäbisch Gmünd, 1613–17:			
Burning #1	6	0	100
Burning #2	5	2	71
Burning #3	6	0	100
Burning #4	9	1	90
Burning #5	2	0	100
Burning #6	1	1	50
Burning #7	5	0	100
Burning #8	3	0	100
Burning #9	2	0	100
TOTAL	39	4	91
Ortenau, 1627–30:			
1627	4	0	100
1628	33	1	97
1629	20	2	91
1630	10	4	71
TOTAL	67	7	91

TABLE 14 (*continued*)

Place and year	Sex of persons executed		
	Female	Male	Per cent women
Oberkirch, 1631–32:			
Cappel, 1631	16	4	80
Ulm, 1631	7	2	78
Renchen, 1632	15	8	65
Sasbach, 1632?	41	23	64
Oppenau, 1631–32	40	10	80
TOTAL	119	47	72
Wertheim, 1616–44:			
1616–17	Sex unknown		
1629	9	1	90
1630–32	2	0	100
1633	Sex unknown		
1634	16	0	100[a]
1641	2	0	100
1642	4	0	100
1644	2	1	67
TOTAL	35	2	95
Baden-Baden, 1627–31:			
Steinbach, 1628	24	9	73
Bühl, 1628–29	47	23	67
Baden, 1627–31	Sex unknown		
TOTAL	71	32	69
Offenburg, 1627–29:			
1627	6	1	86
1628	22	0	100
1629	21	11	66
TOTAL	49	12	80
Mergentheim, 1628–31:			
Jan. 1–May 4, 1629	34	2	95
May 17–Dec. 31, 1629	44	15	75
1630	8	5	62
1631	0	1	0
TOTAL	102	24	81
Esslingen, 1662–65	15	22	41
Reutlingen, 1665–66	11	3	79
Calw, 1683–84	1	1	50
TOTAL, 6 witch hunts before 1627	580	88	87
TOTAL, 9 witch hunts after 1627	470	150	76
GRAND TOTAL	1,050	238	82

[a] Sex unknown, but the implication is that all were women. By implication we can often surmise that only women were involved when words like "sagae" or "veneficae" were used.

[b] The implication is that all were women until 1602, and that from 1602 to 1609, 14 were female and 3 male.

TABLE 15

Würzburg Witchcraft Trials, 1627–1629

Execution groups (in time sequence)	Total executed			Children			Adults			Per cent adults in total
	F	M	%F	F	M	%F	F	M	%F	
1–5	22	4	85%	0	0	0%	22	4	85%	100%
6–10	16	12	57	2	0	100	14	12	54	93
11–15	10	4	71	2	1	67	8	3	73	79
16–20	15	13	54	6	11	35	9	2	82	39
21–25	7	27	21	1	13	7	6	14	30	59
26–29	9	21	30	2	3	40	7	18	28	83
SUBTOTAL	79	81	49%	13	28	32%	66	53	55%	74%
TOTAL	160			41			119			

four executions. The same pattern prevails for girls and boys, with a drop from 100 per cent to 7 per cent, and with a recovery to 40 per cent in the last four burnings. Among adults only, the drop was more rapid, but recovery set in earlier, to be followed in executions 21–29 by another drop in the percentage of women burned. When we look at the proportions of adults and children, we notice an identical pattern, starting with all adults, declining to only 39 per cent adults in burnings 16–20, with a subsequent recovery to levels still well below the first ten burnings. Overall, the breakup of stereotypes is clear. In fact, the first eight persons executed were exclusively adult women. Slowly age and sex came to matter less, leaving society with no protective stereotypes, no sure way of telling who might be, and who could not be, a witch.

Despite these significant increases in men and children, witch panics almost always singled out adult women for special attention. This is not the place to review all of the suggested reasons for this emphasis, but a few salient points deserve mention.[57] First, women were viewed as particularly prone to diabolical contracts, not only because they were thought weak of mind but also and especially because they were lusty. Unlike the Victorian woman from whose standard women have only recently and imperfectly escaped, women in the sixteenth and seventeenth centuries were supposedly aggressive and lustful.[58] Sexual intercourse was an explicit delight for women. Other women were pictured whose primary desire was the satisfaction of sensuality. Only a background of this sort made the stories of seduction by the devil, repeated endlessly in confessions, at all psychologically plausible. The judges could understand, apparently, that a woman would feel drawn to a man and succumb to him on first meeting because such behavior accorded well with ideas of female nature. Just as common are the confessions that intercourse with the devil turned out to be far less enjoyable than with their own husbands, owing to the devil's "hard and cold nature." Regardless of the origin of such confessions, whether spontaneous or suggested, these details provided a convincing rationale for witch hunters trying to explain why women fell prey to the devil in such large numbers.[59]

Beyond psychological plausibility, women seemed also to provoke somehow an intense misogyny at times. In some instances this hatred reflected traditionally tense family relationships. In the case of Barbara Rüfin of Ellwangen we noticed a mother-in-law problem that had got totally out of hand. Such relationships, in which hate could not easily be admitted, might occasionally have disintegrated into wild name-calling of the sort that led to examinations and trials.[60] But surely a bad relation with one's mother-in-law or other kinsman could not have soured whole groups of men against women. And the literary tradition of Eve, Circe, Hecate, and Jezebel cannot explain much more than literary convention. We touch at last a sensitive nerve in the passing observation that during plagues men sometimes suffered and died at a rate six to ten times that of women, perhaps because women stayed at home more than men.[61] Even if the ratio in Germany never reached these heights, it is easy to imagine that occasional disproportions of this sort might have led examiners to look especially diligently for the *women* responsible for plague.[62] More work on plague needs to be done before we can make this more than a rather unlikely suggestion, but at least here one would have a real cause of resentment.[63] It is not enough to assert that a particular social group has been chosen as a scapegoat. One must also examine the reasons why that group *attracted* to itself the scapegoating mechanism.[64]

A much more attractive explanation of the attack on women in witch hunts could also be constructed on what we know of the changing role of women in the early modern period. Scholars have often remarked that the sixteenth century was one of the most bitterly misogynistic periods ever known.[65] Some have attempted to tie this new flood of anti-feminine attitudes to the Renaissance or to the Reformation,[66] an attack that has naturally provoked vigorous rebuttal.[67] No scholars have until now been successful in tying such ideas to more than literary tradition. The attempts at a psychology of misogyny have also shown pronounced weakness in explaining why the sixteenth century brought anything new.[68] Recently, however, it has become clear that the sixteenth century brought one of the most profound demographic changes that Europe ever experienced. John Hajnal has demonstrated that the "European marriage pattern" dates roughly from the fifteenth or sixteenth century, a pattern characterized by late marriage and large proportions of both men and women who never married at all.[69] For the first time in all Western history, it seems, men's ages at first marriage rose to 25 or even 30, whereas women's ages at marriage rose to 23 and up to 27. The proportion remaining single probably rose from about 5 per cent to 15 per cent or even 20 per cent. In specific instances we now know that these numbers were even higher.[70] In nineteenth-century Carinthia, to take an extreme case, 45 per cent of all women never married.[71] In sixteenth-century Württemberg we can see "hints . . . of a non-European marriage pattern in the earlier centuries."[72] In southwestern Germany, therefore, like the rest of Western Europe, the sixteenth century seems to have brought a profound shift in family patterns. The causes of such a change are as yet poorly understood.[73]

The massive implications are only now being explored.[74] In addition to obvious ramifications in the field of economic history, this shift toward later marriage would lay a social basis for trends toward crystalization of the nuclear family as well as emphasis on marriage by choice (and not by arrangement) found among Lutherans and Puritans alike.[75] Just as important no doubt was the social impact of a large proportion of people who never married at all. In a society accustomed to placing 95 per cent of all women in marriage, the identity problems and role conflict of perhaps 20 per cent of all women might now prove enormous. Here for the first time in European history was a large group of women who remained spinsters. Their numbers were of course augmented by widows, who often formed 10–20 per cent of the tax-paying population. We know from other studies that such sexual disbalance away from marriage provoked social problems and affected social attitudes.[76] We know that theoretically, legally, and perhaps emotionally the patriarchal family was considered the basis of society.[77] In the light of these concepts, the growing number of unmarried women would have appeared as a seditious element in society, especially after the death of their fathers removed them from patriarchal control altogether. Nunneries even in Catholic countries seem to have been in decline in the sixteenth century. Until society learned to adjust to the new family patterns, one could argue that unmarried women would have been especially susceptible to attack.

This conclusion would support the commonplace observation that widows and spinsters were most commonly accused of witchcraft, far out of proportion to their numbers in society. Certainly it was against them that many hunts were initially directed; later when that stereotype dissolved, large numbers of married women and young unmarried girls were suspected, accused, and convicted of witchcraft. Much more demographic work needs to be done to turn these conjectures into demonstrations. But the model of changing social roles holds out more hope of solving the knotty problem of sixteenth-century misogyny than a dozen studies of classical or biblical origins.

Two attributes of women did obviously increase the likelihood that they would be suspected of witchcraft. One was melancholy, a depressed state characterized occasionally by obscure or threatening statements and odd behavior. Many women in their confessions emphasized the fact that they were seduced into witchcraft at a time when they were sad, dejected, or even desperate—often because of ill treatment by husbands. Johann Weyer found melancholy so frequently among old women accused of witchcraft that he made it central to his picture of the poor deluded witch.[78]

The other dangerous attribute, as already suggested, was isolation. Women belonged under the protection and legal power of their father until they married.[79] When they married, their husbands took over this power intact. Maids and servants too were part of the household in which they lived and were subject to the discipline of the family.[80] The structure of society was so completely geared to the family that persons without families were automatically peculiar, unprotected, and suspect. Widows in particular were defenseless until they remarried.[81] So were spinsters. For this reason, husbands urged their wives to remarry if death should separate them. Thomas Schreiber, the unfortunate innkeeper in Mergentheim, wrote to his wife shortly before his execution, lamenting that "I can no longer be your father," but urging her to remarry "on account of the children, for widows and orphans are despised and pushed down in this vile world."[82] In some cases the courts even seemed to recognize that the problem of dangerous women was related to their unattached, uncontrolled existence. In 1571 the court at Horb, a few miles up the Neckar from Rottenburg, released Agatha, the widow of Hanns Bader of Bildechingen, on the condition that she swear "to live quietly and chastely, and not to leave the jurisdiction of Bildechingen any more, and to stay day and night in the household of her son-in-law."[83] Putting her under masculine rule would help solve the problem. We are now in a better position to reflect on the impact a larger proportion of unmarried women might have on such a society.

The family context in which witch trials took place often complicated the trials. In a large panic in a small town, it is clear that the judges or jurymen might quickly come to situations in which their own relatives, even wives, were suspected. The chance for political accusation was large and inviting, but it is very difficult without diaries or personal letters to prove this sort of motivation in any specific case. Factionalism, however, may have played a larger role than most historians have assumed. Julio Caro Baroja, the anthropologist, has drawn the suggestive parallel between medieval feuding and witch hunting, but he had little evidence to support it.[84]

It has been commonplace since Michelet to remark the high incidence of trials in which mother and daughter(s) were executed. In Mergentheim nearly one-half of the persons arrested for witchcraft were related to at least one other suspect. In the case of the Weit family, eight members were tried and executed between November 1628 and June 1630. In a story included by Martin Crusius in his chronicle, certain features of factional tension between town and village emerge with startling clarity. Although he did not label it an example of witchcraft, the details are so exceptionally similar that we can be fairly sure that it was. In 1588 it seems that the wine steward at a tavern in Habsburg Bernau[85] failed to keep accurate records. Wine was missing and unaccounted for. The innkeeper stayed in his wine cellar overnight and watched as 17 old women "poured wine for themselves and drank joyously with one another according to their established custom." When the innkeeper brought charges against them, they admitted that they had done this and "other such evil deeds for the past 17 years; therefore, they were burned to death. But some of them had relatives in a village of that region, and they came to Bernau around the first of January, 1589, and set it afire at five places; 129 buildings burned down including the town hall and all its contents, and 23 persons besides."[86] Here at least was a perfectly clear case of family factionalism and the dire effects it could have in witch panics. It was perhaps a fear that family complications would develop that led the magistrates to pause so long in the case of Thomas Schreiber. We may recall that his friends and relatives from several surrounding towns petitioned for his release. Certainly the courts had to be circumspect before taking action. Only after receiving advice from the learned of Würzburg did they feel confident enough to torture, condemn, and execute Schrieber.

Turning from the family nexus in which early modern society both thought and acted, we may treat briefly a few of the persistent questions regarding the status and character of those executed for witchcraft. It is sometimes asserted that witchcraft was a *Modeverbrechen*, a fashionable crime under which many old-fashioned, genuine crimes were subsumed. There can be no doubt that in the many small, isolated witchcraft trials that went on throughout the sixteenth and seventeenth centuries, many crimes like fornication, abortion, infanticide, and poisoning were connected to witchcraft.[87] It is another matter, however, to assert that those caught up in severe witch panics were real criminals. One would then be faced with explaining a sudden crime wave of enormous proportions. The persons caught up in such years of terror ranged from the ugliest hag to the Bürgermeister himself. Often accusations at first were aimed at the stereotyped examples of old, secluded, peculiar women. It is false to assume that this stereotype originated only in the modern age, as many scholars assert. The age of witch hunts thought first in terms of old women, just as we do. But the mechanism of the hunt has shown us in many cases what happened. Denunciations spread rapidly from tortured suspects until a hundred or more persons were implicated. Those who accumulated the most denunciations were of two groups: (1) the people of notoriously bad reputation (especially midwives), and (2) the better known men and women of a town, like magistrates, teachers, innkeepers, wealthy merchants, and their wives. Our analysis of confiscations confirmed the early interest of the courts both in the very poor and in men of wealth. One cannot simply speak glibly of who "the witch" was, what his or her character reveals. We must learn to deal with sixteenth-century stereotypes and become sensitive to the crisis that developed when stereotypes broke down, especially in the seventeenth century.

Historians have also noted occasionally that wealthy persons sometimes received better treatment and less severe torture than their poorer neighbors. Judging by modern standards, they have assumed that bribery eased the lot of the wealthy. Of course it was true that wealthy persons could afford to buy better food than prison fare and to keep warmer in their cells. But by imperial law, persons of high estate were actually entitled to better treatment and less degrading punishments. The *Carolina*, for example, referred often to "estate" (*Stand*) and gave alternatives in punishment in 19 articles.[88] Later interpreters used Roman law to argue that social class was always a relevant factor in determining punishment.[89] We noticed in our account of the witch hunt at Rottenburg (p. 91) that Agatha von Sontheim escaped the full extent of the ordinary law and was released in return for money and a change in religion.

It may well be generally true that the nobility received light treatment, since we know of only two other instances in the German Southwest in which persons of the nobility were even accused of witchcraft between 1500 and 1700. In one case, the knight Hans Ritter von Gnöztheim was executed in 1591 for practicing "unchristliche Zauberei."[90] In the other case, Sabina von Schellenberg (née von Freiberg) was accused of witchcraft in 1635. The court at Bräunlingen arrested her, but finally let her go without seriously questioning her.[91] In a few other incidents, nobles appeared as plaintiffs, as in 1590 when Leo von Freiberg tried and executed a man for witchcraft after aspersions had been cast on Freiberg's wife.[92] Again in 1621 a certain Jacob der Schwabe zu Bamlach was executed at Kleinkems for having used magic to kill Junker Dietrich von Andlaw.[93] An exactly similar case in 1737 in which a person was executed for bewitching Count Neipperg concludes our series.[94] It is evident from so short a list that the nobility did not in this period play anything like the major role it had in the witch trials of the Middle Ages. In that earlier period nobles were often suspected of using magic for political and personal ends.[95] The crucial element of this shift would seem to lie in the group of people who feared the action of witchcraft. As long as kings, princes, and the high nobility feared the effects of evil magic, we can expect that they would have concentrated on rivals and schemers within their own ranks.[96] But in an age when the populace at large lived in fear of witchcraft, the prince or lord was too remote to seem a likely suspect. At most the town magistrates or the administrators of the lord would fall prey to the suspicions of the populace. That, in fact, did happen.[97] Doctors, lawyers, and university professors, in addition to the nobility, seemed to enjoy considerable immunity from witchcraft accusations. Often they too legally avoided the grossest tortures.[98] Even university students who came under suspicion were generally punished by expulsion only.[99]

Aside from these generally privileged groups, it seems clear that Jews and Gypsies were almost never accused of witchcraft. We know of no instance in the German Southwest in which they were victims of witch trials. The standard explanation for this phenomenon has been that witchcraft was a heresy, and therefore one had to be a Christian to become a witch.[100] That made good theological sense, and Christian Thomasius emphasized the point while attacking the witch hunt. "No one," he said, "calls Jews or Gypsies witches (*Hexenmeister*) or says that they have a pact with the devil," despite their common reputation for magic.[101] Yet the most severe judges of witchcraft scoffed at this distinction. Jean Bodin, for example, argued learnedly in 1580 that even pre-Christian Rome and Greece had had witches. They were persons who renounced their own religion and gave themselves to the devil.[102] In struggling to make the classical world relevant to Renaissance Europe, Bodin was continually forced to generalize, and to define matters in such a way that uniquely Christian doctrines became culturally relative. Bodin, therefore, opened the door to witchcraft to even Jews and Gypsies. Similarly in 1667 Johann Jacob Faber asserted that Gypsies actually *were* witches.[103] In 1581 a woman from Cappel near Rottweil even described the devil as a Gypsy.[104] No doubt there were ways of getting around a strict reading of theology if there had been any desire to persecute Jews and Gypsies as witches. After all, the *Carolina* had said nothing of heresy; it spoke only of harmful or harmless magic. It seems necessary to conclude that these two groups were simply not appropriate scapegoats in the sixteenth and seventeenth centuries.[105] Perhaps after the great pogroms of the fifteenth and early sixteenth centuries, the Jews found a social position, in villages and small towns, that was less threatening to their neighbors. Gypsies on the other hand were migrant. They never stayed long enough in one place to become part of the local social structure, and perhaps for that reason were suspected only of thefts and other secular crimes. Gypsies were continually forced and herded from one place to another without becoming part of a witch hunt.[106] Perhaps too their well-known elusiveness made apprehension impossible.

MAGISTRATES AND THE MOB

After examination of the problems of confiscation and the social status of persons convicted of witchcraft, there remains one major question concerning the social forces in witch hunting, namely, the origin of the panic. Far too much has been written concerning the mindless "mass mania" that supposedly was at work during the "witch craze." In quite appropriate reaction against such formulations, a recent scholar has suggestively argued that witch hunts were examples of "bureaucratized mass madness," a terror that gripped the magistrates and brought them to acts that the common people rejected. "The Enlightenment concerning witch trials rose from the bottom to the top."[107] It is refreshing to see new formulations, but this surely goes too far. Witch trials broke out repeatedly after disasters, not because the magistrates felt compelled to find a reason, a scapegoat, but because popular pressures demanded one.

A model example comes from the township of Balingen in Württemberg.[108] In 1672 a huge fire consumed much of the town; by October three women had been arrested on suspicion of witchcraft. When the magistrates consulted the legal faculty of Tübingen concerning the case, they were disappointed to learn that torture would not be permissible even for the prime suspect. In a mood of desperation they wrote to the Oberrat (Superior Council) in Stuttgart explaining that the rabble demanded punishment, and would prove uncontrollable if the three were not executed.

They would not only kill them but would place the magistrates in great personal danger. . . . [Therefore,] in order that we might give the vulgar a sop and silence their mouths, we have been moved to petition your princely grace graciously to allow us to consult a different faculty, like Strasbourg, since as is well known the legal faculty of Tübingen is much too lenient in criminal matters and especially in *delictis occultis* and are always inclined to the more gentle.

The faculty of Tübingen had indeed urged that there were insufficient *indicia* against the prime suspect and that she should simply forswear vengeance and be let go. The magistrates were granted permission to consult elsewhere, but even the torture permitted by Strasbourg failed to produce any confession. The Oberrat then ordered the woman to be banished. As the poor woman was being taken through the streets of the city, she was set upon by the rabble, stoned, and so badly hurt that she died a few days later.

Here as clearly as in Calw and in other places, we see the wrath of a populace unwilling to abide by the rule of law and the helpless position of the magistrates. This was not mass madness to be sure, but it most certainly was not the madness or delusion of a small class of bureaucrats either. It presents a situation that the dukes of Württemberg came to handle by the use of troops, as in Calw.

In general, therefore, it is inaccurate to speak of "enlightenment" proceeding from the bottom upward. It would also be misleading to restate the traditional view that men of learning and wise magistrates slowly but surely fought down the tide of popular superstition. Forty years after giving such sensible advice to Balingen, the Tübingen legal faculty had developed a harder line against witches.[109] As we learned in the largest witch trials in the German Southwest, enlightenment came not from one group to another, not from books, but from the shattering realization that witch hunts could destroy all sense of community, and all inhabitants as well. It was not a lesson easily learned, especially in the smaller trials, which persisted well into the eighteenth century. But those communities that had had a large-scale panic had watched every stereotype break down as soon as everyone was suspected. Spee was, therefore, wrong when he feared that without princely intervention trials would spread like a forest fire, each convict producing the denunciations for the next trial.[110] Instead, by an agonizing process, towns and finally whole regions came to reject the procedure of torture and denunciation.[111] The small trial could live on, proof that men's attitudes toward the devil had not changed fundamentally, that skepticism was not yet in the air. These small trials were viable, since they never had depended on mass denunciations.

But the large panic trial, the severe social purgation, was dead by its own hand. Even Würzburg, where trials had raged until 1630, produced a solemn reconsideration when Bishop Philipp Adolf von Ehrenberg found both his chancellor and himself accused of witchcraft. In an about-face that symbolizes the whole process throughout southwestern Germany, the bishop prohibited further trials and established regular memorial services for the innocent victims of justice.[112]

Chapter Eight

Conclusion

IN CONCLUSION, a few salient points have emerged from this study. First, it seems clear that neither the sixteenth nor the seventeenth century saw any unanimity regarding the essence of witchcraft. To most thinkers it was a curious amalgam of heresy and actual physical crime. Those who argued against the plain words of the *Carolina* and concluded that witchcraft was essentially apostasy or heresy never gained a true consensus. Most trials continued throughout the seventeenth century to emphasize both spiritual and physical damage. In addition, from Johann Weyer on, a large tradition developed among scholars who doubted such fundamental matters as the pact. It is important to realize that there was far more opposition to the full-blown theories of witchcraft than has been commonly recognized. Controversy continued to be common.

In the German Southwest much of this opposition or moderation in matters of witchcraft came from preachers. They were not forerunners of Enlightenment skepticism but pious men of the *Episcopi* tradition, who insisted on interpreting disasters as warnings from God rather than as the results of magic. They insisted that man's proper response to hardship was repentance and reform of life, not the pursuit of witches. Exponents of this view were particularly strong in Württemberg, where they formed an unchallenged orthodoxy from 1540 through the 1620's. Yet moderate exponents of this spiritualizing view of witchcraft could also be found among the Catholics and Calvinists, at least up to 1590 or 1600. This theological diversity of attitude was widespread and an essential determinant of regional variations in the severity of witch hunting. When the Catholics moved to expunge the *Episcopi* tradition and form ranks behind the *Malleus* tradition, we observe a marked intensification of Catholic witch hunting. In contrast, regions like Württemberg went far toward making the *Episcopi* tradition into orthodoxy. Such territories did not need to become skeptical or rationalist in their understanding of the world before they brought large witch trials to an end. They already had a tradition on which to draw to explain why the large witch hunt was not a wise or appropriate response to misfortune. This kind of moderation, of course, did not uproot all witch trials, and we find a series of small trials stretching to the mid-eighteenth century, trials no doubt approved by many exponents of the moderate, *Episcopi* tradition.

This observation regarding small trials brings up again the distinction that we have repeatedly found so significant for an understanding of witch panic at its worst. Large panic trials were basically different from the smaller trials in that they depended on masses of denunciations whose truth was hardly doubted. As a series of witch trials progressed, the typical stereotype of the old woman, living a solitary and eccentric existence, usually began to break down. As witches were tortured into denouncing others whom they had seen at the sabbath, age and sex barriers crumbled until anyone, even the magistrates, could be accused of witchcraft. This progress toward anarchy corrected itself by controls within society in every large hunt known in the German Southwest. Not the Swedes, but a crisis of confidence in the judicial procedures, brought panic to a halt. We found signs of this crisis in the statements of magistrates as well as from members of the populace who came to realize that if the law were given free rein, no one would be safe from its relentless grasp. We suggested that this crisis was especially evident where stereotypes broke down most completely. Thus Rottenburg, which hunted only older women as witches for 30 years, seems to have experienced no real crisis of confidence until the first decades of the seventeenth century, significantly after men and high officials came to be suspected and even convicted of witchcraft.

The climax seems to have come between 1627 and 1631 in the wake of a terrible plague. The lesson learned in those panics may have provided immunity from witch trials after the even more destructive plagues of 1633–35. The fact that the war was by then being fought all over the German Southwest may even have given the common people a new target for their hatred, the soldier, who for some years took the blame previously heaped on old women. Whenever the crisis did come, people seem to have found their own diverse theological traditions rich enough to provide new answers to the old problems. There was no sudden burst of rationalism, no birth of the critical Enlightenment in the villages, unless perhaps a more moderate, Job-oriented theological tradition can be called enlightened. After the great hunts passed in 1666, therefore, small trials of the traditional scapegoat, old and unattached women, could persist despite the new-found abhorrence of severe witch panic. Only the analysis of the large trial as a special type and of the ways that stereotypes broke down exposes these complex dynamics of action and emotion under stress.

Finally, this study underlines the ambiguity of the charge that certain classes of people were especially singled out as victims. It is of course true that midwives and tavernkeepers were common targets. It is hard to find a common implication or thrust in the attack on these two groups. In general it may be said that the first persons attacked for witchcraft were the most suspect elements of society, including widows, spinsters, and midwives. But as soon as a large trial got under way, the most vulnerable targets were the better known elements of society, like tavernkeepers and other wealthy men or their wives. Since formal proceedings depended on the agreement usually of three or even five denunciations, it was inevitable that the more socially prominent would play a large role in most trials for which documentation is available. Analysis of confiscation records makes this clear, but also reveals that the wealthy were not taxed more severely than other classes. At Mergentheim and Ellwangen, on the average, "confiscation" usually amounted to 10 or 15 percent of a man's property—certainly less "confiscatory" than many modern inheritance taxes. When unjust economic motives did come into play, we usually hear of it in protests that even led to the prohibition of such abuses. The new alchemy that changed blood into gold and silver was, therefore, probably neither as widespread nor generally as severe as modern critics have assumed.

Turning briefly to the larger social question of function, we can concede that the small trials may indeed have served a function, delineating the social thresholds of eccentricity tolerable to society, and registering fear of a socially indigestible group, unmarried women. This seems especially likely if it turns out that the sixteenth century really did see the beginning of a new marriage pattern that left many more women unmarried than had ever been the case before. Until single women found a more comfortable place in the concepts and communities of Western men, one could argue that they were a socially disruptive element, at least when they lived without family and without patriarchal control. In this restricted sense the small witch trial may have even been therapeutic, or functional. In its larger form, however, these panics were clearly dysfunctional. They produced fear rather than dissipating it; they increased social tensions rather than relieving or purging them. These large trials involving hundreds of denunciations came to be feared, attacked, and distrusted generally. When communities recognized that torture might be more a battle of nerves than a struggle with the devil, and when courts began to grasp that persons under torture might invent thoroughly consistent stories to escape further anguish, a link in the old system was gone.

The crisis of confidence in judicial procedures may have forced men to search their traditions for a new understanding of the interrelations of God, the devil, and the world. Only rarely did such reevaluation produce a genuine disbelief in the devil or a denial of witchcraft. We know of no such denials in the German Southwest. Men had lost instead the ability accurately to detect witches. From their own experience men had learned that the attempt to purge the body politic was not worth the agony that resulted. In this tormented way the West took a crucial step toward disenchantment.

Appendix

Appendix

Witch Trials in the German Southwest

The Appendix lists chronologically all of the Southwest German witch hunts that I have discovered either in the secondary literature or in archival collections. The list is fairly complete and exhaustive for the secondary literature, but is highly arbitrary in the treatment of archival materials. The old state of Württemberg is particularly well represented. Despite these imbalances, however, the list does provide a preliminary indication of what sorts of witch trials were conducted in southwestern Germany.

A few remarks on the meaning of various entries are necessary. With regard to the "number involved," I have attempted to give rough estimates of the numbers of persons executed or tried, when the source permitted. Often, however, the source said simply that "several" or "many" persons were involved. I have transmitted this ambiguity through the use of two signs, * and **. In compiling Tables 1 and 2 from this Appendix, I have been concerned to establish absolute minimum figures for numbers of persons tried or executed. I have, therefore, interpreted "several" and "many" as "three" in every case. Where no indication of result was evident, I have simply recorded a question mark.

The confession, Catholic or Protestant, of a territory or city is in every case the official confession, the one sanctioned by the ruler or magistracy. In a few cases, this method breaks down. Parity cities, for example, allowed both Catholic and Protestant confessions to exist. Such cases have been labeled "Par." In some other cases, a Protestant ruler governed a Catholic land with no attempt to change the religion of the land. In such cases, I have labeled the confession "P-C." For the reverse situation of Catholic rule or force governing a Protestant land, I have used "C-P."

The sources cited are often only the major reference to a series of trials, rather than a list of all of the literature in which the trials are mentioned. In most cases the author's name and page number are a sufficient reference to the work, cited in full in the Bibliography. In some cases, however, special abbreviations have been employed.

The following summary of symbols for confessions and unknown numbers may be helpful:

C	Catholic
P	Protestant
Par	Parity: both Catholic and Protestant
P-C	Protestant ruler governing a Catholic land
C-P	Catholic ruler governing a Protestant land
*	"Several"
**	"Many"

The following abbreviations and short forms are used in the sources column. For full publication data on works cited in short form, see the Bibliography.

Burkarth	"Hexenprozesse in Hohenzollern." Includes a list of all witch trials on pp. 16–21.
Crusius	*Schwäbische Chronik.*
Dengler	"Das Hexenwesen im Stifte Obermarchtal." Includes a list of 80 persons tried for witchcraft.
Diefenbach	*Der Hexenwahn.*
DvS	*Diözesanarchiv von Schwaben, 1884–1912.*
FDA	*Freiburger Diözesan-Archiv, 1865– .*
GLAK	Baden, Generallandesarchiv Karlsruhe.
GSS	*Geschichte der Stadt Stuttgart.*
HSASt	Württemberg, Hauptstaatsarchiv Stuttgart.
LBSt	Württemberg, Landesbibliothek Stuttgart.
OAB	*Beschreibung der württembergischen Oberämter.*
Riezler	*Geschichte der Hexenprozesse in Bayern.* Includes a list of witch trials mostly from southern Germany and Austria on pp. 141–46.
SASigm	Württemberg, Staatsarchiv Sigmaringen.
Schreiber	*Die Hexenprozesse.*
Soldan-Heppe	*Geschichte der Hexenprozesse.*
Tirol LA	Tirol, Landesregierungsarchiv Innsbruck.
UATüb	Tübingen Universität, Universitätsarchiv.
Willburger	"Hexenverfolgung in Württemberg."
WKG	*Württembergische Kirchengeschichte.*
WSAL	Württemberg, Staatsarchiv Ludwigsburg.
WVLG	*Württembergische Vierteljahrshefte für Landesgeschichte, 1878–1936.*
ZC	K. A. Barack, ed., *Zimmerische Chronik.*

Date, place, and confession	Number involved		Source
	Suspected	Executed	
1300. Freiburg (C)	1	?	Vierordt II, 118
1432. Constance (C)	1	1	A. Rapp (1935)
1446–47. Heidelberg (C)		*	Vierordt II, 118
1450. Ettenheim (C)	1	?	Hansen, *Quellen*, 555
1453. Constance (C)		*	Vierordt II, 118
1458. Constance (C)		*	*Ibid.*
1476. Diersburg (C)		2	Kähni (1964), 33
1480's			
Königsheim (C)		?	Riezler, 94–95; Müller (1910), 397
Waldshut (C)		?	*Ibid.*
Breisach		?	*Ibid.*
Fürstenberg (C)		?	*Ibid.*
1482–86. Constance & Ravensberg (C)		48	*Malleus Maleficarum* II, Q.1, c.4
1484–89. Ravensberg (C)	6	0	Müller (1910), 397, 407–8
1485. Röthenbach (C)	1	0	Riezler
1486. Triersberg (C)	1	?	FDA (1882), 95 *et seq.*
1491			
Veringen (C)		1	Burkarth, p. 14
Pforzheim (C)		?	Vierordt II, 120
1493. Constance (C)	1	0	*Ibid.*, p. 119
1495. Stein a. R. (C)	1	0	Tüchle II, 307
1504. Bretten (C)		*	Vierordt II, 121
1505. Tübingen (C)		1	Plantsch; Crusius II, 163
1507. Ringingen (C)		?	Tüchle II, 307
1507–8. Blaubeuren (C)	2	1	Sauter, 37–38; Soldan-Heppe I, 460
1508. Saulgau (C)		*	Mehrle, 93; Vochezer II, 255
1509. Brackenheim (C)	1	0	Demarce, 79
1510. Villingen (C)		?	A. Rapp (1935)
1512. Pforzheim (C)		?	Riezler; Vierordt II, 120
1517. Pforzheim (C)		?	*Ibid.*
1515–18. Ellwangen (C)	2	2	*Hillersche Chronik* 541
1518. Waldsee (C)		1	Willburger, 137; *WKG* 238
1524. Pforzheim (C)		?	Riezler; Vierordt II, 120
1527. Stuttgart (C)	1	0	Gehring; *GSS*, 19
1528			
Ellwangen (C)	1	?	WSAL B412/52; B412/79
Rottenburg (C)		1	*OAB Rottenburg* I, 412
1530. Rottenburg (C)	5	3	*Ibid.*
1531–33. Pforzheim (C)		?	Riezler; Vierordt II, 120
1532. Grossbottwar (C)	1	1	Bossert (1948), 11–14
1533			
Oberndorf (C)	1	1	Mayer, 73; *ZC* III, 80
Schiltach (C)	1	1	Crusius, II, 236; Vierordt II, 124; *ZC* III, 1–4; Bonnekamp, 16

Date, place, and confession	Number involved		Source
	Suspected	Executed	
1533 (*continued*)			
Hechingen (C)	1	1	*ZC* IV, 311; Speidel, 225; Bonne-kamp, 16, 78
1538			
Ulm (P)	1	0	Schilling, 137
Gundelfingen (C)		?	Riezler
1539			
Mergentheim (C)	3	?	WSAL B262/2&7
Schw. Hall (P)	*	?	Willburger; Brenz, *Ein Predigt von dem Hagel*
1540ff. Ensisheim (C)		**	Vierordt II, 124
1540–57. Renchen (C)		**	GLAK 169/285–87
1542. Weissenhorn (C)		?	Riezler
1546			
Esslingen (P)		2	Reuss, 147
Freiburg (C)		1	Vierordt II, 125; Schreiber, 13–15; Janssen VIII, 681
1547–55. Constance (P&C)		7	Vierordt II, 123
1549. Dornstetten (P)		1	Crusius II, 275
1551. Esslingen (P)	2	1	Willburger, 138; Diefenbach, 90–93
1552			
Crailsheim (P)		1	Schumm, 308
Oberkirch (C)	1	0	GLAK 169/270
1553. Waldangelloch (C)		?	GLAK 61/14877
1556. Hohebach (P)		?	Eyth, 106; *OAB Künzelsau*, 742
1557			
Ortenau (C)	2	2	Volk 5–6, 7, 23; GLAK 119/830
Zell a. H. (C)		1	A. Rapp (1935)
1558. Waldangelloch (C)		?	GLAK 61/14878
1559			
Heilbronn (P)	1	1	Dürr, 129
Horb (C)	1	2	Giefel, 91
1560. Horb (C)	1	0	*Ibid.*; HSASt B46/2
1561			
Wertheim (P)		8	A. Rapp (1935)
Esslingen (P)		?	Diefenbach, 91 n.2
Oberkirch (C)	1	0	GLAK 169/274
Rottweil (C)		1	Ruckgaber, 183
1562			
Prechtal (C)	1	0	Vierordt II, 125
Hochberg (P)		1	*Ibid.*, 123
Stuttgart (P)		11	*GSS*, 19; Landenberger, 11–12
Haslach (C)		?	Riezler
Esslingen (P)	3	0	Pfaff (1856), 258–59
Böblingen (P)		1	Schön, 107–8
Sindelfingen (P)	3	2	Weisert, 119

Date, place, and confession	Number involved		Source
	Suspected	Executed	
1562–63			
Wiesensteig (P)		63	Crusius II, 304; *Warhafftige* (1563); Diefenbach, 91
Mergentheim (C)	1	?	WSAL B262/42
1562–65. Cannstatt (P)	*	?	WSAL A209
1563			
Esslingen (P)	3	1	Pfaff (1856), 268–71
Gemmingen (C)		1	B. Schwarz, 1, 108
Böblingen (P)		3	Schön, 107–8
Sindelfingen (P)	1	?	*Ibid.*
Cannstatt (P)	1	?	WSAL A209
1564			
Horb (C)	4	1	Giefel, 91; HSASt B46/3
Wolfach (C)	1	1	Disch, 377–78
Grünmettstetten (C)	2	1	Willburger, 138
1566. Rottweil (C)		1	Ruckgaber, 183
1569			
Appenweyer (C)	5	3	Volk, 8–9
Ortenau (C)	2	?	GLAK 119/830
1570			
Markgräflerland (C)		?	A. Rapp (1935)
Villingen (C)		?	*Ibid.*
Badenweiler (P)		1	Vierordt II, 123
Unlingen (C)		*	Mehrle, 93 n.214; Vochezer III, 5
Ellwangen (C)		1	Willburger, 138
1571. Bildechingen (C)	1	0	Giefel, 91; HSASt B46/3
1572			
Rottweil (C)	2	2	Ruckgaber, 184, 191
Baden (town) (C)		2	Vierordt II, 51–52; Schott, 214
Baden-Baden (Margravate) (C)		4	Vierordt II, 51; Duhr I, 752
Schillberg (C)		?	Vierordt II, 51
Breisgau (C)	1	?	GLAK 79/3388
1573			
Gengenbach (C)	10	7	Hellinger, 390–94
Rotweil (Kaiserstuhl) (C)		2	Heilig, 416–18
Wolfach (C)	6	5	Disch, 377–78
Ortenberg (C)		1	Volk, 9; GLAK 119/830
Ersingen & Bilfingen (C)		*	Janssen VIII, 681; Pflüger, 212
Harmersbach (C)	1	?	GLAK 229/38630–38885
1574			
Bühl (C)		3	Kähni (1964), 28
Schw. Hall (P)	1	1	German, 250
Rottweil (C)		2	Ruckgaber, 191
Stuttgart (P)		1	R. Roth, 295
Ortenberg (C)		1	Volk, 9

Date, place, and confession	Number involved		Source
	Suspected	Executed	
1574–78. Überlingen (C)	8	8	Harzendorf, 110
1575			
Ortenau (C)		3	Volk, 9–10, 23; GLAK 119/830
Heilbronn (P)		1?	Dürr, 129
Rottweil (C)		1	Ruckgaber, 191
Memmingen (P)		10	Riezler; Baumann III
Wurzach (C)		16	Vochezer III, 477; Mehrle, 93
Mergentheim (C)	1	?	WSAL B262/43
1576			
Wurzach (C)		16	Vochezer III, 477; Mehrle, 93
Ersingen & Bilfingen (C)		*	Janssen VIII, 681; Pflüger, 212
Waldkirch (C)	10	6	*Newezeitung . . . 55 unhulden* (1576)
Eltzach (C)		14	*Ibid.*
Bürgach (C)		8	*Ibid.*
Wezelberg (C)		6	*Ibid.*
Sarna (C)		8	*Ibid.*
Falckenburg (C)		5	*Ibid.*
Stauffach (C)		5	*Newe Zeittung . . . 136. Unholden* (1576)
Spalt (C)		1	*Ibid.*
Bingach (C)		6	*Ibid.*
Endingen (C)		3	*Ibid.*
Cussach (C)		3	*Ibid.*
Rossach (C)		4	*Ibid.*
Rottweil (C)		**	*Ibid.*
Baden (mgf) (C)		2	*Ibid.*
Gersbach (C)		5	*Ibid.*; cf. also Janssen VIII, 680–81; Weller, *Annalen* 1, Abt. 2, 244
Hohenzollern (C)		1	Burkarth, 16–21
Breisgau (C)		1	GLAK 79/3389
1576–80			
Baden (town) (C)		4	Vierordt II, 125
Ettlingen (C)		1	*Ibid.*
1577			
Ersingen & Bilfingen (C)		*	Janssen VIII, 681; Pflüger, 212
Horb (C)		9	R. Roth, 295
Rottweil (C)		2	Ruckgaber, 191–92
1578			
Horb (C)		9	*Warhafftige* (1578), Crusius II, 339; Vierordt II, 125
Rottenburg (C)		7	*Warhafftige* (1578)
Uffburgk (C)		6	*Ibid.*
Allgäu et al. (C)		40+	*Ibid.*

Date, place, and confession	Number involved		Source
	Suspected	Executed	
1579			
Baden-Durlach (P)		3	Vierordt II, 123
Rottweil (C)		1	Ruckgaber, 192
Waldshut (C)		?	A. Rapp (1935)
Freiburg (C)		3	Vierordt II, 126; Riezler; Geiges, 44–45
Reichenau (C)		?	GLAK 96/436–39
Breisgau (C)		?	GLAK 79/3387, 3388
Schwaben (Habsburg) (C)		?	GLAK 65/728
1579–80			
Beuren (C)	1	?	Steigelmann, 53–54, 57
Ailringen (C)	*	?	*OAB Künzelsau*, 329
1580			
Wurzach (C)		9	Mehrle, 93 n.214; Vochezer III, 504
Rottweil C)		30?	Ruckgaber, 188–92; *Newe Zeitung* (1580)
Wangen (C)		9	*Newe Zeitung* (1580)
Horb & Rottenburg (C)		9	*Ibid.*
Rastatt (C)		7	*Ibid.*
Baden (C)		5	*Ibid.*
Füssach & Wolfach (C)		11	*Ibid.*
Constance (C)		2	*Ibid.*
Überlingen (C)		3	*Ibid.*
Kuppenheim (C)		6	*Ibid.*
Wantzenau (C)	5	4	*Ibid.*
Burgau (C)		6	*Ibid.*
Breisgau (C)		?	GLAK 79/3387
Leutkirch (P)		4	*Newe Zeitung* (1580)
Isny (P)		3	*Ibid.*
Biberach (Par)		5	*Ibid.*
1580. Heiligkreuztal (C)		1	Willburger
1581			
Rottweil (C)		9	Ruckgaber, 192
Waldsee (C)		9	Willburger, 138; Janssen VIII, 682; Vochezer III, 513; *WKG*, 475
Obermarchtal (C)		1	Dengler
1582			
Rottenburg (C)		8?	Crusius II, 350–51
Niedernhall (P)	1	?	*OAB Künzelsau*, 742
Reute (Waldkirch) (C)		38	Riezler, 145
Freiburg (C)		3	Vierordt II, 126
Mergentheim (C)	1	?	WSAL B262/44
Breisgau (C)	5	?	GLAK 79/3387, 3388
1583			
Rottenburg (C)		12	Crusius II, 353; Westenhoeffer, 87

Date, place, and confession	Number involved		Source
	Suspected	Executed	
1583 (*continued*)			
Horb (C)		13	*Ibid.*
Rottweil (C)		6	Ruckgaber, 192
Wiesensteig (C)		25	Crusius II, 354
Hechingen (C)		15	*Ibid.*
Breisgau (C)	2	?	GLAK 79/3387
Hohenzollern (C)		1	Burkarth, 16
1584			
Schwaben (Habsburg) (C)		5	GLAK 65/728
Mergentheim (C)	*	?	WSAL B262/46
Breisgau (C)		?	GLAK 79/3388
1585			
Waldsee (C)		7	Vochezer III, 513
Rottenburg (C)		9	Crusius II, 359; Günther, 9; West-enhoeffer, 87
Rottweil (C)		2	Ruckgaber, 192
Schwaben (Habsburg) (C)		?	GLAK 65/728
1586			
Offenburg (C)	1	0	Volk, 32
Waldsee (C)		16	Vochezer III, 513; Mehrle, 93 n.214
Heilbronn (P)		1	*WKG*, 407; Dürr, 129
Mergentheim (C)		*	WSAL B262/45
Schwaben (Habsburg) (C)		?	GLAK 65/728
Breisgau (C)		1	GLAK 79/3387
Obermarchtal (C)		22	Dengler; *OAB Riedlingen*, 458; *OAB Ehingen* I, 265; *WKG*, 414
1587			
Obermarchtal (C)		25	Dengler
Riedlingen (C)		2	Willburger, 138
Forbach (C)		?	Riezler, 145
Wolfach (C)		1	Disch, 377–78
Ortenau (C)		2	GLAK 119/830
Ettingen (C)		1	Tirol LA A/XVI/4
Unlingen (C)		**	Willburger, 138; *DvS* (1899), 139
Schwaben (Habsburg) (C)		15	GLAK 65/728
1586–87. Mergentheim (C)		7	WSAL B262/48
1588			
Hecklingen (C)	1	0	Schott, 220
Neuenburg (Rhein)	4	0	Schott, 221
Rottweil (C)		1	Ruckgaber, 192
Hohenzollern (C)	3	1	Burkarth
Ellwangen (C)		?	WSAL B412/53
Obermarchtal (C)		6	Dengler

Date, place, and confession	Number involved		Source
	Suspected	Executed	
1589			
Rottweil (C)		2	Ruckgaber, 192–93
Horb (C)		5	Crusius II, 378
Bernau ? (C)		17	*Ibid.*
Balingen (P)		*	Crusius II, 419
Giengen (P)		1	*WKG*, 463–64
Schömberg (C)		*	Willburger, 138; Sauter, 14; Crusius II, 419
Biberach (Par)		?	Riezler
Reutlingen (P)		1	Honecker, 11
Cannstatt (P)	1	?	WSAL A209
Hirsau (P)	*	?	*Ibid.*
Bebenhausen (P)	1	?	*Ibid.*
Breisgau (C)	2	?	GLAK 79/3387, 3388, 3390
Hohenzollern (C)	3	3	Burkarth, 16–21
Mergentheim (C)		?	WSAL B262/47
Obermarchtal (C)		1	Dengler
1589–90. Sindelfingen (P)		3	Weisert, 120
1589–92. Mergentheim (C)		**	WSAL B262/49–60
1589–95. Lauffen (P)	2	?	WSAL A209/1424
1590			
Kirchheim u. T. (P)		1	Mayer, 76
Rottenburg (C)		3	*OAB Rottenburg*, 413; Hassler, 141
Stuttgart (P)	1	0	*GSS*, 19
Wolfach (C)	?	?	Disch, 377–78
Heinsheim (P)		1	Neuwirth
Gengenbach (C)		1	Hellinger, 395
Sindelfingen (P)	1	0	Weisert, 120
Homburg (C)		?	Riezler, 145
Memmingen (P)		**	*Ibid.*
Schwaben (Habsburg) (C)	2	?	GLAK 65/728
Breisgau (C)	2	?	GLAK 79/3388
Obermarchtal (C)		3	Dengler
Böblingen (P)		3	Schön, 135–36
1590–93. Freudenberg (P)	10	9	Diefenbach, 12–20
1590–94. Nördlingen (P)		35	Willburger, 168; Janssen VIII, 718
1591			
Böblingen (P)		1	Schön, 135–36
Calw (P)	1	0	WSAL A209
Niederstetten (P)		1	Walcher, 345; *WVLG* (1892); Willburger, 139
Baden-Durlach (P)	1	?	A. Ludwig, 64
Öttingen-Wallerstein (C)		22	Schumm, 308
Schw. Hall (P)		1	German 251
Rottweil (C)		1	Ruckgaber, 193

Date, place, and confession	Number involved		Source
	Suspected	Executed	
1591 (*continued*)			
Riedlingen (C)		1	Willburger, 138
Biberach (Par)	3	?	GLAK 65/728
1592			
Ingelfingen (P)		14	Willburger, 139
Breisgau (C)	1	?	GLAK 79/3387
Schwaben (Habsburg) (C)	3	?	GLAK 65/728
Obermarchtal (C)		3	Dengler, SASigm 30/6/254
1592–93			
Niedernhall (P)		3	*Festschrift* 52
Reichenbach (P)	4	1	WSAL A209
1593			
Wolfach (C)		2	Disch, 377–78
Wallerstein (C)		?	Riezler
Oberndorf (C)	10+	?	GLAK 65/728
Obermarchtal (C)		4	Dengler
1594			
Schorndorf (P)	1	?	WSAL A209
Gaildorf (P)		2	*WKG* 466
Heilbronn (P)		2	*WKG* 463; Dürr, 129
Crailsheim (P)	9	4	Schumm, 308
1594–95. Sachsenheim (P)	1	?	WSAL A209
1594–97. Überlingen (C)		6	Harzendorf, 110
1594–1619. Cannstatt (P)	1	?	WSAL A209
1594–1618. Calw (P)	1	?	*Ibid.*
1595			
Ortenau (C)		7	Volk, 10–13; GLAK 119/830
Reutlingen (P)		5	Honecker, 11
Rottenburg (C)		6	Birlinger I, 132–52
Brackenheim (P)		1	WSAL A209
Breisgau (C)	1	?	GLAK 79/3387
Weil der Stadt (C)		1	Schön, 135–36
1596			
Rottenburg (C)		36	Birlinger I, 132–52; Crusius, *Diarium* I, 89, 103, 135
Kenzingen (C)		12–13	A. Ludwig, 55
Endingen (C)		4	*Ibid.*
Trochtelfingen (C)		13	Burkarth
Ortenberg (C)		2	Volk, 14–15; GLAK 119/830, 1108
Sulz (P)		5	Willburger, 139
Esslingen (P)	1	0	Pfaff (1856), 285–86
Böblingen (P)	3	?	Weisert, 120–21; WSAL A209
Riedlingen (C)		1	Willburger, 138

| Date, place, and confession | Number involved | | Source |
	Suspected	Executed	
Rammersweier (C)		?	Kähni (1964), 98
Obermarchtal (C)		1	Dengler
1597			
Sulz (P)	1	1	WSAL A209; Willburger, 139
Vöhringen (C)		1	Willburger, 139
Boll (P)		1	*Ibid.*
Wolfach (C)	1	0	Disch, 379
Schwaben (Habsburg) (C)	1	?	GLAK 65/728
Brackenheim? (P)	1	?	UATüb. 85/2
1597–99. Offenburg (C)	6	4	Volk, 32
1598			
Hohenzollern (C)	17	11+	Burkarth
Schiltach (C)		2	Mayer, 73
Rottenburg (C)		1	Willburger, 139
Sulz (P)		1	*Ibid.*
Wolfach (C)		15+	Disch, 379
Haigerloch (C)		1	Hodler, 303; Schnell, 91
Cannstatt (P)	1	?	WSAL A209
Herrenalb (P)	1	?	*Ibid.*
1598–1600. Balingen (P)	1	0	*Ibid.*; Seeger, 94–95
1598–1607. Alpirsbach (P)	1	?	WSAL A209
1599			
Rottenburg (C)		10	Birlinger I, 132–52
Gengenbach (C)	*	?	Hellinger, 80
Ortenau (C)		6	Volk, 15; GLAK 119/830
Freiburg i. Br. (C)		18	Janssen VIII, 681; Schreiber, 43 *et seq.*; Vierordt II, 126
Horb (C)	2	1	Giefel, 91
Rammersweier (C)		?	Kähni (1964), 98
Beilstein (P)	1	?	WSAL A209
Breisgau (C)	6+	?	GLAK 79/3387, 3388
1600			
Württemberg (P)	2	0	Seeger, 31
Wurzach (C)	5	4	Mehrle, 95
Offenburg (C)	2	0	Volk, 33–34
Oberndorf a. N. (C)		7	Köhler (1836), 165
Rottenburg (C)		17	Birlinger I, 132–52
Sulz (P)		?	Willburger, 139
Dornstetten (P)	1	?	WSAL A209
1600–1602. Mergentheim (C)	**	?	WSAL B262/61–64
Ca. 1601–4			
Lauda (P)		*	Vierordt II, 127, cf. p. 72
Marbach (P)		*	*Ibid.*
Krautheim (P)		*	*Ibid.*
Königshofen (P)		7	*Ibid.*
Ca. 1601. Breisgau? (C)	2	?	Schott, 225

Date, place, and confession	Number involved		Source
	Suspected	Executed	
1601			
Beilstein (P)	1	0	WSAL A209
Rottenburg (C)		15	Crusius, *Diarium* III, 305, 334
Offenburg (C)	5	3	Volk, 34–41
Mönsheim (P)	1	?	Hoffmann, 181
Sulz (P)		11	Willburger, 139
Schw. Gmünd (C)	2	?	HSASt B177/122 no. 7
Breisgau (C)	3	?	GLAK 79/3387, 3390
1602			
Offenburg (C)	1	0	Kohler, 218–24
Rottenburg (C)		1	*OAB Rottenburg*, 414
Esslingen (P)	1	0	Riezler, 144; Pfaff (1856), 286
Breisgau (C)	5	?	GLAK 79/3390
Böblingen (P)	1	?	WSAL A209
Neuenstadt (P)	1	?	UATüb. 84/1:13–15
Waiblingen (P)	1	?	UATüb. 84/1:15–18
1603			
Freiburg (C)		13	Vierordt II, 126; Geiges, 44–45
Breisgau (C)	3+	?	GLAK 79/3387
Ortenau (C)		?	GLAK 119/834
Hohenzollern (C)		1	Burkarth; Hodler, 303; Schnell, 90
Rottenburg (C)		6	Crusius, *Diarium* III, 614
Freudenstadt (P)		2	Eimer, 91–92; *WVLG* (1886)
Lauda (P)		1	Rommel (1938–39)
Ortenberg (C)		2	Volk, 16
Offenburg (C)		2	Volk, 52–53
Reutlingen (P)		3	Honecker, 11
Wollbach (P)		1	A. Ludwig, 55–56
Sulz (P)	2	1	Willburger, 139
Beilstein (P)	1	?	UATüb. 84/1:300–301
Schorndorf (P)	1	?	UATüb. 84/1:303–4
Kirchheim? (P)	1	?	UATüb. 84/1:226–27
Stuttgart (P)	1	?	UATüb. 84/1:311
Rosenfeld (P)		*	WSAL A209
1604			
Esslingen (P)	1	0	Riezler, 144; Pfaff (1856), 288
Gengenbach (C)	1	?	Hellinger, 86–88
Offenburg (C)		1	Volk, 53–54
Sulz (P)		?	Willburger, 139
Dornstetten (P)	1	?	WSAL A209
Hohenzollern (C)		2	Burkarth
Ca. 1604. Helfenstein (C)		14	D. Meder, 36[r–v]
1604–5			
Mergentheim (C)		?	WSAL B262/65
Brackenheim (P)	1	?	WSAL A209

Date, place, and confession	Number involved		Source
	Suspected	Executed	
1605			
Waldsee (C)		**	*WKG* 475
Urach (P)		?	*WKG* 452
Sulz (P)		?	Willburger, 140
Horb (C)		16	Crusius, *Diarium* III, 768
Rottenburg (C)		6	Crusius, *Diarium* III, 769
Lichtenau (P)	1	0	Lauppe, 106
Schorndorf? (P)	1	?	UATüb. 84/1:501–6, 517–18
Gröningen (P)	1	?	WSAL A209
Besigheim (P)	1	?	*Ibid.*
1606			
Oberndorf a. N. (C)	2	?	Köhler (1836), 167
Schwaben (Habsburg) (C)	*	?	GLAK 65/728
Wildberg (P)	1	?	UATüb. 84/1:794–96
Stuttgart (P)	1	1	UATüb. 84/1:849–51
1607			
Stuttgart (P)	1	?	UATüb. 84/1:958–61
Tübingen (P)	1	?	UATüb. 84/1:972–74
Dornhan (P)	1	?	UATüb. 84/2:11–12
1607–9. Urach (P)	1	?	WSAL A209
1608			
Offenburg (C)	16	11–14	Vierordt II, 126; Volk, 53–54
Weingarten (C)		?	Willburger, 140
Dornhan (P)		6	UATüb. 84/2:134; WSAL A209
Heidenheim (P)		*	UATüb. 84/2:82, 125; WSAL A209
Sindelfingen (P)	1	?	WSAL A209
1608–10. Überlingen (C)		4	Harzendorf, 110
1609			
Oberndorf a. N. (C)		21	Köhler (1836), 166
Rottenburg (C)		4	*WKG* 722; Birlinger I, 152–57
Sindelfingen (P)	7	4	Weisert, 121–26
Breisgau (C)	1	?	GLAK 79/3390
Herrenberg (P)	1	?	UATüb. 84/2:243
Stuttgart (P)	1	?	UATüb. 84/2:244
Sindelfingen (P)	1	?	UATüb. 84/2:214–15
Vaihingen (P)	1	?	UATüb. 84/2:192–93
Böblingen (P)	2	?	WSAL A209
1610			
Heilbronn (P)	2	1	Dürr, 141
Erlach (P-C)		*	Börsig, 76
Urach (P)	5	3	Willburger, 140; UATüb. 84/2:284–85, 289
Backnang (P)	3	1	UATüb. 84/2:275
Breisgau (C)	8+	?	GLAK 79/3390
Hohenzollern (C)		8	Burkarth

Date, place, and confession	Number involved		Source
	Suspected	Executed	
1610–11. Heilbronn (P)		3	*WKG* 463; Willburger, 140
1611			
Breisgau (C)	2	?	GLAK 79/3390
Hohenzollern (C)		1	Burkarth
Wiesensteig (C)		4	GLAK 65/728
Sindelfingen (P)	1	0	Weisert, 128
Lohr (C)		15	Rommel, 13
Heilbronn (P)		1	Dürr, 142; UATüb. 84/3:15–19
Gaildorf (P)		4	*WKG* 466
Dornstetten (P)	1	?	WSAL A209
Asperg (P)	1	?	*Ibid.*; UATüb. 84/3:31–32
Sundelfingen (P)	1	?	UATüb. 84/3:34–36
Hornberg? (P)		1	UATüb. 84/3:44–45
Heidenheim (P)	2	?	UATüb. 84/3:55
Beilstein? (P)	1	?	UATüb. 84/2:327
Leonberg (P)	1	?	UATüb. 84/2:333–35
Ellwangen (C)		Ca. 100	WSAL B412; Janssen VIII, 680; Zeller, 87; Duhr II, ii, 486f
1612			
Ellwangen (C)		Ca. 160	*Ibid.*
Gaildorf (P)		6	*WKG* 466
Niedernhall (P)	1	?	*OAB Künzelsau*, 742
Ulm (P)		1	Sauter, 12
Esslingen (P)	1	0	Pfaff (1856), 289
Breisgau (C)	4	?	GLAK 79/3390
Kirchheim? (P)	1	?	UATüb. 84/3:134
Urach (P)	1	?	UATüb. 84/3:142–43
Stuttgart (P)	1	?	UATüb. 84/3:144–45
Bietigheim? (P)	3	?	UATüb. 84/3:162–63
Leonberg (P)	2	?	UATüb. 84/3:122
Neuffen (P)	2	?	WSAL A209
1613			
Ellwangen (C)		Ca. 50	WSAL B412; Janssen VIII, 680; Zeller, 87; Duhr II, ii, 486f
Wolfach (C)		8+	Disch, 379
Aalen (P)		?	Zeller, 88; Klaus, 15
Heilbronn (P)		1	Dürr, 143–44
Rottenburg (C)	**	0	*OAB Rottenburg*, 414
Niedernhall (P)		2	*OAB Künzelsau*, 742
Burkheim (Habsburg) (C)		7	Vierordt II, 126
Oehringen (P)		*	Willburger, 140; Bacmeister, 182–92
Hüfingen (C)		*	Strukat, 139
Ochsenhausen (C)	3	?	Willburger, 140; Janssen VIII, 723–24
Freiburg (C)	1	0	Janssen VIII, 681 n. 2

Date, place, and confession	Number involved		Source
	Suspected	Executed	
Ulm (P)		1	Willburger, 140; *WKG* 464; Schilling, 138
Schw. Gmünd (C)		11	HSASt B177/122; Zeller, 88; Klaus (1902), 15; *WKG* 475; *1962 Schw. Gmünd*, 45
Gaildorf (P)		1	*WKG* 466
Ettenheim (C)		3	Rest, 44–45; GLAK 169/288
Schwaben (Habsburg) (C)	1	?	GLAK 65/728
Schliengen (C)	*	?	GLAK 176
Oberkirch (P-C)	3	?	GLAK 169/288
Breisgau (C)	2	?	GLAK 79/3390
Tübingen (P)	1	?	UATüb. 84/2:170–71
Heilbronn (P)	*	?	UATüb. 84/3:202–4
Güglingen (P)	1	?	WSAL A209
1614			
Kraichgau (Grombach) (P)		1	Vierordt II, 123
Niedernhall (P)		2	*OAB Künzelsau*, 742
Burkheim (C)		1	Heilig, 418
Schw. Gmünd (C)		27	HSASt B177/122; Zeller, 88; Klaus (1902), 15; *WKG* 475; *1962 Schw. Gmünd*, 45
Altensteig (P)	1	?	UATüb. 84/3:362–63
Bottwar (P)	1	?	UATüb. 84/3:345, 359–60; WSAL A209
Brackenheim (P)	*	?	WSAL A209
Heidenheim (P)	1	?	*Ibid.*
Ellwangen (C)		Ca. 27	WSAL B412; Janssen VIII, 680; Zeller, 87; Duhr II, ii, 486f
1615			
Schw. Gmünd (C)		**	HSASt B177/122; Zeller, 88; Klaus (1902), 15; *WKG* 475; *1962 Schw. Gmünd*, 45
Ellwangen (C)		Ca. 33	WSAL B412; Janssen VIII, 680; Zeller, 87; Duhr II, ii, 486f
Wurzach (C)	1	1	Vogel, 19, 73 n. 9; Mehrle, 95
Langenargen (C)		1	Kichler, 97–99
Hohenzollern (C)		5	Schnell, 91; Burkarth
Rottweil (C)		1	Ruckgaber, 195
Haslach (C)	12	10	Göller, 79–80
Mühringen (C)	6	6	H. Günther, 8
Oberndorf (C)		6	Köhler (1836), 167
Brackenheim (P)	2	?	WSAL A209
Böblingen (P)	1	?	*Ibid.*
Backnang (P)	1	?	UATüb. 84/4:27
Leonberg (P)	1	?	UATüb. 84/4:30
Ortenau (C)	2	?	GLAK 119/834

Date, place, and confession	Number involved		Source
	Suspected	Executed	
1615–16			
Leonberg (P)		6	Caspar, 282; UATüb. 84/4:48; WSAL A209, 1054–56
Sindelfingen (P)	19	12	UATüb. 84/4:23; Weisert, 128–31
1615–17. Dornstetten (P)	**	1+	WSAL A209
1615–21. Weil der Stadt (C)	2	1	Willburger, 141
1616			
Württemberg (P)	**	?	Willburger, 140
Ulm (P)		1	Schilling, 138 *et seq.*; *WKG* 464
Ettenheim (C)	1	0	Rest, 44–45
Oberkirch (P-C)	1	0	Rösch, 31–32
Ellwangen (C)		Ca. 13	WSAL B412; Janssen VIII, 680; Zeller, 87; Duhr II, ii, 486f
Saulgau (C)		1	*WKG* 475; Sauter, 23, 35–36
Göppingen (P)	1	?	WSAL A209
Gröningen (P)	1	?	*Ibid.*
Sündelfingen (P)	1	?	UATüb. 84/4:148–49
Tübingen (P)	1	?	UATüb. 84/4:158
Limpurg (P)	1	?	UATüb. 84/4:370–71
Breisgau (C)	5+	?	GLAK 79/3387, 3388, 3390
Hohenzollern (C)	2	2	Burkarth
1616–17			
Freudenberg (C-P)		50+	Vierordt II, 68, 127
Trauchburg (C)		9	Mehrle, 93–96
Schw. Gmünd (C)		?	HSASt B177/122; Zeller, 88; Klaus (1902), 15; *WKG* 475; *1962 Schw. Gmünd*, 45
Mergentheim (C)	5+	?	WSAL B262/66–67
1616–18. Tübingen (P)	1	0	WSAL A209
1617			
Saulgau (C)		1	*WKG* 475; Sauter, 23, 35–36
Hohenzollern (C)	5	5	Burkarth; Schnell, 88–91
Gengenbach (C)	1	0	Hellinger, 90–91
Oberkirch (P-C)	1	?	GLAK 169/289
1617–18. Calw (P)	1	?	WSAL A209
1618			
Ellwangen (C)		Ca. 10	WSAL B412; Janssen VIII, 680; Zeller, 87; Duhr II, ii, 486f
Breisgau (C)	12	?	GLAK 79/3387, 3390
Ettenheim (C)	1	0	Rest, 44–45
Freiburg i. Br. (C)	1	0	Schott, 231
Wimpfen (P)		2	Frohnhäuser
Neibsheim (C)		3	Vierordt II, 126
Lehen (C)		2?	Schreiber (1837), 35–38
Freiburg? (C)		?	Schreiber (1837), 38
Schiltach (C)		1	Mayer, 72

Date, place, and confession	Number involved		Source
	Suspected	Executed	
Dornhan (P)	1	?	WSAL A209
Calw (P)	2	?	*Ibid.*; UATüb. 84/5:15–16
Heidenheim (P)	1	?	UATüb. 84/4:396–97
Wildberg (P)	1	?	UATüb. 84/4:418–19
Stuttgart (P)	1	?	UATüb. 84/4:422
Lauffen (P)	1	?	UATüb. 84/4:442–43
1618–19. Brackenheim (P)	1	?	WSAL A209
1619			
Geroldseck (P)	1	1	Vierordt II, 123; A. Ludwig (1930), 109
Schiltach (C)		4	Mayer, 72
Schorndorf (P)	1	?	UATüb. 84/5:103–4
Urach (P)	1	?	UATüb. 84/5:106–7
Göppingen (P)	1	?	UATüb. 84/5:218–20
Kirchheim (P)	2	?	UATüb. 84/5:269–70
Besigheim (P)	1	?	WSAL A209
Herrenberg (P)	1	?	*Ibid.*
Blaubeuren (P)	1	?	*Ibid.*
1620			
Altensteig (P)	1	0	Willburger (1932), 138; WSAL A209
Oppenau (P-C)	1	0	Rösch, 32
Mergentheim (C)		?	WSAL B262/68
Backnang (P)	1	?	UATüb. 84/5:385–86; WSAL A209
Heidenheim (P)	1	?	WSAL A209
1620–21. Schiltach (C)		1	Mayer, 72–73
1621			
Ulm (P)		1	Schilling, 138 *et seq.*; Haas, 87
Güglingen (P)	1	?	WSAL A209; UATüb. 84/5:462–63
Herrenberg (P)	1	?	WSAL A209
Ebingen (P)	1	?	*Ibid.*
Freudenstadt (P)	1	0	*Ibid.*
Wildberg (P)	1	?	UATüb. 84/5:465
Kleinkems (P)	1	1	A. Ludwig, 73
Horb (C)	6	0	Giefel, 91; WSAL B46/3
Reutlingen (P)		1	Honecker, 11
Sulz (P)		2	Willburger, 141
1622			
Trauchburg (C)	2	1	Mehrle, 96
Mengen (C)	1	?	Bicheler, 79
Ortenau (C)	1	0	Volk, 18, 23–24
Horb (C)	2	1	Willburger, 141; Giefel, 91
Ebingen (P)	1	?	WSAL A209
Gröningen (P)	1	1	*Ibid.*
1623			
Cannstatt (P)	1	?	UATüb. 84/6:264–65

Date, place, and confession	Number involved		Source
	Suspected	Executed	
1623 (*continued*)			
Neuenburg (P)	1	?	UATüb. 84/6:185–86
Göppingen (P)	1	?	WSAL A209
Altensteig (P)	1	?	*Ibid.*
Heidenheim (P)	1	?	*Ibid.*
Ca. 1624			
Kenzingen (C)		*	A. Ludwig, 74
Black Forest (?)		*	*Ibid.*
1624			
Wolfach (C)	1	0	Disch, 379–80
Freiburg (C)		1+	Geilen, 44–45
Buchau (C)		1	Willburger, 141
Güglingen (P)	1	?	WSAL A209
Mergentheim (C)	1	?	WSAL B262/70
1624–26. Ettenheim (C)		Ca. 13	A. Rapp (1935); Rest, 47–49
1625			
Kenzingen (C)		*	Kürzel, 142–44
Hohenzollern (C)		1	Burkarth; Schnell, 90
Langenargen (C)		1	Kichler, 97–99
Sulz (P)		9	Willburger, 141
Tettnang (C)		1	*WKG* 475; G. Schneider, 71
Tübingen (P)	1	?	UATüb. 84/6:626–28
Urach (P)	1	?	UATüb. 84/6:784–85
Altensteig (P)	1	?	WSAL A209
Limpurg (P)	1	?	WSAL B120/Rep. p. 59
1625–26			
Oberkirch (P-C)	5+	?	GLAK 169/290–91
Cannstatt (P)	1	?	WSAL A209
1626			
Werstein (C)	2	1	Schnell, 91; Burkarth
Haigerloch (C)		1	Hodler, 303
Esslingen (P)	1	0	Pfaff, 289–91
Bebenhausen (P)	1	?	WSAL A209
Sulz (P)	1	?	*Ibid.*; UATüb. 84/6:901
Calw (P)	2	?	WSAL A209
Lauffen (P)	1	?	*Ibid.*
Brackenheim (P)	1	?	*Ibid.*
Stuttgart (P)	1	?	UATüb. 84/6:964
1626–28. Sulz (P)	4	*	WSAL A209; UATüb. 84/6:965, 1023–25; Willburger, 141
1626–29. Böblingen (P)	3	?	WSAL A209
1627? Rastatt? (C)		1?	Ruppert, 472
1627			
Hohenzollern (C)	3	3	Burkarth
Offenburg (C)		7	Volk, 58–61
Mühringen (C)		3	H. Günther, 8–9

Date, place, and confession	Number involved		Source
	Suspected	Executed	
Ortenau (C)		4	Volk, 24; GLAK 119/1102, no. 1
Obermarchtal (C)		7	Dengler
Limpurg (P)	*	?	UATüb. 84/6:1063–65, 1072, 1086
Göppingen (P)	1	0	UATüb. 84/6:1071, 1078; WSAL A209
Urach (P)	2	?	UATüb. 84/6:1107–8, 1122–23
Mergentheim (C)		?	WSAL B262/69
Zell a. H. (C)	*	?	GLAK 119/1102, nos. 10, 40, 94
1627–28			
Esslingen (P)		4	Pfaff, 291; Riezler, 144
Offenburg (C)		5	Volk, 64–66, 72
1627–31			
Gengenbach (C)		70?	A. Rapp, 193
Baden (town) (C)		70?	Hermann, 1–4; Ruppert, 454
[1627–31]. Bishopric of Würzburg (parts are in Baden-Württ.) (C)		219	Vierordt II, 127–28
1628			
Steinbach (C)		33	Reinfried, 50
Offenburg (C)		17	Volk, 72–78
Freudenstadt (P)		*?	Eimer, 91
Buchau (C)		2	Willburger, 141
Weil der Stadt (C)		1	*WKG* 475
Sindelfingen (P)	1	0	Weisert, 131
Ortenau (C)		39	Volk, 3, 24–25
Wertheim (P)		?	Diefenbach, 11
Sulz (P)	4	?	Willburger, 141; UATüb. 83/2
Erstein? (?)		1	A. Ludwig, 110
Schwaben (Habsburg) (C)	4	?	GLAK 65/728
Rottenburg (C)	1	?	*Ibid.*
Oberndorf (C)	1	?	*Ibid.*
Obermarchtal (C)		1	Dengler
Göppingen (P)	1	?	WSAL A209
Winnenden (P)	1	?	*Ibid.*
Calw? (P)	1	?	UATüb. 84/6:1217–18
Waiblingen (P)	1	?	UATüb. 84/6:1266–67, 1293–94
Schw. Hall (P)	1	?	UATüb. 84/6:1247–52, 1326–27, 1362–66
Schorndorf (P)	1	?	UATüb. 84/6:1225
Mergentheim (C)		17	WSAL B262; *WKG* 475
1628–29			
Alpirsbach (P)	10	?	WSAL A209
Bühl (Baden) (C)		70	Duffner, 49; Reinfried (1916), 6–19
1628–30. Bohlsbach (C)		3	Kähni (1964), 25
1628–31. Alpirsbach (P)	1	0	Giefel, 92

| Date, place, and confession | Number involved | | Source |
	Suspected	Executed	
1629			
Ortenau (C)		22	Volk, 19–26
Offenburg (C)		32	Volk, 79–86
Wertheim (P)		10	Diefenbach, 20–34
Mergentheim (C)		94	WSAL B262; *WKG* 475
Kapplertal (C)		1	Rösch, 32
Hofweier (C)		6	Kähni (1964), 58
Achern (C)		*	Reinfried (1916), 19 n. 25
Schw. Hall (P)	1	0	German, 251
Schutterwald (C)		10	Kähni (1964), 107
Oppenau (P-C)	1	0	Rösch, 32
Kloster Wittich (C)	1	0	Vochezer III, 694–95
Rottweil (C)		1	Sauter, 17
Sulz (P)	4	1+?	Willburger, 141; UATüb. 84/6: 1284–86, 1301–4, 1304–6
Urach (P)	1	?	UATüb. 84/6:1329–30, 1334–36
Heidenheim (P)	1	?	UATüb. 84/6:1342–44
Bebenhausen (P)	1	?	WSAL A209
Leonberg (P)	2	?	*Ibid.*
Blaubeuren (P)	1	?	*Ibid.*
Hohenzollern (C)		2	Burkarth
Breisgau (C)	1	?	GLAK 79/3389
Ellwangen (C)		?	WSAL B412/64, 65
1629–30			
Sulz (P)	1	?	WSAL A209
Offenburg (C)	4	0	Volk, 86–88
1629–31. Dürmentingen (C)	*	1	Willburger, 142
Ca. 1630. Cannstatt (P)	1	?	WSAL A209
1630			
Sulz (P)	1	?	UATüb. 84/7:22–23
Wertheim (P)		?	UATüb. 84/7:81–83; Diefenbach, 36–41
Marbach (P)		1	Haug, 259
Glatt (C)	1	?	Schnell, 89
Mergentheim (C)		13	WSAL B262; P. Beck (1884); Burkarth
Haigerloch (C)		2	Schnell, 90; Hodler, 303; Burkarth
Ortenau (C)		14	Volk, 27
Mengen (C)		2	Bicheler, 79
Haslach (C)		6	Göller, 81
Esslingen (P)		1	Pfaff, 291–94
Breisgau (C)	2	?	GLAK 79/3387
1630–31			
Offenburg (C)	3	1	Volk, 88–89; Schreiber, 22
Alpirsbach (P)	4	?	WSAL A209
1630–32. Wertheim (P)		2	Rommel

Date, place, and confession	Number involved		Source
	Suspected	Executed	
1631? Sasbach (P-C)		63	GLAK 169/292–98; Börsig, 76–79, 334–37; Rösch, 33–37; Vierordt II, 123
1631			
Cappel (P-C)		20	*Ibid.*
Ulm (Oberkirch) (P-C)		9	*Ibid.*
Mergentheim (C)		1	WSAL B262
Marbach (P)		1	Haug, 259; UATüb. 84/7:116–18
Hüfingen (C)	11	10	Balzer, 7; Franck, 14–15
Lahr (P)		1	Vierordt II, 123
Herbertingen (C)	13	8+	Mehrle, 93 n. 214; Vochezer III, 383
Haslach (C)		3	Göller, 83
Altenheim (Lichtenberg) (P)		1	A. Ludwig (1930), 109
Hornberg (P)	1	?	WSAL A209
Lauffen (P)	3	?	*Ibid.*
Dornhan (P)	6	5	*Ibid.*
Beilstein (P)	1	?	*Ibid.*
Sulz (P)	1	?	UATüb. 84/7:118–20
1631–32. Oppenau (P-C)		50	GLAK 169/292–98; Börsig, 76–79; Rösch, 33–37; Vierordt II, 123
1632			
Oppenau (P-C)	5	0	Vierordt II, 124
Hüfingen (C)		*	Schreiber, 23
Donaueschingen (C)	7	7?	Strukat, 139
Haslach (C)		1	A. Rapp (1935)
Renchen (P-C)		12	GLAK 169/292–98
Schorndorf (P)	1	?	UATüb. 84/8:1–2
Heidenheim (P)	2	1	WSAL A209
Bräunlingen (P)	2	2	Schreiber, 24–26; Balzer, 9–24; Schott, 233
Neuenburg (P)	1	?	WSAL A209
Dornstetten (P)	2	?	*Ibid.*
1633. Wertheim (P)	60	11	Diefenbach, 55; Rommel
1634			
Wertheim (P)	16	16?	*Ibid.*
Calw (P)	1	?	UATüb. 84/8:397–400
1635			
Bräunlingen (C)	9	5	Balzer, 25–42; Schreiber, 33–34
Stuttgart (P)	1	?	UATüb. 84/8:421–22
1636			
Mühringen (C)	**	1	H. Günther, 8–9; Willburger, 142; *WKG* 475
Sulz (C-P)	**	5	Willburger, 142; WSAL A209
1637			
Holzhausen (P?)		1	Willburger, 142

Date, place, and confession	Number involved		Source
	Suspected	Executed	
1637 (*continued*)			
Herrenberg (P)	1	?	WSAL A209
Reutlingen (P)	1	?	UATüb. 84/8:543–45
Stuttgart (P)	1	?	UATüb. 84/8:546
Oberkirch (P-C)	2	0	GLAK 169/300–301
1637–40. Oberndorf (C)		6+	Köhler (1836), 172–75; *WKG* 475
1638			
Stuttgart (P)	1	?	UATüb. 84/8:548–50
Reutlingen (P)	1	0	Honecker, 111
1639			
Wertheim (P)	1	0	Diefenbach, 55–56
Offenburg (C)	1	0	Bechtold (1914), 29; Volk, 89
Wolfach (C)	2	?	Disch, 379–80
Herrenberg (P)	1	?	WSAL A209
Ca. 1640. Herrenberg (P)	1	?	*Ibid.*
1640			
Wolfach (C)		3	Disch, 377–78, 380
Oberkirch (P-C)	1	1	GLAK 169/302
Ca. 1641. Wolfach (C)	1	0	Disch, 379
1641			
Wertheim (C-P)	2	2	Rommel, 19; Diefenbach, 56
Villingen (C)		19	A. Rapp (1935)
Offenburg (C)	1	?	Bechtold (1914), 29
Leonberg (P)	2	?	UATüb. 84/8:633–37
Sulz (P)	1	?	UATüb. 84/8:612–17
1641–42. Offenburg (C)	1	1	Bechtold (1914), 30
1642			
Wertheim (C-P)	18+	4	Rommel, 23; Diefenbach, 56
Bietigheim (P)	1	?	WSAL A209
Möckmühl (P)	2	?	UATüb. 84/8:666–71
1642–50. Schwaben (Habsburg) (C)	11?	?	GLAK 65/728
1643			
Durlach (C-P)	*	0	Bechtold (1917), 141–42
Hohenzollern (C)	1	1	Burkarth
1644			
Wertheim (C-P)	13	3+?	Rommel, 23–24
Mösskirch (C)	7	?	GLAK 65/728
Reutlingen (P)		1	Willburger, 142; Honecker, 12
Schw. Hall (C-P)	**	**	Krüger, 53; German, 242–43; Riegler, 71 n. 204
Hornberg (P)	1	?	WSAL A209
1645			
Waldsee (C)	*	1?	*WKG* 475; Sauter, 36
Stuttgart (P)		1	UATüb. 84/9:669–79

Date, place, and confession	Number involved		Source
	Suspected	Executed	
1645–46. Sulz (P)		?	WSAL A209
1646. Reutlingen (P)	1	0	Honecker, 11–12
1647			
Bietigheim (P)	1	?	Roemer
Schramberg (C)		2	Willburger, 142
Kirchheim (P)	1	1	WSAL A209
Beilstein (P)	2	?	*Ibid.*
1648			
Wertheim (P)	5	?	Rommel, 24–25
Oberndorf (C)		2	Köhler (1836), 179
Kirchheim (P)	1	?	WSAL A209; UATüb. 84/9:761–70
Esslingen (P)	1	?	UATüb. 84/9:27–48
Hohenzollern (C)	2	1	Burkarth
1648–77. Klettgau (C)	1	?	Schott, 234
1649			
Hohenzollern (C)	1	0	Burkarth; Schnell, 80
Biberach (P)	5	?	UATüb. 84/9: 98–110
Hornberg (P)	1	?	WSAL A209
1650. Rottenburg (C)		?	*WKG* 475; Willburger, 142; Birlinger I, 157–75
Ca. 1650. Freudenstadt (P)	1	?	Zingeler (1886), 148–53; Willburger, 142
1651			
Reichenbach (P)	1	?	WSAL A209
Tübingen (P)	1	?	*Ibid.*
Haigerloch (C)		1	Hodler, 303; Schnell, 87; Burkarth
Waldulum (Oberkirch) (P-C)	2	?	Eimer (1941), 214
1651–52			
Mergentheim (C)	*	?	WSAL B246/250
Rosenfeld (P)	1	?	WSAL A209
1652			
Werstein (C)	1	?	Schnell, 91
Haigerloch (C)		2	Hodler, 303; Burkarth
Hohenzollern (C)	1	?	GLAK 79/3387
Schw. Gmünd (C)		1	*1962 Schw. Gmünd,* 46; *WKG* 541
Winnenden (P)	1	?	WSAL A209
Balingen (P)	1	?	*Ibid.*
1652–53. Tuttlingen (P)	1	?	*Ibid.*
1652–54. Zell a. H. (C)	*	?	GLAK 228
1652–55. Breisgau (C)	6	?	GLAK 79/3390
1653			
Haigerloch (C)		2	Schnell, 90–91; Burkarth
Hohebach (P)	1	?	Eyth, 222
Cannstatt (P)	3	?	WSAL A209; UATüb. 84/10:176–81

Date, place, and confession	Number involved		Source
	Suspected	Executed	
1653–57. Grafenhausen (C)	*	?	GLAK 169/303–4
1654			
Oberkirch (P-C)		?	GLAK 169/303
Köngen (P)	1	?	UATüb. 84/10:490–94
Marbach (P)	1+	0	Haug, 259
Neufra (C)		?	Willburger, 142
1654–58. Ettenheim (C)	6	1+?	Rest, 49–51
1655			
Schorndorf (P)	1	?	WSAL A209
Lahr (C)	3	2	A. Ludwig (1930), 108, 112–14
Breisgau (C)	1	?	GLAK 79/3389
1656			
Herrenberg (P)	1	?	WSAL A209
Tübingen (P)	1	?	*Ibid.*
Schorndorf (P)	1	?	UATüb. 84/11:207–19
Oppenau (P-C)	1	?	WSAL A444/13
1656–57. Winningen (C)	1	?	GLAK 65/729
1656–58. Neuenstadt, Weinsberg, Möckmühl (P)	32	4	Willburger, 142; WSAL A209/1610
1657			
Gammertingen Hettingen (C)	1	1	Schnell, 88; Burkarth
Mösskirch (C)	1	?	GLAK 65/728
Oberkirch (P-C)		?	GLAK 169/303–4
Obermarchtal (C)	2	1	Dengler
Neustadt (P)	1	?	UATüb. 84/11:317–27
Herrenberg (P)	1	?	UATüb. 84/11: 330–31, 417–22
1657–59. Leonberg (P)	*	?	WSAL A209
1657–65. Möckmühl (P)	*	?	*Ibid.*
1658			
Hohenzollern (C)	2	1	Schnell, 88; Burkarth
Heidenheim (P)	1	?	WSAL A209
Bietigheim (P)	1	?	*Ibid.*
Neuenstadt a. K. (P)	**	?	*Ibid.*
Kirchheim (P)	1	?	*Ibid.*; UATüb. 84/11:900–904
Obersontheim (P)	1	?	UATüb. 84/11:837–47
1659			
Horb (C)	1	?	HSASt B46/1
Gengenbach & Zell (C)	*	?	Hellinger, 396
Sulz (P)		1	Willburger, 142; UATüb. 84/12:723–36, 778–82, 910–18; WSAL A209
Schorndorf (P)	1	?	UATüb. 84/12:887–910; 84/14:67–72
Leonberg (P)	1	?	UATüb. 84/12:426–50
Beilstein (P)	1	?	UATüb. 84/12:711–15

Date, place, and confession	Number involved		Source
	Suspected	Executed	
Calw (P)	1	?	WSAL A209
Sachsenheim (P)	2	?	*Ibid.*
1659–60			
Böblingen (P)	1	?	*Ibid.*
Schorndorf (P)	1	?	*Ibid.*
1660			
Böblingen (P)	1	?	*Ibid.*
Sachsenheim (P)	1	?	*Ibid.*
Balingen (P)	*	?	*Ibid.*
Kirchheim (P)	1	?	*Ibid.*
Leonberg (P)		?	*Ibid.*
Marbach (P)	1	?	*Ibid.*
Urach (P)	1	?	UATüb. 84/14:154–55, 182–91, 249–75
Hohenzollern (C)	1	1	Schnell, 88; Burkarth
Freiburg i. Br. (C)	1	?	Schott, 77 n. 15
Owen (P)	1	0	Rooschüz, 46
Schwaben (Habsburg) (C)	1	?	GLAK 65/728
1660–61. Urach (P)	1	0	WSAL A209
1660–67. Liebenzell (P)	1	1	*Ibid.*
1660–70. Fellbach (P)	*	1+	Fleck, 62
1661			
Nürtingen (P)		?	WSAL A209
Urach (P)	1	?	*Ibid.*
Brackenheim (P)	1	?	*Ibid.*
Reutlingen (P)	1	0	Honecker, 12
Wolfach (C)	*	?	Disch, 387
Gengenbach (C)		2	Hellinger, 396
Esslingen (P)	1	?	UATüb. 85/1
Herrenberg (P)	1	?	UATüb. 84/14:791–806
Köngen (P)	1	?	UATüb. 84/14:983–98
1661–62. Weinsberg (P)	3+	?	UATüb. 84/15:344–46, 548–75; WSAL A209
1662			
Lauffen (P)	1	?	WSAL A209
Waiblingen (P)	1	0	*Ibid.*
Villingen (C)	1	1	A. Rapp (1935)
Gengenbach (C)	3	2	Schaaf, 149; Hellinger; Rapp
Buchau (C)	2	2	Willburger, 143
Esslingen (P)		Ca. 28	Pfaff, 347–71, 441a–62a; UATüb. 84/16:180–91
Sulz (P)	1	?	UATüb. 84/15:1209–17
1662–63. Marbach (P)	1	?	WSAL A209; UATüb. 84/16:240–62
1662–64. Sulz (P)	*	?	WSAL A209

Date, place, and confession	Number involved		Source
	Suspected	Executed	
1662–65. Mergentheim (C)		?	WSAL B262/111
1663			
Nürtingen (P)	2	1?	Kocher III, 249–59; WSAL A209; UATüb. 84/16:766–71, 915–25, 992–95
Ettenheim (C)		?	A. Rapp (1935)
Hohenzollern (C)	1	?	Burkarth; Schnell, 80
Fellbach (P)		1	Honecker, 22
Schorndorf (P)	1	?	WSAL A209
Rosenfeld (P)	1	?	*Ibid.*; UATüb. 84/16:749–57
Winnenden (P)	1	?	WSAL A209
Wildbad (P)		?	*Ibid.*
Böblingen (P)	1	?	*Ibid.*
Leonberg (P)	1	?	UATüb. 84/13:190–204; 84/16:854–59
Hohenzollern (C)	2	?	UATüb. 84/16:771–81; Burkarth
Urach (P)	1	?	UATüb. 84/16:888–94
Stuttgart (P)	5	?	UATüb. 84/16:894–97, 925–26; 565–66, 630–42; 995–1008; 566–71, 642–44, 728–31, 744–49, 847–49, 859–62; 1008–14
Cannstatt (P)	1	?	UATüb. 84/16:652–58, 742–44
1663–64			
Esslingen (P)	**	Ca. 1	Pfaff, 347–71; 441a–62a; UATüb. 84/16:1068–74, 1065–68
Tübingen (P)	1	?	WSAL A209
1663–66. Nagold (P)	2	?	*Ibid.*
1664			
Pforzheim (P)	1	?	Stolz, 113
Kirchheim (P)	2	?	WSAL A209
Nürtingen (P)	2	?	*Ibid.*
Waiblingen (P)	1	?	*Ibid.*; UATüb. 84/17:43–47
Cannstatt (P)	2	?	WSAL A209
Stuttgart (P)	1	?	UATüb. 84/16:1074–91
1665			
Hohenzollern (C)	2	?	Schnell, 80; Burkarth
Königsegg (C)		2	Buck, 108–15; Sauter, 35; Willburger, 143
Esslingen (P)		Ca. 8	Pfaff, 347–71, 441a–62a
Sindelfingen (P)	1	0	Weisert, 131–32
Herrenberg (P)	1	?	UATüb. 84/17:370–78; WSAL A209
Cannstatt (P)	1	0	WSAL A209
Bebenhausen (P)	1	?	*Ibid.*
1665–66. Reutlingen (P)		14	UATüb. 84/17:314–24; 84/19:293–96; Honecker, 13–21

Date, place, and confession	Number involved		Source
	Suspected	Executed	
1666			
Hohenzollern (C)	3	2	Schnell, 80; Burkarth
Heidenheim? (P)	1	?	WSAL A209
1666–73. Weinsberg (P)	20+	?	*Ibid.*
1667			
Reutlingen (P)	1	?	UATüb. 84/20:10–12
Ettenheim (C)	1	1	GLAK 169/305; Rest, 51–56; Bechtold (1914), 125
Kirchheim (P)	1	?	WSAL A209; UATüb. 84/20:69–70, 80–87
Böblingen (P)	1	?	WSAL A209; UATüb. 84/19:397–407
Hornberg (P)	1	?	UATüb. 84/19:546–52; WSAL A209
Tübingen (P)	1	?	WSAL A209
Möckmühl (P)	1	?	*Ibid.*
Gengenbach (C)		2	Bechtold (1914), 125
Heilbronn (P)		1	Dürr, 195
Altshausen (C)		1	Sauter, 12, 34–35
1667ff. Cannstatt (P)		**	Honecker, 29
1668			
Hohenzollern (C)		1	Burkarth; Schnell, 80
Bietigheim (P)	1	?	Roemer
Marbach (P)	1	?	WSAL A209
Kirchheim (P)	1	?	*Ibid.*
Möckmühl (P)		?	*Ibid.*
Schorndorf (P)	1	?	*Ibid.*
Münsingen (P)	3	?	*Ibid.*
Gröningen (P)	1	?	*Ibid.*
Bebenhausen (P)	*	?	*Ibid.*
1668–69. Cannstatt (P)	1	?	*Ibid.*
1669			
Nimburg (P)		1	Vierordt II, 124
Sindelfingen (P)	1	0	Weisert, 132; WSAL A209
Urach (P)	2	?	UATüb. 84/22:1–11; 84/23:149–61
1670			
Ettenheim (C)	1	0	Bechtold (1914), 126
Hohenzollern (C)	1	0	Schnell, 81; Burkarth
Leonberg (P)	1	?	WSAL A209
Nürtingen (P)	1	?	*Ibid.*; UATüb. 84/24:137–45
Rosenfeld (P)	1?	?	WSAL A209
Waiblingen (P)	1	?	*Ibid.*
Bietigheim (P)	1	?	*Ibid.*
Neuhausen a. d. Fildern (P)	1	?	UATüb. 84/24:8–13

Date, place, and confession	Number involved		Source
	Suspected	Executed	
1671			
Friedingen (C)	1	?	UATüb. 84/24:478–87
Freudenstadt (P)	1	?	WSAL A209
Leonberg (P)	2	?	*Ibid.*
Neuffen (P)	1	?	*Ibid.*
Hornberg (P)	1	?	*Ibid.*
Tübingen (P)	1	?	*Ibid.*
1671–72. Weinsberg (P)	1	?	*Ibid.*
1672			
Cannstatt (P)	**	?	*Ibid.*
Altdorf-Weingarten (C)		?	*Altdorf-Weingarten,* 76
Kappel (C)	3	0	Bechtold (1914), 127–29
Wolfach (C)		1	Disch, 387
Hosskirch (C)		1	Buck, 135; Sauter, 12; Willburger, 143
1672–73. Balingen (P)	1	0	WSAL A209
1673			
Derendingen (P)	1	0	M .Brecht (1967), 97
Bottwar (P)	1	?	WSAL A209
Göppingen (P)	2	?	UATüb. 84/25:279–82
Calw (P)		?	Willburger, 143
1674			
Derendingen (P)	*	0	M. Brecht (1967), 96
Cannstatt (P)	1	?	WSAL A209
Ettenheim (C)	1	?	Rest, 51–56
Saulgau (C)	*	1+	Sauter, 24–26, 34
Schwaben (Habsburg) (C)	3	?	GLAK 65/728
1675			
Derendingen (P)	1	0	M. Brecht (1967), 97
Gröningen (P)	1	?	WSAL A209
Cannstatt (P)	1	?	*Ibid.*
Calw (P)	1	?	WSAL A209; UATüb. 84/28:508–10
Nagold (P)	1	?	UATüb. 84/28:478–79
1676			
Alpirsbach (P)	1	?	WSAL A209
Cannstatt (P)	1	?	*Ibid.*
Freudenstadt (P)	3	?	WSAL A209; UATüb. 84/29:312–15, 337–45
Mösskirch (P)	1	?	UATüb. 84/29:57–58
Königsegg (C)		1	Buck, 108
Weingarten (C)		1	Willburger, 143
1677			
Alpirsbach (P)	1	?	WSAL A209
Neuffen (P)	1	?	*Ibid.*

Date, place, and confession	Number involved		Source
	Suspected	Executed	
Böblingen (P)	1	?	*Ibid.*
Calw (P)	1	?	*Ibid.*; UATüb. 84/718–36
Brackenheim (P)	1	?	WSAL A209
Marbach (P)	1	?	UATüb. 84/26:unpaged
Knittlingen (P)	1	?	UATüb. 84/29:586–89, 589–97
Breisgau (C)	1	?	GLAK 79/3390
1677–79. Oberkirch (C)	**	?	Bechtold (1914), 126
1678			
Blaubeuren (P)	1	?	WSAL A209
Besigheim (P)	1	0	*Ibid.*
1678–80. Stetten (P)	1	?	WSAL A209; UATüb. 84/30:557–62
1679			
Cannstatt (P)	1	?	*Ibid.*; UATüb. 84/31:184–90
Böblingen (P)	1	?	WSAL A209
Backnang (P)	2	?	*Ibid.*
Feuchtwangen (P)	3	?	UATüb. 84/30:692–710; 84/31:169–81
Hohenzollern (C)	2	2	Schnell, 81; Burkarth
Freiburg i. Br. (C)	1	?	GLAK 79/3390
Ettenheim? (C)	1	0	Bechtold (1914), 126
1680			
Cannstatt (P)	1	?	WSAL A209
Ulm (P)	1	1	Willburger, 144; LBSt Cod. hist. 2°, fol. 1045
Rabenau (P)	1	?	UATüb. 84/34:268–84
Heidenheim (P)	1	?	UATüb. 84/32:193–231
Waldsee (C)		1	Sauter, 10
Veringenstadt (C)		1	*Handbuch hist. Stätten*, 705
Hohenzollern (C)		1	Burkarth
1681			
Schmiedelfelden (Limburg) (P)		1	UATüb. 84/35:303–18
Schorndorf (P)	1	?	UATüb. 84/37:172–81
Stuttgart (P)	2	?	UATüb. 84/38:198–220; 84/35:318–27
Imperial Knight (?)	1	?	UATüb. 84/38:312–20
Heidenheim (P)	1	?	WSAL A209/1156
Möckmühl (P)	1	?	WSAL A209
Beilstein (P)	1	?	*Ibid.*
Alpirsbach (P)	2	?	*Ibid.*
1681–83. Urach (P)	1	?	*Ibid.*
1682			
Mösskirch (C)	3	?	GLAK 65/728
Heidenheim (P)	1	?	WSAL A209

Date, place, and confession	Number involved		Source
	Suspected	Executed	
1682 (*continued*)			
Neydingen (P)	1	?	UATüb. 84/39:312–30
Ettenheim (C)	1	0	A. Rapp (1935); Rest, 51–56
Gengenbach (C)		2	Hellinger
1683–86. Calw (P)	9	2	WSAL A209; UATüb. 84/22:931–77
1683			
Altensteig (P)	1	0	Willburger (1932), 138–39; WSAL A209
Leonberg (P)	1	?	WSAL A209
Brackenheim (P)	1	?	*Ibid.*
1684			
Balingen (P)	1	?	*Ibid.*
Hornberg (P)	1	?	*Ibid.*
Marbach (P)	1	0	Haug, 259
Saulgau (C)	1	1	*Ibid.*
Bietigheim (P)	1	?	Roemer
Schw. Gmünd (C)	4	4	Klaus, 15
Sindelfingen (P)	1	0	Weisert, 132; WSAL A209
Esslingen (P)	5	?	HSASt B177/123
1685			
Weinsberg (P)	1	?	WSAL A209
Bietigheim (P)	1	?	*Ibid.*
Waldsee (C)		1	Sauter, 11
Esslingen (P)	5	?	HSASt 177/123
Mösskirch (C)	1	?	GLAK 65/728
1686			
Calw (P)	1	?	WSAL A209
Leibenzell (P)	1	?	*Ibid.*
Freudenstadt (P)		1	*Ibid.*
Urach (P)	1	?	*Ibid.*
Brackenheim (P)	1	?	*Ibid.*
Tuttlingen (P)	1	?	*Ibid.*
1687			
Blaubeuren (P)		?	*Ibid.*
Kirchheim (P)	1	?	*Ibid.*
1688			
Güglingen (P)	1	?	*Ibid.*
Blaubeuren (P)	1	?	*Ibid.*
Calw (P)	1	?	*Ibid.*
Königseggwald (C)		1	Sauter, 31
Ellwangen (C)		?	WSAL B412/65
1690			
Herrenberg (P)	1	?	WSAL A209
Böblingen (P)	1	0	*Ibid.*

Date, place, and confession	Number involved		Source
	Suspected	Executed	
Rottenburg (C)	1	1	*OAB Rottenburg*, 412–14; Willburger, 144
1692			
Böblingen (P)	1	?	WSAL A209
Schorndorf (P)	1	?	*Ibid.*
1693			
Besigheim (P)	1	?	*Ibid.*
Weinsberg (P)	1	?	UATüb. 84/53:939–66
1694			
Herrenberg (P)	2	?	WSAL A209; UATüb. 84/55:207–56, 541–58
Schorndorf (P)	3	?	WSAL A209; UATüb. 84/54:651–64; 84/55:1707–25
Kirchheim (P)	2	?	WSAL A209
Ellwangen (C)	1	?	UATüb. 84/55:1331–36
1695			
Freudenstadt (P)	1	?	WSAL A209; UATüb. 84/56:1225
Möckmühl (P)	3	?	WSAL A209
Neuenburg (P)	1	?	*Ibid.*
Reutlingen (P)	1	?	UATüb. 84/56:653–69
Aurach? (P)	1	?	UATüb. 84/56:1–23
Herrenberg (P)	2	?	UATüb. 84/56:247–73
Constance, Zeil, Wurzach (C)	1	?	Schott, 237
Heilbronn (P)		1	Dürr, 129
1696			
Waiblingen (P)	1	?	WSAL A209
Blaubeuren (P)	1	?	*Ibid.*
Owen (P)	1	0	Rooschüz, 46–47
1697			
Bietigheim (P)	1	0	Roemer; UATüb. 84/58:648–54
Oberkirch (C)	1	?	GLAK 169/306
1698			
Herrenberg (P)	1	?	WSAL A209
Glatt (C)	2	1	Schnell, 89; Burkarth
1699. Breisgau (C)	1	?	GLAK 79/3389
1700			
Marbach (P)	1	?	WSAL A209
Owen (P)	*	?	Rooschüz, 61
1702–85			WSAL A209 contains materials on magic, witchcraft, blasphemy, and poisoning (now viewed as a purely physical process). Sixty-nine episodes are preserved in this series of records.

Date, place, and confession	Number involved		Source
	Suspected	Executed	
1706 *et seq.*			UATüb. 84 contains materials on magic, witchcraft, blasphemy, and poisoning throughout the eighteenth century.
1702–1800			The secondary literature contains references to at least 26 further episodes of magic, witchcraft, and poisoning in the eighteenth century in southwestern Germany.

In addition to the detailed information on individual witch trials, we know of other series of trials that have not yet been broken down into specific incidents (often because the archives are not in full working order):

Date and place	Number executed	Source
1450–1590. Reichenau	?	GLAK 61/14875
1460–1862. Ziegelhausen	?	GLAK 229/118058–118323
1430–1937. Langensteinbach	?	GLAK 229/58018–58342
1460–1860. Buchen	?	GLAK 229/13852–13964
1248–1859. Zell-Weierbach	?[a]	GLAK 229/117552–117782
1493–1852. Odenheim	?	GLAK 229/79155–79283
1500–1700. Burgheim	?	GLAK 65/142
1557–1603. Ortenau	28	Volk, 23–24; Janssen VIII, 681
1561–1648. Rottweil	113	Ruckgaber, 174–96
1570–1610. Wertheim	80	A. Rapp, 192
1570–1610. Gengenbach	40	*Ibid.*; cf. GLAK 61/5745–5751
1581–1682. Schwaben (Habsburg)	?	GLAK 65/727
1581–1594. Waldsee	38	*WKG* 475
1590–1594. Nördlingen	35	Willburger, 168; Janssen, VIII, 718; Wulz (1938), 42–72; (1939), 95–120
1596–1628. Rammersweier	10	Kähni (1964), 98
1601–1676. Stein a. R.	28	Urner-Astholz, 185
1602–1622. Tuttlingen	**	WSAL A209
1603–1615. Ortenau	?	GLAK 119/834, No. 1–5
1615–1629. Weil der Stadt	38	Caspar, 282
1628–1631. Baden-Baden	?	GLAK 61/5047
1628–1731. Bühl	?	GLAK 61/5445–5450
1645–1652. Schw. Gmünd	?	HSASt B177/123

[a] In 1557–1630 there were four persons executed, according to Kähni [1964], 126.

Notes

Complete authors' names, titles, and publishing data will be found in the Bibliography, pp. 261–300. Complete manuscript sources for the following archive abbreviations, used in the Notes, are given in full in the first part of the Bibliography, pp. 261–62.

GLAK	Baden, Generallandesarchiv Karlsruhe
HSASt	Württemberg, Hauptstaatsarchiv Stuttgart
LBSt	Württemberg, Landesbibliothek Stuttgart
SASigm	Württemberg, Staatsarchiv Sigmaringen
Tirol LA	Tirol, Landesregierungsarchiv Innsbruck
UATüb	Tübingen Universität, Universitätsarchiv
WSAL	Württemberg, Staatsarchiv Ludwigsburg

CHAPTER ONE

1. A wealth of folklore and bibliography may be found in Bächtold-Stäubli's multi-volume *Handwörterbuch des deutschen Aberglaubens*, s.v. Hexe, Zauber, etc.

2. The only convincing case study of such a group appears in Ginzburg's *I benandanti*.

3. Alan Macfarlane purposely eschews the broad interpretive efforts of earlier scholars, who, he suggests, were confined either by their purely literary sources or by their lack of imagination. H. R. Trevor-Roper was a principal target of this criticism. See Macfarlane, *Witchcraft in Tudor and Stuart England*, pp. 9–11.

4. A critical list of important works is provided in Midelfort, "Recent Witch Hunting Research." See also Jackson, "Primitive Medicine."

5. Cf. Macfarlane, pp. 240–49; for an example of overconfidence, see Madsen, "Anxiety and Witchcraft," p. 110.

6. Kittredge, *Witchcraft in Old and New England*.

7. Monter, *European Witchcraft*, p. 47.

8. Erikson, *Wayward Puritans*.

9. Swanson, *Birth of the Gods*.

10. Rosen, *Madness in Society*, p. 17.

11. Martindale, ed., *Functionalism*; Goldschmidt, *Comparative Functionalism*.

12. Macfarlane, pp. 248–49.

13. *Ibid*.

14. See Jacob, "Hexenlehre des Paracelsus," for an example of modern Lower Saxon superstitions.

15. See the intelligent discussion by Henry Guerlac in "George Lincoln Burr."
16. Laslett, *The World We Have Lost*, pp. 159–62.
17. See Thomas, "History and Anthropology."
18. Rossell Hope Robbins makes this a leitmotif in *The Encyclopedia of Witchcraft and Demonology*.
19. Demos, "Underlying Themes."
20. See for example Masters, *Eros and Evil*.
21. Delcambre, "Les procès de sorcellerie en Lorraine," and also "La psychologie des inculpés lorrains de sorcellerie." See especially his *Le concept de la sorcellerie*, Vol. 2, p. 275. As an example of the psychological vogue, Chadwick Hanson assumes that when a society believes in witchcraft, its practice can genuinely cause human disease and suffering; *Witchcraft at Salem*, pp. ix–xiv, 10.
22. See Trevor-Roper, *Crisis*, pp. 138–39, 143; Mandrou, *Magistrats et sorciers*, p. 152.
23. See Trevor-Roper, *Crisis*, pp. 168–78.
24. Baschwitz, *Hexen und Hexenprozesse*, p. 8.
25. Hansen, *Zauberwahn*, pp. 4 et seq.
26. Robbins, p. 219.
27. G. Bader, *Hexenprozesse in der Schweiz*.
28. See the works of Byloff, Ewen, Hoppstädter, Macfarlane, Notestein, Riezler, Schacher, and Volk for the most noteworthy exceptions.
29. Miller, ed., *Baden-Württemberg*, pp. xxxiv–xxxv. For a heroic attempt at a general introduction, cf. K. S. Bader, *Der deutsche Südwesten*.
30. Macfarlane. Also, Monter, "Patterns of Witchcraft in the Jura." I am grateful to Mr. Monter for showing me a copy of this very useful article before publication.

CHAPTER TWO

1. Williams, *Witchcraft*; Caro Baroja, *The World of the Witches*; Soldan-Heppe, *Geschichte der Hexenprozesse*.
2. Williams, p. 127; *Malleus Maleficarum*, Pt. I, Question 2. This tripartite form of analysis was expounded in detail by Abraham Saur in "Ein kurtze newe Warnung."
3. See the monumental collection of such materials in Lea, *Materials*: on Peter Binsfeld, see pp. 576–90; on Thomas Erastus, pp. 430–31; on Martin Delrio, pp. 640–46; on Peter Thyraeus, pp. 624–27. See also Bodin, *De la démonomanie des sorciers*, fols. 6r–v. For Essex, see Macfarlane, *Witchcraft*. For the concept of archaism, see Monter, "Patterns of Witchcraft."
4. For the biblical basis of Catholic demonology, see Hopkin, *The Share of Thomas Aquinas*, and Kelly, *The Devil*. For the Protestant use of the Bible, see Paulus, *Hexenwahn*, pp. 67–100.
5. Kittredge, *Witchcraft in Old and New England*, p. 356, gives a clear view of these matters from a seventeenth-century standpoint.
6. Ross, *Aristotle*, pp. 94–95; Aristotle, *Metaphysics*, XII: 7.
7. Hopkin, p. 36; Hansen, *Zauberwahn*, pp. 196–204; Collins, *Thomistic Philosophy of the Angels*, pp. 307–15.
8. *Malleus Maleficarum*, Pt. I, Q. 7, p. 49.
9. *Ibid.*, Pt. II, Q. 1, chap. 3, p. 106.
10. Bodin, fols. 90r–91v.
11. On Mancini, see Thorndike, *History*, VI: 518–19; on Vanini, VI: 570; on da Vinci, V: 33; on Fortunatus Affaytatus, V: 270; on Cardan, V: 567–68; on Pomponazzi, V: 100–103; see also Walker, *Spiritual and Demonic Magic*, pp. 107–11.

12. Schmid, *Doctrinal Theology*, pp. 204–16.

13. *Ibid.*, pp. 205–6; Collins, p. 315; Hopkin, pp. 36, 110–24; Bodin, fol. 115r; Erastus, *Deux Dialogues*, pp. 484–87.

14. *Malleus Maleficarum*, Pt. III, pp. 195ff; Bodin, fols. 6r-v, 28r-v; Weyer, *De Praestigiis Daemonum* (I have used the reprint of the Paris, 1579, translation, *Histoires, disputes et discours*, pp. 105, 143, 148).

15. This was the response of George Gifford; cf. Teall, "Witchcraft and Calvinism"; Hitchcock, "George Gifford."

16. Bodin, fol. 196v.

17. *Ibid.*, fols. 217r-v; cf. fol. 235v.

18. *Malleus Maleficarum*, Pt. I, Q. 12, p. 68.

19. *Malleus Maleficarum*, Pt. I, Q. 2, p. 20.

20. *Ibid.*, p. 15.

21. This was the theory of, among others, Lambert Daneau, a prominent Calvinist witchcraft theorist; cf. Paulus, *Hexenwahn*, p. 180.

22. Bodin, pp. 236–40.

23. Tobias Wagner, *Casual Predigten,* "Kohlschwartze Teufel" (pp. 3–72), and "Apologia" (pp. 73–116), contain examples, taken from Wagner's pastoral experience, of two persons who signed pacts with the devil. Wagner reported that he saw the pacts. Cf. also Baschwitz, *Hexen und Hexenprozesse*, p. 27.

24. Pratt, *The Attitude of the Catholic Church*; Robbins, *Encyclopedia.*

25. Hopkin.

26. *Ibid.*, p. 183.

27. Augustine has been baffling, seeming both skeptical and superstitious to various scholars. Caro Baroja (*World of the Witches*, p. 43) classifies him as a rationalist, since he explained the flight of women as mere illusion. For the opposite view, cf. Merzbacher, *Hexenprozesse in Franken*, p. 9.

28. Soldan-Heppe, *Geschichte der Hexenprozesse*, I: 102.

29. *Ibid.*, I: 112–16; Robbins, pp. 74–75. An unpublished seminar paper by John L. Teall encouraged my own thought on this point.

30. Robbins, p. 76. "Innumera multitudo hac falsa opinione decepta haec vera esse credit et credendo a recte fide deviat et errore paganorum revolvitur, cum aliquid divinitas aut numinis extra unum Deum arbitratur," in Hansen, *Quellen*, pp. 38–39.

31. Robbins, p. 77; Kelly, pp. 50–52; Hansen, *Quellen*, p. 39.

32. Hansen, *Quellen*, p. 39.

33. Robbins, pp. 75–76; Kelly, p. 50; Hansen, *Quellen*, p. 38.

34. Robbins, p. 75.

35. *Ibid.*, p. 370.

36. *Ibid.*, p. 550; see also pp. 7, 369–79.

37. *Ibid.*, p. 9.

38. Hobbes said: "For as for witches, I think not that their witchcraft is any real power, but yet that they are justly punished for the false belief they have that they can do much mischief, joined with their purpose to do it if they can." Hobbes, *Leviathan*, p. 31. For Bayle's comments, which are similar, see "Reponse aux questions d'un provincial," in *Oeuvres diverses*, III: 562–65.

39. Bainton, *Burr*, pp. 172–75.

40. Hopkin, pp. 150–51; Zwetsloot, *Friedrich von Spee*, pp. 38, 46. In any study of magic we must remain sensitive to the real ambivalence contained within the concept, for "magia" was both Eastern wisdom and the practical art. Thorndike suggested

that only in the sixteenth century did the distinction between natural and demonic magic become generally accepted; Thorndike, *History*, V: 13–14. For a brilliant analysis of the ambivalence toward magic in the sixteenth century, see Walker, *Magic*, especially pp. 75–85, 112–19, 205–12.

41. Hopkin, pp. 91–95, 106–10. It was generally held that the good angels would not answer man's needs except through prayer to God.

42. Zwetsloot, p. 36; cf. Merzbacher, *Hexenprozesse in Franken*, p. 11. The analysis of the precisely heretical aspect of diabolical magic became very complex, as is evident in the delicate distinctions in Bernard Basin; see Thorndike, *History*, IV: 491–93.

43. Hopkin, pp. 149–51; Hansen, *Quellen*, pp. 56–57.

44. Schweizer, "Der Hexenprozess," p. 10; Robbins, pp. 287–88; Soldan-Heppe, pp. 199–200; Thorndike, *History*, III: 30–31.

45. Hopkin, pp. 180–83; Robbins, pp. 245, 270–71; Feine, *Kirchliche Rechtsgeschichte*, I: 441–42; Plöchl, *Geschichte des Kirchenrechts*, II: 317–18.

46. We owe the conclusive proof of the relationship between heresy and witchcraft to Jeffrey B. Russell, whose unpublished paper before the American Historical Association in December 1969 forms the basis of my conclusions in this matter.

47. Caro Baroja, *World of the Witches*, pp. 84–86; Hansen, *Quellen*, pp. 450–53; Robbins, pp. 272, 414–24, 516–17.

48. Schweizer, p. 11; Hopkin, p. 178.

49. Robbins, pp. 75, 143.

50. Actually, the sixteenth-century Italian and Spanish Inquisitions did conduct moderate witchcraft trials, since they forbade the use of torture to discover accomplices. See Paulus, *Hexenwahn*, pp. 261–76.

51. Robbins, pp. 268–69; cf. Shannon, "Secrecy of Witnesses."

52. Robbins, pp. 54–55, 498; Soldan-Heppe, I: 463–65.

53. Caro Baroja, *World of the Witches*, p. 82.

54. Macfarlane's evidence from Essex shows very little of this emphasis on devil and pact, and instead a constant stress on maleficium. In this example one can see not only the primitiveness of English witchcraft, but the extent to which the English legal tradition remained free from the influence of canon law.

55. Before him, almost every pope of the fourteenth and fifteenth centuries had condemned the sorcery of some group or region; see Robbins, p. 263; Hansen, *Quellen*, pp. 1–24.

56. Robbins, pp. 264–66; Hansen, *Quellen*, pp. 25–27. It is worth noting that this bull makes no mention of the sabbath or of the witches' flight. As noted earlier, these were not essential to the crime of witchcraft.

57. Karl O. Müller, "Heinrich Institoris," pp. 397–98, n. 2; cf. *Malleus Maleficarum*, Pt. II, Q. 1, chap. 4.

58. Hansen, *Zauberwahn*, pp. 478–93.

59. It suggested this emphasis in its title, "Maleficarum." Witches could also be known as veneficae, lamiae, magae, sagae, sortilegii, fascinarii, haeretici, mathematici, pithonissae, and stregones; see Hansen, *Quellen*, pp. 614ff.

60. Hansen, *Zauberwahn*, pp. 478–81; *Quellen*, p. 360.

61. Hansen, *Zauberwahn*, pp. 491–94.

62. *Ibid.*, p. 524.

63. Radbruch, *Peinliche Gerichtsordnung*, p. 76; hereafter cited as *Carolina*.

64. *Carolina*, Arts. 106, 107, 108, 116, 172.

65. Robbins, p. 540.

66. *Ibid.*, pp. 215, 549; Soldan-Heppe, I: 399.

67. Soldan-Heppe, I: 399.

68. The learned Jesuit, Martin Delrio, mentioned several such thinkers in his *De magia*: Martin de Arles, Ponzinibio, "Fray Samuel," Porta, Alciatus, Duaren, Aerodius, Montaigne, Camerarius, Molitor, John of Salisbury; see Caro Baroja, *World of the Witches*, p. 278, n. 15.

69. Soldan-Heppe, I: 254.

70. Riezler, *Hexenprozesse in Bayern*, p. 123; L. Rapp, *Hexenprozesse und ihre Gegner aus Tirol*, pp. 9–12; Robbins, pp. 347–48. In the fifteenth century we find similar denials of flight and sabbath in Socinus of Siena, William Becchius of Florence, and Peter Mamoris; see Thorndike, IV: 297, 299, 301–2. The same is true of Alphonsus de Spina; see Hansen, *Quellen*, pp. 147–48.

71. Champier: Thorndike, V: 117; Johann Fichard: Soldan-Heppe, I: 467. In Hansen: *Quellen*: Alciatus, pp. 310–11; de Cassinis, pp. 262ff; Ponzinibio, p. 313; Montaigne, pp. 312–13, n. 1. This list could be extended to include many more sixteenth-century thinkers.

72. Thorndike, VI: 535–37; Paulus, *Hexenwahn*, p. 124.

73. U. F. Schneider, "Das Werk 'De Praestigiis Daemonum,'" pp. 10–18, 53; Walker, *Magic*, pp. 93–94, 105–6, 152–56.

74. Weyer's disappointment with men like Brenz was obvious; see his *Liber apologeticus* attached to the *De Praestigiis* beginning with the edition of 1577.

75. Robbins, p. 539; Soldan-Heppe, I: 459.

76. U. F. Schneider, pp. 1–3, 73–91; but see also Burr in Bainton, p. 183.

77. In Germany alone the list includes H. J. Höcker, H. Hammelmann, J. Ewich, J. G. Gödelmann, H. Neuwaldt, H. Witekind (A. Lercheimer), C. Loos, A. Praetorius, C. Anten, T. Thumm, M. Biermann, and the anonymous author of the *Malleus Judicum*; see U. F. Schneider, pp. 83–91, 93.

78. Weyer, *Histoires, disputes et discours*, Vol. I, chap. 24, especially pp. 143–48.

79. Samuel de Cassinis at the beginning of the sixteenth century argued that spirits can only move other things according to the nature of those things, and that it was not human nature to fly; Hansen, *Quellen*, p. 511. Applied systematically, this sort of argument might have been as radical as Weyer's.

80. Cf. Dijksterhuis, *Mechanisierung*; Westfall, *Science and Religion*.

81. One might have argued that Christ broke the power of the devil, but unfortunately figures like Simon Magus appear in the New Testament. Ponzinibio tried to argue against witchcraft in this way, but this approach was not common; see Thorndike, VI: 538.

82. U. F. Schneider, p. 18.

83. Allen, *Doubt's Boundless Sea*; Glanvill, *Sadducismus Triumphatus*; Bodin, pp. i, ii verso.

84. Robbins, pp. 45–46.

85. Robbins, pp. 496–97; Conrad, *Deutsche Rechtsgeschichte*, II: 438; Wolf, *Grosse Rechtsdenker*, pp. 395ff. For the qualifications of Thomasius's views, cf. Philipp, *Zeitalter der Aufklärung*, pp. 289–95.

86. Merzbacher, *Hexenprozesse in Franken*, pp. 111–12; Fehr, "Gottesurteil und Folter"; Lea, *Superstition and Force*, pp. 371–524; Hansen, *Quellen*, pp. 167–68: "neque hoc genus demoniorum eici potest, nisi cum tortura et quaestione."

87. *Carolina*, Arts. 60, 69; Geilen, "Auswirkungen der 'Cautio Criminalis,'" pp. 12–19.

88. *Carolina,* pp. 16–17; Fehr, "Gottesurteil und Folter," pp. 240–50.

89. *Carolina,* Arts. 33–47.

90. Hansen, *Quellen,* p. 311.

91. Robbins, p. 539.

92. U. F. Schneider, pp. 76–77; Thorndike, VI: 535.

93. The learned jurist Johann Fichard offered just such a legal objection to illegal uses of torture; U. F. Schneider, pp. 89–90.

94. Robbins, pp. 78–79.

95. U. F. Schneider, p. 91; Merzbacher, *Hexenprozesse in Franken,* pp. 24–25; Geilen, p. 41.

96. Robbins, p. 480. Spee marks the high point of opposition to legal abuses. Adam Tanner and Paul Laymann, both Jesuits, used similar arguments before and after Spee's time.

97. Robbins, pp. 273, 479–84; Spee, *Cautio Criminalis* (1939 ed.), Q. 22, p. 104.

98. Geilen, pp. 45–50; Robbins, pp. 220, 492; Trevor-Roper, "European Witch-Craze."

99. Geilen, pp. 45–50; Merzbacher, *Hexenprozesse in Franken,* pp. 36–37. Hermann Knapp tried to debunk this as mere legend by pointing out that there were trials again in the eighteenth century. They were minor in comparison to the seventeenth century. Certainly Leibniz cannot be accused of lying about events that were still more than fifty years off. Knapp, *Zenten des Hochstifts Würzburg,* II: 588–89.

100. Robbins, p. 269; but cf. Paulus, *Hexenwahn,* pp. 270–75.

101. Geilen, p. 44; Christian Meyfarth took many of his arguments from Spee in his *Christliche Erinnerung* of 1635.

102. Geilen, p. 44.

CHAPTER THREE

1. Hansen, *Zauberwahn,* p. 4; this attitude was vigorously opposed by Nikolaus Paulus and other nineteenth-century Catholics.

2. Macfarlane, *Witchcraft,* shows that this was the case in Essex.

3. Diefenbach, *Hexenwahn,* pp. 301–23; Paulus, *Hexenwahn,* pp. 48–100.

4. Thorndike, *History,* VI, 156 et seq.

5. Jacob, "Hexenlehre," pp. 16–43, esp. p. 34; Walker, *Spiritual and Demonic Magic;* Yates, *Giordano Bruno;* Nauert, *Agrippa.*

6. The work is relatively rare and has never been evaluated by a competent historian of late medieval theology.

7. A study should be undertaken to determine if *via moderna* and *via antiqua* had distinct positions regarding witchcraft. If they did, the difference may well have lain in divergent conceptions of God's will.

8. "Hoc documentum contra multos est, quidem enim laedantur vel laesiones petiuntur, inculpant seu accusant astra, alii daemones, tertii fortunam illi phytonissas [sic] alii incantatores," *Opusculum,* sig. B3v.

9. *Ibid.,* sig. f1v to g4v.

10. Laistner, "Western Church and Astrology"; Allen, *Star Crossed Renaissance;* Burckhardt, *Renaissance,* pp. 484–94.

11. Cassirer, *Individual and Cosmos,* p. 101.

12. *Ibid.,* pp. 117–22.

13. Klibanski et al., *Saturn and Melancholy,* pp. 245–46.

14. Pagel, *Paracelsus,* p. 50; Yates, pp. 60, 114–15; Cassirer, p. 111.

15. Koestler, *Watershed*, pp. 38–42.

16. Warburg, "Heidnisch-antike Weissagung," pp. 492–97; Rauscher, "Halleysche Komet," pp. 259–76; Graubard, "Astrology's Demise."

17. Boas, "Establishment," pp. 424–26; Calvin, *Institutes*, I, v, 5; I, xiv, 22.

18. Zanta, *Renaissance du stoïcisme*, pp. 47–73.

19. Saunders, *Justus Lipsius*, pp. 157ff; Oestreich, "Calvinismus"; Brunner, *Adeliges Landleben*, pp. 128–30.

20. Ringgren, *Fatalistic Beliefs*, gathers expert treatments of fate from cultures all over the world, thus pointing up the complexities involved in doctrines of fate.

21. A few scholars of course have recognized this, e.g. Williams, *Witchcraft*; Teall, Witchcraft and Calvinism"; Rosen, *Madness in Society*, pp. 14–17.

22. Brenz, *In Hiob* (1527); I have also used the German translation of 1530, *Der Job ussgelegt*; cf. M. Brecht, "Chronologie," p. 54; and M. Brecht, *Die frühe Theologie*, pp. 153–67.

23. "Permittit Satanae, ut per maleficos & incantatores, aut miraculas edat, aut praestigiis suis oculos spectatorum perstringat, & factis phantasmatibus illudat," *Operum . . . Brentii . . . Tomus Septimus*, p. 158.

24. The lectures were given April 1537 to April 1538: *Operum . . . Tomus Primus* (1576) (Köhler No. 541), p. 496; cf. Schäfer, *Kirchengeschichte*, p. 51; and cf. M. Brecht, "Chronologie," pp. 58–59.

25. Brenz, "Ein Predig von dem Hagel und Ungewitter"; this sermon was preached in 1539 but not published until 1557, when it appeared as "Homilia de grandine" in *Pericopiae evangeliorum quae usitato more in praecipuis Festis legi solent expositae per Iohan. Brent* (1557; Köhler No. 333); it was reprinted in this form in 1560 (K. 372) and in 1572 (K. 531). Jacob Gretter translated it into German with the other feast and festival sermons in 1558 (K. 347). It was reprinted in this form in 1561 (K. 397), 1565 (K. 445), and 1572 (K. 527). It also appeared separately in German in 1565 (K. 459, K. 460), and 1570 (K. 514). Johann Weyer included it in the Apologia for his *De Praestigiis Daemonum* (1577 and 1583), and it appears in the German version of *De Praestigiis* published as the second volume of *Theatrum de Veneficis* (Frankfurt, 1586) and again in Weyer's *Opera Omnia* (Amsterdam, 1660). It was probably in Weyer's work that Reginald Scot read it; cf. Scot's *The Discoverie of Witchcraft* (ed. Williamson), p. 26. It seems clear, therefore, that Brenz's sermon enjoyed a modest success. I am grateful to Dr. Martin Brecht for help in working out this publication history.

26. The argument was first formulated by Ulric Molitor, a jurist at the episcopal curia of Constance in 1489. See above, p. 24. Molitor's work was also reprinted in the *Theatrum de Veneficis*, mentioned in the preceding note. See Janssen, *Geschichte*, VIII: 601–2, for full quotations from Molitor and comparisons with Johann Weyer.

27. See Brenz, "Ob ein Weltliche Obrigkeit . . . die Widertauffer . . . vom Leben zum Tod richten lassen möge," in *Consiliorum Theologicorum Decas IV*, ed. Bidembach (Lauingen, 1607), pp. 211–34. Brenz never satisfactorily cleared up his paradoxical view that witches deserved death while Anabaptists should be treated with the spiritual sword only. Weyer attacked Brenz at exactly this point in correspondence with Brenz during 1565 and 1566. The letters and Brenz's reply appear in Weyer's "Liber apologeticus" attached to *De Praestigiis Daemonum* (Basel, 1577), pp. 818 et seq.

28. Brenz, Commentarius Posterior in Exodum, *Operum . . . Tomus Primus* (1576) (Köhler No. 541), p. 676.

29. *Samuelis Liber prior* (1554); *Operum . . . Tomus Tertius* (1578) (K. 546), p. 1423; *Operum . . . Tomus Septimus* (1588) (K. 568), pp. 806, 886. Martin Brecht makes this point in *Die frühe Theologie*, pp. 11–12.

30. Hellmann, "Meteorologie," pp. 21–22.

31. Sachs, "Ein spiel," pp. 63–64.

32. Spreter, *Hexen Büchlein*, bound to his *Christenliche Instruction* (Basel, 1540); on Spreter, cf. Bossert, "Johann Spreter," and Paulus, "Johann Spretter."

33. Paulus, "Johann Spretter," p. 251.

34. *Ibid.*, pp. 261–62.

35. Crusius, *Schwäbische Chronik*, II: 304.

36. *Erschreckliche Nüwe Zytung* (1562), fol. 2v; this was found in the Bayerische Staatsbibliothek, Munich; it is cited in Emil Weller, *Zeitungen*, pp. 173–74, No. 256.

37. Alber and Bidembach, *Summa etlicher Predigen* (1562), sig. A2v. This work was even translated into Croatian in 1563. Köhler (No. 426) mistakenly attributed it to Brenz. Felix Bidembach reprinted this tract 40 years later, explaining that the "foolish rabble" were still wrongly accusing witches; *Consiliorum Theologicorum Decas I* (1608), fol.):( ):(, r–v, and pp. 118–33.

38. Alber and Bidembach, sig. A3v–A4r.

39. *Ibid.*, fols. B2v–B3r.

40. This was, however, a favorite maxim repeated even by the most resolute witch hunters. Cf. Paulus, "Johann Spretter," p. 257, and his "Württembergische Hexenpredigten," p. 85.

41. "Eng recht, weit unrecht," cf. Kisch, *Erasmus*.

42. In many of these statements they borrowed verbatim from Brenz.

43. Alber and Bidembach, sig. C1v.

44. Heerbrand, *Disputationes Theologicae*, p. 467.

45. "Sunt enim tantum inania verba, et murmur quoddam, ad decipiendos homines, arte diabolica conficta et composita, quae nullus sequitur effectus, neque ex ordinatione divina, neque ex causis naturalibus." *Ibid.*, p. 469.

46. *Ibid.*, p. 471. Cf. also Heerbrand's *Compendium Theologiae*, "De Miraculis," p. 435: "Quorum opera utitur, ut sibi devinctos retineat et alios in errorem inducat."

47. Heerbrand, *Predig von dem Wunderzeichen* (1577), pp. 8–11; cf. Rauscher, "Halleysche Komet."

48. *Predig Vom Straal* (1579), fol. 4r–v.

49. *Ibid.*, fol. 6r.

50. Platz, *Kurtzer Nottwendiger unnd Wollgegrundter Bericht*. I have also used the reprint in Bidembach, ed., *Consiliorum Theologicorum Decas II*, pp. 50–80.

51. Platz, *Newe Zeitung* (1584), p. 10.

52. *Ibid.*, p. 14.

53. *Ibid.*, pp. 17–20.

54. Pflacher, *Weinthewre*. Pflacher was a minister in the imperial city of Kempten and preached these two sermons on December 8 and 12, 1588. In traditional manner he discounted secondary causes and emphasized God as the true cause of man's troubles. High wine prices were of course punishment for the sin of drunkenness. See also Wilhelm Bidembach, "Wie zur Zeit der Thewrung und Hungersnoth, die einfältige Pfarrer und Kirchendiener das Volck ermahnen, lehren, und trösten sollen," first printed in 1570 and reprinted in Felix Bidembach, ed., *Consiliorum Theologicorum Decas II*, No. 7.

55. This was an image of some importance for European intellectual history. For

the necessity of "governors" for clockwork in the age before Huygens, see Cipolla, *Clocks and Culture*, pp. 41, 122–23. By the sixteenth century some thinkers saw the clock image as a threat to the Christian idea of providence. Johann Hasler argued that God was not a clockmaker but that he sat behind the scenes and constantly controlled everything, just as the "Kuntzenjäger seine Bildlin hintern grünen Tüch selbs hin und her heben," *Astrologische Practica*, sig. A2r. See also Thompson, "Time, Work-Discipline, and Industrial Capitalism," pp. 56–57. For Elizabethan usage of the same image, cf. Stürzl, *Zeitbegriff*, pp. 126–27. For a recent treatment of this image, see Popper, *Of Clouds and Clocks*.

56. *Wetter Glöcklin*, pp. 15–16. I have used the second edition of 1603. The first edition would seem to have been 1599 (p. 5). On p. 151 Schopff refers to "this present year, '98," making 1598 the likely year of composition for this work.

57. *Ibid.*, pp. 68–69.

58. *Ibid.*, pp. 72–73.

59. Sigwart, *Predigt Von dem Erdbidemen*, fol. 10r–10v.

60. *Predigt Vom Reiffen*; cf. the interesting speculations in *Zwo Hexenzeitung*, fols. 3v–4r.

61. *Predigt Vom Hagel*, pp. 16–17.

62. *Brunstpredigt*, p. 14.

63. For an origin of this image, cf. Plato, *The Republic*, V: 469.

64. Lotter, *Gründtlicher und nothwendiger Bericht*, pp. 10–11. A first edition appeared in 1613, but I have been able to locate only the second edition of 1615.

65. *Ibid.*, pp. 15–16.

66. *Ibid.*, pp. 27–28.

67. *Ibid.*, p. 35.

68. *Ibid.*, pp. 110–15.

69. Karl Gödecke was the first to identify this work; cf. his *Grundriss*, Vol. II, *Reformationszeitalter* (2d ed.; Dresden, 1886), p. 387. For Birck, see Hugo Holstein, "Thomas Birck"; Holstein did not know of the *Hexenspiegel*. For an account of the printing of *Hexenspeigel*, cf. Sievers, "Notizen"; however, Seivers had not examined the copy in the Stuttgart Landesbibliothek. It is clear from Birck's account that only these nine signatures (72 pp.) were printed. We know of no MS of the whole work. For a sensational and distorted description of the *Hexenspiegel*, cf. Janssen, *Geschichte*, VI, 382–85.

70. *Hexenspiegel*, p. 1.

71. Gödecke, p. 387; Janssen, VI: 382–85.

72. *Hexenspiegel*, pp. 16, 31, 32.

73. *Ibid.*, pp. 66–68.

74. *Zwo Hexen Zeitung* (1616), fol. 4r.

75. Graeter, *Hexen oder Unholden Predigten*, sig. A2v–B1r.

76. *Ibid.*, sig. B1r–v.

77. *Ibid.*, sig. C1r.

78. *Ibid.*, sig. C4v–D2v.

79. *Ibid.*, sig. B2v–B3r.

80. Janssen, VIII, 638–41; but see Lea, *Materials*, p. 647.

81. *Acht Hexenpredigten*, Vorrede.

82. *Ibid.*, fol. 12v–13r.

83. *Ibid.*, fol. 56v.

84. *Ibid.*, fols. 67r, 75v, 91r.

85. *Ibid.*, fol. 75v.
86. *Ibid.*, fol. 76r.
87. *Ibid.*, fol. 109r.
88. *Ibid.*, fol. 114r-v.
89. *Ibid.*, fol. 114r.
90. *Ibid.*, fol. 115r.
91. Hartmann, *Chronik*, p. 78. Schrötlin was born of a distinguished line of preachers. His father was a Württemberg preacher and superintendent; his mother was the daughter of Matthaeus Alber. Cf. Hützelin, *Zwo Christliche Leich Predigten.*
92. *Tractatus Theologicus*, pp. 91–106; the first edition was in 1621. Cf. Paulus, *Hexenwahn*, pp. 114–15; Thorndike, *History*, VIII: 557–58.
93. Gehring, "Hexenprozess," p. 169.
94. Seeger, *Consilia Tubingensia*, pp. 56–61.
95. *Ibid.*, pp. 61, 94 et seq.
96. The Consilium is lengthy by sixteenth-century standards. It was printed in Thumm, *Tractatus Theologicus*, pp. 76–90.
97. Gehring, "Hexenprozess," I (1937): 179–80.
98. *Ibid.*, p. 181.
99. *Ibid.*, pp. 182–83.
100. Dieterich, *Sonderbahrer Predigten*, pp. 19–22.
101. *Specimen Zeli.*
102. *Ibid.*, pp. 24–25, 28.
103. *Ibid.*, p. 97.
104. *Ibid.*, p. 116.
105. Gehring, "Hexenprozess," I (1937): 186–88.
106. Mauritius, *Consiliorum Chiloniensium*, Pt. II, pp. 310–11; cf. Gehring, "Hexenprozess," p. 186.
107. Wagner, *Kohlschwartze Teuffel*, pp. 71–79, 85–86; cf. Wagner's *Casual Predigten*, pp. 73–116. This latter item is an "Apologia, das ist: Gründlicher Gegenbericht, Auff das zu Dillingen wider obige Predigt, den genanten Kohlschwartzen Teuffel, Unter dem Namen eines Einfältigen Teuffels von Esslingen, Cum Facultate Superiorum aussgesprenfte Passquill." I could not locate a copy of this Catholic attack from Dillingen.
108. Wagner, "Apologia," p. 77.
109. Faber, *Specimen Zeli*, sig. C1.
110. *Commentarius in Pentateuchum*, I: 226–27.
111. *De Magia*. Gehring felt moved to complain that it "würfelt alles, was je über das Thema geschrieben wurde, in beispielloser Weitschweifigkeit, Kritiklosigkeit und Fruchtlosigkeit durcheinander," "Hexenprozess," I (1937): 177n; cf. Thorndike, *History*, VII: 359.
112. Osiander, *De Magia*, p. 293; my italics.
113. *Ibid.*, pp. 294, 311.
114. "Heberlin," *Historische Relation*, p. 27.
115. *Ibid.*, pp. 36–37; cf. Holl, "Bedeutung der grossen Kriege," pp. 313–14. A. D. J. Macfarlane argues the opposite, i.e. that Protestant doctrine tended to increase the terror of the unknown and unaccountable; *Witchcraft*, p. 195.
116. I have used the faithful reprint (Paris, 1885) of the 1579 French translation, *Deux Dialogues*, p. 438; cf. Thorndike, *History*, V: 652–67.
117. Lea, *Materials*, p. 552; Erastus, *Deux Dialogues*, pp. 498–505, 532, 538.

118. Vierordt, *Geschichte*, II, 122; Janssen, *Geschichte*, VIII: 637–38; Heidelberg's legal faculty was not consistent in this position. Cf. Carl Binz's introduction to his edition of Witekind, *Augustin Lercheimer*.

119. Vierordt, *Geschichte*, II: 122. Balduin was a jurist at Heidelberg, 1556–61.

120. Binz, *Augustin Lercheimer*, pp. 7–8, 45, 52, 82.

121. *Ibid.*, pp. 49–50.

122. *Ibid.*, p. 157.

123. Vierordt, *Geschichte*, II: 122.

124. Karl F. Vierordt noticed the same sharp contrast when he listed the writers of sixteenth-century Baden. He had no trouble listing over 30 Protestant writers, but he could find no more than four Catholics; *Geschichte*, II, 114–16. Suffragan Bishop Forner of Bamberg noted with dismay in 1625, "I know of scarcely any [Catholic] preachers who confront this plague [of witchcraft] and try to heal it." Duhr, *Geschichte der Jesuiten*, Vol. II, Pt. 2, p. 499.

125. Zinccius, "De potestate Daemonum"; on Zink, cf. Schreiber, *Geschichte der Albert Ludwigs Universität*, II: 218–19, 266; and Zedler, *Universal-Lexikon*, Vol. 62, cols. 850–51.

126. Zink, "De potestate Daemonum," fol. 57r.

127. *Ibid.*, fol. 79v.

128. *Ibid.*, fol. 80r-v.

129. Cf. Riezler, *Hexenprozesse in Bayern*, pp. 233–34.

130. Schreiber, *Geschichte der Albert Ludwigs Universität*, II: 159; cf. Zedler, *Universal-Lexikon*, Vol. 28, cols. 70–71; and Thorndike, *History*, VI: 399–405.

131. Pictorius, *Pantopōlion*, pp. 31–32.

132. *Ibid.*, p. 38.

133. "Non ideo tantum, quod a Christianorum, collegio, mente et corpore turpiter sese subtrahunt, et particulari cuidam daemoni obsceno servituto velut mancipio astringent; aut ut verius loquar, in hunc finem adpropriant, ut se in homines quos odio habent, rite ulciscantur, hos laedant, gravent et interficiant quandoque." *Ibid.*, p. 78.

134. *Ibid.*, p. 79. "Obijcimus quod harum Erynnarum numerus in tam immensum ecrescit mare, ut nemo ab earum incantationibus et expiationibus tutus versari queat, si non cremantur." *Ibid.*, p. 80.

135. Wagner, *Catechesis*, p. 412; on Wagner, cf. Zedler, *Universal-Lexikon*, Vol. Vol. 52, col. 641.

136. Feucht, *Neun und dreissig Catholische Predigen*, pp. 422–24, 502–10.

137. Lutz, *Warhafftige Zeittung* (1571), in *Theatrum de Veneficis*, p. 5. On Lutz, cf. Paulus in *Diözesanarchiv aus Schwaben*, 13 (1895): 81ff, and Zedler, *Universal-Lexikon*, Vol. 18, cols. 1354–55.

138. *Warhafftige Zeittung*, p. 5.

139. On Lorichius, cf. Schreiber, *Geschichte der Albert Ludwigs Universität*, II: 308; Zedler, *Universal-Lexikon*, Vol. 18, col. 460; and especially Ehses, "Jodocus Lorichius."

140. *Aberglaub*, pp. 382–85.

141. *Ibid.*, p. 119.

142. *Ibid.*, p. 126.

143. For this problem see Bauer, *Frühgeschichte der theologischen Fakultät*. For a selection of Catholic sermons from the sixteenth and seventeenth centuries, see Brischar, *Die katholischen Kanzelredner*, Vols. 1–3. For preaching traditions in the German Southwest before the Reformation, cf. Kerker, "Zur Geschichte des Predigtwe-

sens." A step in the direction of a history of Catholic teaching in the German Southwest after the Reformation was taken by Lauer, in "Theologische Bildung."

144. Martini, *De Ivre Censuum* (1604); another edition appeared in Cologne, 1660. I cite the 1604 edition. The "nova interpretatio" of arts. 109 and 218 runs from p. 519 to p. 544. On Martini, cf. Stintzing, *Geschichte der deutschen Rechtswissenschaft*, I: 672.

145. *De Ivre Censuum*, p. 518.

146. *Ibid.*, p. 519.

147. *De Ivre Censuum*, pp. 530–32.

148. See my dissertation, "The Social and Intellectual Foundations of Witch Hunting in Southwestern Germany, 1562–1684," Yale University, 1970, pp. 129–30, for details of this matter.

149. For the whole idea of the construction of a confessional image, consult the seminal article by Ernst Walter Zeeden, "Grundlagen und Wege der Konfessionsbildung."

150. Heerbrand, "De Magia," p. 478.

151. E.g. Heilbronner, *Daemonomania*, pp. 12–17.

152. Sigwart, *Predigt Vom Reiffen*, fol. 3v.

153. Graeter, *Hexen oder Unholden Predigten*, sig. A2v–B1r.

154. Längin, *Religion und Hexenprozess*, pp. 133–34.

155. Stähelin, *Brunstpredigt*, p. 12; Platz, *Newe Zeitung*, p. 14.

156. Janssen, *Geschichte*, VIII, 632. This was the explicit view of Peter Binsfeld; cf. Lea, *Materials*, II: 578. Delrio also supported this view; cf. Lea, *Materials*, II: 643–44.

157. Spee, *Cautio Criminalis*.

158. Martini, *De Ivre Censuum*, p. 519.

159. This connection was drawn by the "counterconsultant," who attacked Leonhard Kager's views; HSASt B177, Büschel 122.

160. Osiander, *De Magia*, p. 293.

CHAPTER FOUR

1. Hansen, *Quellen*, pp. 516–613; Soldan-Heppe, *Geschichte der Hexenprozesse*, I: 213–19.

2. Thirteen editions are known from 1487 to 1520 and another sixteen from 1576 to 1660. Burr noted that not one important witchcraft treatise appeared between 1520 and 1563.

3. Cf. Schweizer, "Der Hexenprozess," pp. 32–33, for Zwingli.

4. Diefenbach, *Zauberglaube*, pp. 1 et seq.; Paulus, *Hexenwahn*, pp. 48–66; the sixteenth-century Jesuit Martin Delrio blamed the rise of witchcraft on the Reformation.

5. Diefenbach, *Hexenwahn*, pp. 289–300.

6. Trevor-Roper, *Crisis*, pp. 140–45; Robbins, *Encyclopedia*, p. 218; Burns, *Counter Reformation*, pp. 78–80.

7. Soldan-Heppe, *Geschichte der Hexenprozesse*, I: 508; II: 53; Robbins, *Encyclopedia*, p. 218.

8. Duhr, *Stellung der Jesuiten*, p. 96.

9. Burr, *Selections from His Writings*, pp. 228–30.

10. *Carolina*, Introduction, pp. 15–16; cf. Articles 12, 13, 14, 61.

11. Merzbacher, *Hexenprozesse in Franken*, p. 153; Delcambre, "Les procès de sorcellerie en Lorraine"; Schwerin, *Grundzüge*, pp. 351–53; Planitz, *Deutsche Rechts-*

geschichte, pp. 256–57, 259, 303, 305–7; Conrad, *Deutsche Rechtsgeschichte,* II: 429–34, 339–42; Schmidt, *Einführung,* pp. 86–107, 194–211.

12. Burr, *Selections,* pp. 182–83.

13. Gehring, "Hexenprozess," I (1937): 157–88, esp. p. 167.

14. Soldan-Heppe, *Geschichte der Hexenprozesse,* I: 399.

15. *Carolina,* Articles 24–44; Altona, "Stellung," pp. 909–13.

16. Osborn, *Teufelliteratur,* p. 22; Gödecke, *Grundriss,* II: 476–83; Grimm, Teufels-bücher," pp. 513–15; Ohse, "Teufelliteratur"; this dissertation contains an excellent bibliography. Freiherr von Liliencron also noted the rise of miraculous and supersti-tious accounts after 1550, in "Mitteilungen," p. 139.

17. Osborn, *Teufelliteratur,* pp. 3–22; cf. the representative collection of such works in *Theatrum Diabolorum,* ed. Feyrabend (1569).

18. Grimm, "Teufelsbücher," s.v. 1552.

19. *Theatrum Diabolorum;* in the first edition, only the "Pestilenzteuffel" of Her-mann Straccus had not appeared in an earlier edition.

20. Cf. Gödecke, *Grundriss,* II: 564–69, for a list of the numerous early editions. There were four reprints in the first year, 1587–88.

21. The *Theatrum Diabolorum* contains works by Jodocus Hocker, a follower of Weyer, and by the more credulous Ludwig Millich. The *Theatrum de Veneficis* contains works by Weyer and his disciple Ewich, as well as by the witch-hunting Calvinist Lambert Daneau.

22. In cities now in Württemberg, epidemics came in the 1560's to Brackenheim, Heilbronn, Lauffen, Neuenstadt, Schwäbisch Hall, Stuttgart, Ulm, Waiblingen, Wimpfen, Sulz, and Wangen. The 1570's were no healthier. Cf. Keyser, *Deutsches Städtebuch,* IV: 2, 2, under the names of these cities.

23. The few other regions for which we have adequate accounts tend to support this conclusion, especially those by G. Bader, Schacher, Byloff, Notestein, Ewen, Reiz-ler, Merzbacher, H. Klein, Krämer, Hoppstädter.

24. WSAL A209 (Oberrat), Bü. 1424.

25. Monter, *Calvin's Geneva,* p. 72.

26. Recent studies of prejudice have made good use of the concept; e.g. Berkowitz, "Anti-Semitism," and Berkowitz and Green, "Stimulus Qualities."

27. G. Bader, *Hexenprozesse in der Schweiz,* esp. the tables at the end. See also Monter, "Patterns of Witchcraft in the Jura."

28. Trevor-Roper, *Crisis,* p. 160.

29. Zwetsloot, *Friedrich von Spee,* pp. 282–83.

30. Franz, *Der dreissigjährige Krieg,* p. 43.

31. Cf. Freytag, "Der dreissigjährige Krieg." For the wrath of peasants against soldiers, cf. Redlich, *De Praeda Militari,* p. 7.

32. Bechtold, "Hexen im bayrischen Lager," p. 141.

33. Wedgwood, *Thirty Years War,* p. 376.

34. Bechtold, "Hexen im bayrischen Lager," pp. 141–42; for witches in the Swedish army, cf. Rommel, "Beiträge," pp. 19–20.

35. German, *Chronik,* pp. 242–43; Gmelin, *Hällische Geschichte,* p. 817; Riegler, *Reichsstadt Schwäbisch Hall,* p. 71; Krüger, *Schwäbisch Hall,* p. 43.

36. Charles Tilly's study, *The Vendée,* is a model example.

37. For such regions the most useful general works are Huttenlocher, *Baden-Württemberg;* Gradmann, *Süddeutschland;* Grube, *Vogteien;* Grube, "Vogteien-Ämter-Landkreise"; and K. S. Bader, *Der deutsche Südwesten.*

38. Trevor-Roper, pp. 105–6.

39. Bitter, *Massenwahn*, discussion of papers, pp. 239, 254–55.

40. David Sabean of the University of Pittsburgh is at work on varying patterns of family structure in the German Southwest.

41. Neither series of records has been fully exploited, although Paul Gehring used the Tübingen *consilia* for his study (without full footnotes to the archival materials). The records of the Oberrat are now held at the State Archive in Ludwigsburg under the rubric A209. Further study of the Tübingen *consilia* may be facilitated by the catalog of witchcraft cases that I prepared and left in the Tübingen University Archive.

42. *Carolina*, Art. 109.

43. Giefel, "Hexenprozesse in Horb," p. 91.

44. Disch, *Chronik der Stadt Wolfach*, pp. 379–80.

45. Haug, *Marbacher Dorfbuch*, p. 259.

46. Weisert, *Geschichte der Stadt Sindelfingen*, pp. 131–32.

47. A. Rapp, "Scheiterhaufen am Oberrhein," p. 52.

48. Weingarten (city), *Altdorf-Weingarten*, p. 76.

49. Bechtold, *Grimmelshausen und seine Zeit*, pp. 127–29.

50. Brecht, *Kirchenordnung*, pp. 96–97.

51. Rest, "Ettenheimer Hexenprozesse," pp. 55–56.

52. On the whole subject of this genuine ritual tradition, cf. Butler, *Ritual Magic*, esp. pp. 213 et seq.

53. Brecht, *Kirchenordnung*, p. 98.

54. WSAL A209 (Oberrat), cf. Schorndorf, 1705; and Maulbronn, 1730.

55. Stevenson, *Meaning of Poison*.

56. For this case and the other generalizations in this paragraph I have relied on the catalog of the papers of the Württemberg Oberrat, A209 in Staatsarchiv Ludwigsburg.

57. Willburger, "Hexenprozesse im Nagolder Wald."

58. WSAL A209 (Oberrat), cf. Nagold, 1742.

CHAPTER FIVE

1. For this account on Weisensteig, see Wurm, *Chronik*, pp. 11–17; Kerler, *Geschichte*, pp. 141–48; Veesenmeyer, *Sammlung*, pp. 1–38.

2. Crusius, *Schwäbische Chronik*, II: 304.

3. Pfaff, "Hexenprozesse zu Esslingen," pp. 257–58; for Naogeorgus and his witchcraft beliefs, see *Allgemeine deutsche Biographie*, 23 (1886): 245–50; *Religion in Geschichte und Gegenwart* (3d ed., 1960), Vol. 4, col. 1306; Theobald, *Das Leben und Wirken*, p. 32.

4. Pfaff, "Hexenprozesse zu Esslingen," pp. 263–65.

5. Crusius, *Schwäbische Chronik*, II: 304.

6. Schön, "Was in den Jahren 1555–96," p. 108.

7. *Warhafftige und Erschreckliche Thatten* (1563); for some unexplained reason, Wurm in his *Chronik*, p. 17, reports that Ulrich executed 70 in one day. He cites no source.

8. Miller, *Baden-Württemberg*, pp. 747–48.

9. Oswald Gabelkofer was born in 1539 and served 37 years as personal physician to the dukes of Württemberg; see LBSt, his "Chronik der Grafen von Helfenstein," p. 746. Gabelkofer notes that "What else there is to report of the life and deeds of these famous princely counts, especially concerning the changes in religion or the

burning of the many witches, and much else besides, my gracious Lord Count Rudolf, your Grace's only son, will be able to learn from your Grace if you think it proper."

10. Stälin, *Wirtembergische Geschichte*, IV: 644–46; *Allgemeine deutsche Biographie*, 4 (1876): 639.

11. Paulus too assumes this to be the case; see his *Hexenwahn*, pp. 108–9.

12. Pfaff, "Hexenprozesse zu Esslingen," pp. 265 et seq.

13. Crusius used the polemical language of the 1590's when he called Naogeorgus a "Calvinist." We must be cautious here and should perhaps merely suggest some sort of Zwinglian unorthodoxy; *Schwäbische Chronik*, II: 308.

14. Crusius, *Schwäbische Chronik*, II: 354.

15. Meder, *Acht Hexenpredigten*, fol. 36r-v.

16. GLAK 65 (Handschriften), Bü. 728 (Originalakten über Hexenprozesse in Schwaben, 1581–1682), fol. 80.

17. Keyser, *Deutsches Städtebuch*, IV, 2, 2, s.v. Rottenburg.

18. Bossert, "Rottenburg"; Stemmler, *Grafschaft Hohenberg*, pp. 5–6.

19. *Beschreibung des Oberamts Rottenburg*, II: 412–13. Four women and one man were accused and three of the women executed in 1530. Despite strappado 186 times, these three confessed nothing until Dr. Wolf Wischler of Balingen brought them the mysterious drink. A similar potion was used at Esslingen by a Tübingen surgeon in 1562; Pfaff, "Hexenprozesse zu Esslingen," pp. 258, 260.

20. *Warhafftige und ein erschröckliche Neuwe Zeitung*, sig. A4r.

21. Crusius, *Schwäbische Chronik*, II: 339. The witches at Horb were executed on June 7, only 23 days after the storm.

22. *Newe Zeitung Von den Hexen* (1580), sig. A2r; cf. the same account in *Zwo Newe Zeittung. Was man für Hexen oder Unholden verbrendt hat* (1580), sig. A1v.

23. Crusius, *Schwäbische Chronik*, II: 350–51; several scholars have read *vier* for *viel* and thus confidently add up the year's total as eight, e.g. Willburger, "Hexenverfolgung."

24. Crusius said that 19 were executed in Rottenburg in 1583, but the Thann chronicle cited only 12. Following Crusius are *Beschreibung des Oberamts Rottenburg*, II: 413; Vierordt, *Geschichte*, II: 126. Following the Thann chronicle is Janssen, *Geschichte*, VIII: 725. Cf. Westenhoeffer, *Reformationsgeschichte*, pp. 86–87. The chronicler mistakenly gloats on p. 87 over the work of the devil in Rottenburg— which he assumes to be Protestant!

25. Westenhoeffer, *Reformationsgeschichte*, p. 87; see also Günther, "Mühringer Hexenprozesse," pp. 5–9.

26. Crusius, *Schwäbische Chronik*, II: 378.

27. Crusius, *Schwäbische Chronik*, II: 385; cf. Hassler, *Chronik*, p. 141.

28. *Beschreibung des Oberamts Rottenburg*, II: 413–14.

29. I was unable to turn up the original documents for Rottenburg's witch trials.

30. Birlinger, *Aus Schwaben*, I: 131–84, esp. 142–45.

31. *Ibid.*, p. 146; cf. Schön, "Was in den Jahren," pp. 135–36.

32. Birlinger stated that 19 were executed on June 11, but this may be a mistake, since Crusius would hardly have failed to mention so large an execution; Birlinger, *Aus Schwaben*, I: 151; Crusius, *Diarium*, I: 135.

33. Birlinger, I:150.

34. *Ibid.*, pp. 151–52; Crusius, *Diarium*, II: 333; Crusius's nephew witnessed the execution of ten women on August 17, 1599 (*cum permissu meo!*).

35. Birlinger, I: 132, 136.

36. Crusius, *Diarium*, III: 305, 334.

37. *Ibid.*, p. 132.

38. *Beschreibung des Oberamts Rottenburg*, II: 414.

39. "Magus esse fertur," Crusius, *Diarium*, III: 781.

40. *Ibid.*, pp. 614, 769; 16 witches were executed at Horb in 1605 (*ibid.*, p. 768).

41. Birlinger, I: 152–57.

42. *Beschreibung des Oberamts Rottenburg*, II: 414.

43. Birlinger, I: 175.

44. Miller, *Baden-Württemberg*, pp. 568–73; Keyser, *Deutsches Städtebuch*, IV, 2, 2, p. 430.

45. Ruckgaber, "Hexenprozesse"; Rottweil Stadtarchiv, Criminalakten: II/I/V/-9/#14–26, Repertoria by Mack, Vols. 12–14. Ruckgaber counted only 32 executions for the years 1561–1600, but it seems clear that 60 is closer to the truth.

46. *Zwo Newe Zeittung. Was man für Hexen oder Unholden verbrendt hat* (1580), sig. A1v; for the same account cf. *Newe Zeitung Von den Hexen* (1580), sig. A2r. Aldenberger, *Fewerspiegel* (1610) is said to contain the same report, but I have been unable to examine it.

47. Ruckgaber, "Hexenprozesse," pp. 179–80.

48. *Ibid.*, pp. 182, 190–96. Rottweil Stadtarchiv, Criminalakten: II/I/V/9/#14–26; see the cases of Hans Tresell and Ursula Stramin.

49. Rottweil Stadtarchiv, Repertorium, Vol. 13, 1582–89: see letter of April 14, 1582, with regard to a "Gesellschaft der Brenner." For witches as arsonists, see Haslach in 1533 and Stuttgart in 1563; Pfaff, *Geschichte der Stadt Stuttgart*, I: 218; Crusius, *Schwäbische Chronik*, II: 236; *Ein erschröcklich geschicht Vom Tewfel* (1533).

50. Miller, *Baden-Württemberg*, pp. 497–98; Dengler, "Hexenwesen," p. 104.

51. Walter, *Kurze Geschichte*, pp. 77–78.

52. Dengler, "Hexenwesen." Except for a few false transcriptions of names from the documents and a large number of facile generalizations from inadequate acquaintance with the secondary literature, Dengler's study is reliable, even if it is a perfect specimen of *Gründlichkeit*. His dissertation bulks almost as large as the total sum of manuscript sources used.

53. *Ibid.*, p. 7; this claim makes no sense at all.

54. *Ibid.*, trial no. 1.

55. *Ibid.*, trials nos. 2–49.

56. SASigm, Repositur 30 (Thurn und Taxissches Archiv Obermarchtal), Paket 254 (Marchtaler Hexenprozesse), Dep. 6.

57. The *stygma diabolicum* did play a definite role in the witchcraft trial of 1745; see Dengler, p. 63.

58. SASigm, Repositur 30, Pkt. 254.

59. Dengler, trials nos. 65–72.

60. *Ibid.*, p. 63; trials nos. 29, 32, 58, 61; 25, 41, 57, 59.

61. *Ibid.*, p. 60.

62. Miller, *Baden-Württemberg*, p. 145.

63. Pfeifer, *Verfassungs- und Verwaltungsgeschichte*, p. 104.

64. Reinhard, "Untersuchungen," I: 318, 334.

65. Pfeifer, p. 154.

66. Pfeifer, pp. 158–59.

67. *Ibid.*, p. 159.

68. *Ibid.*, pp. 159–60.

69. *Ibid.*, p. 160.

70. WSAL B412 (Stift Ellwangen, Strafakten), Bü. 1 (Criminal-Processordnung im Stift Ellwangen).

71. Pfeifer, p. 171.

72. WSAL B412, Bü. 25–26: Informatio. Maintzischen Process wieder die Unholden (1612); Directorium wie mit Unholden in den Österreichischen Herrschaften Bregentz und Hohenegkh procedirt würdet (n.d.); see also Byr, "Hexenprozesse in Bregenz," pp. 215–26.

73. WSAL B412, Bü. 25–26: Interrogatoria Generalia So anno 1611 angefangen wieder die Unholden von Herrn Dr. Carl Kiblern Fürstl. Ellwangischen und Alten Cantzlern, circa materiam actuum strygimagiae, verfast.

74. WSAL B412, Bü. 25–26: Copia Churfürstlichen Maintzischen Mandats wie es mit der Confiscations Straff der Hexen Persohnen Zuhalten, proclaimed by Elector Johann Schweickhardt on April 13, 1612.

75. Pfeifer, p. 160, asserts that the court of Ellwangen did not consult other legal experts in the sixteenth and seventeenth centuries. Yet the records of a 1615 consultation with both Freiburg i. Br. and Ingolstadt exist; WSAL B389 (Stift Ellwangen), Bü. 230d (Strafakten). It seems likely that records of other such instances would emerge from an exhaustive survey of the trial records.

76. Keyser, *Deutsches Städtebuch*, IV, 2, 2, s.v. Ellwangen. Cf. Schabel, *Stadt und Garnison*, pp. 33–34, and Müller, "Zur Geschichte der Seuchen," pp. 83–86.

77. WSAL B387, Bü. 65 (Ellwangen Hofratsprotokolle); B387, Bü. 798 (Ellwangen Kapitel-Rezesse 1611–21), fols. 121v, 218v, 319r.

78. WSAL B389, Bü. 230f (Ellwangen Strafakten).

79. The richest materials are in WSAL B412 and B389. If placed in a pile, the Ellwangen records of this panic alone would surely rise 15 feet in height. It is curious that this wealth of material has provoked so little scholarly interest.

80. WSAL B412, Bü. 58, no. 2.

81. WSAL B412, Bü. 58, no. 4.

82. WSAL B412, Bü. 58, no. 5.

83. WSAL B412, Bü. 58, no. 8; cf. Rosen, *Madness in Society*, pp. 13–14.

84. WSAL B412, Bü. 58, no. 11.

85. WSAL B412, Bü. 58, no. 18.

86. WSAL B412, Bü. 58, no. 19.

87. Duhr, *Geschichte der Jesuiten*, p. 489. It was cheaper to execute several at one time. See also Zeller, "Hexenbrände," pp. 86–88.

88. Duhr, *Geschichte der Jesuiten*, p. 489.

89. See above, n. 79.

90. This was one of Margaret Murray's gravest errors in *Witch Cult*.

91. This account is drawn from a mass of witch confessions and testimony in Ellwangen: WSAL B412, Bü. 21, 52–54, 57–75, 78–90, 93–96; WSAL B389, Bü. 230a-f. See also Ellwangen, Pfarrarchiv, "Hillersche Chronik," pp. 521–41, for an account of 13 cases from Ellwangen in 1611–16. This chronicle is of great use for Ellwangen history, but in the matter of witchcraft it simply recounts these cases with no concern for generalizations. The MS was completed by Josef Friedrich von Hiller, Dr. jur., in 1844; for a description of it, see Häcker, "Die Hillerische und Schillerische Chronik."

92. The Southwest German sources almost never use the term "sabbat" or "sabbath" for witches. Instead, men spoke of "Hexentanz" or "conventum sagarum," or other such descriptive names.

93. WSAL B412, Bü. 65.

94. WSAL B412, Bü. 75.

95. WSAL B412, Bü. 65; the references to Anno 88 are to 1588.

96. WSAL B389, Bü. 230f.

97. WSAL B387, Bü. 64 (Ellwangen Hofratsprotokolle), fol. 334v.

98. WSAL B387, Bü. 799 (Ellwangen Kapitelrezesse), fols. 262r–264r.

99. WSAL B412, Bü. 82.

100. This account is based on WSAL B412, Bü. 82, and on Laun, "Die Gegen-schreiberin."

101. Bodin, *De la démonomanie*, sig. aiii verso.

102. For this case, see WSAL B412, Bü. 78 and Bü. 81.

103. Duhr, *Geschichte der Jesuiten*, p. 489.

104. WSAL B389, Bü. 230d ("Facti Species").

105. WSAL B389, Bü. 230d (Consultations from the Universities of Freiburg and Ingolstadt); for other voluntary confessions, cf. Maria Bautzin's confession (B412, Bü. 78) and that of Barbara Schneider (B412, Bü. 62).

106. WSAL B412, Bü. 82.

107. WSAL B412, Bü. 62.

108. WSAL B389, Bü. 230f.

109. By 1515-18 this problem had arisen. See Ellwangen, Pfarrarchiv, "Hillersche Chronik," p. 541.

110. This, at least, is the charge of Franz Kropf, S.J., in his history of the Upper German province (I: 65) cited in Duhr, *Geschichte der Jesuiten*, p. 489.

111. WSAL B389, Bü. 230f.

112. Cf. WSAL B412, Bü. 64–65.

113. Duhr, *Geschichte der Jesuiten*, p. 489.

114. Keyser, *Deutsches Städtebuch*, IV, 2, 2, s.v. Schwäbisch Gmünd.

115. For a fascinating analysis of social and religious problems in Gmünd, see Naujoks, *Obrigkeitsgedanken*, pp. 21–39, 71–102, 177–95. See also E. Wagner, "Reichs-stadt Schwäbisch Gmünd," pp. 161, 464.

116. Keyser, *Deutsches Städtebuch*, IV, 2, 2, s.v. Schwäbisch Gmünd.

117. HSASt B177, Bü. 122 (Gmünd: Korrespondenzen); WSAL B412, Bü. 79–80 (Ellwangen: Strafakten). Cf. *1962 Schwäbisch Gmünd*, and Klaus, "Geschichtliches."

118. HSASt B177, Bü. 122.

119. Note the "Verzaichnus der Unholden so alhie zue Schw. Gmündt seindt ver-brent worden," in HSASt B177, Bü. 122.

120. *1962 Schwäbisch Gmünd*, p. 46; *Württembergische Kirchengeschichte*, p. 475.

121. *1962 Schwäbisch Gmünd*, pp. 45-46; HSASt B177, Bü. 122.

122. *1962 Schwäbisch Gmünd*, p. 45.

123. HSASt B177, Bü. 122 (Urfehde June 30, 1616).

124. HSASt B177, Bü. 122 (Kager, "Consilium in Causa Malef.").

125. *Ibid.*, pp. 38–42.

126. *Ibid.*, pp. 5–7, 59.

127. *Ibid.*, pp. 45–46, 43–44.

128. *Ibid.*, p. 24.

129. *Ibid.*, pp. 48–49.

130. HSASt B177, Bü. 122, Part 7 ("Edict des Raths zu Gmünd betr. Verbot leichtfertiger Beschuldigung der Hexen"). This document is undated and marked ca. 1600 by an archivist. Obviously it was written in 1613.

131. HSASt B177, Bü. 122, Kager, "Consilium," p. 56.

132. HSASt B177, Bü. 122 ("Fernere information Juris und Erinnerung. In causa maleficarum"), fol. 5r.

133. HSASt B177, Bü. 122, Kager, "Consilium," pp. 57–58, citing canon *Episcopi*, G. Everhard, Ponzinibio and J. G. Gödelmann.

134. *Ibid.*, pp. 60–62.

135. This massive tract of 121 folio pages is without title and may even be missing the first few pages. We shall refer to it as the "Counter-Consilium," and to its author as the Counter-consultant; HSASt B177, Bü. 122.

136. "Doch de Magia in specie sic dicta zuverstehn quatenus illa excludit Maleficum et Magum comprehendit, qualis fuit Scotus. Est enim differentia inter inter [sic] maleficum et Magum."

137. His authorities were Binsfeld, Delrio, and Bartholomaeus de Spina.

138. See p. 26 and note 80, p. 235; Gödelmann was originally from Swabia and studied at Tübingen. Cf. Crusius, *Schwäbische Chronik*, II: 389, and index s.v. Gödelmann.

139. WSAL B412, Bü. 80 (Ellwangen: Strafakten); Anna Schmidin claimed to have seen them at a witches' dance in Schwäbisch Gmünd.

CHAPTER SIX

1. For Oberndorf, Sulz, and Hechingen, see F. Köhler, *Oberndorf*, p. 166; F. Köhler, *Sulz*, pp. 237–39; Crusius, *Schwäbische Chronik*, II: 354; and Burkarth, "Hexenprozesse in Hohenzollern." The last-mentioned study is excellent.

2. Consult the map facing p. 1 and the Appendix for orientation and literature.

3. Trevor-Roper, *Crisis*, p. 3.

4. Franz, *Der dreissigjährige Krieg*, pp. 5–7; Kamen, "Economic and Social Consequences," pp. 49–50.

5. Franz, pp. 43–44.

6. Sebastian Bürster, quoted in Jessen, *Der dreissigjährige Krieg*, pp. 254–55.

7. Baden-Durlach had taken over the lands of Baden-Baden in 1594 when Eduard Fortunat proved himself incompetent. See Bartmann, *Kirchenpolitik*, pp. 224–27.

8. J. Bader, *Badische Landesgeschichte*, p. 506.

9. Wedgwood, *The Thirty Years War*, p. 210.

10. Duhr, *Geschichte der Jesuiten*, p. 130.

11. Kamen, "Economic and Social Consequences," p. 61.

12. Ritter, *Deutsche Geschichte*, III: 373, 421–23.

13. *Ibid.*, p. 429.

14. Trevor-Roper, pp. 156, 161. This is clearly an oversimplification.

15. One of these six, Oberkirch, was under Württemberg's jurisdiction for the time, but was undisturbed in its Catholicism.

16. Cf. Kähni, "Reformation und Gegenreformation," pp. 28–29; materials regarding these disputes are in GLAK 119, Bü. 888 and 967–68.

17. Kähni, "Reformation und Gegenreformation," pp. 29–30, 34; in 1559 the Landvogt of the Ortenau complained to the Habsburg government in Innsbruck that Offenburg's council was partly Lutheran! A strange complaint from a land only recently returned from Lutheranism. Cf. J. V. Wagner, *Graf Wilhelm von Fürstenberg*.

18. GLAK 119 (Ortenau: Verbrechen), Bü. 830, Bü. 834, Bü. 1102.

19. Volk, *Hexen.*

20. *Ibid.,* pp. 3, 24–27; Volk failed to include in his own summary (p. 3) five persons condemned to death. It is not clear where Kähni (*Offenburg,* p. 75) gets a total of 160 executions in the Ortenau.

21. GLAK 119, Bü. 834, no. 50.

22. Volk, p. 17.

23. *Ibid.,* p. 18.

24. Cf. J. Kohler, "Die Carolina," pp. 218–24.

25. Kähni, "Die Beziehungen," pp. 109–23.

26. The town itself had wavered until 1531, when it swung decidedly to Catholicism.

27. Kähni, "Reformation und Gegenreformation," pp. 20–37, 32–33.

28. *Ibid.,* pp. 33, 35.

29. It is obvious that this is the same sort of organic moral concern shown by those imperial cities that went over to a Swiss-inspired Reformation; cf. Moeller, *Reichsstadt und Reformation.*

30. Vierordt, *Geschichte,* II: 126. This despite the fact that at least 11 persons were executed at Offenburg in 1608 for witchcraft; Volk, pp. 53–57.

31. Volk, p. 39.

32. Offenburg, Stadtarchiv, Ratsprotokolle (1627), fols. 270v and 273v.

33. *Ibid.,* fol. 270v.

34. *Ibid.,* fol. 273r et seq.; Volk, p. 103; Kähni, *Offenburg,* pp. 71–75.

35. Stadtarchiv Offenburg, Ratsprotokolle (Nov. 14, 19, 22, Dec. 1, 4, 1627), fols. 274r–281v; Volk, pp. 58–63.

36. Volk, pp. 72–86; Kähni seems to have counted incorrectly in *Die Stadt und Landgemeinden,* p. 83.

37. Volk, p. 70.

38. *Ibid.,* p. 71.

39. *Ibid.,* pp. 73–77.

40. *Ibid.,* p. 77.

41. *Ibid.,* pp. 74–79.

42. *Ibid.,* pp. 84–85.

43. *Ibid.,* pp. 85–86.

44. There seems to be no justification for Robbins's assertion that the rich were sought out in Offenburg, or that rewards were offered for accusations; Robbins, *Encyclopedia,* pp. 221–22. The deputy who had to arrest an accused witch was, of course, paid for his labors; Volk, pp. 111–12.

45. Stadtarchiv Offenburg, Ratsprotokolle (Dec. 3, 1629), fol. 41r.

46. *Ibid.,* fol. 41r.

47. *Ibid.,* fols. 57v–58r. Offenburg must have had some liaison with the imperialist armies, but it was apparently not occupied by troops during 1629–30.

48. *Ibid.,* fols. 58r-v, 59v, 61v, 63v.

49. Volk, p. 88–89; Schreiber, *Hexenprozesse,* p. 22; Bechtold, *Grimmelshausen und seine Zeit,* pp. 29–30.

50. Volk, pp. 88–89.

51. *Ibid.;* Kähni, *Offenburg,* p. 75.

52. Volk, p. 90–91.

53. *Ibid.,* p. 90.

54. Keyser, *Deutsches Städtebuch*, IV, 2, 1: 243.

55. Hellinger, "Die Carolina in Gengenbach," pp. 80, 86–88, 90–91; Hellinger, "Die Carolina und die Hexenverfolgung," pp. 390–93, 394, 395, 396, 500.

56. A. Rapp, *Deutsche Geschichte am Oberrhein*, p. 193; A. Rapp, "Scheiterhaufen am Oberrhein," No. 11 (March 16, 1935): 42–43. The sensationalist tone of Rapp's writing lends an air of fable to his "history."

57. It may be that Rapp got his figure of 70 for the period 1627–31 by telescoping the data from 1610 to 1682. Marie Sonneborn counted 70 executions in Gengenbach in 1610–82 ("Hexenprozesse in Gengenbach," pp. 76, 84–85). Cf. J. Köhler, "Bemerkungen," pp. 387–89, and Schaaf, *Gengenbach*, pp. 148 et seq. The archival materials for the trials at Gengenbach were locked up in Karlsruhe while the Generallandesarchiv was being remodeled.

58. Ruppert, "Ein badischer Hexenrichter," pp. 447–48; Albert Ludwig, *Die evangelischen Pfarrer*. For rebuttal, cf. Janssen, *Geschichte*, VIII: 680, n. 5; Duhr, *Geschichte der Jesuiten*, p. 498.

59. Vierordt, *Geschichte*, p. 127; Hermann, *Die Hexen von Baden-Baden*, pp. 5–6; Albert Ludwig, *Die evangelischen Pfarrer*, p. 55.

60. These Protokolle were not available to me because of renovation of the GLAK.

61. Reinfried, "Auszüge," pp. 20–21; Reinfried, "Kulturgeschichtliches," p. 50.

62. Reinfried, "Auszüge," p. 3.

63. We are told by Hermann (pp. 1–4) and by Ruppert (p. 454) that records of 200 trials remain. Of them 33 trials are from Steinbach and 70 from Bühl (with all persons executed). This leaves 97 unaccounted for. We also know that six or seven persons withstood torture in Baden and were set free. We may conclude that 90 or 91 persons were executed in Baden. Others have assumed that nearly all of the 200 trials mentioned were in Baden alone and that 193 persons were executed there. The confusion stems from use of the name "Baden-Baden," meaning both the territory and the town. Until the documents are again open to inspection, we cannot be sure which interpretation is correct.

64. Ruppert, pp. 470–71.

65. *Ibid.*, pp. 464 et seq.; Hermann, pp. 9–11; Vierordt, *Geschichte*, p. 127.

66. Hermann, pp. 45–46; Ruppert, p. 471.

67. The bishop of Strasbourg found this arrangement (1604–34, 1649–65) necessary to cover the costs occasioned by the famous Strasbourg chapter fight of the late sixteenth century. See Miller, *Baden-Württemberg*, pp. 493–94, and Eimer, "Das bischöfliche Amt Oberkirch."

68. Börsig, *Geschichte*, p. 76.

69. *Ibid.*, pp. 76–77; Eimer, "Das bischöfliche Amt Oberkirch" (1929), p. 639.

70. GLAK 169 (Oberkirch), Bü. 292.

71. For this consilium, see GLAK 169, Bü. 294.

72. See GLAK 169, Bü. 298. In some cases these additional persons were denounced six to ten times and their names were then crossed off. Since the judges paid close attention to the number of times suspects were denounced, it is unlikely that those denounced five and more times would have escaped execution more frequently than those denounced only four times. Therefore, since ten of the 14 persons denounced four times were executed, we may assume that about 10/14 of those denounced five to seven times were executed. In addition we may also assume that all persons denounced eight or more times were executed. This procedure adds 16 or 17 probable victims to our firm figure of 47, or 63 to 64 executed in all.

73. GLAK 65, Bü. 1849 (Oberkircher Gerichtsbuch). July and August alone had seen 32 executions. Cf. Börsig, p. 77.

74. GLAK 169, Bü. 294. In addition, perhaps 30 to 40 more denunciations entailed persons already dead or unknown in Oppenau.

75. GLAK 65, Bü. 1849; Börsig, p. 78. The Strasbourg jurists stated this position very learnedly and at length in the curiously obscure copy of their opinion for the city "O" in 1608 (Oberkirch? Offenburg?) housed in WSAL A209 (Oberrat), Bü. 2104.

76. Vierordt's explanation was the presence of the Swedes; *Geschichte*, 11: 124.

77. *Ibid.*, pp. 68, 127.

78. Miller, *Baden-Württemberg*, p. 188; Kretschmer, *Historische Geographie*, pp. 576, 578; Keyser, *Deutsches Städtebuch*, IV, 2, 1: 66–67.

79. Vierordt, *Geschichte*, II: 68, 127.

80. Cf. Diefenbach, Duhr, Janssen, Ruppert. Other accounts of Julius Echter also omit this episode, e.g. Specker, "Reformtätigkeit."

81. Not all members of their government were superstitious. Councilor Philipp Reinhard was skeptical of magic and witchcraft and lamented the role he had to play in witchcraft trials. See Rommel, "Beiträge," p. 13.

82. Diefenbach, *Hexenwahn*, p. 21; Rommel, p. 13.

83. Diefenbach, *Hexenwahn*, pp. 21–22.

84. Confessions came quickly after shaving the old lady from head to toe in search of the devil's mark.

85. Diefenbach, *Hexenwahn*, p. 23–34; Rommel, p. 16.

86. *Newer Tractat Von der Verführten Kinder Zauberey* (1629), pp. 7–11; on the concept of "supplying the years" cf. *Carolina*, Art. 164; Bonnekamp, *Die Zimmerische Chronik*, p. 23.

87. *Newer Tractat*, pp. 15–18, 21–22, 23, 29, 31.

88. Diefenbach, *Hexenwahn*, p. 51; cf. also Notestein, *History*, pp. 146ff., 209 et seq., 221 et seq., 274–76, etc.; G. Bader, *Hexenprozesse*, p. 100.

89. Rommel, p. 17.

90. *Ibid.*

91. See Diefenbach, *Hexenwahn*, p. 34 (for a rebuke concerning acceptance by the judges of a bucket of wine, vintage 1624—a great year—from one of the suspects), and pp. 41–44, 50, 61. See Rommel, pp. 14–16, for the close control and interest of the counts, reprinting a number of letters.

92. Diefenbach, *Hexenwahn*, p. 48.

93. Vierordt, *Geschichte*, II: 124. This point seems to have eluded the polemical mind of Diefenbach, who treated all of the Wertheim trials as Protestant affairs.

94. Diefenbach, *Hexenwahn*, p. 73.

95. This might have implications for literary theory. See, e.g., Abrams, *The Mirror and the Lamp*, pp. 11, 33, 48–49.

96. Diefenbach, *Hexenwahn*, pp. 79–80.

97. *Ibid.*, p. 81.

98. A trial was begun in 1648 when three children denounced three women and two other children, but the results of this last trial in Wertheim are lost.

99. Keyser, *Deutsches Städtebuch*, IV, 2, 2: 162–64.

100. This of course takes into account only those lands around Mergentheim. The Order owned other lands throughout the Empire.

101. Generally in Germany the largest witch hunts occurred at Trier, Bamberg, Fulda, and Würzburg, all ecclesiastical lands.

102. Materials are found in great abundance in WSAL B262 (Strafprozesse zu Mergentheim), Bü. 71–110, enough to keep a German Ph.D. candidate busy for years. German studies of such massive evidence are nonexistent. For the only study of the Mergentheim trials beyond passing reference, see the summary in *Württembergische Kirchengeschichte*, Calw, p. 175, of the *Beschreibung des Oberamts Mergentheim* (1880). But see also Beck, "Hexenprozesse aus dem Fränkischen."

103. A formal extradition declaration was necessary on Würzburg's part, stating that friendly cooperation with the Würzburg judicial authorities implied no legal subjection to Würzburg or diminution of sovereignty.

104. From an account for Mergentheim on April 8, 1628; WSAL B262, Bü. 91; the rest of the materials for this case are also in this *Büschel*.

105. Cf. letter of the Bishop of Würzburg on May 10 and 23, 1628, and the reply of Johann Caspar on May 29, 1628.

106. WSAL B262, Bü. 83, pt. 1.

107. WSAL B262, Bü. 106 (Allgemeines betr. Hexenprozesse 1628–29).

108. WSAL B262, Bü. 90.

109. WSAL B262, Bü. 79 and Bü. 81. A different source gives October 29, 1628, as the date of the first burning: WSAL B262, Bü. 71.

110. WSAL B262, Bü. 82.

111. Cf. WSAL B262, Bü. 71; and B262, Bü. 77.

112. WSAL B262, Bü. 82, pt. 1; B262, Bü. 82, pt. 3.

113. WSAL B262, Bü. 83, pt. 1.

114. WSAL B262, Bü. 85.

115. One is easily misled by the statistics at the back of G. Bader, *Hexenprozesse*.

116. For an example of lack of caution, cf. Monter, "Trois historiens," p. 212.

117. Mandrou, *Magistrats et sorciers*, p. 111.

118. For the crisis in the use of spectral evidence at Salem, cf. Starkey, *Devil in Massachusetts*.

119. WSAL B262, Bü. 71 and Bü. 77.

120. For the whole case, see WSAL B262, Bü. 103.

121. Faber, *Specimen Zeli justi Theologici contra Maleficos*.

122. *Ibid.*, p. 228.

123. Vaihingen was a small parcel of land dependent on and subject to Esslingen. It lay about ten miles west of Esslingen and is not to be confused with Vaihingen an der Enz.

124. K. Pfaff, "Hexenprozesse zu Esslingen," pp. 351 and 450 et seq. One of the persons under examination sickened and died before she could be sentenced.

125. *Ibid.*, p. 359.

126. UATüb. 85 (Consilia juridica), Bü. 1 (unbound consilium of 1661); UATüb. 84, Vol. 16, pp. 180–91 (consilium from 1662); pp. 1068–74 (consilium from 1664); pp. 1065–68 (Facultatis Medicae Responsum).

127. K. Pfaff, "Hexenprozesse zu Esslingen," p. 459.

128. *Ibid.*, pp. 459–62.

129. Salzmann, *Hexenprozesse*, pp. 13–16. In most respects this study is far inferior to the earlier one by K. Pfaff.

130. *Ibid.*, p. 19.

131. K. Pfaff, "Hexenprozesse zu Esslingen," p. 459.

132. Riezler, *Geschichte der Hexenprozesse in Bayern*, p. 144; Willburger, "Hexenverfolgung in Württemberg," pp. 142–43; K. Pfaff, "Hexenprozesse zu Esslingen," pp. 347–71, 441a–62a. Otto Schwister asserted that, in all, 375 were accused of witchcraft in Esslingen, *Kirchengeschichte*, pp. 229–32.

133. They were Vaihingen and Möhringen; cf. Riezler, *Geschichte der Hexenprozesse in Bayern*, p. 144, who lists 165 suspects from these two villages alone.

134. Liebel, "The Bourgeoisie"; G. Fischer, "Freie Reichsstadt Reutlingen," pp. 41, 206.

135. Forderer, *Reutlingen*, p. 34; Honecker, "Hexenprozesse," p. 3, 8.

136. Minor trials had occurred in 1589, 1595, 1603, 1621, 1638, 1644, and 1646.

137. Honecker, pp. 13–21, 44–45. For these trials and for opinions relating to the children, cf. "Liber sententiarum," UATüb. 84, Vol. 17, fol. 314–24v; Vol. 19, fol. 293–96v; Vol. 20, fol. 10–12.

138. Honecker, pp. 8, 15–20.

139. The link of *venenum* to *veneficium* is an obvious example.

140. Honecker, pp. 24–25.

141. *Ibid.*, pp. 30–33.

142. Mehring, "Aus der Zeit." Mehring reprinted *in toto* this interesting song: "Ein erschröckliche, jedoch warhafftige und erbärmliche Newe-Zeitung von Häxenmeisteren und Zauberern... theils aber bey 42 vom Leben zum Todt erbärmlich seynd hingerichtet worden. Geschehen zu Reüdlingen im Hertzogthumb Wirtenberg" (Augsburg: bey Christoff Schmid, 1666).

143. Miller, *Baden-Württemberg*, pp. 110–11.

144. Cf. Mönch, *Heimatkunde vom Oberamt Calw*, pp. 61–65; Rheinwald and Rieg, *Calw*, pp. 129–38.

145. UATüb. 84, Vol. 28, fols. 508–10v.

146. UATüb. 84, Vol. 29, pp. 718–36; Vol. 42, pp. 242–43.

147. Häberlin, *Historische Relation*, pp. 9–10.

148. WSAL A209, Bü. 691, 52, pp. 36–37.

149. UATüb. 84, Vol. 42, pp. 244–48.

150. UATüb. 84, Vol. 42, fols. 283v, 290r-v; Vol. 22, fols. 931–32.

151. UATüb. 84, Vol. 22, pp. 956, 958. For the witch trials at Mora in 1669 and later, cf. Soldan-Heppe, *Geschichte der Hexenprozesse*, II: 172–75; and Rose, *Razor for a Goat*, Appendix.

152. The cover of their report bears the motto "Periculum in mora."

153. WSAL A209, Bü. 691, 52, p. 2.

154. *Ibid.*, pp. 42, 43.

155. P. Stälin, *Geschichte der Stadt Calw*, pp. 105–6.

156. WSAL A209, Bü. 691, 52, pp. 57, 54.

157. Scharfe, "Soziale Kontrolle."

158. Häberlin, *Historische Relation*, pp. 16–27.

159. *Ibid.*, pp. 36–47.

160. WSAL A209, Bü. 691, 52, p. 51.

CHAPTER SEVEN

1. Robbins, *Encyclopedia*, p. 221.

2. Probably one reason why the historical study of Roman law in Germany waited

until the nineteenth century was that it had to wait until such study was no longer useful.

3. *Carolina*, Art. 218, clause 6: "Item an etlichen orten so eyn übelthetter ausserhalb des lasters unser beleidigten Majestet oder sunst in andern fellen, so der übelthetter leib unnd gut nit verwirckt vom leben zum todt gestrafft, werden weib und kinder an bettelstabe, unnd das gut dem herren zugewiesen, und die und dergleichen gewonheyt, Wollen wir dass eyn jede oberkeyt abschaffen und daran sein soll, dass sie hinfürther nit geübt, gebraucht oder gehalten werden als wir dann auss Keyserlicher macht die selben hiemit auffheben, vernichtigen unnd abthun, und hinfürther nit eingefürt werden sollen."

4. For the attitude of Julius Clarus and Peter Binsfeld, cf. Soldan-Heppe, *Geschichte der Hexenprozesse*, I: 413–14.

5. Martini, *De Ivre Censuum*, p. 538.

6. *Ibid.*, pp. 541–43, where the reforms of Justinian are closely argued.

7. HSASt B177, Bü. 122: Kager, "Consilium in Causa Malef., Lamiarum et Venef.; Appendix," October 10, 1613, p. 51.

8. *Ibid.*; for the *Polizeiordnungen* of the sixteenth century, cf. Segall, *Geschichte*, an excellent and thorough study of a much neglected topic.

9. HSASt B177, Bü. 122: Kager, "Consilium; Appendix," p. 53.

10. "Counter Consilium," HSASt B177, Bü. 122, fols. 57–58 (unnumbered).

11. *Ibid.*, fols. 58–59.

12. Goldast, *Rechtliches Bedencken*, pp. 133–34; Goldast seems to have finished this learned work on October 24, 1629. Read in Goldast's way, the text of the *Carolina* ran, "so ein übelthetter (ausserhalb des Lasters der Beleydigung Unserer Majestätt oder sonst in anderen Fällen so der Übelthäter Leib und Guth *mit* verwürcket) vom Leben zum Todt gestraffet, Weib und Kind an Bettelstab, und das Guth dem Herren zugewiesen."

13. Cf. *Carolina*, fn. to Art. 218 on p. 145, and Art. 135, where suicide to escape punishment is explicitly punished by confiscation.

14. WSAL B412, Bü. 26 (Copia Churfürstlichen Maintzischen Mandats Wie es mit der Confiscations Straff der Hexen Persohnen Zuhalten); thus those with three surviving children would pay the state one-fourth of the total sum allotted to the children.

15. For this earlier procedure, cf. Huffschmid, "Zur Criminalstatistik," p. 413.

16. Gehring, "Der Hexenprozess," 2 (1938): 38. To be sure, Gehring goes too far in asserting that legal minds were united against confiscations in the seventeenth century (n. 171). In Rottweil, if confiscations had been collected, we would hear of it in the Ratsprotokolle, which are silent on this point. Cf. the case of Hans Engel in 1580, whose property was divided among his heirs after his execution: Rottweil Stadtarchiv, (1) Ratsprotokolle, esp. Vol. 1 (1580–82): 96; (2) Criminalakten, April 29, 1580. For Offenburg the same considerations apply; cf. also Volk, *Hexen*, pp. 104–5.

17. Birlinger, *Aus Schwaben*, I: 171. We noted earlier that an official was punished in 1605 in Rottenburg for extortion.

18. Goldast, *Rechtliches Bedencken*, p. 174. Despite Goldast's hard line on confiscation, he agreed that out of equity for the surviving family, only those lands were to be confiscated that lay in the jurisdiction where the person was executed.

19. A copy of the decree is found in GLAK 119, Bü. 1102.

20. Ruppert, "Ein badischer Hexenrichter," p. 450.

21. *Ibid.*, p. 463.

22. Honecker, "Hexenprozesse," p. 5; *Carolina*, Art. 205, and note on p. 145.

23. E.g. Rest, "Ettenheimer Hexenprozesse," pp. 42–43.

24. Robbins exaggerates when he writes, "In Germany the educated, wealthy, young and respected were the most numerous of those burned," *Encyclopedia*, p. 543; cf. also pp. 220–22.

25. Diefenbach, *Hexenwahn*, p. 92.

26. GLAK 169, Bü. 289; Bü. 285; Bü. 302.

27. For Wertheim we have only Vierordt's assertion that confiscation played a major role in the Counter-Reformation policy of Bishop Julius Echter von Mespelbrunn (*Geschichte*, II: 68, 127) and the provision for regulating the property of witches, 1629, printed in Rommel, "Beiträge," p. 15. For Esslingen we hear of very high "costs," with 2,300 gulden spent by June 30, 1663, on witch trials, prisons, food, etc. At that time only 2,045 gulden had been collected, so that Esslingen was not even breaking even. It is not clear where Soldan-Heppe got the idea that Esslingen stopped trying witches only when the officials had taken all they could; Soldan-Heppe, *Geschichte der Hexenprozesse*, I: 440.

28. WSAL B412, Bü. 26 (Informatio Maintzischen Process wieder die Unholden). The chapter had decided a few cases dealing with confiscation in 1611; WSAL B387 (Kapitel-Rezesse), Bü. 798, fols. 94v, 111r.

29. WSAL B412, Bü. 54 (Supplicationes betr. Confiscationsgelder): cf. B412, Bü. 101 (Ellwangen: Strafbuch, 1614–17).

30. The question of confiscation had arisen by 1515 in Ellwangen; cf. Ellwangen, Pfarrarchiv, "Hillersche Chronik," p. 541.

31. WSAL B412, Bü. 63.

32. A barrel of about 1,000 litres of wine was reckoned in 1629 at 12 gulden; WSAL B262, Bü. 78 (a disorderly bundle of cost lists and confiscations), no. 8. Board per person in prison cost one-quarter gulden a day for food "from the kitchen" (i.e. not bread and water); B262, Bü. 80, no. 3.

33. WSAL B412, Bü. 77 (Rechnung von Jacob Weiss); B412, Bü. 92 (Strafgelt); B412, Bü. 101 (Strafbuch).

34. WSAL B262, Bü. 75 (Scharfrichterzettel, auch Confiscationen).

35. E.g. WSAL B262, Bü. 80, nos. 1 and 2.

36. WSAL B262, Bü. 80, no. 5.

37. WSAL B262, Bü. 81, no. 3; B262, Bü. 87–89.

38. Cf. Mehrle, *Die Strafrechtspflege*, p. 97; Göller, "Hexen," p. 80.

39. WSAL B262, Bü. 88, no. 27 (confiscations ordered on May 15, 1629), item 6.

40. *Ibid.*, item 9.

41. WSAL B262, Bü. 88, no. 1 (Verzaichnus dern . . . undern Ambt Newenhauss verhafften nunmehr . . . hingerichten Persohnen vermögen), item 6; B262, Bü. 88, no. 3; B262, Bü 88, no. 6.

42. WSAL B262, Bü. 79, no. 1. He was caught and executed on November 7, 1629.

43. WSAL B262, Bü. 88, no. 26; cf. no. 31, a letter of May 11, 1629, requesting advice in the matter.

44. All that remains is an order that 110 gulden be paid and an inventory of her property as worth only 80 gulden. We do not know what the heirs finally did pay. WSAL B262, Bü. 79, no. 1; B262, Bü. 89, no. 24.

45. In 1652 at the wealthy episcopal town of Bruchsal, 17.92 per cent of the population owned more than 1,000 gulden (Drollinger, *Kleine Städte*, p. 118). In the villages of Württemberg in 1544 only 3.5 per cent of the inhabitants had more than 500

gulden, and only 0.84 per cent had more than 1,000 gulden; cf. Clasen, *Die Wieder-täufer*, p. 205. Adding the cities of Württemberg would probably raise these figures to perhaps 6 or 7 per cent over 500 gulden, and 2 or 3 per cent over 1,000 gulden. Even allowing for money devaluation and the price rise of the sixteenth century, one could scarcely anticipate anything like 20 per cent in 1630 owning more than 1,000 gulden. From inventories we know that a man could own a large house (more than seven rooms), a horse, three cows, three calves, pigs, geese, and chickens, and be assessed at 1,158 gulden. That was clearly a wealthy man (WSAL B262, Bü. 88, no. 6—Peter Weit). Another person owned a house, barn, one calf, and one cow, as well as six parcels of land, and was assessed for taxes at a valuation of 352 gulden. She was comfortably in the middle (B262, Bü. 81, no. 7—Dorothea Weit). Again, Georg Reuss owned two houses, had 14 parcels of land including several acres of vineyard, and had 145 gulden worth of material in his tailor shop. He was obviously wealthy, and his tax assessment valued him at 1,284 gulden. It seems evident that anyone with over 1,000 gulden was part of the wealthy elite, who numbered perhaps 15 per cent of the population at the most.

46. WSAL B262, Bü. 78, no. 10, pt. 1.

47. WSAL B262, Bü. 78, no. 10, pt. 4.

48. *Cautio Criminalis*, Q. 15 and Q. 16, no. 3.

49. Janssen, *Geschichte*, VIII: 633.

50. Faber, *Specimen Zeli*, p. 91.

51. WSAL B262, Bü. 87, no. 4 (Georg Feygenbutz).

52. Obermarchtal was an exception, although the men there usually seem to have been ordinary criminals who had the charge of witchcraft merely added to their list of crimes; cf. Dengler, "Hexenwesen," pp. 62–63.

53. For a not very novel use of dissonance theory, cf. Rosenthal and Siegel, "Magic and Witchcraft."

54. Cf. Tramer, "Kinder im Hexenglauben."

55. Karl Vierordt characteristically saw even this incident as a persecution of Protestantism. *Geschichte*, II: 127–28.

56. Soldan-Heppe, *Geschichte der Hexenprozesse*, II: 17–20.

57. For general treatments see Hansen, "Die Zuspitzung des Hexenwahns auf das weibliche Geschlecht," *Quellen*, pp. 416–44; Paulus, *Hexenwahn*, pp. 195–247; Caro Baroja, *World of the Witches*, pp. 18–40, 47–48, 101–4; Harper, "Fear and the Status of Women."

58. R. Schmidt, *Die Frau*, pp. 40, 122–28, 134; Janssen, *Geschichte*, VI: 430–37.

59. These details may be found in virtually any of the confessions throughout the German Southwest. Cf. esp. Mergentheim and Ellwangen, whose trials produced hundreds of them.

60. Middleton and Winter, *Witchcraft and Sorcery*, pp. 18–19.

61. Wilson, *The Plague*, p. 3, n. 3.

62. Carl Bücher thought that he saw this phenomenon in fourteenth- and fifteenth-century Frankfurt, since the number of widows on tax lists rose after plague years. This was faulty reasoning, since when women died, there was no change in a man's tax status, whereas a husband's death brought the widow into the tax lists; Bücher, *Frauenfrage*, pp. 6, 58.

63. It would seem unlikely that this kind of disproportion in favor of women in plague could have been at all common without provoking comment. What we know of later plagues certainly fails to show any violent disproportion. Women usually

suffered on an equal basis with men in early modern Germany too. Cf. Woehlkens, *Pest und Ruhr*, p. 91. Cf. also the recent dispute between Russell, "Effects of Pestilence," and Thrupp, "Plague Effects."

64. Berkowitz and Green, "Stimulus Qualities."

65. Kelso, *Doctrine for the Lady*, pp. 6, 10–13.

66. Janssen, *Geschichte*, VI: 430–37.

67. Kawerau, "Lob und Schimpf des Ehestandes"; Siegel, "Milton."

68. Cf. Rogers, *Troublesome Helpmate*, pp. 100–134; Powell, *English Domestic Relations*, pp. 147–78.

69. Hajnal, "European Marriage Patterns in Perspective." Many scholars have endorsed these views: Wrigley, "Family Limitation," p. 87; Spengler, "Demographic Factors"; Van de Walle, "Marriage," p. 489; Demeny, "Early Fertility Decline," pp. 514–16.

70. Cf. Litchfield, "Demographic Characteristics," p. 197. Between 1450 and 1649 men married between 29 and 35 years of age, and 30 to 55 per cent of all daughters were still single at age 50.

71. Demeny, p. 514.

72. Hajnal, p. 116.

73. Noonan, "Intellectual and Demographic History," pp. 480–81.

74. Spengler, "Demographic Factors"; Hajnal, p. 132.

75. Ariès, *Centuries of Childhood*, pp. 69–75, 403–4; Morgan, *Puritan Family*, chaps. 2 and 3; Luther, "Das Elltern die Kinder zur Ehe nicht zwingen."

76. Moller, "Sex Composition."

77. The structure of Althusius's thought regarding politics revolves constantly around the family. Morgan's conclusions (pp. 78–89) would seem to apply far beyond the restricted New England horizon.

78. E. William Monter has asserted that Bodin was correct in rejecting Weyer's claim that witches were melancholy, befuddled old women. Bodin had argued that such women *could* not be melancholiacs. Such a statement merely proves Bodin's ignorance of the state of the literature in the sixteenth century and his total reliance on the classics. Galen was not accepted uncritically in the sixteenth century as Monter implies, "Inflation and Witchcraft," p. 382. Cf. Babb, *Elizabethan Malady*, p. 191 (for a *lady* suffering from melancholy), p. 28 (for "uterine" melancholy). Melancholy was itself often pictured as a woman; cf. Klibansky, Panofsky, and Saxl, *Saturn and Melancholy*, pp. 220 et seq., 376 et seq., and the plates. For Bodin and melancholy, cf. Brann, "Renaissance Passion of Melancholy," pp. 361–67, with the proof of how thoroughly out of tune Bodin was with contemporary thinkers on the subject.

79. Eberle, "Probleme," p. 91–92.

80. Morgan, pp. 62–77, 84–87.

81. R. Schmidt, *Die Frau*, p. 125.

82. WSAL B262, Bü. 103 (undated letter to his wife).

83. Giefel, "Zur Geschichte der Hexenprozesse."

84. Caro Baroja, *World of the Witches*, pp. 89–91. He says that inquisitors thought of witches as an organized band, hardly a novel observation.

85. Bernau is about five miles northwest of St. Blasien.

86. Crusius, *Schwäbische Chronik*, II: 378.

87. This appears very clearly in the consultations of the Tübingen legal faculty throughout the seventeenth century: UATüb 84, Vols. 1–60.

88. Gwinner, *Der Einfluss des Standes*, pp. 43–46, 87–89, 117, 125.

89. For Rome, cf. Garnsey, "Legal Privilege."

90. Walcher, "Ein Hexenprozess," p. 345.

91. Balzer, "Die Bräunlinger Hexenprozesse," p. 24; cf. the weak study by Heinrich Schreiber, *Die Hexenprozesse*, pp. 25–32.

92. Meyer, *Heimatbuch*, p. 76.

93. Albert Ludwig, *Die evangelischen Pfarrer*, p. 73.

94. Willburger, "Hexenverfolgung in Württemberg," p. 144.

95. Caro Baroja, *World of the Witches*, p. 83.

96. A late example is the famous Voisin affair in France, 1676–87; see Mandrou, *Magistrats et sorciers*, pp. 468–72.

97. Franck, "Der Hexenprozess"; Balzer, p. 7; Strukat, "Hexenprozesse."

98. Gwinner, *Der Einfluss des Standes*, pp. 203–4.

99. E.g. in Freiburg i. Br. in 1613; Janssen, *Geschichte*, VIII: 681, n. 2. In 1588 two Tübingen students received light punishment for their version of Faust in verse; cf. Boeckh, *Geschichte*, p. 421; Engel, *Bibliotheca*, no. 212, pp. 67–71. The unique copy of this version is in Copenhagen.

100. "Only a Christian could be a witch"; Robbins, *Encyclopedia*, p. 550.

101. Philipp, *Zeitalter der Aufklärung*, pp. 291–92.

102. Ordinary pagans were idolators whose religion at least "restrains men somehow by the barriers of the law of nature," Bodin, *De la démonomanie*, fols. 69r–79r.

103. Faber, *Specimen Zeli*, p. 12.

104. Ruckgaber, "Die Hexenprozesse," pp. 184 et seq.

105. Trevor-Roper oversimplifies when he suggests that Jews and witches were interchangeable victims of pressures for social conformity. He fails to analyze the specific cases in which it was either Jews or witches who were persecuted; *Crisis*, p. 112.

106. As in Rottweil; Stadtarchiv, Repertorium, Vols. 12–13, 1570–89. In 1580 Rottweil was much taken up with the problems of Gypsies.

107. Baeyer-Katte, "Die historischen Hexenprozesse," p. 224.

108. For the Balingen account, see WSAL A209, Bü. 165.

109. Gehring, "Der Hexenprozess," 1: 187–88.

110. Spee, *Cautio Criminalis*, Q. 8, p. 11: "Up to today every trial has had to be ended by a command. It never found its own end." Spee's assertion made good polemic but was poor social analysis.

111. Cases of hysterical contagion seem also to be self-limiting; cf. Back and Kerckhoff, *The June Bug*.

112. Solleder, "Hexenwahn," p. 183.

Bibliography

The Bibliography is divided into three parts: Manuscript Sources, Primary Printed Sources, and Secondary Sources.

MANUSCRIPT SOURCES

Baden, Generallandesarchiv Karlsruhe.
Repertorium 61. Protokolle.
Repertorium 65/142. Burgheim Gerichtsbuch.
Repertorium 65/727-29. Originalakten über Hexenprozesse in Schwaben.
Repertorium 65/1849. Oberkirch Gerichtsbuch.
Repertorium 79/3384-3416. Breisgau Verbrechen.
Repertorium 96/436-39. Reichenau Verbrechen.
Repertorium 119/829-34, 1099-1102. Ortenau.
Repertorium 169/285-306. Oberkirch.
Repertorium 176. Schliengen.
Repertorium 228. Zell am Harmersbach.
Repertorium 229. Buchen, Harmersbach, Langensteinbach, Neidingen, Odenheim, Zell-Weierbach, Ziegelhausen.
Bayern, Staatsbibliothek München. Cod. lat. monach. 3757: Johann Zink (Zinccius), De potestate daemonum et sagarum (ca. 1549). Copied by Johann Waltenberger.
Ellwangen, Pfarrarchiv. Josef Friedrich von Hiller, "Hillersche Chronik."
Ellwangen, Stadtarchiv. Karl Gottfried von Schiller, "Schillersche Chronik."
Offenburg, Stadtarchiv. Ratsprotokolle.
Rottweil, Stadtarchiv. Ratsprotokolle.
Tirol, Landesregierungsarchiv Innsbruck. Sammelakten A/XVI/4. Ettingen Hexenprozess.
Tübingen Universität, Universitätsarchiv.
84/1-70. Libri Sententiarum . . . facultatis jur.
85/2. Fragmenta Consiliorum.
Württemberg, Hauptstaatsarchiv Stuttgart.
Repertorium A444. Oberkirch.
Repertorium B19-22. Hohenberg.
Repertorium B23-28. Vorderösterreich.
Repertorium B41-42. Hohenberg.
Repertorium B34-46. Horb.
Repertorium B95-97. Helfenstein.
Repertorium B169-74. Reichsstadt Esslingen.

Repertorium B177. Reichsstadt Gmünd.
Repertorium B535. Stift Wiesensteig.
Repertorium H44. Oberamt Saulgau.
Württemberg, Landesbibliothek Stuttgart.
Cod. hist. fol. 393: Oswald Gabelkofer, Chronik der Grafen von Helfenstein.
Cod. hist. fol. 689: Christian Friedrich Bauer, Chronik der Stadt Mergentheim, bearbeitet von Archivar Breitenbach (1837–1838).
Württemberg, Staatsarchiv Ludwigsburg.
Repertorium A209. Württemberg Oberratsprotokolle.
Repertorium B17–18. Schwabenbücher Hohenberg.
Repertorium B120. Limpurger Erbschenkenarchiv.
Repertorium B262. Mergentheim Gerichtsakten.
Repertorium B387. Ellwangen Hofratsprotokolle und Kapitelrezesse.
Repertorium B389. Ellwangen Gerichtsakten.
Repertorium B412. Stift Ellwangen, Kriminal-Gerichtswesen und Gerichtsakten.
Württemberg, Staatsarchiv Sigmaringen. Repositur 30, Paket 254. Marchtaler Hexenprozesse.

PRIMARY PRINTED SOURCES

Alber, Matthaeus, and Wilhelm Bidembach. *Ein Summa etlicher Predigen vom Hagel und Unholden gethon in der Pfarrkirch zuo Stuottgarten im Monat Augusto, Anno MDLXII . . . sehr nutzlich und tröstlich zuo diser zeit zuo lesen.* Tübingen, 1562. Also printed in *Consiliorum Theologicorum Decas I,* ed. Felix Bidembach (Frankfurt, 1608).

Albrecht, Bernhard. *Magia, Das ist: Christlicher Bericht von der Zauberey und Hexerey. . . . Item: dass eine Christliche Obrigkeit recht daran thue, wann sie Hexen . . . straffet.* Leipzig, 1628.

Andreae, Jakob. *Drey und dreissig Predigten von fürnemsten Spaltungen in der Christlichen Religion, so sich zwischen den Bäptischen, Lutherischen, Zwinglischen, Schwenckfeldern und Widerteuffern halten. . . .* Tübingen, 1568.

Anhorn, Bartholomäus. *Magiologia: Christliche Warnung für dem Aberglauben und Zauberey.* Basel, 1674.

Barack, K. A., ed. *Zimmerische Chronik.* New ed. by Paul Hermann. 4 vols. Meersburg, 1932.

Bayle, Pierre. "Réponse aux questions d'un provincial," in *Oeuvres diverses avec une introduction par Elisabeth Labrousse.* Hildesheim, 1966.

Besold, Christoph, *Consiliorum Iuridicorum Decas Una.* Tübingen, 1626.

Besold, Christoph, ed. *Consiliorum Tubingensium sive Illustrium Iuris Responsorum & Consultationum. . . .* Vol. 6. Tübingen, 1661.

Bidembach, Felix. *Manuale ministrorum Ecclesiae, Handbuch für die junge angehende Kirchendiener im Herzogthumb Würtemberg zugericht.* Tübingen, 1603.

Bidembach, Wilhelm. "Wie zur Zeit der Thewrung und Hungersnoth, die einfältige Pfarrer und Kirchendiener das Volck ermahnen, lehren, und trösten sollen" (1570), in *Consiliorum Theologicorum Decas II,* ed. Felix Bidembach (Frankfurt, 1608), pp. 168–75.

Bildstein, Leonard. *Geomagus in Archiducali Universitate Friburgo Brisgoia, Praeside Leonardo Bildstein . . . academico examini publici propositus per Adamum Peterman, Ehingensem. . . .* Freiburg, 1631.

[Birck, Thomas]. *Hexenspiegel, Ein uberaus schöne und wolgegründte Tragedi darinnen augenscheinlich zusehen, was von Unholden und Zauberern zuhalten seie*. . . . Tübingen, 1600.

Blarer, Ambrosius. *Ain New geschicht wie ain Knäblein bey Yssne umb zwelff jar underbarliche gesicht gehabt, unnd von mancherlay tröwung der straff Gottes darinn geredt habe*. N.p., 1533.

Bocer, Heinrich. *Tractatus de Omnis Generis Homicidis*. Tübingen, 1629.

Bodin, Jean. *De la démonomanie des sorciers*. Paris, 1580.

Brenz, Johannes. "Epistola Brentii de muliercula, quae in oppidulo Waldenberg consuetudinem habuit cum Diabolo," in *Consiliorum Theologicorum Decas VII*, ed. Felix Bidembach (Frankfurt, 1611), pp. 144–47.

——. *Etzliche Buss Predigten Auss den schrecklichen Historien von der Sündfluth und dem Exempel des Zorns Gottes*. . . . Trans. Theophilo Glaser. Dresden, 1595.

——. *Der Job ussgelegt . . . im Latein unnd yetzt Verdeutscht*. N.p., 1530.

——. "Ob die Obrigkeit inn Glaubens sachen mit Gewalt handeln, unnd uber die Gewissen herschen möge," in *Consiliorum Theologicorum Decas III*, ed. Felix Bidembach (Lauingen, 1607), pp. 196–202.

——. "Ob ein Weltliche Obrigkeit in Gottlichen und billichen Rechten die Widertauffer durch Fewr oder Schwert vom Leben zum Tod richten lassen möge," in *Consiliorum Theologicorum Decas IV*, ed. Felix Bidembach (Lauingen, 1607), pp. 211–34.

——. *Operum Reverendi et Clarissimi Theologi D. Ioannis Brentii*. 8 vols. Tübingen, 1576–90.

——. "Ein Predig von dem Hagel und Ungewitter." First published as "Homilia de grandine" in *Pericopiae evangeliorum quae usitato more in praecipuis Festis legi solent, expositae per Iohan. Brent* (Frankfurt, 1557). Its first printing in German was in Jacob Gretter's translation of these festival sermons (1558). (Köhler No. 347.)

——. *Samuelis Liber prior, Sexagintasex Homiliis*. Frankfurt, 1554.

——. "Von dem Hagel und Ungewitter," in *Evangelien der fürnembsten Fest- und Feyertagen . . . sampt . . . andern . . . Predigten*, trans. Jacob Gretter (Frankfurt, 1558). (Köhler No. 347.)

——. "Wie man sich in sterbenden Läufften, zur Zeit der Pestilenz, Christlich halten solle," in *Consiliorum Theologicorum Decas II*, ed. Felix Bidembach (Frankfurt, 1608), pp. 81–98.

Bullinger, Heinrich. *The Decades of Henry Bullinger*. Ed. Thomas Harding. Cambridge, Eng., 1849.

Calvin, Jean. *Institutes of the Christian Religion*. Ed. J. T. McNeill. Philadelphia, 1960.

Carolina. Die peinliche Gerichtsordnung Karls V. von 1532 (Carolina). Ed. Gustav Radbruch. Stuttgart, 1962.

Churfürstlich-Mayntizische Land-Recht und Ordnungen für samtliche Chur-Mayntzische Landen. Mainz, 1755.

Chur-Fürstl. Pfaltz Landts Ordnung. Heidelberg, 1582.

Cotta, Johann Friedrich. *Dissertatio Historiam Succinctam Dogmatis Theologici de Angelis Exhibens*. 2 vols. Tübingen, 1765–66.

Crusius, Martin. *Diarium*, ed. W. Göz et al. 4 vols. Tübingen, 1927–61.

——. *Schwäbische Chronik, worinnen zu finden ist, was sich von Erschaffung der Welt an biss auf das Jahr 1596 in Schwaben . . . zugetragen. . . . Aus dem Lateinischen erstmals übersetzt, und mit einer Continuation vom Jahr 1596 biss 1733 . . . versehen*. Ed. and trans. Johann Jacob Moser. 2 vols. Frankfurt, 1733.

Dieterich, Conrad. *Institutiones Catecheticae Depromptae E. B. Lutheri Cathechesi ...Editio novissima.* Leipzig, 1663.

———. *Philosophischer und theologischer Traumdiscurss von nachtlichen Träumen.* Ulm, 1624.

———. *Sonderbahrer Predigten So von unterschiedenen Materien hiebevor zu Ulm ...gehalten...Dritter Theil. Darinn die Kriegs- und Busspredigten...begriffen werden.* Leipzig, 1635.

Einfeltiger, Christlicher und nutzlicher Bericht von den Exorcismus unnd Teuffels Beschwerungen, so dieses verschienene 1603 Jahr zu Offenburg fürgenommen worden. N.p., 1603.

Erastus, Thomas. *Deux Dialogues...Touchant le pouvoir des sorcières: et de la punition qu'elles méritent.* Paris, 1579; reprinted Paris, 1885.

———. *Disputatio de Lamiis seu Strigibus.* Basel, 1577.

Erschreckliche Nüwe Zytung. Warhafftiger und gründlicherbericht, wie das Wetter im Wirttenberger land so grossen schaden gethan hat, einem guten Fründ zugeschriben. N.p., 1562.

Ein erschröckliche geschicht so zu Derneburg in der Graffschafft Reinstein am Hartz gelegen von dreyen Zauberin unnd swayen Mannen...1555. Nuremberg, n.d.

Ein erschröcklich geschicht Vom Tewfel und einer unholden, beschehen zu Schilta bey Rotweil in der karwochen MDXXXIII Jar. N.p., [1533].

Erschröckliche Newe Zeytung. Lauingen, 1583.

Faber, Johann Jakob. *Specimen Zeli justi Theologici contra Maleficos et Sagas. Das ist Muster und Prob eines recht Theologischen Eifers wider die Zauberer und Hexen.* Foreword by Tobias Wagner. Stuttgart, 1667.

Faberius, Vitus. *Sechs und Viertzig Discursus oder Predigten uber alle Feyertäg dess gantzen Jahrs.* Würzburg, 1680.

———. *Supplementum Oder Neuer Zusatz dess Historien-Predigers Uber das völlige A.B.C. auf gleiche Form und Art dess Ersten und Andern Theils....*Würzburg, 1686. Pp. 485–512: "Das böse Weib."

Feucht, Jacob. *Neun und dreissig Catholische Predigen, zu underschiedlichen zeiten und von mancherley Materien vormalen verfertiget....*Cologne, 1578.

Feyrabend, Sigmund. *Theatrum Diabolorum.* Frankfurt, 1569.

Frisius, Paul (Nagoldanus). *Dess Teuffels Nebelkappen, Das ist Kurtzer begriff, dess gantzen Handels, der Zauberey belangend, zusamengelesen.* N.p., 1583; reprinted in [Saur], *Theatrum de Veneficis.*

Glanvill, Joseph. *Sadducismus Triumphatus.* London, 1680.

Gödelmann, Johann Georg. *Tractatus de Magis, Veneficis et Lamiis, deque his recte cognoscendis et puniendis.* Frankfurt, 1601.

Goldast, Melchior (von Haimins-Feld). *Rechtliches Bedencken Von Confiscation der Zauberer- und Hexen-Güther....*Bremen, 1661.

Graeter, Jacob. *Hexen oder Unholden Predigten. Darinnen zu zweyen underschiedlichen Predigten auff das kürtzest unnd ordenlichest angezeigt würdt, was in disen allgemeinen Landklagen, uber die Hexen und Unholden, von selbigen warhafftig und Gottseelig zu halten.* Tübingen, 1589.

Der Graffschafft Hohenlohe gemeinsames Land-Recht. Öhringen, 1738.

Grimmelshausen, H. J. C. von. *The Adventurous Simplicissimus.* Trans. A. T. S. Goodrick. Lincoln, Neb., 1962.

Häberlin, Georg Heinrich ("Heberlin"). *Historische Relation von denen In der Hochfürstl. Würtemb....Stadt Calw einiger Zeit her Der Zauberey halber beschreyten*

Kindern, und andern Personen. Sambt einer Christlichen Predigt Wie solchen... *Satanischen Anläufften Christlich zu begegnen.* Stuttgart, 1685.

Hafenreffer, Matthias. *Loci Theologici: certa methodo ac ratione in Tres Libros tributi.* Tübingen, 1600.

Harpprecht, Ferdinand Christoph. *Consiliorum Tubingensium.* 6 vols. Tübingen, 1695–98.

Hasler, Johann. *Astrologische Practica Auff das 1590. Jar.* Basel, [1589?].

Hauber, Eberhard David, ed. *Bibliotheca, Acta et Scripta, Magica, gründliche Nachrichten....* 36 parts in 3 vols. Lemgo, 1738–45.

Heerbrand, Jacob. *Compendium Theologiae, Quaestionibus Methodi Tractatum.* Tübingen, 1573.

———. *Disputationes Theologicae in Inclyta Tubingensia Academia....* Tübingen, 1575.

———. *Ein Predig Vom Straal so zuo Tübingen den XIX. Brachmonats diss 1579 Jar eingeschlagen. Gehalten den ersten Sontag nach Trinitatis zu Tübingen.* Tübingen, 1579.

———. *Ein Predig, Von dem erschrockenlichen Wunderzeichen am Himmel, dem newen Cometen oder Pfawenschwantz.* Tübingen, 1577.

Heilbronner, Jacob. *Daemonomania Pistoriana. Magica et cabalistica morborum curandorum ratio, a Ioanne Pistorio Niddano... Cum Antidoto prophylactico Iacobi Heilbronneri.* Lauingen, 1601.

Hobbes, Thomas. *Leviathan.* New York, 1955.

Hondorff, Andreas. *Promptuarium Exemplorum. Das ist Historien und Exempelbuch nach ordnung und Disposition der heiligen Zehen Gebott Gottes.* 3d ed. Frankfurt, 1574.

Hossmann, Abr. *De tonitru et tempestate, Bericht von Donnern und Hagelwettern, wannen und woher sich dieselben verursachen, ob sie natürlich; item ob Teufel und Zauberer auch Wetter machen können.* Leipzig, 1612.

Hützelin, Johann. *Zwo Christliche Leich Predigten. Die Erste... Daniel Schrötlins ... den 17. Decembris Anno 1623... eingeschlafen.* Stuttgart, 1625.

J. R. G. F. *Erschröckliche Newe Zeitung Von der Grausame, Ubernaturliche Wundergeschicht, dess Blutbrunnens zu Görlingen im Landt zu Wirtemberg, Leonberger Vogtei.* Augsburg, 1592.

Land Recht Der Fürstenthummer und Landen Der Marggraffschafften Baaden und Hachberg, Landgraffschafft Sausenberg und Herrschafft Rötteln, Badenweiler, Lahr, und Mahlberg, etc. Durlach, 1710.

Lipsius, Justus. *Two Bookes of Constancie.* Trans. J. Stradling. London, 1595.

Lorichius, Gerhard (Hadamarius). *Bibliae Totius Brevis et Compendiosa Elucidatio.* Cologne, 1563.

Lorichius, Jodocus. *Aberglaub. Das ist kurtzlicher bericht. Von verbottenen Segen, Artzneyen, Künsten, vermeinten Gottsdienst, und andern spottlichen Beredungen. ... 2d. ed.* Freiburg, 1593.

———. *Fortalitium Christianae Fidei ac Religionis Adversus Haereses Horum Temporum....* Rottweil, 1606.

Lotter, Tobias. *Gründtlicher und nothwendiger Bericht, Was von denen ungestümmen Wettern, verderblichen Hägeln und schädlichen Wasserflutten, mit welchen Teutschland an sehr viel Orten, in dem 1613. Jahr ernstlich heimgesucht worden, zuhalten seye....* Stuttgart, 1615.

Luther, Martin. "Das Elltern die Kinder zur Ehe nicht zwingen noch hyndern, und die Kinder on der elltern willen sich nicht verloben sollen" (1524), in *D. Martin Luthers Werke* (Weimar, 1883–), 15: 163–69.

Lutz, Reinhard. *Warhafftige Zeittung. Von Gottlosen Hexen, auch Ketzerischen und Teuffels Weibern, die zu Schlettstadt. des H. Römischen Reichsstadt in Elsass, auff den XXII Herbstmonat des 1570. Jahrs... sindt verbrennt worden.* 1st ed. 1571; reprinted in [Saur], *Theatrum de Veneficis*, pp. 1–11.

Malleus Maleficarum. By Jacob Sprenger and Heinrich Institoris (1486). Ed. and trans. Montague Summers. London, 1948.

Marstaller, Christophorus. *Der Pfarr und Pfründ Beschneiderteuffel.* Nuremberg, 1575.

Martini, Friedrich. *De Ivre Censuum seu annorum redituum... commentarius.... Cui, eodem authore, ad calcem adnexa est nova Carolin. Constitution 109 & 218 in praxi frequentissimarum interpretatio.* Freiburg, 1604; another ed., Cologne, 1660.

Mauritius, Erich. *Consiliorum Chiloniensium Specimen sive Responsa de Jure XXX.* Kiel, 1669.

Meder, David. *Acht Hexenpredigten. Darinnen Von des Teuffels Mord Kindern, der Hexen... erschrecklichem Abfalle, Lastern und Ubelthaten, dadurch die Göttliche Maiestet gelestert, und Menschen und Viehe, etc. verderblicher Schaden zugefüget. ...* Leipzig, 1605.

Metzger, Thomas. *Criminalia et resolutiones... de captura et tortura reorum... quibus accesserunt Consilia quaedam criminalia....* Freiburg, 1618.

Molitor, Ulric. *De lamiis et phitonicis mulieribus* (1489). Translated into German as "Von Hexen und Unholden" in [Saur], *Theatrum de Veneficis.*

Ein newe und warhafftige Zeittung von einer wunderbarlichen schröcklichen und abschewlichen Geburt. Strassburg, 1569.

Newe Zeittung, und wahre Geschicht, dises LXXVI Jars geschehen im Breissgaw, wie man da in etlichen Stätten, und Flecken, inn die 136. Unholden gefangen, und verbrendt hat, ... im thon Kompt her zu mir spricht Gottes Sohn. N.p., n.d.

Newe Zeitung Von den Hexen oder Unhulden, so mann verbrend hat von dem 7. Februari an biss auff den 25 Junii dises 1580. Jar.... In ein Liedt verfasst Im Thon All die ir jetzund Leiden, verfolgung trübsal und schmach. N.p., 1580.

Newe Zeitunge. Von einem Manne Hans Bader genennt, wie dem der Teüfel mit Stricken... beyde Hände auff den Rugken bindet.... Augsburg, 1562.

Newer Tractat Von der Verführten Kinder Zauberey. In welchem mit reifflichem Discurs und muthmässigem Bedencken vorgehalten wirdt, auss was Ursachen viel unerwachsene, und unmündige Kinder, so noch zur zeit scheinnen unschuldig zu seyn, zu der verdampten Geister, und Zauberer Gesellschafft gebracht und unerhörter weiss verführt werden.... Aschaffenburg, 1629.

Newezeitung Und ware geschicht, dieses 76. Jars geschehen im Breissgaw, wie man da in etlichen Stätten und Flecken in die 55 unhulden gefangen und verbrent hat ... In ein Lied verfasset, im Thon. Kompt her zuo mir spricht Gottes [sic]. Hof, 1576.

Osiander, Andreas. "Wie und wohin ein Christ für der grausamen Plag der Pestilenz fliehen sol, aus dem 91. Psal.," in *Consiliorum Theologicorum Decas I,* ed. Felix Bidembach (Frankfurt, 1608), pp. 133–56.

Osiander, Johann Adam. *Commentarius in Pentateuchum.* Tübingen, 1676.

———. *Tractatus Theologicus de Magia.* Tübingen, 1687.

Osiander, Lucas. *Bawrenpostilla, Das ist Einfältige, jedoch Sämdtliche Ausslegung der Episteln und Evangelien... Für das einfältige Christliche Völcklein auff den Dörffern.* Tübingen, 1601.

————. *Ein Predigt vom Reiffen welcher drey Tag nach einander nämlich, den 21. 22. und 23. Aprilis Anno etc. 1602 gefallen....* Tübingen, 1602.

————. *Ein Predig Uber das Evangelium, wölches man auff den tag der heyligen Aposteln Petri und Pauli...ausszulegen pflegt.* Tübingen, 1583.

————. 'Wie die Christen in dieser Welt mit gutem Gewissen, frölich sein, unnd Schwermütigkeit von sich treiben mögen und sollen" (1583), in *Consiliorum Theologicorum Decas II*, ed. Felix Bidembach (Frankfurt, 1608), pp. 192–202.

Pflacher, Moses. *Weinthewre. oder Bericht auss Gottes Wort, woher und auss was Ursachen dise jetzige Weintewrung entstanden, auch wie dieselbige abzustellen....* Tübingen, 1589.

Pictorius, Georg. *Pantopōlion, continens omnium ferme quadrupedum...naturas carmine elegiaco...de apibus methodo....De Illorum Daemonum qui sub lunari collimitio versantur, ortu, nominibus, officiis, illusionibus, potestate, vaticiniis, miraculis, & quibus mediis in fugam compellantur....Quibus accedit de speciebus magiae ceremonialis, quam Goetiam vocant epitome, eodem Pictore collectore, et an Sagae vel Mulieres quas expiatrices nominamus ignis mulcta sint damnandae, resolutio.* Basel, 1562.

Plantsch, Martin. *Opusculum de sagis maleficis Martini Plantsch concionatoris Tubingensis.* Pforzheim, 1507.

Platz, Conrad Wolffgang. *Kurtzer Nottwendiger unnd Wollgegrundter Bericht, Auch Christliche vermanung von der Grewlichen, in aller Welt gebreuchlichen Zauberey Sünd dem zauberischen Beschwören un Segensprechen. Predigweiss gethon zu Biberach.* N.p., 1565.

————. *Newe Zeitung und Busspiegel. Von dem Straal so zu Biberach dises lauffenden 84. Jars, den 10. Tag Maii in den Kirchen unnd Glockenthurm eingeschlagen. ...*Tübingen, 1584.

————. "Ob Segensprechen und beschwören auch für Zauberey sind zurechnen...," in *Consiliorum Theologicorum Decas II*, ed. Felix Bidembach (Frankfurt, 1608), pp. 50–80.

Plaustarius, Johann. *Prognosticon, Oder Weissagung auff diese jetzige Zeit, darinn vermeldet, wie GOTT der Allmächtige die gantze Welt, ihrer Sünde wegen, daheim suchen wolle....*N.p., 1621.

Praetorius, Johann (Schultz). *Blockes-Berges Verrichtung.* Leipzig, 1668.

Radbruch, Gustav, ed. *Die peinliche Gerichtsordnung Karls V. von 1532 (Carolina).* Stuttgart, 1962.

Rivandrum, Zacharias. "Ob auch die Hexen und Unholden die Menschen durch ihre Zauberey, in Wölffe, Bären, und andere wilde und unvernünfftige Thier, verwandlen können," in *Consiliorum Theologicorum Decas VII*, ed. Felix Bidembach (Frankfurt, 1611), pp. 132–43.

Rose, William R., ed. *The Historie of the Damnable Life and Deserved Death of Doctor John Faustus.* South Bend, Ind., 1963.

Sachs, Hans. "Ein spiel mit 4 person zw spielen: Sankt Petter leezet sich mit sein freunden unden auf erden," in *Zwölf Fastnachtspiele aus den Jahren 1554 bis 1556 von Hans Sachs*, ed. Edmund Goetze (Halle, 1886).

Sammlung der Landrechte, Landes-Ordnung der Markgrafschaft Baden-Baden; wie auch der Statuten...Offenburg, Gengenbach, und Zell....Nebst einem Anhange von allen späteren Verordnungen welche das Bad.-Badische Landrecht abgeändert haben. 2 vols. Karlsruhe, 1805–6. A copy is in the Landesbibliothek Karlsruhe.

Saur, Abraham. "Ein kurze newe Warnung Anzeige und Underricht ob auch zu dieser Zeit under uns Christen Hexen Zäuberer und Unholden vorhanden. Und was sie aussrichten können," in [Saur], *Theatrum de Veneficis*, pp. 202–14.

[Saur, Abraham]. *Theatrum de Veneficis. Das ist: Von Teuffels gespenst Zauberern und Gifftbereitern, Schwartzkünstlern, Hexen und Unholden.... Sampt etlicher hingerichten Zauberischer Weiber gethaner Bekanntnuss.* Frankfurt, 1586.

[Schnauss, Cyriacus]. *Newe Zeytung Vom Teüffel. Wie newlich der Bapst und sein gesell/ Der öberst Sathanus auss der hell/ Von ihrer gesellschaft und disem Krieg/ Sprach gehalten.* N.p., 1546.

Schopff, Johann. *Wetter Glöcklin, das ist Erinnerung und Auffmunderung, Wie jetziger Zeit vilfältige schwere Wetter zubetrachten.... Auch werden unter andern die jenige hierinnen widerlegt, so solche Wetter den Hexen und Unholden freuenlich und unbedächtig zuschreiben.* Tübingen, 1603.

Scot, Reginald. *The Discoverie of Witchcraft* (1584). Ed. H. R. Williamson. London, 1964.

Ein sehr schröckliche und abscheuliche Wundergeburt. Strassburg, 1569.

Sigwart, Johann Georg. *Eilff Predigten Von den Vornemsten unnd zu ieder zeit in der Welt gemeinsten Lastern sampt derenselben entgegen gesetzten Tugenten.* Tübingen, 1603.

——. *Ein Predigt Vom Hagel und Ungewitter, Im Jahr Christi 1613, den 30. May ...(als am Sambstag Abends zuvor Nachmittag vor 5. Uhren ein schröcklicher Hagel gefallen)....* Tübingen, 1613.

——. *Ein Predigt Vom Reiffen und Getröst, Den 25. Aprilis ... 1602 (als die nächste Tag zuvor, nemblich den 21. 22. und 23. gemelten Monds das Rebwerck erfroren).* ... Tübingen, 1602.

——. *Ein Predigt Von dem Erdbidemen Als den Achten Septemb dieses 1601. Jahrs, das Erdreich an vil underschidlichen orten hefftig gebebet.* Tübingen, 1601.

Spee, Friedrich von. *Cautio Criminalis oder rechtliches Bedenken wegen der Hexenprozesse* (1632). Ed. and trans. Joachim-Friedrich Ritter. 2d. ed. Weimar, 1967.

Sprenger, Jacob, and Heinrich Institoris. *Malleus Maleficarum* (1486). Ed. and trans. Montague Summers. London, 1948.

Spreter, Johann. *Christenlich Instruction und ware erklärung furnemlicher artickel des Glaubens.* Basel, 1543.

——. *Ein kurtzer Bericht, was von den Abgötterischen Sägen und Geschweren zuhalten, wie der etlich volbracht, unnd das die ein Zauberney, auch greüwel vor Gott dem Herren seind.* Basel, 1543.

[Spreter, Johann]. *Hexen Büchlein, das ist, ware entdeckung und erklärung oder Declaration fürnämlicher Artikel der Zauberey, und was von Zauberern, Unholden, Hengsten, Nachtschaden, Schüssen, auch der Hexen händel ... zu halten sey.... Etwan durch den Wolgeborenen Herren Herr Jacob Freyherr von Liechtenberg auss ihrer gefengknuss erfahren und jetzt durch ein gelerten Doctor zusammen bracht* (bound to Spreter's *Christenliche Instruction*). [Basel, 1540.]

Stähelin, Christoph. *Brunstpredigt, Behalten zu Dornstätten am Schwarzwald auff den Sontag der H. Dreyfaltigkeit im Jar ... 1607 ... als zuvor den 18. Monats Aprilis ein fewriger Straal gegen Abend daselbsten eingeschlagen.* Tübingen, 1607.

Theatrum de Veneficis. Das ist: Von Teuffels gespenst Zauberern und Gifftbereitern, Schwartzkünstlern, Hexen und Unholden.... Sampt etlicher hingerichten Zauberischer Weiber gethaner Bekanntnuss. [By Abraham Saur.] Frankfurt, 1586.

Thumm, Theodor. *Tractatus Theologicus de Sagarum Impietate, nocendi imbecillitate et poenae gravitate etc. Partim ex private experientia, partim veris historiis & relationibus aliorum.* Tübingen, 1667.

Voltz, Valentinus. *Commentarii Duo. I. De Inquisitione: sive ad L.2 ... adjectis duobus Consiliis, ad eandem materiam spectantibus. II. In Tit. Digest. ad leg. Cornel. de sicar. etc.... Uterque Notis hinc indo illustratus: per Dn. Georgium Adalbertum Burchardum.... Nunc cum Notis uberioribus, Summarius & Indice in lucem editus, cura ac studio Jacobi Schytzii.* Tübingen, 1620.

———. *De inquisitione seu processibus contra sagas.* Solisbaci [Sulzbach], 1695.

Wagner, Bartholomeas. *Cathchesis oder Catholische Kinder Lehr oder die für-nembste Stuck unsers ... Glaubens ... in LXXXIX Predig deduciert ... volgends aber jede Predig Frag and Antwort gestellt.* Freiburg, 1609.

Wagner, Tobias. *Casual Predigten über allerhand bedenckliche schwere Fäll Welche sich in nechst verflossenen Jahren und gefährlichen Zeiten haben begeben.... Stuttgart, 1658.*

———. *Der kohlschwartze Teuffel. Das ist: Eine scharffe Predig vom und wider den Teuffel.... Auch sambt Historischer Erzelung dess schweren Gewissenfalls selbsten. ... Ulm, 1643.*

Warhafftige und ein erschröckliche Neuwe zeitung des grossen Wasser guss so den 15. May diss lauffenden 78. Jahrs zu Horb geschehen, dem löblichen Hauss Oesterreich gehörig, wie man hernach alda etlich Unholden verbrent hatt, wie sie schröcklich ding bekendt haben.... Im Thon wie man Den König Lassla singt. Antorff, [1578].

Warhafftige und Erschreckliche Thatten und handlungen der LXIII Hexen und Unholden, so zu Wisenstaig mit dem Brandt gericht worden seindt. Anno MDLXIII. N.p., 1563.

Warhafftige und glaubwirdige Zeyttung von Hundert und vier und dreyssig Unholden. So umb irer Zauberey halben diss verschinen 1582 Jars, zu Gefencknus gebracht, und den 15. 19. 24. 28. October auff ihr unmenschliche Thaten und graewliche aussag ... zum Fewer verdampt und verbrennet worden. Strasbourg, 1583.

Westenhoeffer, Johann, ed. *Die Reformationsgeschichte von einem Baarfüsser Mönche. Auszug aus der Thanner Chronik.* Leipzig, 1882.

Weyer, Johann. *Histoires disputes et discours des illusions et impostures des diables, des magiciens infames.... Le tout compris en six livres.* Ed. E. Bourneville. Paris, 1885.

———. *Opera Omnia.* Amsterdam, 1660.

———. *De Praestigiis Daemonum.* Basel, 1577. Also printed in Weyer, *Opera Omnia.*

———. *De Praestigiis Daemonum. Von Teuffels ge-spenst Zauberern und Gifftbereitern ... durch D. Johannem Weier in Latein ... von Johanne Fuglino verteutscht ... auffs neuen ubersehen und mit vielen heilsamen nützlichen Stücken: auch sonderlich ... Zusätzen, so im Lateinischen nicht gelesen, so der Bodinus mit gutem Grund nicht widerlegen kan.* Frankfurt, 1586. (Vol. 2 of [Saur], *Theatrum de Veneficis.*)

Wild, Johann. *Epitome Semonorum ... Dominicalium ... Anno MDLVI in Cathedrali Vvormatiensi ... habita.* Antwerp, 1562.

Wildersin, Bernhard. *Wunder- und Buss-Spiegel, Das ist: Eine Christliche Predigt Vom Blut-Regen, auch andern Wundern und Zeichen, so dieser Zeit im Hertzogthum Wirtemberg begeben und sehen lassen.* Schwäbisch Hall, 1643.

Wyerman, Johann. *Practica Uff das MDLXV Jar, Von künfftigen Kranckheyten, Kriegen, Todt, Thüre und anderen dingen so sich diss Jars alls zu besorgen, allenthalben zutragen.* Zürich, 1564.

Zeiller, Martin. *Chronicon parvum Sueviae oder kleines schwäbisches Zeitbuch.* Ulm, 1653.

Zeitung von der greulichen Zauberei in deutscher Nation. Erfurt, 1613.

Zwo Hexen Zeitung, Die Erste: Auss dem Bissthumb Würtzburg, Das ist, Gründliche Erzehlung wie der Bischoff zu Würtzburg das Hexenbrennen im Franckenlande angefangen.... Die Ander, Auss dem Hertzogthumb Würtenberg, Wie der Hertzog zu Würtenberg, in unterschiedlichen Stätten das Hexenbrennen auch angefangen. Tübingen, 1616.

Zwo Hexenzeitung, Die Erste Von dreyen Hexen-Pfaffen, unnd einem Organisten zu Ellwang, wie dieselbe Christo abgesagt unnd dem bösen Geist mit Leib und Seel sich ergeben.... Die ander: Von einer Unholdin oder Hexen, wie sie mit ihren Gespilen alles zu verderben unterstanden, der Satan aber ihnen ursachen.... Nuremberg, 1615.

Zwo Newe Zeittung. Was man für Hexen oder Unholden verbrendt hat, von dem siebenden Hornung an biss auff den zwentzigsten Höwmonat diss MDLXXX. Jars, auch darbey angezeigt, an was ohrt und enden, auch was sie bekendt haben, etc. Die ander, Von der grausammen Wüterey des Türcken.... Hof, 1580.

SECONDARY SOURCES

Abrams, M. H. *The Mirror and the Lamp. Romantic Theory and the Critical Tradition.* New York, 1958.

Adam, Albert Eugen. *Württembergische Landtagsakten unter Herzog Friedrich I (1599–1608).* Stuttgart, 1911.

Adelmann, P. "Teufelsbesessenheit und Teufelsaustreibung. Kulturgeschichtliches über Dämonenglauben im Schwarzwald, auf der Baar, und am Bodensee," *Oberländer Chronik,* No. 195 (1958).

A. G. "Der Hexenglaube im Schwabenland," *Württemberger Zeitung* (Stuttgart), No. 300 (1910): 9.

Allen, Don Cameron. *Doubt's Boundless Sea. Skepticism and Faith in the Renaissance.* Baltimore, 1964.

———. *The Star-Crossed Renaissance. The Quarrel About Astrology and Its Influence in England.* Durham, N.C., 1941.

Allgemeine deutsche Biographie. 56 vols. Leipzig, 1875–1912.

Altona. "Stellung des Reichskammergerichts zu den Hexenprozessen," *Zeitschrift für die gesamte Strafrechtswissenschaft,* 12 (1892): 909–13.

Altotting, Franz Xaver von. "Konrad von Monheim, O.F.M. Cap. (1643–1712), als Seelsorger bei den Geislinger Hexen," in *Miscellanea Melchor de Pobladura,* 2. Rome, 1964. Pp. 377–91.

Die Archivpflege in den Kreisen und Gemeinden. Lehrgangsbericht und Hilfsbuch für den Archivpfleger in Württemberg und in Hohenzollern. Stuttgart, 1952. No. 5 of the Veröffentlichungen der württembergischen Archivverwaltung.

Ariès, Philippe. *Centuries of Childhood.* New York, 1962.

Autenrieth, Johannes. *Die Handschriften der württembergischen Landesbibliothek, Stuttgart.* Ser. 2, Vol. 3: *Codices iuridici et politici, Patres.* Wiesbaden, 1963.

Babb, Lawrence. *The Elizabethan Malady. A Study of Melancholia in English Literature from 1580 to 1640.* East Lansing, Mich., 1951.

Bächtold-Stäubli, Hanns. *Handwörterbuch des deutschen Aberglaubens.* 10 vols. Berlin and Leipzig, 1930–31.

Back, Kurt W., and Alan C. Kerckhoff. *The June Bug. A Study of Hysterical Contagion.* New York, 1968.

Bacmeister, Karl A. W. "Zur Geschichte der Hexenprozesse. Concept eines Bedenkens über die zu Niedernhaal um Hexerei und Zauberei willen in Verhaft liegende

Susann Michel Lunge's Weib, deren Aussage, und noch weiters angebene Personen," *Württembergische Vierteljahrshefte für Landesgeschichte* (1886), pp. 282–92.

Bader, Guido. *Die Hexenprozesse in der Schweiz.* Dr. jur. dissertation, Zürich University. Affoltern, 1945.

Bader, Josef. *Badische Landesgeschichte von den ältesten bis auf unsere Zeiten.* 2d ed. Freiburg, 1834.

———. "Die ehemalige strassburgische Herrschaft Oberkirch," *Badenia*, 2 (1840): 219–37.

Bader, Karl S. *Der deutsche Südwesten in seiner territorialstaatlichen Entwicklung.* Stuttgart, 1950.

Baeyer-Katte, Wanda von. "Die historischen Hexenprozesse. Der verbürokratisierte Massenwahn," in *Massenwahn in Geschichte und Gegenwart, ein Tagungsbericht der Stuttgarter Gemeinschaft 'Arzt und Seelsorger' im Sommer 1964*, ed. Wilhelm Bitter (Stuttgart, 1965), pp. 220–31.

Bainton, Roland H. *George Lincoln Burr: His Life, by Roland H. Bainton; Selections from His Writings, Ed. by Lois Oliphant Gibbons.* Ithaca, N.Y., 1943.

Baltl, Hermann. "Folklore Research and Legal History in the German Language Area," *Journal of the Folklore Institute*, 5 (1968): 142–51.

Balzer, Eugen. "Die Bräunlinger Hexenprozesse," *Alemannia*, 3d series, 2 (1910): 1–42.

Barnett, Bernard. "Witchcraft, Psychopathology and Hallucinations," *British Journal of Psychiatry*, 111, No. 474 (1965): 439–45.

Barth, Hans-Martin. *Der Teufel und Jesus Christus in der Theologie Martin Luthers.* Göttingen, 1967.

Bartmann, Horst. *Die Kirchenpolitik der Markgrafen von Baden-Baden im Zeitalter der Glaubenskämpfe, 1535–1622.* Freiburg, 1961.

Baschwitz, Kurt. *Hexen und Hexenprozesse. Die Geschichte eines Massenwahns.* Munich, 1966.

Basso, Keith Hamilton. "Heavy with Hatred: An Ethnographic Study of Western Apache Witchcraft." Unpublished Ph.D. dissertation, Stanford University, 1967.

Batzer, Ernst. "Der Hexenfang in Schutterwald 1629," *In und um Offenburg*, 3 (1920): 29–31.

Bauer, Johannes Joseph, S.J.C. *Zur Frühgeschichte der theologischen Fakultät der Universität Freiburg i. Br., 1460–1620.* Freiburg, 1957. No. 14 of the Beiträge zur Freiburger Wissenschafts- und Universitätsgeschichte.

Baumann, Franz Ludwig. *Geschichte des Allgäus.* 3 vols. Kempten, 1894.

Baumann, Werner. *Ernst Friedrich von Baden-Durlach. Die Bedeutung der Religion für Leben und Politik eines süddeutschen Fürsten im Zeitalter der Gegenreformation.* Stuttgart, 1962. Ser. B (Forschungen), vol. 20 of the Veröffentlichungen der Kommission für geschichtliche Landeskunde in Baden-Württemberg.

Baumgärtel, Gottfried. *Die Gutachter- und Urteilstätigkeit der Erlanger Juristenfakultät in dem ersten Jahrhundert ihres Bestehens.* Erlangen, 1962. Ser. A, Vol. 14 of the Erlanger Forschungen.

Baur, Fritz, ed. *Bibliography of German Law.* Trans. Courtland H. Peterson. Karlsruhe, 1964.

Bausinger, H. "Aufklärung und Aberglaube," *Deutsche Vierteljahrschrift für Literaturwissenschaft und Geistesgeschichte* (Stuttgart), 37 (1963): 345–62.

Bechtold, Artur. "Hexen im bayrischen Lager bei Durlach (1643)," *Alemannia*, 44 (1917). 138–44.

————. *Johann Jacob Christoph von Grimmelshausen und seine. Zeit.* Heidelberg, 1914.

Beck, Paul. "Die Bibliothek eines Hexenmeisters," *Zeitschrift des Vereins für Volkskunde* (Berlin), 15 (1905): 412–24.

————. " 'Hexenbründe' in Sulz a. N.," *Diözesanarchiv aus Schwaben,* 10, supplement 20 (1892): 37–40.

————. "Hexenprozesse aus dem Fränkischen," *Württembergische Vierteljahrshefte für Landesgeschichte,* 6 (1883): 247–53, 304–10; 7 (1884): 76–80, 157–60, 297–302.

————. "Hexenprozesse im Limpurgischen," *Ipf- und Jagstzeitung* (Ellwangen), No. 141 (1909): 5.

Becker, Albert. "Hexen im Odenwald," *Die Starkenburg,* 29, No. 5 (1952).

Belling, Dieter. "Das Strafrecht des Schwabenspiegels. Ein Beitrag zur Geschichte des deutschen Strafrechts." Unpublished Dr. jur. dissertation, Tübingen University, 1949.

Bender, K. L. "Die Reformation in Gengenbach," *Veröffentlichungen des Vereins für Kirchengeschichte in der evangelischen Landeskirche in Baden,* 22 (1962): 5–27.

Berger, Adolf. *Encyclopedic Dictionary of Roman Law.* Philadelphia, 1953. N.S. 43, pt. 2 of the Transactions of the American Philosophical Society.

Berkowitz, Leonard. "Anti-Semitism and the Displacement of Aggression, *Journal of Abnormal and Social Psychology,* 59 (1959): 182–87.

Berkowitz, Leonard, and J. A. Green. "The Stimulus Qualities of the Scapegoat," *Journal of Abnormal and Social Psychology,* 64 (1962): 293–301.

Beschreibung der württembergischen Oberämter. Ed. Königliches Statistisches Landesamt, Stuttgart. 64 vols. (1824–86); N.S., 11 vols. (1893–1930).

Beste, August Friedrich Wilhelm. *Die bedeutendsten Kanzelredner der älteren lutherschen Kirche von Luther bis Spener.* 3 vols. Leipzig, 1856–86.

Bezold, Friedrich von. "Astrologische Geschichtskonstruktionen im Mittelalter," in *Aus Mittelalter und Renaissance. Kulturgeschichtliche Studien* (Munich, 1918), pp. 165 et seq.

Biberstein-Krasicky, Dennis Graf von. "Das Prozessrecht der Gerichts- und Landesordnungen der fürstenbergischen Territorien im 16. und beginnenden 17. Jahrhundert." Unpublished Dr. jur. dissertation, Freiburg University, 1947.

Bicheler, D. *Die ehemalige vorderösterreichische Donaustadt Mengen, in Krieg und Frieden.* Mengen, 1957.

Binz, Carl, ed. *Augustin Lercheimer [Hermann Witekind] und seine Schrift wider den Hexenwahn.* Strassburg, 1888.

Birlinger, Anton. *Aus Schwaben. Sagen, Legenden, Aberglauben, Sitten, Rechtsbräuche, Ortsneckereien, Lieder, Kinderreime.* 2 vols. Wiesbaden, 1874.

Birnbaum, Norman. "Social Structure and the German Reformation." Unpublished Ph.D. dissertation, Harvard University, 1958.

Bitter, Wilhelm, ed. *Massenwahn in Geschichte und Gegenwart.* Stuttgart, 1-965.

Boas, Marie. "The Establishment of the Mechanical Philosophy," *Osiris,* 10 (1952): 412–541.

Boeckh, Joachim G., et al. *Geschichte der deutschen Literatur von 1480 bis 1600.* Berlin, 1961.

Bog, Ingomar. "Wachstumsprobleme der oberdeutschen Wirtschaft, 1540–1618," *Jahrbücher für Nationalökonomie und Statistik,* 179 (1966): 493–537.

Bonnekamp, Carl Georg. *Die Zimmerische Chronik als Quelle zur Geschichte des Strafrechts, der Strafgerichtsbarkeit und des Strafverfahrens in Schwaben im Aus-

gang des Mittelalters. Dr. jur. dissertation, Bonn. Strafrechtliche Abhandlungen, No. 411. Breslau-Neukirch, 1940.

Bonomo, Giuseppe. *Caccia alle streghe.* Palermo, 1959.

Börsig, Josef. *Geschichte des Oppenauer Tales.* Karlsruhe, 1951.

Borst, Otto. *Esslingen am Neckar. Ein Brevier seiner Geschichte und Kunst.* Esslingen, 1962.

––––––. "Die Kulturbedeutung der oberdeutschen Reichsstadt am Ende des alten Reiches," *Blätter für deutsche Landesgeschichte,* 100 (1964): 159–246.

Bossert, Gustav. "Johann Brenz, 'der Reformator Wurttembergs,' und seine Toleranzideen," *Blätter für württembergische Kirchengeschichte,* N.S. 15 (1911): 150–61; N.S. 16 (1912): 25–47.

––––––. "Johann Spreter von Rottweil," *Blätter für württembergische Kirchengeschichte,* N.S. 15 (1911): 103–25.

––––––. "Die Reformation im heutigen Dekanatsbezirk Sulz a. N.," *Blätter für württembergische Kirchengeschichte,* N.S. 38 (1934): 205–57.

––––––. "Rottenburg und die Herrschaft Hohenberg am Ausgang des Reformationszeitalters, 1540–1561," *Blätter für württembergische Kirchengeschichte,* N.S. 39 (1935): 1–30.

––––––. "Die Visitationsprotokolle der Diözese Konstanz von 1574 bis 1581," *Blätter für württembergische Kirchengeschichte,* 6 (1891): 1–5.

––––––. *Württemberg und Janssen.* Halle, 1884. No. 5 of the Schriften des Vereins für Reformationsgeschichte.

Bossert, Gustav, Jr. "Ein Hexenprozess in Grossbottwar im Jahr 1532," *Blätter für württembergische Kirchengeschichte,* 48 (1948): 11–14.

Brandi, Karl. *Deutsche Geschichte im Zeitalter der Reformation und Gegenreformation.* 3d ed. Munich, 1960.

––––––. *Gegenreformation und Religionskriege.* 2 vols. Leipzig, 1927–30.

Brann, Noel Lacy. "The Renaissance Passion of Melancholy: The Paradox of Its Cultivation and Resistance." Unpublished Ph.D. dissertation, Stanford University, 1965.

Brauns, K. "Der schwäbische Reichskreis, ein Vorläufer des Südwestens," *Hohenzollerische Jahreschefte,* 11 (1951): 47–64.

Brecht, Alfred. *Johann Brenz, der Reformator Württembergs.* Stuttgart, 1949.

Brecht, Martin. "Die Chronologie von Brenzens Schriftauslegungen und Predigten." *Blätter für württembergische Kirchengeschichte,* 64 (1964): 53–74.

––––––. "Die Entwicklung der alten Bibliothek des Tübinger Stifts in ihrem theologic- und geistesgeschichtlichen Zusammenhang. Eine Untersuchung zur württembergischen Theologie." Unpublished Th.D. dissertation, Tübingen University, 1961. Published in shortened form in *Blätter für württembergische Kirchengeschichte,* 63 (1963): 3–103.

––––––. *Die frühe Theologie des Johannes Brenz.* Tübingen, 1966. No. 36 of the Beiträge zur historischen Theologie.

––––––. *Kirchenordnung und Kirchenzucht in Württemberg vom 16. bis 18. Jahrhundert.* Stuttgart, 1967. No. 1 of the Quellen und Forschungen zur württembergischen Kirchengeschichte.

Breiden, Heribert. "Die Hexenprozesse der Grafschaft Blankenheim von 1589 bis 1643. Eine rechtsgeschichtliche und prozessrechtliche Untersuchung." Unpublished Dr. jur. dissertation, Bonn University, 1954.

Breining, Friedrich. *Alt-Besigheim in guten und bösen Tagen.* Besigheim, 1925.

Breitling, Richard. "Hexereien auf dem Rotenberg," *Untertürkheimer Zeitung*, No. 32 (1931).

Brietzmann, F. *Die böse Frau in der deutschen Literatur des Mittelalters*. Berlin, 1912. No. 42 in the Sammlung Palästra.

Brischar, Johann Nepomuk. *Die katholischen Kanzelredner Deutschlands seit den drei letzten Jahrhunderten. Als Beitrag zur Geschichte der deutschen Kanzelberedsamkeit.* 5 vols. Schaffhausen, 1867–71.

Brückner, Wolfgang. "Popular Piety in Central Europe," *Journal of the Folklore Institute*, 5 (1968): 158–74.

Brunner, Otto. *Adeliges Landleben und europäischer Geist. Leben und Werk Wolf Helmhards v. Hohberg 1612–1688.* Salzburg, 1949.

———. *Land und Herrschaft. Grundfragen der territorialen Verfassungsgeschichte Österreichs im Mittelalter.* 5th ed. Vienna, 1965.

Bücher, Carl. *Die Frauenfrage im Mittelalter.* Tübingen, 1882.

Buck, Michael R. "Hexenprozesse aus Oberschwaben," *Alemannia*, 11 (1883): 108–35.

Buhrlen, R. "Der wirtschaftliche Niedergang Esslingens im 16. und 17. Jahrhundert." Unpublished Ph.D. dissertation, Tübingen University, 1928.

Burckhardt, Jacob. *The Civilization of the Renaissance in Italy.* New York, 1964.

Bürger. "Beitrag zum Hexenwesen. Auszug aus dem Kirchenbuch zu Unterregenbach," *Zeitschrift des historischen Vereins für das württembergische Franken*, 8, No. 3 (1870): 502–4.

Burkarth, Rolf. "Hexenprozesse in Hohenzollern (mit den 1803 dazugekommenen Gebieten)." Unpublished thesis, Pädagogische Hochschule, Reutlingen, 1965.

Burkhardt, Felix. "Der Zauberer von Oberriexingen. Neue Funde zu Zauber und Segen," *Württembergisches Jahrbuch für Volkskunde* (1961–64): 109–15.

Burkhardt, Georg. *Geschichte der Stadt Geislingen a. d. Steige.* Vol. 1. Konstanz, 1963.

Burland, C. A. "Modern Swabian Folk-Beliefs About Witches," *Folklore* (London), 68 (1957): 495–97.

Burns, Edward McNall. *The Counter Reformation.* Princeton, N.J., 1964.

Burr, George Lincoln. *Selections from His Writings.* Ed. Lois Oliphant Gibbons. Ithaca, N.Y., 1943.

———. "The Witch Persecutions," *Translations and Reprints from the Original Sources of European History*, 3, No. 4. New York, 1903.

Burr, Viktor, ed. *Ellwangen 764–1964. Beiträge und Untersuchungen zur Zwölfhundertjahrfeier.* 2 vols. Ellwangen, 1964.

Butler, Eliza M. *Fortunes of Faust.* Cambridge, Eng., 1952.

———. *The Myth of the Magus.* Cambridge, Eng., 1948.

———. *Ritual Magic.* Cambridge, Eng., 1949.

Byloff, Fritz. *Das Verbrechen der Zauberei (crimen magiae). Ein Beitrag zur Geschichte der Strafrechtspflege in Steiermark.* Graz, 1902.

Byr, Robert. "Hexenprozesse in Bregenz (1596–1651)," in *Schriften des Vereins für Geschichte des Bodensees* (Lindau, 1886), pp. 215–26.

Carlebach, Rudolf. *Badische Rechtsgeschichte. I. Das ausgehende Mittelalter und die Rezeption des römischen Rechts unter Mitteilung der wichtigeren bisher ungedruckten Landesordnungen. II. Das Zeitalter des 30 jährigen Kriegs unter Mitteilung einiger bisher ungedruckten Aktenstücke.* Heidelberg, 1906–9.

Caro Baroja, Julio. *Vidas Magicas e Inquisicion.* 2 vols. Madrid, 1967.

———. *The World of the Witches.* Chicago, 1964.

Cartellieri, Otto. "Von Zauberei und Ketzerei in alten Zeiten," *Pfälzisches Museum,* 43 (1926): 3 et seq.

Carus, Paul. *The History of the Devil and the Ideal of Evil.* Chicago, 1900.

Cassirer, Ernst. *The Individual and the Cosmos in Renaissance Philosophy.* New York, 1964.

Cipolla, Carlo M. *Clocks and Culture, 1300–1700.* London, 1967.

Clasen, Claus-Peter. *The Palatinate in European History, 1555–1618.* Oxford, 1963.

———. *Die Wiedertäufer im Herzogtum Württemberg und in benachbarten Herrschaften. Ausbreitung, Geisteswelt und Soziologie.* Stuttgart, 1966. Vol. B/32 of the Veröffentlichungen der Kommission für geschichtliche Landeskunde in Baden-Württemberg.

Collins, James. *Thomistic Philosophy of the Angels.* Washington, D.C., 1947. Vol. 89 of the Catholic University of America Philosophical Studies.

Conrad, Hermann. *Deutsche Rechtsgeschichte.* 2 vols. Karlsruhe, 1966.

Cramer, J. *Die Grafschaft Hohenzollern. Ein Bild süddeutscher Volkszustände, 1400–1850.* Stuttgart, 1873.

Croissant, Werner. "Die Berücksichtigung geburts- und berufständischer und soziologischer Unterschiede im deutschen Hexenprozess." Unpublished Dr. jur. dissertation, Mainz University, 1953.

Cruel, R. *Geschichte der deutschen Predigt im Mittelalter.* Detmold, 1879.

Davies, R. Trevor. *Four Centuries of Witch Beliefs.* London, 1947.

Dehlinger, Alfred. *Württembergs Staatswesen.* Stuttgart, 1951.

Delcambre, Etienne. *Le concept de la sorcellerie dans le duché de Lorraine au XVIe et XVIIe siècle.* 3 vols. Nancy, 1948–51.

———. "Les procès de sorcellerie en Lorraine. Psychologie des juges," *Tijdschrift voor Rechtsgeschiedenis,* 21 (1954): 389–419.

———. "La psychologie des inculpés lorrains de sorcellerie," *Revue historique de droit français et étranger,* 32 (1954): 383–403, 508–26.

Demarce, Virginia Easley. "The Official Career of Georg III Truchsess von Waldburg: A Study in the Administration of Religious Policy by a Catholic Government during the First Years of the Reformation." Unpublished Ph.D. dissertation, Stanford University, 1967.

Demeny, Paul. "Early Fertility Decline in Austria-Hungary: A Lesson in Demographic Transition," *Daedalus,* 97 (1968): 502–22.

Demos, John. "Underlying Themes in the Witchcraft of Seventeenth-Century New England," *American Historical Review,* 75 (1969–70): 1311–26.

Dengler, Robert. "Das Hexenwesen im Stifte Obermarchtal von 1581 bis 1756." Unpublished Ph.D. dissertation, Erlangen University, 1953.

Diefenbach, Johann. *Besessenheit, Zauberei und Hexenfabeln.* Frankfurt, 1893.

———. *Der Hexenwahn vor und nach der Glaubensspaltung in Deutschland.* Mainz, 1886.

———. *Der Zauberglaube des 16. Jahrhundert nach den Catechismen Dr. Martin Luthers und des Petrus Canisius.* Mainz, 1900.

Diehm, Franz. *Geschichte der Stadt Bad Mergentheim. Äusseres Schicksal und innere Verhältnisse.* Bad Mergentheim, 1963.

Dijksterhuis, E. J. *Die Mechanisierung des Weltbildes.* Trans. Helga Habicht. Berlin, 1956.

Dillingen und Schwaben. Festschrift zur 400-Jahr-Feier der Universität Dillingen 1949. Dillingen, 1949.

Disch, Franz. *Chronik der Stadt Wolfach*. Wolfach, 1920.

Distel, Theodor. "Strafrechtsgeschichtliche Findlinge," *Zeitschrift für die gesamte Strafrechtswissenschaft*, 10 (1890): 431–46.

Doren, A. *Fortuna im Mittelalter und in der Renaissance*. Hamburg, 1923.

Döttinger, Karl, ed. *Heimatbuch des Kreises Heidenheim*. Heidenheim, 1962.

Drollinger, Kuno. *Kleine Städte Südwestdeutschlands. Studien zur Sozial- und Wirtschaftsgeschichte der Städte im rechtsrheinischen Teil des Hochstifts Speyer bis zur Mitte des 17. Jahrhunderts*. Stuttgart, 1968. Vol. B/48 of the Veröffentlichungen der Kommission für geschichtliche Landeskunde in Baden-Württemberg.

Duffner, Alfons. *Heimatbuch der Gemeinde Bühlertal*. Bühlertal, 1954.

Duhr, Bernhard. *Geschichte der Jesuiten in den Ländern deutscher Zunge*. Vol. 2, pt. 2. Freiburg, 1913.

———. *Die Stellung der Jesuiten in den deutschen Hexenprozessen*. Cologne, 1900.

Duncker, Max. *Die Pfarr- und Gemeinde-Registraturen des Oberamts Rottenburg*. Stuttgart, 1913. No. 8 of the Württembergische Archivinventare.

———. *Verzeichnis der württembergischen Kirchenbücher*. Stuttgart, 1938.

Dürr, Fr. *Heilbronner Chronik*. Heilbronn, 1895.

Eberle, Ernst. *Probleme zur Rechtsstellung der Frau nach den kursächsischen Konstitution von 1572*. Dr. jur. dissertation, Heidelberg University, 1964; published Stuttgart, 1964.

Eckstein, Franz. "Zum Diersburger Hexenprozess vom Jahre 1486," *Zeitschrift für die Geschichte des Oberrheins*, N.S. 40 (1927): 635–36.

Ehses, Stephan. "Jodocus Lorichius, katholischer Theologe und Polemiker des 16. Jahrhunderts," in *Festschrift zum elfhundertjährigen Jubiläum des deutschen Campo Santo in Rom,* ed. Stephan Ehses (Freiburg, 1897), pp. 242–55.

Eimer, Manfred. "Das bischöfliche Amt Oberkirch unter württembergischer Pfandherrschaft," *Zeitschrift für die Geschichte des Oberrheins*, N.S. 42 (1928): 132–46; N.S. 43 (1929): 610–39.

———. *Geschichte der Stadt Freudenstadt*. Freudenstadt, 1937.

———. "Eine Hexe in Waldulum," *Die Ortenau*, 28 (1941): 214.

Engel, Karl. *Bibliotheca Faustiana. Zusammenstellung der Faustschriften vom 16. Jahrhundert bis Mitte 1884*. 2d ed. Oldenbourg, 1885.

Erikson, Kai. *Wayward Puritans*. New York, 1966.

Ernst, Fritz. "Geschichtliche Grundlagen," in *Baden-Württemberg. Staat, Wirtschaft, Kultur*, ed. Theodor Pfizer (Stuttgart, 1963).

Ernst, Viktor, ed. *Der Briefwechsel des Herzogs Christoph von Württemberg*. 4 vols. Stuttgart, 1899–1907.

Estes, James Martin. "Johannes Brenz and the Problem of Church Order in the German Reformation." Unpublished Ph.D. dissertation, Ohio State University, 1964.

Evans, Austin P. "Hunting Subversion in the Middle Ages," *Speculum*, 33 (1958): 1–22.

Ewen, Cecil L'Estrange. *Witchcraft and Demonianism*. London, 1933.

———. *Witch Hunting and Witch Trials*. London, 1929.

Eyth, Ludwig. *Chronik von Hohebach a. d. Jagst*. Stuttgart, 1904.

Falk, Franz. "Das Corpus Catholicorum," *Der Katholik*, 3d series, 3 (Mainz, 1891): 440–63. Continued by Nikolaus Paulus as "Katholische Schriftsteller aus der Reformationszeit," *Der Katholik*, 3d series, 5 (1892): 544–64; Vol. 8 (1893): 213–23.

———. "Die deutsche Postillen-Literatur des 16 Jahrhunderts," *Wissenschaftliche Beilage zur Germania* (1909): 57–61.

Febvre, Lucien. "Sorcellerie: Sottise ou révolution mentale?" *Annales: Economies, Sociétés, Civilisations,* 3 (1948): 9–15.

Fehr, Hans. "Gottesurteil und Folter. Eine Studie zur Dämonologie des Mittelalters und der neueren Zeit," in *Festgabe für Rudolf Stammler,* ed. Edgar Tatarin-Tarnheyden (Berlin and Leipzig, 1926), pp. 231–54.

———. "Tod und Teufel im alten Recht," *Zeitschrift der Savigny-Stiftung für Rechtsgeschichte, Germanistische Abteilung,* 67 (1950): 50 et seq.

———. "Zur Erklärung von Folter und Hexenprozess," *Zeitschrift für schweizerische Geschichte,* 24 (1944): 581–85.

Feine, Hans Erich. *Kirchliche Rechtsgeschichte.* 2 vols. Weimar, 1954–55

Feist, E. "Castellio's *De Arte Dubitandi* and the Problem of Religious Liberty," in *Autour de Michel Servet et de Sebastien Castellion,* ed. B. Becker (Haarlem, 1953), pp. 244–58.

Feller, R. *Geschichte Berns von der Reformation bis zum Bauernkrieg, 1516–1653.* Bern, 1953.

Festschrift zur 600-Jahr-Feier der Stadt Niedernhall. Niedernhall, 1956.

Fetzer, A. *Das heutige Oberamt Heidenheim im dreissigjährigen Kriege.* Published Ph.D. dissertation, Tübingen University, 1933.

Fischer, Gerhard. "Die freie Reichsstadt Reutlingen. Die Verfassung ab 1500 und das Strafrecht." Unpublished Dr. jur. dissertation, Tübingen University, 1959.

Fischer, Wolfram. *Das Fürstentum Hohenlohe im Zeitalter der Aufklärung.* Tübingen, 1958. No. 10 of the Tübinger Studien zur Geschichte und Politik.

Fischlin, Ludovicus Melchior. *Memoria Theologorum Wirtembergensium.* Ulm, 1709.

Fladt, Wilhelm. "Hexen und böse Geister," *Mein Heimatland,* 3 (1916): 71–73.

Fleck, Egid, et al. *Fellbach.* Fellbach, 1958.

Flemming, Willi. *Deutsche Kultur im Zeitalter des Barocks (Handbuch der Kulturgeschichte,* Sect. 1, No. 6). 2d ed. Konstanz, 1960.

———. *Das deutsche Schrifttum von 1500 bis 1700.* Potsdam, 1943.

Forderer, J. *Reutlingen. Leben und Streben einer schwäbischen Reichsstadt.* Tübingen, 1948.

Franck, Wilhelm. "Der Hexenprozess gegen dem Fürstenbergischen Registrator, Obervogteiverweser und Notar Mathias Tinctorius und Consorten zu Hüfingen. Ein Sittenbild aus den 30er Jahren [1630's]," *Zeitschrift der Gesellschaft für Beförderung der Geschichts- Altertums- und Volkskunde von Freiburg, dem Breisgau und den angrenzenden Landschaften,* 2 (1870–72): 1–42.

———. "Zum Hexenwesen" [punishments and tortures at Donaueschingen and Wolfach], *Zeitschrift der Gesellschaft für ... Volkskunde von Freiburg ...,* 2 (1870–72): 430–31.

Franz, Günther. *Der dreissigjährige Krieg und das deutsche Volk.* 3d ed. Stuttgart, 1961.

Freytag, Gustav. "Der dreissigjährige Krieg. Die Dörfer und ihre Geistlichen," in his *Bilder aus der deutschen Vergangenheit,* Vol. 3 (Leipzig, 1890), pp. 100–144.

Fritz, Ernst. "Neckartäler Hexengeschichten und ihre Deutung," *Unter der Dorflinde im Odenwald,* 36 (1954): 16 et seq.

Fritz, Friedrich. "Die evangelische Kirche Württembergs im Zeitalter des Pietismus," *Blätter für württembergische Kirchengeschichte,* 55 (1955): 68–117; 56 (1956): 99–168.

————. "Theodor Thumm, ein Vorkämpfer der lutherischen Kirche in der Zeit des dreissigjährigen Krieges," *Luthertum* (1939): 202–30.

————. "Ulmische Kirchengeschichte vom Interim bis zum 30jährigen Krieg (1548–1612)," *Blätter für württembergische Kirchengeschichte,* N.S. 35 (1931): 130–206; N.S. 36 (1932): 1–62; N.S. 38 (1934): 51–132.

————. "Die württembergischen Pfarrer im Zeitalter des 30jährigen Krieges," *Blätter für württembergische Kirchengeschichte,* N.S. 29 (1925): 129–68.

Frohnhäuser, Ludwig. *Geschichte der Reichsstadt Wimpfen.* Darmstadt, 1870.

Futter, Kurt. "Die kirchlichen Zustände in der Grafschaft Hohenlohe im Zeitalter nach der Reformation," *Blätter für württembergische Kirchengeschichte,* N.S. 53 (1953): 64–82.

Gallinek, A. "Psychogenic Disorders and the Civilization of the Middle Ages," *American Journal of Psychiatry,* 98 (1942): 42–54.

Galling, Kurt, ed. *Religion in Geschichte und Gegenwart.* 7 vols. 3d ed. Tübingen, 1957–65.

Garnsey, Peter. "Legal Privilege in the Roman Empire," *Past & Present,* No. 41 (1968): 3–24.

Gayler, Christoph F. *Historische Denkwürdigkeiten der ehemaligen freien Reichsstadt . . . Reutlingen vom dritten Viertel des 16ten bis gegen die Mitte des 18ten Jahrhunderts.* Reutlingen, 1845.

Gehring, Paul. "Der Hexenprozess und die Tübinger Juristenfakultät. Untersuchungen zur württembergischen Kriminalrechtspflege im 16. und 17. Jahrhundert," *Zeitschrift für württembergische Landesgeschichte,* 1 (1937): 157–88, 370–405; 2 (1938): 15–47.

Geiges, Hermann. "Hexen und Hexenprozesse im Breisgau," *Schauinsland,* 1 (1873–74): 44–45, 48, 56.

Geilen, Heinz Peter. "Die Auswirkungen der 'Cautio Criminalis' von Friedrich von Spee auf den Hexenprozess in Deutschland." Unpublished Dr. jur. dissertation, Bonn University, 1963.

Geipel, Jochen. *Die Konsiliarpraxis der Eberhard-Karls-Universtät und die Behandlung der Ehrverletzung in den Tübinger Konsilien.* Stuttgart, 1965. No. 4 of the Schriften zur südwestdeutschen Landeskunde.

German, Wilhelm. *Chronik von Schwäbisch Hall und Umgebung.* Schwäbisch Hall, [1900?].

Geschichte der Stadt Stuttgart. Stuttgart, 1905.

Giefel, J. "Zur Geschichte der Hexenprozesse in Horb und Umgebung," *Reutlinger Geschichtsblätter,* 13 (1902): 90–92.

Ginzburg, Carlo. *I benandanti. Ricerche sulla stregoneria e sui culti agrari tra Cinquecento e Seicento.* Turin, 1966.

Glass, David Victor, and D. E. C. Eversley. *Population in History: Essays in Historical Demography.* Chicago, 1965.

Gmelin, Julius. *Hällische Geschichte. Geschichte der Reichsstadt Hall und ihres Gebiets.* Schwäbisch Hall, 1896.

Gmelin, Moriz F. "Aus Visitationsprotokollen der Diözese Constanz von 1571–1586," *Zeitschrift für die Geschichte des Oberrheins,* 25 (1873): 129–204.

Gödecke, Karl. *Grundriss zur Geschichte der deutschen Dichtung aus den Quellen.* Vol. 2: *Das Reformationszeitalter.* 2d ed. Dresden, 1886.

Goldschmidt, Walter. *Comparative Functionalism.* Berkeley, 1966.

Göller, Otto. "Hexen in Haslach und Umgebung," *Die Ortenau,* 27 (1940): 79–85.

Gradmann, Robert. *Süddeutschland*. 2 vols. Stuttgart, 1931.

Graesse, Johann Georg. *Bibliotheca magica et pneumatica*. Leipzig, 1843.

Graubard, Mark. "Astrology's Demise and Its Bearing on the Decline and Death of Beliefs," *Osiris*, 13 (1958): 210–61.

Grimm, Heinrich. "Die deutschen 'Teufelbücher' des 16. Jahrhunderts," *Börsenblätter für den deutschen Buchhandel*, 15 (1959): 1733–92.

———. "Die deutschen 'Teufelsbücher' des 16. Jahrhunderts. Ihre Rolle im Buchwesen und ihre Bedeutung," *Archiv für Geschichte des Buchwesens*, 16 (1959): 513–70.

Grube, Walter. *Vogteien, Ämter, Landkreise in der Geschichte Südwestdeutschlands*. Stuttgart, 1960.

———. "Vogteien-Ämter-Landkreise. Verwaltungsgeschichtliche Entwicklungen im südwestdeutschen Raum," *Das Landkreis. Zeitschrift für kommunale Selbstverwaltung* (1960): 392–98.

Guerlac, Henry. "George Lincoln Burr," *Isis*, 35 (1944): 147–52.

Günther, H. "Mühringer Hexenprozesse," *Reutlinger Geschichtsblätter*, 22–23 (1911–12): 5–9.

Günther, Ludwig. *Ein Hexenprozess. Ein Kapitel aus der Geschichte des dunkelsten Aberglaubens*. Giessen, 1906.

Gürsching, Heinrich. "Jakob Andreae und seine Zeit," *Blätter für württembergische Kirchengeschichte*, 54 (1954): 123–56.

Gwinner, Heinrich. *Der Einfluss des Standes im gemeinen Strafrecht*. Dr. jur. dissertation, Breslau-Neukirch University, 1934. Published as No. 345 of the Strafrechtliche Abhandlungen.

———. "Ein Hexenprozess aus der Reichsstadt Lindau im Bodensee, aus dem Jahr 1730," *Bodensee-Heimatschau* (Lindau), 17, Nos. 1 and 2 (1937).

Haalck, Jürgen, and Norbert Trotz. "Die Hexenverfolgung in der Spruchpraxis der Rostocker Juristenfakultät. Eine Studie zur Universitätsgeschichte," *Wissenschaftliche Zeitschrift der Universität Rostock, Gesellschaftliche und sprachwissenschaftliche Reihe*, 13 (1964): 227–37.

Haas, Carl. *Die Hexenprozesse. Ein culturhistorischer Versuch nebst Dokumenten*. Tübingen, 1865.

Häcker, O. "Die Hillerische und Schillerische Chronik. Ein Beitrag zur Ellwanger Litteraturgeschichte," *Schwäbisches Archiv* (ed. Beck), 27 (1909): 177–84.

Haendke, Berthold. *Deutsche Kultur im Zeitalter des dreissigjährigen Krieges*. Leipzig, 1906.

Hagelstange, Alfred. *Süddeutsches Bauernleben im Mittelalter*. Leipzig, 1898.

Hajnal, John. "European Marriage Patterns in Perspective," in *Population in History* (ed. D. V. Glass and D. E. C. Eversley, Chicago, 1965), pp. 101–43.

Hampp, Irmgard. "Untersuchung zum Zauberspruch auf Grund von Sammlungen aus Württemberg wie aus deutschen und ausländischen Vergleischsgebieten." Unpublished Ph.D. dissertation, Tübingen University, 1955.

Hansen, Joseph. *Quellen und Untersuchungen zur Geschichte des Hexenwahns und der Hexenverfolgungen im Mittelalter*. Bonn, 1901.

———. *Zauberwahn, Inquisition und Hexenprozess im Mittelalter*. Munich and Leipzig, 1900.

Hanson, Chadwick. *Witchcraft at Salem*. New York, 1969.

Harper, Edward B. "Fear and the Status of Women," *Southwestern Journal of Anthropology*, 25 (1969): 81–95.

Hartmann, Julius. *Chronik der Stadt Stuttgart. Sechshundert Jahre nach der ersten denkwürdigen Nennung der Stadt (1286)*. Stuttgart, 1886.

Hartung, Fritz. *Deutsche Geschichte im Zeitalter der Reformation, Gegenreformation, und des dreissigjährigen Krieges*. 2d ed. Berlin, 1963.

Harzendorf, Fritz. Überlinger Hexenprozess im Jahre 1596," *Schriften des Vereins für Geschichte des Bodensees und seiner Umgebung*, 67 (1940): 108–41.

Hase, Karl August von. *Handbuch der protestantischen Polemik gegen die römisch-katholische Kirche*. 7th ed. Leipzig, 1900.

Hasselhorn, Martin. *Der altwürttembergische Pfarrstand im 18. Jahrhundert*. Stuttgart, 1958. Ser. B, No. 6 of the Veröffentlichungen der Kommission für geschichtliche Landeskunde in Baden-Württemberg.

Hassler, Ludwig Anton. *Chronik der königl. Württemb. Stadt Rottenburg und Ehingen am Neckar . . . 1200–1819*. Rottenburg, 1819.

Haug, Franz. *Marbacher Dorfbuch*. Ellwangen, 1959.

Hauger, Emil. *Wolterdingen. Geschichte eines Baardorfes*. Wolterdingen, 1960.

Hayes, H. R. *The Dangerous Sex: The Myth of Feminine Evil*. New York, 1964.

Hebeisen, Gustav. "Die Bedeutung der ersten Fürsten von Hohenzollern und des Kardinals Eitelfriedrich von Hohenzollern für die katholische Bewegung Deutschlands ihrer Zeit," *Mitteilungen des Vereins für Geschichte und Altertumskunde in Hohenzollern*, 54–57 (1920–23): 1–178.

Heeger, Fritz. "Volkskundliches aus Hexenprozessakten des badischen Frankenlandes," *Mein Heimatland*, 9 (1922): 91–95.

Heilig, Otto. "Zur Kenntnis des Hexenwesens am Kaiserstuhl," *Zeitschrift des Vereins für Volkskunde*, 14 (1904): 416–18.

Heinzelmann, Matthias. "Aus dem Hexenprozess der Adlerwirtin Katharina Memler von Melchingen," *Hohenzollerische Heimat*, 5, No. 4 (1955): 50–53.

Heitz, Paul, and Fr. Ritter. *Versuch einer Zusammenstellung der deutschen Volksbücher des 15. und 16. Jahrhunderts nebst deren späteren Ausgaben und Literatur*. Strassburg, 1924.

Hellinger, Karl. "Die Carolina in Gengenbach," *Archiv für Strafrecht und Strafprozess*, 59 (1912): 78–94.

———. "Die Carolina und die Hexenverfolgung in Gengenbach," *Archiv für Strafrecht und Strafprozess*, 59 (1912): 389–97, 497–500.

Hellmann, Gustav. "Aus der Blütezeit der Astrometeorologie," *Beiträge zur Geschichte der Meteorologie* (Berlin), Nos. 1–5 (1914). No. 273 of the Veröffentlichungen des kgl. preuss. meteorol. Instituts.

———. "Meteorologie in deutschen Flugschriften des 16. Jahrhunderts," *Abhandlungen der preussischen Akademie der Wissenschaften: Physikalisch-mathematische Klasse*, No. 1 (1921).

Hellwig, A. "Der Hexenmord zu Forchheim," *Alemannia*, Ser. 3, 2 (1910): 43–47.

Hemphill, R. E. "Historical Witchcraft and Psychiatric Illness in Western Europe," *Proceedings of the Royal Society of Medicine*, 59 (1966): 891–902.

Hermann, Ernst. *Die Hexen von Baden-Baden. Nach den Original-Akten des allgemeinen Landes-Archivs in Karlsruhe*. Karlsruhe, 1890.

Hermelink, Heinrich. *Geschichte der evangelischen Kirche in Württemberg von der Reformation bis zur Gegenwart. Das Reich Gottes in Wirtemberg*. Stuttgart and Tübingen, 1949.

"Hexenprozesse," *Neues Tagblatt*, No. 99 (1900): 1.

"Hexenprozesse" [Sulz], *Schuhkraffts Unterhaltungsblatt*, No. 80 (1820).

"Der Hexenprozess zu Hüfingen gegen den Fürstenbergischen Registrator, Obervogteiverweser und Notar Mathias Tinctorius und Consorten," *Die Heimat. Blätter für Baar und Schwarzwald*, Nos. 17–21 (1933), No. 1 (1934).

"Die Hexe von Schwaigern," *Schwäbische Chronik von Elben* (1898): 2449.

Heyd, Wilhelm, et al. *Bibliographie der württembergischen Geschichte*. Ed. Württembergischen Kommission für Landesgeschichte. 10 vols. Stuttgart, 1895–1967.

Heyse, Karl, ed. *Bücherschatz der deutschen Nationallitteratur des XVI. und XVII. Jahrhunderts*. Berlin, 1854.

Hinschius, Paul. *Das Kirchenrecht der Katholiken und Protestanten in Deutschland*. 6 vols. Berlin, 1870–97.

Hirsch, Rudolf. *Printing, Selling and Reading, 1480–1550*. Wiesbaden, 1966.

Hitchcock, James. "George Gifford and Puritan Witch Beliefs," *Archiv für Reformationsgeschichte*, 58 (1967): 90–99.

Hodler, Franz Xaver. *Geschichte des Oberamts Haigerloch*. Hechingen, 1928.

Hoenninger, Waldemar. "Heidelberger Zauberinnen," *Mannheimer Geschichtsblätter*, 23 (1922): 113–19.

Hoensbroech, Graf von. *Das Papstthum in seiner sozialkulturellen Wirksamkeit*. 2 vols. Leipzig, 1900–1902.

Hoffmann, Gustav. *Geschichte des Dorfes Mönsheim, Oberamt Leonberg*. Self-published, 1904.

Hofmann, Katharina. *Das Erbe der Helfensteiner*. Freiburg, 1918.

Holborn, Hajo. *A History of Modern Germany*. 3 vols. New York, 1959–69.

Holl, Karl. "Die Bedeutung der grossen Kriege für das religiöse und kirchliche Leben innerhalb des deutschen Protestantismus," in *Gesammelte Aufsätze zur Kirchengeschichte* (3 vols., Tübingen, 1928), Vol. 3, pp. 302–84.

Holstein, Hugo. "Der Dramatiker Thomas Birck," *Zeitschrift für deutsche Philologie*, 16 (1884): 71–85.

Hölzle, Erwin. *Der deutsche Südwesten am Ende des alten Reiches. Geschichtliche Karte des reichsdeutschen und benachbarten Gebiets*. Stuttgart, 1938.

Honecker, F. "Hexenprozesse im alten Reutlingen," *Reutlinger Heimatschriften*, 3 (1926): 1–47.

Hopkin, Charles E. *The Share of Thomas Aquinas in the Growth of the Witchcraft Delusion*. Philadelphia, 1940.

Hoppstädter, K. "Die Hexenverfolgungen im saarländischen Raum," *Zeitschrift für die Geschichte der Saargegend*, 9 (1959): 210–67.

Huber, Manfred. "Die Durchführung der tridentinischen Reform in Hohenzollern, 1567–1648." Unpublished Ph.D. dissertation, Tübingen University, 1963.

Huffschmid, E. Ph. "Zur Criminalstatistik des Odenwaldes im XVI. und XVII. Jahrhundert," *Zeitschrift für deutsche Kulturgeschichte*, 4 (1859): 409–34.

Hunt, Morton M. *The Natural History of Love*. New York, 1959.

Hurter, Hugo, S.J. *Nomenclator Literarius Theologiae Catholicae Theologos exhibens aetate, natione, disciplinis distinctos*. 5 vols. Innsbruck, 1903–13.

Huttenlocher, Friedrich. *Kleine geographische Landeskunde von Baden-Württemberg*. Karlsruhe, 1962.

———. "Zusammenhänge zwischen ländlichen Siedlungsarten und geschichtlichen Wirtschaftsweisen im südwestdeutschen Raum," *Zeitschrift für württembergische Landesgeschichte*, 1 (1937): 68–87.

Imhof, Eugen. *Blaubeurer Heimatbuch*. Blaubeuren, 1950.

Ingelfinger, Franz Kuno. *Die religiös-kirchlichen Verhältnisse im heutigen Württem-*

berg am Vorabend der Reformation. Th.D. dissertation, Tübingen University, 1939; published, Stuttgart, 1940.

The Interpreter's Dictionary of the Bible. 4 vols. New York, 1962.

Jackson, S. W., and J. K. Jackson. "Primitive Medicine and the Historiography of Psychiatry," in *Psychiatry and Its History: Methodological Problems in Research,* ed. George Mora and Jeanne Brand (Springfield, Ill., 1970).

Jacob, Mechtild. "Die Hexenlehre des Paracelsus und ihre Bedeutung für die modernen Hexenprozesse. Ein Beitrag zur Geschichte der Entwicklung des Hexenglaubens seit dem Mittelalter. Unter besonderer Berücksichtigung der Überlieferung aus dem Raum Gifhorn [Lower Saxony]." Unpublished Ph.D. dissertation, Göttingen University, 1960.

Jäger, Karl. *Mitteilungen zur schwäbischen und fränkischen Reformationsgeschichte.* Stuttgart, 1828.

Janssen, Johannes. *Geschichte des deutschen Volkes seit dem Augsgang des Mittelalters.* 8 vols. 15th ed. Freiburg i. Br., 1924.

Jehle, A. "Theologische Articul, darauff die Hexen sollen examiniert werden," *Blätter für württembergische Kirchengeschichte,* 9 (1894): 80.

Jessen, Hans. *Der dreissigjährige Krieg in Augenzeugenberichten.* Düsseldorf, 1963.

Joerres, Johann Arnold Clemens. "Die Verordnung Margarethas, gefürsteter Gräfin zu Arenberg, über die Verfolgung und Bestrafung der Zauberei, Hexen . . . und Wiedersherstellung eines religiösen Lebens in der Grafschaft Arenberg vom 30.11. 1593." Unpublished Dr. jur. dissertation, Bonn University, 1950.

Kaelbling, R. "Comparative Psychopathology and Psychotherapy," *Acta Psychotherapeutica,* 9 (1961): 10–28.

Kähni, Otto. "Die Beziehungen zwischen der Reichsstadt Offenburg und der Landvogtei Ortenau im 16. und 17. Jahrhundert," *Die Ortenau,* N.S. 1 (1949): 109–23.

———. *Offenburg. Aus der Geschichte einer Reichsstadt.* Offenburg, 1951.

———. "Reformation und Gegenreformation in der Reichsstadt Offenburg und in der Landvogtei Ortenau," *Die Ortenau,* N.S. 2 (1950): 20–37.

———. *Die Stadt und Landgemeinden des Kreises Offenburg. Ein historisch-topographisches Ortslexikon.* Bühl, 1964.

Kamen, Henry. "The Economic and Social Consequences of the Thirty Years' War," *Past & Present,* No. 39 (Apr. 1968): 44–61.

Kantzenbach, Friedrich Wilhelm. *Orthodoxie und Pietismus.* Gütersloh, 1966.

———. "Stand und Aufgaben der Brenzforschung," *Theologische Literaturzeitung,* 85 (1960), Col. 851.

Kawerau, W. "Lob und Schimpf des Ehestandes in der Litteratur des 16. Jahrhunderts," *Preussische Jahrbücher,* 69 (1892): 760–81.

Kelly, Henry Ansgar. *The Devil, Demonology and Witchcraft: The Development of Christian Beliefs in Evil Spirits.* Garden City, N.Y., 1968.

Kelso, Ruth. *Doctrine for the Lady in the Renaissance.* Urbana, Ill., 1956.

Kerker. "Zur Geschichte des Predigtwesens in der letzten Hälfte der [sic] XV. Jahrhunderts mit besonderer Rücksicht auf das südwestliche Deutschland," *Theologische Quartalschrift,* 44 (1862): 267–301.

Kerler, H. F. *Geschichte der Grafen von Helfenstein.* Ulm, 1840.

Keyser, Erich. *Deutsches Städtebuch,* IV, 2. 1: *Badisches Städtebuch.* 2: *Württembergisches Städtebuch.* Stuttgart, 1959–62.

———. "Neue deutsche Forschungen über die Geschichte der Pest," *Vierteljahrsschrift für Sozial- und Wirtschaftsgeschichte,* 44 (1957): 243–53.

Kichler, Johann B. *Die Geschichte von Langenargen und des Hauses Montfort.* Friedrichshafen, 1926.

Kisch, Guido. *Erasmus und die Jurisprudenz seiner Zeit. Studien zur humanistischen Rechtsdenken.* Basel, 1960. No. 56 of the Basler Studien zur Rechtswissenschaft.

———. *Zasius und Reuchlin. Eine rechtsgeschichtlichvergleichende Studie zum Toleranzproblem im 16. Jahrhundert.* Konstanz-Stuttgart, 1961. No. 1 of the Pforzheimer Reuchlinschriften.

Kittredge, George Lyman. *Witchcraft in Old and New England.* Cambridge, Mass., 1929.

Klaus, Bruno. "Geschichtliches und Kulturgeschichtliches aus Gmünd," *Württembergische Jahrbücher* (1902): 1–25.

Klein, Anton. "In und um Baden. [Part] 6: St. Anton, unsere süddeutschen Volksheiligen und der Teufel im vorderen Schwarzwald," *Badener Tagblatt* (June 1909).

Klein, Herbert. "Die älteren Hexenprozesse im Lande Salzburg," *Mitteilungen der Gesellschaft für Salzburger Landeskunde,* 97 (1957): 17–50.

Klibansky, Raymond, Erwin Panofsky, and Fritz Saxl. *Saturn and Melancholy: Studies in the History of Natural Philosophy, Religion and Art.* London, 1964.

Klinckowstroem, Carl Graf von. "Bibliographie des deutschsprachigen Schrifttums über Aberglauben bis 1800," *Börsenblatt für den deutschen Buchhandel,* 14 (1958): 1290–92.

Knapp, Hermann. *Das Übersiebnen der schädlichen Leute in Süddeutschland.* Berlin, 1910.

———. *Die Zenten des Hochstifts Würzburg. Ein Beitrag zur Geschichte des süddeutschen Gerichtswesens und Strafrechts.* 2 vols. in 3. Berlin, 1907.

Koch, Hugo. *Hexenprozesse und Reste des Hexenglaubens in der Wetterau.* Giessen, 1935. No. 37 of the Giessener Beiträge zur deutchen Philologie.

Kocher, Anton von. "Rottweiler Hexenprozesse," *Neues Tagblatt* (Stuttgart), No. 50 (1909): 7–8.

Kocher, J. *Geschichte der Stadt Nürtingen.* 3 vols. Stuttgart, 1928.

Koenigsberger, H. G., and G. L. Mosse. *Europe in the Sixteenth Century.* New York, 1968.

Koestler, Arthur. *The Watershed. A Biography of Johannes Kepler.* Garden City, N.Y., 1960.

Köhler, Friedrich August. *Oberndorf am Neckar. Beschreibung und Geschichte der Stadt und ihres Oberamts-Bezirks.* Sulz, 1836.

———. *Sulz am Neckar. Beschreibung und Geschichte der Stadt.* Sulz, 1835.

———. *Tuttlingen. Beschreibung und Geschichte dieser Stadt und ihres Oberamts-Bezirks. Ein merkwürdiger Beitrag zur Vaterlandskunde.* Tuttlingen, 1839.

Kohler, Josef. "Aus der Geschichte der Karolina," *Die Ortenau,* 3 (1912): 87–90.

———. "Bemerkungen zu den Gengenbacher Hexenprotokollen," *Archiv für Strafrecht und Strafprozess,* 59 (1912): 387–89.

———. "Die Carolina in den freien Reichsstädten Offenburg und Zell am Harmersbach," *Archiv für Strafrecht und Strafprozess,* 59 (1912): 218–24.

Köhler, Walter. *Bibliographia Brentiana. Bibliographisches Verzeichnis der gedruckten und ungedruckten Schriften und Briefe.* Leipzig, 1904.

Kolb, Christoph. "Die Kompendien der Dogmatik in Altwürttemberg," *Blätter für württembergische Kirchengeschichte,* 51 (1951): 4–19.

Kollnig, Karl. "Die Landesordnungen von Hohenzollern-Hechingen," *Hohenzollerische Jahreshefte,* 5 (1938): 159–88.

Kopfmann, Karl. *Die untere Herrschaft Ulms im dreissigjährigen Krieg.* Published Ph.D. dissertation, Tübingen University, 1934.

Krämer, Wolfgang. *Kurtrierische Hexenprozesse im 16. und 17. Jahrhundert vornehmlich an der unteren Mosel. Ein Beitrag zur Kulturgeschichte.* Munich, 1959.

Kraus, Johann Adam. "Aus den Visitationsakten des ehemaligen Kapitels Trochtelfingen, 1574–1709," *Freiburger Diözesan-Archiv,* Ser. 3, 5 (1953): 145–81.

———. "Opfer des Hexenwahns in Hohenzollern," *Hohenzollerische Heimat,* 17 (1967): 1–3.

———. "Zu den Zollerischen Landesordnungen," *Hohenzollerische Jahreshefte,* 6 (1939): 1–15.

Krebs, Manfred. *Gesamtübersicht der Bestände des Generallandesarchivs Karlsruhe.* 2 vols. Stuttgart, 1954–57. Nos. 1 and 2 of the Veröffentlichungen der Staatlichen Archivverwaltung Baden-Württembergs.

Krenzlin. A. "Die Kartierung von Siedlungsformen im deutschen Volksgebiet," *Berichte zur deutschen Landeskunde,* 3 (1943): 259–66.

Kretschmer, Konrad. *Historische Geographie von Mitteleuropa.* Munich, 1904.

Krick, Friederich. "Ein Hexenprozess gegen eine Ulmerin—Aus dem Ilmer Winkel," *Mitteilungen des historischen Vereins Neu Ulm* (1913): 5–6, 9–10, 13–14. Also in *Schwabenspiegel,* 6 (1912–13): 245 et seq.

Kriegstoetter, F. X. "Über Hexenprozesse," *Donauboten* (1878): 123.

Krüger, Eduard. *Schwäbisch Hall. Mit Grosskomburg, Kleinkomburg, Steinbach und Limpurg.* Schwäbisch Hall, 1953.

Kull, E. "Die Verteilung des landwirtschaftlich benutzten Grundbesitzes in Württemberg nach der Aufnahme vom 10. Januar 1873," *Württembergische Jahrbücher* (1881): 1–238.

Kürzel, Albert. "Hexenglaube als Veranlassung zur Einsetzung der Scapulier-Bruderschaft in dem Gotteshause Ettenheim-Münster," *Zeitschrift der Gesellschaft für Beförderung der Geschichts- Altertums- und Volkskunde von Freiburg, dem Breisgau und den angrenzenden Landschaften,* 2 (1870–72): 143–44.

Ladewig, Paul. "Eine Zauberin zu Todtnau," *Zeitschrift für die Geschichte des Oberrheins,* 41 (1887): 236–40.

Laistner, M. L. W. "The Western Church and Astrology during the Early Middle Ages," *Harvard Theological Review,* 34 (1941): 251–75.

Lampe, Hans-Sirks. "Die Darstellung des Teufels in den geistlichen Spielen Deutschlands. Von den Anfängen bis zum Ende des 16. Jahrhunderts." Unpublished Ph.D. dissertation, Munich University, 1963.

Landenberger, Johannes. *Stuttgarter Hexengeschichten; kulturgeschichtliche Bilder.* Lorch, 1904.

Längin, Georg. *Religion und Hexenprozess. Zur Würdigung des 400 jährigen Jubiläums der Hexenbulle und des Hexenhammers sowie der neuesten katholischen Geschichtsschreiber auf diesem Gebiet.* Leipzig, 1888.

Laslett, Peter. *The World We Have Lost.* New York, 1965.

Lauer, Hermann. "Die theologische Bildung des Klerus der Diözese Konstanz in der Zeit der Glaubenserneuerung," *Freiburger Diözesan-Archiv,* 20 (1919): 113–64.

Laufs, Adolf. "Reichsstädte und Reichsreform," *Zeitschrift der Savigny-Stiftung für Rechtsgeschichte, Germanistische Abteilung,* 84 (1967): 128–201.

———. *Die Verfassung und Verwaltung der Stadt Rottweil, 1650–1806.* Stuttgart, 1963.

Laun, F. "Die Gegenschreiberin [Hexenprozessakten]," *Ellwanger Jahrbuch* (1911): 79–85.

Lauppe, Ludwig. "Hexenverfolgung im ehemaligen hanaulichtenbergischen Amte Lichtenau," *Die Ortenau*, 5 (1914): 106.

Lautenschlager, Friedrich, ed. *Bibliographie der badischen Geschichte*. 2 vols. Karlsruhe, 1929–38. Continued in 2 further vols. by W. Schulz. Stuttgart, 1961–63.

Lea, Henry Charles. *A History of the Inquisition of the Middle Ages*. 3 vols. London, 1888.

———. *Materials Toward a History of Witchcraft*. Ed. Arthur C. Howland. 3 vols. Philadelphia, 1939.

———. *Superstition and Force*. 3d ed. Philadelphia, 1878.

Lecler, Joseph. *Toleration and the Reformation*. 2 vols. London, 1960.

Lederle, Karl F. "Zur Geschichte der Reformation und Gegenreformation in der Markgrafschaft Baden-Baden vom Tode Philiberts bis zum Ende der kirchlichen Bewegungen (1569–1635)," *Freiburger Diözesan-Archiv*, 47 (1919): 1–45.

Lefebvre, Georges. *La grande peur de 1789*. Paris, 1932.

Leidlmair, Adolf. "Württemberg und die Auswanderung aus den österreichischen Alpenländern," in *Studien zur südwestdeutschen Landeskunde. Festschrift . . . Friedrich Huttenlocher*. Bad Godesberg, 1963.

Lempens, Carl. *Geschichte der Hexen und Hexenprozesse*. St. Gall, 1880.

Lieban, Richard W. "Sorcery, Illness and Social Control in a Philippine Municipality," *Southwestern Journal of Anthropology*, 16 (1960): 127–43.

Liebel, Helen Pauline Grit. "The Bourgeoisie in Southwestern Germany 1500–1789: A Rising Class?" *International Review of Social History*, 10 (1965): 283–307.

Liliencron, Freiherr von. "Mittheilungen aus dem Gebiete der öffentlichen Meinung in Deutschland während der zweiten Hälfte des 16. Jahrhunderts," *Abhandlungen der histor. Classe der Königlich Bayerischen Akademie der Wissenschaften* (Munich), 12, pt. 3 (1874): 105–70.

Linsenmayer, Anton. *Geschichte der Predigt in Deutschland von Karl dem Grossen bis zum Ausgange des 14. Jahrhunderts*. Munich, 1886.

Lipenius, Martinus. *Bibliotheca Realis Universalis omnium materiarum et titulorum in Theologia, Jurisprudentiae, Medicina et Philosophia occurrentium*. 6 vols. Frankfurt, 1685.

Litchfield, R. Burr. "Demographic Characteristics of Florentine Patrician Families, Sixteenth to Nineteenth Centuries," *Journal of Economic History*, 29 (1969): 191–205.

Littmann, Ellen. *Studien zur Wiederaufnahme der Juden durch die deutschen Städte nach dem schwarzen Tode. Ein Beitrag zur Geschichte der Judenpolitik der deutschen Städte im späten Mittelalter*. Ph.D. dissertation, Cologne University; published, Breslau, 1928.

Loeser, J. *Geschichte der Stadt Baden*. Baden-Baden, 1891.

Loomis, Charles Grant. *White Magic: An Introduction to the Folklore of Christian Legend*. Cambridge, Mass., 1948.

Ludwig, Adolf. "Die Malefikantenpredigt. Nachklänge zu einem Hexenprozess in Lahr im Jahr 1655," *Die Ortenau*, 17 (1930): 107–23.

Ludwig, Albert. *Die evangelischen Pfarrer des badischen Oberlandes im 16. und 17. Jahrhundert*. Lahr, 1934. No. 9 of the Veröffentlichungen des Vereins für Kirchengeschichte in der evangelischen Landeskirche Badens.

Macfarlane, A. D. J. *Witchcraft in Tudor and Stuart England*. New York, 1970.

Mack, Karl Conrad. *Die Oberamts- und Seminarstadt Saulgau mit Bezirksgemeinden. Die Geschichte einer württembergischen Oberamtsstadt und ihres Bezirks*. Stuttgart, 1908.

Madsen, W. "Anxiety and Witchcraft in Mexican American Acculturation," *Anthropology Quarterly*, 39 (1966): 110–27.

Maltzahn, Wendelin von. *Deutsche Bücherschatz des 16., 17. und 18. bis um die Mitte des 19. Jahrhunderts, nebst Register*. Jena, 1875–82.

Mandrou, Robert. *Magistrats et sorciers en France au XVIIe siècle*. Paris, 1968.

Mann, Immanuel. "Zur Predigttätigkeit von Brenz in Hall," *Blätter für württembergische Kirchengeschichte*, 45 (1941): 8–49.

Marquardt, Ernst. *Geschichte Württembergs*. Stuttgart, 1961.

Marquart, A. "Eine Hexengeschichte," *Remszeitung*, 102, Nos. 198, 220, and 230 (1905).

———. "Eine Hexengeschichte vom Jahr 1701," *Gmünder Heimatblätter*, 1 (1928): 44–47.

Martens, Karl von. *Geschichte der innerhalb der gegenwärtigen Gränzen des Königreichs Württemberg vorgefallenen kriegerischen Ereignisse vom Jahr 15 vor Christi Geburt bis zum Friedensschlusse 1815*. Stuttgart, 1847.

Martindale, Don, ed. *Functionalism in the Social Sciences*. Philadelphia, 1965. Monograph 5 of the American Academy of Political and Social Science.

Marwick, M. G. "The Sociology of Sorcery in a Central African Tribe," *African Studies*, 22 (1963): 1–21.

Marzell, Heinrich. *Zauberpflanzen, Hexentränke: Brauchtum und Aberglaube*. Stuttgart, 1964.

Masters, R. E. L. *Eros and Evil: The Sexual Psychopathology of Witchcraft*. New York, 1962.

Mauch. "Notizen über das bei Verhandlung der Hexenprozesse im Limburgischen beobachtete Verfahren," *Zeitschrift des historischen Vereins für das württembergische Franken*, 1 (1848): 62–72.

Mauser, Ulrich. *Der junge Luther und die Häresie*. Gütersloh, 1968. No. 184 of the Schriften des Vereins für Reformationsgeschichte.

Mayer, Dieter Wilhelm. "Die Grafschaft Sigmaringen und ihre Grenzen im 16. Jahrhundert." Unpublished Ph.D. dissertation, Tübingen University, 1956.

Mayer, Karl. *Heimat-Buch für Kirchheim unter Teck und Umgebung*. 4th ed. Kirchheim, [1928].

Mayer, M. "Hexenverbrennung in Schiltach," *Die Ortenau*, 8 (1921): 71–73.

Mehring, G. "Aus der Zeit der Hexenverfolgungen in Reutlingen." Reprint of "Ein erschröckliche, jedoch war/ hafftige und erbärmliche/ Newe-Zeitung/ von Häxenmeisteren . . . 1665," *Blätter für württembergische Kirchengeschichte*, N.S. 9 (1905): 187–92.

Mehrle, Paul-Dieter. *Die Strafrechtspflege in der Herrschaft Kisslegg von den Anfängen bis zum Jahre 1633*. Dr. jur. dissertation. Freiburg University, 1961; published Pfullingen, 1961.

Mejer. "Ein Beitrag über Hexenprozesse," *Zeitschrift des historischen Vereins für das württembergische Franken*, 8 (1869): 314–17.

Merzbacher, Friedrich. "Geschichte der Hexenprozesse im Hochstifte Würzburg," *Mainfränkisches Jahrbuch für Geschichte und Kunst* (Würzburg), 2 (1950).

————. *Die Hexenprozesse in Franken.* Munich, 1957. No. 56 in the Schriftenreihe zur bayrischen Landesgeschichte.

Metz, F., ed. *Vorderösterreich. Eine geschlichtliche Landeskunde.* Ed. Alemannisches Institut. 2d ed. Freiburg, 1967.

Meyer, Karl. *Heimatbuch für Kirchheim unter Teck und Umgebung.* 4th ed. Kirchheim, [1928?].

Middleton, John, and E. H. Winter, eds. *Witchcraft and Sorcery in East Africa.* London, 1963.

Midelfort, H. C. Erik. "Recent Witch Hunting Research, or Where Do We Go from Here?" *The Papers of the Bibliographical Society of America,* 62 (1968): 373-420.

————. "Witchcraft and Religion in Sixteenth-Century Germany: The Formation and Consequences of an Orthodoxy," *Archiv für Reformationsgeschichte* 62 (1971) 266-78.

Miller, Max, ed. *Handbuch der historischen Stätten Deutschlands.* VI: *Baden-Württemberg.* Stuttgart, 1965.

Minder, Robert. *Der Hexenglaube bei den Jatrochemikern des 17. Jahrhundert.* M.D. dissertation, Zurich University, 1963; published as N.S., Vol. 12, in the Zürcher medizingeschichtliche Abhandlungen.

Moeller, Bernd. *Reichsstadt und Reformation.* Gütersloh, 1962. No. 180 of the Schriften des Vereins für Reformationsgeschichte.

Moller, Herbert. "Sex Composition and Correlated Culture Patterns of Colonial America," *William and Mary Quarterly,* Ser. 3, 2 (1945): 113-53.

Mönch, W. *Heimatkunde vom Oberamt Calw.* Calw, 1912.

Monfang, C. *Katholische Katechismen des XVI. Jahrhundert in deutscher Sprache.* Hildesheim, 1964. Reprint of the 1881 ed.

Monter, E. William. *Calvin's Geneva.* New York, 1967.

————. *European Witchcraft.* New York, 1969.

————. "Inflation and Witchcraft: The Case of Jean Bodin," in *Action and Conviction in Early Modern Europe: Essays in Honor of E. H. Harbison,* ed. by T. K. Rabb and J. Seigel (Princeton, N.J., 1969), pp. 371-89.

————. "Patterns of Witchcraft in the Jura," *Journal of Social History,* 5 (1971-72): 1-25.

————. "Trois historiens actuels de la sorcellerie," *Bibliothèque d'humanisme et renaissance,* 31 (1969): 207-13.

————. "Witchcraft in Geneva, 1537-1662," *Journal of Modern History,* 43 (1971): 180-206.

Morgan, Edmund. *The Puritan Family.* Boston, 1944.

Müller, Ernst. *Kleine Geschichte Württembergs mit Ausblicken auf Baden.* Stuttgart, 1963.

Müller, Karl Otto. *Gesamtübersicht über die Bestände der staatlichen Archive Württembergs in planmässiger Einteilung.* Stuttgart, 1937. No. 2 of the Veröffentlichungen der württembergischen Archivverwaltung.

————. "Heinrich Institoris, der Verfasser des Hexenhammers, und seine Tätigkeit als Hexeninquisitor in Ravensburg im Herbst 1484," *Württembergische Vierteljahrshefte für Landesgeschichte,* N.S. 19 (1910): 397-417.

————. "Zur Geschichte der Seuchen in Alt-Württemberg," *Zeitschrift für württembergische Landesgeschichte,* 4 (1940): 83-86.

Murray, Margaret Alice. *The Witch Cult in Western Europe.* Oxford, 1921.

Nadel, S. F. "Witchcraft in Four African Societies: An Essay in Comparison," *American Anthropologist*, N.S. 54 (1952): 18–29.

Nauert, Charles G. *Agrippa and the Crisis of Renaissance Thought.* Urbana, 1965. No. 55 of the Illinois Studies in the Social Sciences.

Naujoks, Eberhard. *Obrigkeitsgedanken, Zunftverfassung und Reformation. Studien zur Verfassungsgeschichte von Ulm, Esslingen und Schwäbisch Gmünd.* Stuttgart, 1958.

———. "Reichsfreiheit und Wirtschaftsrivalität. Eine Studie zur Auseinandersetzung Esslingens mit Württemberg im 16. Jahrhundert," *Zeitschrift für württembergische Landesgeschichte*, 16 (1957): 279–302.

Nelson, Benjamin. "The Early Modern Revolution in Science and Philosophy: Fictionalism, Probabilism, Fideism, and Catholic Prophetism," in *Boston Studies in the Philosophy of Science*, Vol. 3 (New York, 1968), pp. 1–40.

Neu, Heinrich. *Pfarrerbuch der evangelischen Kirche Badens von der Reformation bis zur Gegenwart.* 2 vols. Lahr, 1938–39. No. 13 of the Veröffentlichungen des Vereins für Kirchengeschichte in der evangelischen Landeskirche Badens.

Neumayr, M. *Die Schriftpredigt im Barock. Auf Grund der Theorie der katholischen Barockhomiletik.* Paderborn, 1938.

1962 Schwäbisch Gmünd: 800 Jahre Stadt. Schwäbisch Gmünd, 1962.

Neuwirth, Gustav. *Geschichte des Dorfes Heinsheim a. N.* Karlsruhe, 1954.

Neveux, J. B. *Vie spirituelle et vie sociale entre Rhin et Baltique au XVIIᵉ siècle: de J. Arndt à P. J. Spener.* Paris, 1967.

Newald, R. *Die deutsche Literatur vom Späthumanismus zur Empfindsamkeit: 1570–1750.* Vol. 5 of *Geschichte der deutschen Literatur.* Munich, 1951.

Noonan, John T. "Intellectual and Demographic History," *Daedalus*, 97 (1968): 463–85.

Notestein, Wallace. *History of Witchcraft in England from 1558 to 1718.* New York, 1965.

Nottarp, Hermann. *Gottesurteile.* Bamberg, 1949. Nos. 4–8 of the Geschichtliche Reihe, Allgemeine Schriften zur Philosophie, Theologie und Geschichte. Ed. Benedikt Kraft.

Oberschelp, Reinhard. *Die Bibliographien zur deutschen Landesgeschichte und Landeskunde im 19. und 20. Jahrhundert.* Frankfurt, 1967. Special issue No. 7 of the Zeitschrift für Bibliothekwesen und Bibliographie.

Oestreich, Gerhard. "Calvinismus, Neustoizismus, und Preussentum," *Jahrbuch für die Geschichte Mittel- und Ostdeutschlands*, 5 (1956): 157–82.

———. "Justus Lipsius als Theoretiker des modernen Machtstaats," *Historische Zeitschrift*, 181 (1956): 31–78.

Ohse, Bernard. "Die Teufelliteratur zwischen Brant und Luther. Ein Beitrag zur näheren Bestimmung der Abkunft und des geistlichen Ortes des Teufels, besonders im Hinblick auf ihre Ansichten über das Böse." Unpublished Ph.D. dissertation, Freie Universität, Berlin, 1961.

Osborn, Max. *Die Teufelliterature des XVI. Jahrhunderts.* Berlin, 1893.

Overdick, Renate. *Die rechtliche und wirtschaftliche Stellung der Juden in Südwestdeutschland im 15. und 16. Jahrhundert dargestellt an den Reichsstädten Konstanz und Esslingen und an der Markgrafschaft Baden.* Konstanz, 1965. No. 15 in the Konstanzer Geschichts- und Rechtsquellen. Edited by the Stadtarchiv.

Ow Wachendorf, Freiherr H. H. von. "Geständnis einer Hexe," *Reutlinger Geschichtsblätter*, 21 (1910): 10–11.

Pagel, Walter. *Paracelsus. An Introduction to Philosophical Medicine in the Era of the Renaissance.* Basel, 1958.

Parrinder, Geoffrey. *Witchcraft, European and African.* London, 1963.

Patrides, C. A. "Renaissance and Modern Views on Hell," *Harvard Theological Review*, 57 (1964): 217–36.

———. "Renaissance Thought on the Celestial Hierarchy: The Decline of a Tradition," *Journal of the History of Ideas*, 20 (1959): 155–66.

———. "The Salvation of Satan," *Journal of the History of Ideas*, 28 (1967): 467–79.

Pätzold, Gerhard. *Die Marburger Juristenfakultät als Spruchkollegium.* Marburg, 1960. No. 5 of the Beiträge zur hessischen Geschichte.

Paulus, Nikolaus. *Hexenwahn und Hexenprozess vornehmlich im 16. Jahrhundert.* Freiburg, 1910.

———. "Johann Spretter, ein Hexenschriftsteller des 16. Jahrhunderts," *Historisch-politische Blätter für das katholische Deutschland*, 150 (1912): 248–62.

———. "Württembergische Hexenpredigten aus dem 16. Jahrhundert," *Diözesanarchiv von Schwaben*, 15, No. 6 (1897): 81–85; No. 7 (1897): 107–8.

Petersdorff, Egon von. *Dämonologie.* 2 vols. Munich, 1956–57.

Peuckert, Will-Erich. *Die grosse Wende. Das apokalyptische Saeculum und Luther. Geistesgeschichte und Volkskunde.* Hamburg, 1948.

———. "Hexen- und Weiberbünde," *Kairos* (Salzburg), 2 (1960): 101–5.

———. *Pansophie. Ein Versuch zur Geschichte der weissen und schwarzen Magie.* 2d ed. Berlin, 1956.

Pfaff, Friedrich. "Eine Teufelsaustreibung aus dem Jahre 1701" [in Freiburg i. Br.], *Alemannia*, 27 (1900): 29–49.

Pfaff, Karl. *Geschichte der Stadt Stuttgart.* Stuttgart, 1845.

———. "Die Hexenprozesse zu Esslingen im 16. und 17. Jahrhundert, *Zeitschrift für deutsche Kulturgeschichte*, 1 (1856): 253–71, 283–94, 347–71, 441–62.

———. "Württemberg nach seinem natürlichen, statistischen und kommerziellen Zustand zu Ende des 16. und zum Anfang des 17. Jahrhundert," *Württembergische Jahrbücher für vaterländische Geschichte, Geographie, Statistik und Topographie*, No. 2 (1841).

Pfeifer, Hans. *Verfassungs- und Verwaltungsgeschichte der Fürstpropstei Ellwangen.* Stuttgart, 1959. Ser. B, Vol. 7 of the Veröffentlichungen der Kommission für geschichtliche Landeskunde in Baden-Württemberg.

Pfeiffer, Gerhard. "Studien zur Geschichte der fränkischen Reichsritterschaft," *Jahrbuch für fränkische Landesforschung*, No. 22, ed. Institut für fränkische Landesforschung an der Universität Erlangen (Erlangen, 1962): 173–280.

Pfister, Oskar. *Calvins Eingreifen in die Hexer- und Hexenprozesse von Peney 1545 nach seiner Bedeutung für Geschichte und Gegenwart.* Zürich, 1947.

Philipp, Wolfgang, ed. *Das Zeitalter der Aufklärung.* Vol. 7 of *Klassiker des Protestantismus.* Bremen, 1963.

Pickering, F. P. "Notes on Fate and Fortune," in *Medieval German Studies Presented to Frederick Norman.* London, 1965. Pp. 1–15.

Planitz, Hans. *Deutsche Rechtsgeschichte.* 2d ed. Graz-Cologne, 1961.

Plöchl, Willibald M. *Geschichte des Kirchenrechts.* Vienna, 1953.

Poliakov, Leon. *The History of Anti-Semitism.* Vol. 1. New York, 1965.

Popkin, Richard H. *The History of Scepticism from Erasmus to Descartes.* Rev. ed. New York, 1968.

Popper, Karl R. *Of Clouds and Clocks: An Approach to the Problem of Rationality and the Freedom of Man.* The Arthur Holly Compton Memorial Lecture, April 21, 1965. St. Louis, 1966.

Powell, Chilton L. *English Domestic Relations 1487–1653.* New York, 1917.

Pratt, A. M. *The Attitude of the Catholic Church toward Witchcraft.* Washington, D.C., 1915.

Pressel, Th. *Anecdota Brentiana. Ungedruckte Briefe und Bedenken von Johannes Brenz.* Tübingen, 1868.

Price, Harry. *Short-title Catalogue of Works on Psychical Research, Spiritualism, Magic, Psychology, Legerdemain, and Other Methods of Deception, Charlatanism, Witchcraft and Technical Works for the Scientific Investigation of Alleged Abnormal Phenomena from ca. 1450 A.D. to 1929 A.D.* London, 1929.

Rade, Paul Martin. *Zum Teufelsglauben Luthers.* Gotha, 1931.

Rapp, Alfred. *Deutsche Geschichte am Oberrhein.* Karlsruhe, 1937.

———. "Scheiterhaufen am Oberrhein. Ein Bericht von Hexenverfolgung und Hexenverbrennung in unserer Heimat," *Alemannisches Volk,* 3, Nos. 11–13 (1935).

Rapp, Ludwig. *Die Hexenprozesse und ihre Gegner aus Tirol. Ein Beitrag zur Kulturgeschichte.* Innsbruck, 1874.

Rauh, Rudolf. *Systematische Übersicht über die Bestände des Fürstl. von Waldburg-Zeil'schen Gesamtarchivs im Schloss Zeil vor 1806 (1850), Archiv Kisslegg und Archiv Ratzenried.* Stuttgart, 1953. No. 24 of the Württembergische Archivinventare.

Rauscher, Julius. "Der Halleysche Komet im Jahr 1531 und die Reformatoren," *Zeitschrift für Kirchengeschichte,* 32 (1911): 259–76.

———. *Reformation 1500–1559. Württembergische Reformationsgeschichte.* Ed. Calwer Verlagsverein. Stuttgart, 1934. No. 3 in the Württembergische Kirchengeschichte.

Real-Enzyklopädie für protestantische Theologie. 3d ed. 22 vols. Leipzig, 1896–1913.

Redlich, Fritz. *De Praeda Militari. Looting and Booty, 1500–1815.* Wiesbaden, 1956.

Reifferscheid, Alexander. *Quellen zur Geschichte des geistigen Lebens in Deutschland während des 17. Jahrhunderts.* Heilbronn, 1889.

Reinfried, Karl. "Auszüge aus den Hexenprozess-Protokollen des Amts Bühl der Jahre 1628 und 1629," *Alemannia,* 43 (1916): 2–21.

———. "Kulturgeschichtliches aus der Polizei-Ordnung der Stadt und des Amts Steinbach vom Jahre 1673," *Alemannia,* Ser. 3, 2 (1910): 48–54.

———. "Die Stadt- und Pfarrgemeinde Bühl unter Windeck geschichtlich dargestellt," *Freiburger Diözesan-Archiv,* 11 (1877).

Reinhardt, Rudolf. *Restauration, Visitation, Inspiration, Die Reformbestrebungen in der Benediktinerabtei Weingarten von 1567 bis 1627.* Stuttgart, 1960. Ser. B, No. 11 of the Veröffentlichungen der Kommission für geschichtliche Landeskunde in Baden-Württemberg.

———. "Untersuchungen zur Besetzung der Propstei Ellwangen seit dem 16. Jahrhundert," in *Ellwangen. 764–1964,* ed. Viktor Burr (Ellwangen, 1964).

Renz, G. A. "Ein Hexenprozess der Reichsstadt Biberach im Jahr 1647/48," *Schwarzwälder Bote* (Oberndorf), Unterhaltungsblatt, Nos. 61–62 (1908).

Rest, Josef. "Ettenheimer Hexenprozesse im 17. Jahrhundert," *Die Ortenau,* 3 (1912): 38–56.

Reu, Johann Michael. *Quellen zur Geschichte des kirchlichen Unterrichts . . . zwischen 1530 und 1600.* Vol. 1: *Süddeutsche Katechismen.* Gütersloh, 1904.

Reuning, Wilhelm. "Balthasar Bekker der Bekämpfer des Teufel- und Hexenglaubens." Unpublished Ph.D. dissertation, Giessen University, 1925.

Reusch, Franz. *Die deutschen Bischöfe und der Aberglaube.* Bonn, 1879.

Reuss, R. *La sorcellerie au XVIᵉ et au XVIIᵉ siècle particulièrement en Alsace.* Paris, 1871.

Reyscher, August Ludwig. *Vollständige, historisch und kritisch bearbeitete Sammlung der württembergischen Gesetze.* 19 vols. in 28. Stuttgart and Tübingen, 1828–51.

Rheinwald. "Aus den Sindelfinger Hexenprozessakten," *Besondere (literar.) Beilage des Staatsanzeigers für Württemberg* (1904): 16–25.

Rheinwald, Ernst, and Gisbert Rieg. *Calw. Geschichte und Geschichten aus 900 Jahren.* Calw, 1952.

Rhode, Hans Wilhelm. "Evangelische Bewegung und katholische Restauration im österreichischen Breisgau unter Ferdinand I. und Ferdinand II. Studien zur Kirchenpolitik der Habsburger in Vorderösterreich im 16. Jahrhundert." Unpublished Ph.D. dissertation, Freiburg University, 1957.

Richter, Aemilius Ludwig. *Die evangelischen Kirchenordnungen des sechzehnten Jahrhundert.* 2 vols. Weimar, 1846.

Riedle, A. "Bevölkerung und Wirtschaft der Reichsstadt Heilbronn zur Zeit des dreissigjährigen Kriegs." Unpublished Ph.D. dissertation, Tübingen University, 1933.

Riegler, Franz. *Die Reichsstadt Schwäbisch Hall im dreissigjährigen Krieg.* Ed. Württembergischen Kommission für Landesgeschichte. Stuttgart, 1911. No. 7 of the Darstellungen aus der württembergischen Geschichte.

Riezler, Sigmund. "Feuerprobe an einer Hexe (Anna Henni von Rötenbach bei Neustadt im Schwarzwald) 1485," *Anzeiger für Kunde der deutschen Vorzeit,* N.S. 20 (1873): 77–78.

———. *Geschichte der Hexenprozesse in Bayern. Im Lichte der allgemeinen Entwicklung dargestellt.* Stuttgart, 1896.

———. "Paul Laymann und die Hexenprozesse. Zur Abwehr," *Historische Zeitschrift,* 84 (1900): 244–56.

Ringgren, Helmer, ed. *Fatalistic Beliefs in Religion, Folklore, and Literature.* Stockholm, 1967. No. 2 of the Scripta Instituti Donneriani Aboensis.

Ritter, Moriz. *Deutsche Geschichte im Zeitalter der Gegenreformation und des dreissigjährigen Krieges.* 3 vols. Stuttgart, 1889–1908.

Robbins, Rossell Hope. *The Encyclopedia of Witchcraft and Demonology.* New York, 1959.

Roder, Christian. "Ein merkwürdiger Hexenprozess in Villingen 1641," *Schriften des Vereins für Geschichte und Naturgeschichte der Baar,* 9 (1896): 79–88.

Roeder, Philipp Ludwig Hermann. *Geographisch- statistisch- topographisches Lexikon von Schwaben.* 2 vols. Ulm, 1791–92.

Roemer, Hermann. *Geschichte der Stadt Bietigheim an der Enz.* Stuttgart, 1956.

Rogers, Katharine M. *The Troublesome Helpmate: A History of Misogyny in Literature.* Seattle, 1966.

Röhm, Helmut. *Die Vererbung des landwirtschaftlichen Grundeigentums in Baden-Württemberg.* Remagen, 1957. No. 102 of the Forschungen zur deutschen Landeskunde.

Röhrich, Lutz. "Die dämonischen Gestalten der schwäbischen Volksüberlieferung." Unpublished Ph.D. dissertation, Tübingen University, 1949.

Rommel, Gustav. "Beiträge zur Geschichte des Hexenwesens in der Grafschaft Wertheim," *Jahrbuch des historischen Vereins 'Alt-Wertheim'* (1938–39): 10–25.

Rooschüz, Paul. *Owen. Seine Geschichte und seine Denkwürdigkeiten.* Stuttgart, 1884.

Rose, Elliot. *A Razor for a Goat.* Toronto, 1962.

Rosen, George. *Madness in Society: Chapters in the Historical Sociology of Mental Illness.* New York, 1969.

————. "A Study of the Persecution of Witches in Europe as a Contribution to the Understanding of Mass Delusions and Psychic Epidemics," *Journal of Health and Human Behavior*, 1 (1960): 200–211.

Rosenthal, T., and Bernard J. Siegel. "Magic and Witchcraft: Interpretation from Dissonance Theory," *Southwestern Journal of Anthropology*, 15 (1959): 143–67.

Ross, David. *Aristotle.* London, 1964.

Rossi, Paolo. *Francis Bacon: From Magic to Science.* Trans. Sacha Rabinovitch. London, 1968.

Roth, R. "Die Universität Tübingen im Jahre 1577," *Württembergische Jahrbücher* (1871): 280–95.

Rothert, Eduard. *Karten und Skizzen aus der Entwicklung der grösseren deutschen Staaten.* Düsseldorf, 1916.

Rottenkolber, Josef. *Geschichte des Allgäus.* Munich. 1951.

Ruckgaber, Heinrich. *Geschichte der Frei- und Reichsstadt Rottweil.* 2 vols. Rottweil, 1835–38.

————. "Die Hexenprozesse in Rottweil a. N.," *Württembergische Jahrbücher* (1838): 174–96.

Ruf, J., and Franz Rösch. "Ein Einblick in die Renchtäler Hexenprozesse. Nach umfangreichen Materialsammlungen zusammengestellt und neubearbeitet," *Die Ortenau*, 11 (1924): 31–38.

Ruppert, Philipp. "Ein badischer Hexenrichter" [Dr. Matern Eschbach], *Zeitschrift der Gesellschaft für Geschichtskunde von Freiburg*, 5 (1880): 445–73.

Russell, Josiah C. "Effects of Pestilence and Plague, 1315–1385," *Comparative Studies in Society and History*, 8 (1965–66): 464–73.

Salzmann, Val. *Die Hexenprozesse der Reichsstadt Esslingen.* Esslingen, 1887.

Sandermann, Wolfgang. *Die Herren von Hewen und ihre Herrschaft; Ein Beitrag zur politischen Geschichte des schwäbischen Adels.* Freiburg i. Br., 1956.

Sattler, Christian Friderich. *Geschichte des Herzogthums Würtemberg unter der Regierung der Herzogen.* Vol. 4. Tübingen, 1771.

Saunders, Jason L. *Justus Lipsius: The Philosophy of Renaissance Stoicism.* New York, 1955.

Sauter, Johann Georg. *Zur Hexenbulle 1484. Die Hexerei mit besonderer Berücksichtigung Oberschwabens. Eine culturhistorische Studie.* Ulm, 1884.

Schaaf, Paul. *Gengenbach. Vergangenheit und Gegenwart.* Konstanz, 1960.

Schabel, Wilhelm. *Stadt und Garnison Ellwangen.* Frankfurt, 1957.

Schacher von Inwil, Joseph. *Das Hexenwesen im Kanton Luzern (1400–1675).* Luzern, 1947.

Schäfer, Gerhard. *Kleine württembergische Kirchengeschichte.* Stuttgart, 1964.

Scharfe, Martin. "Soziale Kontrolle im Dorf des vorindustriellen Zeitalters. Volkstümliche Rechtsanschauungen im ehemaligen Zeller Stab," *Jahreshefte des Geschichts- und Altertumsvereins Göppingen*, 4 (1965): 75–81.

Schell, Erwin. *Die Reichsstädte beim Übergang an Baden.* Heidelberg, 1929.

Schellhass, Karl. *Gegenreformation im Bistum Konstanz im Pontifikat Gregors XIII.* Karlsruhe, 1925.

————. "Zur Geschichte der Gegenreformation im Bistum Konstanz," *Zeitschrift für die Geschichte des Oberrheins*, 32 (1917): 3–43, 187–240, 375–413, 493–514; 33 (1918): 316–47, 449–95; 34 (1919): 145–81, 273–99.

Schian, M. "Die lutherische Homiletik in der zweiten Hälfte des 16. Jahrhunderts," *Theologische Studien und Kritiken*, 72 (1899): 62–94.

Schib, Karl. *Geschichte der Stadt Rheinfelden*. Rheinfelden, 1961.

Schilliger, J. "Die Hexenprozesse im ehemaligen Fürstbisthum Basel," *Vom Jura zum Schwarzwald*, 8 (1891).

Schilling, Alb. "Drei Hexenverbrennungen zu Ulm," *Württembergische Vierteljahrshefte für Landesgeschichte* (1883): 137–41.

Schmid, Heinrich. *The Doctrinal Theology of the Evangelical Lutheran Church*. Trans. Charles A. Hay and Henry E. Jacobs. Minneapolis, Minn., 1961.

Schmidlin, Josef. *Die kirchlichen Zustände in Deutschland vor dem dreissigjährigen Krieg nach den bischöflichen Diözesanberichten an den Heiligen Stuhl*. 3 vols. in 1. Freiburg, 1908–10.

Schmidt, Eberhard. "Die Carolina," *Zeitschrift der Savigny-Stiftung für Rechtsgeschichte, Germanistische Abteilung*, 53 (1933): 1–34.

———. *Einführung in die Geschichte der deutschen Strafrechtspflege*. 3d ed. Göttingen, 1965.

———. *Inquisitionsprozess und Rezeption. Studien zur Geschichte des Strafverfahrens in Deutschland vom 13. bis 16. Jahrhundert*. Leipzig, 1940. No. 124 of the Leipziger rechtswissenschaftliche Studien.

Schmidt, Friedrich Heinz, ed. *Schwäbische Volkssagen vom Schwarzwald zum Allgäu, von Taubergrund zum Bodensee*. Stuttgart, 1966.

Schmidt, Rudolf. *Die Frau in der deutschen Literatur des 16. Jahrhunderts*. Strassburg, 1917.

Schneider, Gebhard. "Ein Hexenprozess in Tettnang," *Schriften des Vereins für Geschichte des Bodensees und seiner Umgebung* 16 (1887): 68–72.

Schneider, Ulrich Friedrich. "Das Werk 'De Praestigiis Daemonum' von Weyer und seine Auswirkungen auf die Bekämpfung des Hexenwahns." Unpublished Dr. jur. dissertation, Bonn University, 1951.

Schnell, E. "Zur Geschichte der Kriminal-Justiz und besonders der Hexenprozesse in Hohenzollern," *Mitteilungen des Vereins für Geschichte und Altertumskunde in Hohenzollern*, 7 (1873–74): 69–99.

Schnurrer, Chr. Fr. *Erläuterungen der württembergischen Kirchen- Reformations- und Gelehrten-Geschichte*. Tübingen, 1798.

Scholtz, Harald. *Evangelischer Utopismus bei Johann Valentin Andreae. Ein geistiges Vorspiel zum Pietismus*. Stuttgart, 1957. No. 42 of the Darstellungen aus der württembergischen Geschichte hrsg. von der Kommission für geschichtliche Landeskunde in Baden-Württemberg.

Schön, Theodor. "Des Apothekers Heinrich Efferen Kampf gegen den Hexenwahn," *Mittheilungen des Cannstatter Altertumsvereins*, No. 4 (1898).

———. "Was in den Jahren 1555–1596 in und um den Schwarzwald Merkwürdiges passiert ist," *Aus dem Schwarzwald. Blätter des württembergischen Schwarzwaldvereins*, 17 (1909): 107–9, 135–36.

Schott, Clausdieter. *Rat und Spruch der Juristenfakultät Freiburg i. Br*. Freiburg, 1965. No. 30 of the Beiträge zur Freiburger Wissenschafts- und Universitätsgeschichte.

Schraepler, Horst W. *Die rechtliche Behandlung der Täufer in der deutschen Schweiz, Südwestdeutschland und Hessen, 1525–1618*. Tübingen, 1957. No. 4 of the Schriften zur Kirchen- und Rechtsgeschichte.

Schreiber, Heinrich. *Geschichte der Albert Ludwigs Universität zu Freiburg i. Br.* 3 vols. Freiburg, 1857–60.

———. *Die Hexenprozesse zu Freiburg im Breisgau, Offenburg in der Ortenau, und Bräunlingen auf dem Schwarzwalde.* Freiburg i. Br., 1836.

Schrittenloher, Joseph. "Aus der Gutachter- und Urteilstätigkeit der Ingolstädter Juristenfakultät im Zeitalter der Hexenverfolgungen," *Jahrbuch für fränkische Landesforschung,* 23 (1963): 315–53.

Schüling, Hermann. *Bibliographischer Wegweiser zu dem in Deutschland erschienen Schrifttum des 17. Jahrhunderts.* Giessen, 1964. No. 4 of the Berichte und Arbeiten aus der Universitätsbibliothek Giessen.

Schumm, Johann. *Heimatbuch Crailsheim.* Crailsheim, 1928.

Schuster, Otto. *Kirchengeschichte von Stadt und Bezirk Esslingen.* Stuttgart, 1946.

Schwab, F. "Eine neuere Hexengeschichte aus dem Badischen," *Psychische Studien,* 25 (1898): 439–42.

Schwarz, Benedikt. "Ein Hexenprozess im Kraichgau vom Jahre 1563," *Alemannia,* Ser. 3, 5 (1913): 1–17, 99–109, 127–46.

Schweizer, P. "Der Hexenprozess und seine Anwendung in Zürich," *Zürcher Taschenbuch* (Zürich), N.S. 25 (1902): 1–63.

Schwerin, Claudius Freiherr von. *Grundzüge der deutschen Rechtsgeschichte.* Ed. Hans Thieme. 4th ed. Berlin and Munich, 1950.

Schwister, Otto. *Kirchengeschichte von Stadt und Bezirk Esslingen.* Stuttgart, 1946.

Seeger, Hermann. *Die strafrechtlichen Consilia Tubingensia von der Gründung der Universität bis zum Jahre 1600.* Tübingen, 1877.

Segall, Josef. *Geschichte und Strafrecht der Reichspolizeiordnungen von 1530, 1548, und 1577.* Giessen, 1914. No. 183 (1914) of the Strafrechtliche Abhandlungen.

Seger, O. "Der letzte Akt im Drama der Hexenprozesse in der Grafschaft Vaduz und Herrschaft Schellenberg," *Jahrbuch des historischen Vereins des Fürstentums Liechtenstein,* 57 (1957): 135 et seq.

Selig, Theodor. "Aus der Zeit des Hexenwahns," *Sonntagsfreude. Beilage zur Riedlinger Zeitung,* Nos. 20 and 21 (1905).

———. "Die Hexen auf dem Teutschbuch und Emersberg," *Riedlinger Zeitung,* Nos. 197, 199, 200, 204, and 212 (1924).

Seligman, Kurt. *History of Magic.* London, 1953.

Shannon, Albert. "The Secrecy of Witnesses in Inquisitorial Tribunals and in Contemporary Secular Trials," in *Essays in Medieval Life and Thought Presented in Honor of Austin Patterson Evans,* ed. J. H. Mundy (New York, 1955), pp. 59–69.

Siebel, Friedrich W. "Die Hexenverfolgung in Köln." Unpublished Dr. jur. dissertation, Bonn University, 1959.

Sieber, Adolf. *Das heutige Oberamt Besigheim in den Zeiten des dreissigjährigen Kriegs.* Ph.D. dissertation, Tübingen University; published Tübingen, 1935.

Siegel, Paul N. "Milton and the Humanist Attitude toward Women," *Journal of the History of Ideas,* 11 (1950): 42–53.

Sievers, Ed. "Notizen zu Thomas Birck," *Beiträge zur Geschichte der deutschen Sprache und Literatur,* 10 (1885): 199–205, 450.

Soldan-Heppe. *Geschichte der Hexenprozesse.* Ed. Max Bauer. 2 vols. Munich, 1912.

Solleder, Fridolin. "Hexenwahn, Zauberei und Wunderglauben in Franken," *Frankenland,* 1 (1914): 115–26, 176–83.

———. "Wie anno 1567 der Teufel zu Donauwörth einen Knecht geholt," *Das Bayerland,* 30 (1919): 56–58.

Sommerfeldt, Gustav. "Der Protestantismus Süddeutschlands und die Kriegsbefürcht-
ungen des Jahres 1562," *Blätter für württembergische Kirchengeschichte*, N.S. 12
(1908): 174–80.

Sonneborn, Marie. "Hexenprozesse in der ehemaligen Reichsstadt Gengenbach," *Der
Altvater*, 7, Nos. 24 and 26 (1940).

Spamer, A. "Zauberbuch und Zauberspruch," *Deutsches Jahrbuch für Volkskunde*, 1,
Nos. 1 and 2 (1955): 109–26.

Specker, Hans Eugen. "Die Reformtätigkeit der Würzburger Fürstbischöfe Friedrich
von Wirsberg (1558–1573) und Julius Echter von Mespelbrunn (1573–1617),"
Würzburger Diözesanblätter, 27 (1965): 29–125.

———. *Die Reformtätigkeit des Würzburger Fürstbischofs Julius Echter von Mespelbrunn, 1573–1617*. Published Ph.D. dissertation, Tübingen University, 1963.

Speidel, August. *Burladinger Heimatbuch*. Burladingen, 1958.

Spengler, Joseph. "Demographic Factors and Early Modern Economic Development,"
Daedalus, 97 (1968): 433–46.

Stälin, Christoph Friedrich. *Wirtembergische Geschichte*. 4 vols. Stuttgart, 1847–73.

———. *Zur Geschichte der alten und neuen Büchersammlungen in Württemberg*.
Stuttgart and Tübingen, 1838.

Stälin, Paul Friedrich. *Geschichte der Stadt Calw*. Calw and Stuttgart, 1888.

Stapf, Heribert. "Der 'Meister Reuaus' und die Teufelsgestalt in der deutschen Dichtung des späteren Mittelalters." Unpublished Ph.D. dissertation, Munich University,
1956.

Starkey, Marion. *The Devil in Massachusetts*. New York, 1949.

Steigelmann, H. *Der geistliche Rat zu Baden-Baden und seine Protokolle von 1577–
1584*. Stuttgart, 1962.

Stemmler, Eugen. *Die Grafschaft Hohenberg und ihr Übergang an Württemberg,
1806*. Stuttgart, 1950. No. 34 of the Darstellungen aus der württembergischen Geschichte.

Stern, Selma. *The Court Jew. A Contribution to the History of the Period of Absolu-
tism in Central Europe*. Philadelphia, 1950.

———. *Josel von Rosheim. Befehlshaber der Judenschaft im heiligen römischen Reich
deutscher Nation*. Stuttgart, 1959.

Stern-Täubler, Selma. "Die Vorstellung vom Juden und vom Judentum in der Ideo-
logie der Reformationszeit," in *Essays Presented to Leo Baeck on the Occasion of
his Eightieth Birthday* (London, 1954), pp. 194–211.

Stevenson, Lloyd. *The Meaning of Poison*. Lawrence, Kans., 1959. Ser. 7 of the Logan
Clendening Lectures in the History and Philosophy of Medicine.

Stintzing, Rod. von. *Geschichte der deutschen Rechtswissenschaft*. Munich and Leipzig, 1880; reprinted Aalen, 1957.

Stocker, D. "Verbrechen und Strafe in Schaffhausen vom Mittelalter bis in die Neuzeit," *Zeitschrift für schweizer Strafrecht*, 5 (1892): 309 et seq.

Stocker, Franz August. "Die Teufelsbesessene von Murg," *Vom Jura zum Schwarzwald*, 6 (1889): 205–30.

Stolz, Aloys. *Geschichte der Stadt Pforzheim*. Pforzheim, 1901.

Stones, G. B. "The Atomistic View of Matter in the XVth, XVIth, and XVIIth Centuries," *Isis*, 10 (1928): 445–65.

Strukat, A. "Hexenprozesse in den fürstenbergischen Gemeinden," *Aus dem Schwarzwald*, 35 (1927): 139.

Stumpf, Karl. "Die Pest im Frankenland vom 15. bis 17. Jahrhundert," *Fränkische Blätter*, 5, No. 12 (1922).

Stürzl, Erwin. *Der Zeitbegriff in der elisabethanischen Literatur. The Lackey of Eternity.* Vienna-Stuttgart, 1965. No. 69 of the Wiener Beiträge zur englischen Philologie.

Sütterlin, Berthold. *Geschichte Badens.* Karlsruhe, 1965.

Swanson, Guy E. *The Birth of the Gods.* Ann Arbor, Mich., 1960.

Tantsch, Werner Karl. "Deutsche Teufels- und Hexennamen aus Urgichten des 15. bis 18. Jahrhundert." Unpublished Ph.D. dissertation, Heidelberg University, 1958.

Teall, John L. "Witchcraft and Calvinism in Elizabethan England: Divine Power and Human Agency," *Journal of the History of Ideas*, 23 (1962): 21–36.

"Eine Teufelsverschreibung einer Nattheimerin" [Kreis Heidenheim], *Der Heydekopf*, 1 (1921–24): 277ff.

Theobald, Leonhard. *Das Leben und Wirken des Tendenzdramatikers der Reformationszeit Thomas Naogeorgus seit seiner Flucht aus Sachsen.* Leipzig, 1908.

Thoma, Werner. *Die fürstenbergischen Lande im Zeitalter der Glaubenskämpfe.* Ph.D. dissertation, Freiburg University (1960); No. 88 (1962) in the Reformationsgeschichtliche Studien und Texte (Münster).

Thomas, Keith. "History and Anthropology," *Past & Present*, No. 24 (Apr. 1963): 3–24.

———. *Religion and the Decline of Magic. Studies in Popular Beliefs in Sixteenth and Seventeenth Century England.* London, 1971.

Thompson, E. P. "Time, Work-Discipline, and Industrial Capitalism," *Past & Present*, No. 38 (Dec. 1967): 56–97.

Thorndike, Lynn. *A History of Magic and Experimental Science.* 8 vols. New York, 1923–58.

———. "The Place of Magic in the Intellectual History of Europe," *Columbia University Studies*, 24 (1905): 1–10.

Thrupp, Sylvia. "Plague Effects in Medieval Europe," *Comparative Studies in Society and History*, 8 (1965–66): 474–83.

Thudichum, Friedrich. *Die Diözesen Konstanz, Augsburg, Basel, Speier, Worms nach ihrer alten Einteilung in Archidiakonate, Dekanate, Pfarreien.* Tübingen, 1906. Vol. 1, No. 2 of the Tübinger Studien für schwäbische und deutsche Rechtsgeschichte.

———. *Geschichte der Reichsstadt Rottweil und des Kaiserlichen Hofgerichts daselbst.* Tübingen, 1911. Vol. 2, No. 4 of the Tübinger Studien für schwäbische und deutsche Rechtsgeschichte.

Tilly, Charles. *The Vendée. A Sociological Analysis of the Counterrevolution of 1793.* New York, 1967.

Tomek, Ernst. *Kirchengeschichte Österreichs.* Vol. 2: *Humanismus, Reformation, Gegenreformation.* Innsbruck and Vienna, 1949.

Trachtenberg, Joshua. *The Devil and the Jews.* New Haven, Conn., 1943.

Tramer, M. "Kinder im Hexenglaube und Hexenprozess des Mittelalters," *Zeitschrift für Kinderpsychiatrie*, 11 (1945): 140–49, 180–87.

Trevor-Roper, H. R. "The European Witch-Craze of the Sixteenth and Seventeenth Centuries," in *The Crisis of the Seventeenth Century: Religion, the Reformation and Social Change* (New York, 1968), pp. 90–192.

Trimble, William R. *The Catholic Laity in Elizabethan England, 1558–1603.* Cambridge, Mass., 1964.

Tüchle, Hermann. *Kirchengeschichte Schwabens.* 2 vols. Stuttgart, 1950–54.

Tumbült, Georg. *Der Fürstentum Fürstenberg von seinen Anfängen bis zur Mediatisierung im Jahre 1806.* Freiburg, 1908.

Turberville, A. S. *Medieval Heresy and the Inquisition.* London, 1920.

Turner, V. W. "Witchcraft and Sorcery: Taxonomy versus Dynamics," *Africa,* 34 (1964): 314–25.

Tz. "Aus der Hexengeschichte Württembergs," *Neues Tagblatt* (Stuttgart), No. 34 (1910): General Anzeiger, p. 1.

Urner-Astholz, Hildegard, et al. *Geschichte der Stadt Stein am Rhein.* Bern, 1957.

Utsch, Johanna. "Wolfgang Hildebrand und die Magia naturalis." Unpublished Ph.D. dissertation, Göttingen University, 1950.

Van de Walle, Etienne. "Marriage and Marital Fertility," *Daedalus,* 97 (1968): 486–501.

Vanotti, J. N. von. *Geschichte der Grafen von Montfort und von Werdenberg.* Belle-Vue bei Konstanz, 1848.

Veesenmeyer, Georg. *Sammlung von Aufsätzen zur Erläuterung der Kirchen- Litteratur- Münz- und Sittengeschichte besonders des 16. Jahrhunderts.* Ulm, 1827.

Veit, Ludwig Andreas, and Ludwig Lenhart. *Kirche und Volksfrömmigkeit im Zeitalter des Barock.* Freiburg, 1956.

Vierordt, Karl Friedrich. *Geschichte der evangelischen Kirche in dem Grossherzogthum Baden. Nach grossentheils handschriftlichen Quellen bearbeitet.* 2 vols. Karlsruhe, 1847–56.

Vilberg, Max. *Regenten-Tabellen.* Frankfurt a. O., 1906.

Villeneuve, Roland. *Le musée des supplices.* Paris, 1968.

Villinger, Heinz. "Die Tätigkeit des schwäbischen Reichskreises auf dem Gebiet des Polizeiwesens (16. Jahrhundert)." Unpublished Dr. jur. dissertation, Heidelberg University, 1950.

Vochezer, Josef. *Geschichte des fürstlichen Hauses Waldburg in Schwaben.* 3 vols. Kempten, 1888–1907.

Vogel, Ansgar Otto. *Bad Wurzach. Seine Geschichte und sein Recht.* Leutkirch, 1959.

Volk, Franz. *Hexen in der Landvogtei Ortenau und der Reichsstadt Offenburg.* Lahr, 1882.

Wächter, Carl Georg von. *Beiträge zur deutschen Geschichte insbesondere zur Geschichte des deutschen Strafrechts.* Tübingen, 1845.

Wacker, G. *Der Bezirk Böblingen einst und jetzt.* Böblingen, 1910.

Wagner, Emil. "Die Reichsstadt Schwäbisch Gmünd vom Tode Kaiser Maximilians II. 1576 bis zum Anfang des 17. Jahrhunderts," *Württembergische Vierteljahrshefte für Landesgeschichte,* N.S. 10 (1901): 161–99, 464.

Wagner, Johannes Volker. *Graf Wilhelm von Fürstenberg 1491–1549 und die politisch-geistigen Mächte seiner Zeit.* Stuttgart, 1966.

Walcher, Karl. "Ein Hexenprozess im Jahr 1591," *Württembergische Vierteljahrshefte für Landesgeschichte,* N.S. 1 (1892): 345–53.

Waldenmaier, Hermann. *Die Entstehung der evangelischen Gottesdienstordnungen Süddeutschlands im Zeitalter der Reformation.* Leipzig, 1916. Nos. 125–26 of the Schriften des Vereins für Reformationsgeschichte.

Walker, D. P. *Spiritual and Demonic Magic from Ficino to Campanella.* London, 1958.

Walker, Martin. "Das volkstümliche Leben in 15. und 16. Jahrhundert. Nach den Zeugnissen von Dorfordnungen aus dem schwäbischen Teil Württembergs." Unpublished Ph.D. dissertation, Tübingen University, 1954.

Walter, Fr. A. *Kurze Geschichte von dem Prämonstratenserstifte Obermarchtal. Von seinem Anfange 1171 bis zu seiner Auflösung 1802.* Ehingen, 1835.

Wangner, B. "Hexenprozesse aus den Jahren 1635–1636: Löffingen-Blumberg," *Zeitschrift für Volkskunde*, 9 (1935): 109–25.

Warburg, Aby. "Heidnisch-antike Weissagung in Wort und Bild zu Luthers Zeiten," in his *Gesammelte Schriften*, ed. Bibliothek Warburg (Leipzig, 1932).

Wax, Rosalie, and Murray Wax. "The Magical World View," *Journal for the Scientific Study of Religion*, 1 (1962): 179–88.

Weber, Franz Michael. *Ehingen. Geschichte einer oberschwäbischen Donaustadt.* Ehingen, 1955.

Weber, Hellmuth von. "Die peinliche Halsgerichtsordnung Kaiser Karls V," *Zeitschrift der Savigny-Stiftung für Rechtsgeschichte, Germanistische Abteilung*, 77 (1960): 288–310.

Weber, Kilian. "Hexenbrände in Linzgau," *Bodensee-Chronik*, 23, No. 11 (1934).

Weber, Siegfried. *Stadt und amt Stuttgart zur Zeit des dreissigjährigen Kriegs. Bevölkerungsbewegung und Finanzen.* Published Ph.D. dissertation, Tübingen University, 1936.

Weber-Unger, Heinrich. "Strafrecht und Volksglaube. Dargestellt an der Zimmerischen Chronik und dem Buche Weinsberg." Unpublished Dr. jur. dissertation, Heidelberg University, 1947.

Wedgwood, C. V. *The Thirty Years War.* New York, 1961.

Weech, Friedrich von. "Die badischen Landtagsabschiede von 1554–1668," *Zeitschrift für die Geschichte des Oberrheins*, 29 (1877): 323–423.

———. "Eine Teufelsaustreibung in Baden im Jahre 1585," *Zeitschrift für die Geschichte des Oberrheins*, 28 (1876): 179–94.

Wegner, Wolfgang. *Die Faustdarstellung vom 16. Jahrhundert bis zur Gegenwart.* Amsterdam, 1962.

Weingarten (city). *Altdorf-Weingarten. Ein Heimatbuch.* Weingarten, 1960.

Weisert, Hermann. *Geschichte der Stadt Sindelfingen 1500–1807.* Sindelfingen, 1963.

Weller, Emil. *Annalen der poetischen National-Literatur der Deutschen im XVI. und XVII. Jahrhundert.* 2 vols. Freiburg i. Br., 1862–64.

———. *Die ersten deutschen Zeitungen hrsg. mit einer Bibliographie (1505–1599).* Tübingen, 1872. No. 111 in the Bibliothek des literarischen Vereins in Stuttgart.

Weller, Karl. *Württembergische Geschichte.* Ed. Arnold Weller. 5th ed. Stuttgart, 1963.

Welti, Ludwig. *Graf Kaspar von Hohenems, 1573–1640. Ein adeliges Leben im Zwiespalte zwischen friedlichem Kulturideal und rauher Kriegswirklichkeit im Frühbarock.* Innsbruck, 1963.

Weser, R. "Alte Gmünder. XIV. Dr. juris Leonhard Kager. Ein Gmünder Familiensilberschatz," *Remszeitung*, 108, Nos. 197–99 (1911).

West, Robert H. *The Invisible World: A Study of Pneumatology in Elizabethan Drama.* Athens, Ga., 1939.

Westfall, Richard S. *Science and Religion in Seventeenth Century England.* New Haven, Conn., 1958.

Wiegelmann, Günter. "The 'Atlas der deutschen Volkskunde' and the Geographical Research Method," *Journal of the Folklore Institute*, 5 (1968): 187–97.

Wiessner, Hermann. *Sachinhalt und wirtschaftliche Bedeutung der Weistümer im deutschen Kulturgebiet.* Brünn, 1934.

Wiley, Margaret L. *The Subtle Knot.* Cambridge, Mass., 1952.

Willburger, August. "Hexenprozesse im Nagolder Wald," *Aus dem Schwarzwald*, 40 (1932): 137–39.

———. "Hexenverfolgung in Württemberg," *Rottenburger Monatschrift für praktische Theologie*, 13 (1929–30): 135–45, 167–73.

Williams, Charles. *Witchcraft*. London, 1941.

Wilson, F. P. *The Plague in Shakespeare's London*. London, 1963.

Wilson, Monica H. "Witch Beliefs and Social Structure," *American Journal of Sociology*, 56 (1951): 307–13.

Winston, Richard. *Charlemagne: From the Hammer to the Cross*. New York, 1954.

Winterberg, Hans. *Die Schüler von Ulrich Zasius*. Stuttgart, 1961. Ser. B, No. 18 of the Veröffentlichungen der Kommission für geschichtliche Landeskunde in Baden-Württemberg.

Winters, Peter Jochen. *Die "Politik" des Johannes Althusius und ihre zeitgenössischen Quellen. Zur Grundlegung der politischen Wissenschaft im 16. und im beginnenden 17. Jahrhundert*. Freiburg, 1963.

Wintterlin, Friedrich. *Geschichte der Behördenorganisation in Württemberg*. Stuttgart, 1904.

Wirth, Hermann. "Hexenverbrennung zu Heidelberg," *Archiv für die Geschichte der Stadt Heidelberg*, 1 (1868): 99–113.

———. "Zur Topographie der Hexenzusammenkünfte und die Tellsage in der Pfalz," *Archiv für die Geschichte der Stadt Heidelberg*, 1 (1868): 198–200; 2 (1869): 36–39; 3 (1870): 67–68.

Woehlkens, Erich. *Pest und Ruhr im 16. und 17. Jahrhundert*. Hannover, 1954. N.S. 26; Schriften des niedersächsischen Heimatbundes.

Wolf, Erik. *Grosse Rechtsdenker der deutschen Rechtsgeschichte*. 4th ed. Tübingen, 1963.

Wolff, Alfred. *Gerichtsverfassung und Prozess im Hochstift Augsburg in der Rezeptionszeit*. Würzburg, 1913.

Wrigley, E. A. "Family Limitation in Preindustrial England," *Economic History Review*, 19 (1966): 82–109.

Wulz, Gustav. "Nördlinger Hexenprozesse," *Jahrbuch des Historischen Vereins für Nördlingen* (Rieser Heimatverein), 20 (1938): 42–72; 21 (1939): 95–120.

———. "Die Nördlinger Hexen und ihre Richter," *Der Rieser Heimatbote* (Zeitungsbeilage), Nos. 142–47 (1939).

Wunderlich, Peter, "Das Recht der Reichsstadt Isny vom Beginn der Zunftherrschaft bis zur Reformation." Unpublished Dr. jur. dissertation, Tübingen University, 1958.

Wurm, Theodor. *Chronik der Stadt Wiesensteig*. Geislingen, 1957.

Würtenberger, Thomas. *Die Strafrechtswissenschaft in der Freiburger Rechts- und Staatswissenschaftlichen Fakultät*. Freiburg, 1957. No. 15 of the Beiträge zur Freiburger Wissenschafts- und Universitätsgeschichte.

Württembergische Kirchengeschichte. Ed. Calwer Verlagsverein. Calw and Stuttgart, 1893.

Yates, Frances. *Giordano Bruno and the Hermetic Tradition*. London, 1964.

Zanta, L. *La renaissance du stoïcisme au XVIᵉ siècle*. Paris, 1914. N.S., No. 5 in the Bibliothèque littéraire de la renaissance.

Zauberei und Frömmigkeit; Volksleben. Untersuchungen des Ludwig-Uhland-Instituts der Universität Tübingen. Vol. 13. Tübingen, 1966.

Zedler, J. H. *Grosses vollständiges Universal-Lexikon*. 63 vols. and 4 suppl. vols. Leipzig and Halle, 1732–54; reprinted Graz, 1961–64.

Zeeden, Ernst Walter. *Deutsche Kultur in der frühen Neuzeit*. Frankfurt, 1960. Handbuch der Kulturgeschichte, ed. E. Thurnher: Sec. 1, Zeitalter deutscher Kultur; No. 5.

———. *Die Entstehung der Konfessionen. Grundlagen und Formen der Konfessionsbildung im Zeitalter des Glaubenskämpfe*. Munich, 1965.

———. "Grundlagen und Wege der Konfessionsbildung in Deutschland im Zeitalter der Glaubenskämpfe," *Historische Zeitschrift*, 185 (1958): 249–99.

———. *Katholische Überlieferungen in den lutherischen Kirchenordnungen des 16. Jahrhunderts*. Münster i. W., 1959. No. 17 of the Katholisches Leben und Kämpfen im Zeitalter der Glaubenspaltung; Vereinsschriften der Gesellschaft zur Herausgabe des Corpus Catholicorum.

———. *Das Zeitalter der Gegenreformation*. Freiburg, 1967.

Zeller, Joseph. "Hexenbrände in Ellwangen vor 300 Jahren," *Ellwanger Jahrbuch*, 4 (1914): 86–88.

Zimmermann, Karl. "Hexenwesen und Hexenverfolgung in der Grafschaft Baden von 1574 bis 1600," *Badener Neujahrsblatt* (1950): 40–55.

Zingeler. "Ein Hexenprozess zu Freudenstadt aus dem 17 Jahrhundert," *Württembergische Vierteljahrshefte für Landesgeschichte*, 9 (1886): 148–53.

Zoepfl, Friedrich. *Geschichte der Stadt Mindelheim in Schwaben*. Munich, 1948.

———. "Hexenwahn und Hexenvergolgung in Dillingen," *Zeitschrift für Bayerische Landesgeschichte*, 27 (1964): 235–44.

Zoepfl, Heinrich. *Deutsche Rechtsgeschichte*. 3 vols. Braunschweig, 1871–72.

Zwengel, Otto. *Das Strafverfahren in Deutschland von der Zeit der Carolina bis zum Beginn des 19. Jahrhundert*. Niederlauke/Taunus, 1963.

Zwetsloot, Hugo. *Friedrich von Spee und die Hexenprozesse*. Trier, 1954.

Index